NO CITIZEN LEFT BEHIND

NO CITIZEN LEFT BEHIND

Meira Levinson

HARVARD UNIVERSITY PRESS
Cambridge, Massachusetts & London, England 2012

KH

Library of Congress Cataloging-in-Publication Data

Levinson, Meira.
  No citizen left behind / Meira Levinson.
    p. cm.
  Includes bibliographical references and index.
  ISBN 978-0-674-06578-9 (alk. paper)
  1. Citizenship—Study and teaching (Middle school)—United States.
2. Democracy and education—United States. I. Title.
  LC1091.L39 2012
  370.11′5—dc23   2011048024

4/15/13

To my students,

past and present

CONTENTS

NO CITIZEN LEFT BEHIND

If there is no struggle there is no progress. Those who profess to favor freedom and yet depreciate agitation, are men who want crops without plowing up the ground, they want rain without thunder and lightning. They want the ocean without the awful roar of its many waters. This struggle may be a moral one, or it may be a physical one, and it may be both moral and physical, but it must be a struggle. Power concedes nothing without a demand. It never did and it never will.

—*Frederick Douglass*

Kurt Cobain versus Master P

On October 13, 1998, I am coaching my school's National Academic League quiz bowl team in our first match. I teach at Walden Middle School, a fairly typical institution in the Atlanta Public Schools. Our student body is entirely African American and poor. Our teachers and students are deeply committed and hard working, but we struggle academically nonetheless. A colleague and I decided to start the quiz bowl team this year as a way of encouraging academically aspiring kids. We've had fun at the practices so far, and it's been great to see how many kids voluntarily stay after school to develop their academic skills and knowledge. At the moment, though, I'm not sure if anyone is having much fun.

We are competing against Sutton Middle School, one of the two so-called "White" middle schools in the district. We are getting creamed. No, not just creamed—massacred. Totaled. Buried. The National Academic League is set up to allow any team of fifteen to forty students to participate in the game, and we had made the decision before the match to include all students who had regularly attended practices, regardless of their ability. It's a decision that the team had agreed on, but I am beginning to wonder about the wisdom of our decision. Participation is great, but nobody likes to lose—let alone be humiliated.

National Academic League matches have four different quarters, and we're in the middle of the team versus team quarter: five of our best students against five of theirs, each accompanied by a set of five back-ups eager to rotate in. The questions are designed to require teamwork in coming up with the answer. Whichever team buzzes in first and answers correctly earns two points; if a team buzzes in with the wrong answer, though, it loses one point. As the judge pulls out the next question card and places it for both teams to see, I'm hoping that we'll score a lucky break—or at least, that our team won't continue its trend of buzzing in and losing points.

Please match the people on the left to the correct description on the right.

a. Richard Nixon   1. composed "Raindrops Keep Falling on My Head" and other hits

b. Burt Bacharach   2. founded the band Nirvana and wrote the hit song, "Smells Like Teen Spirit"

c. Bjorn Borg   3. won the Wimbledon tennis tournament five years in a row

d. John Wayne   4. resigned as president of the United States because of the Watergate scandal

e. Kurt Cobain   5. acted in over 200 films, many of them Westerns

When I see the question, I am livid. The point of the National Academic League is to inspire students to study harder the material they are learning in school; all questions, therefore, are supposed to be tied to the English, math, science, and social studies curriculum. This question comes out of nowhere—we did not sign up to compete in a trivia game. Also, all of the people listed are White men: I know my students will be able to identify Richard Nixon and Kurt Cobain, but I'm less sure about John Wayne, and I'll be shocked if they've ever even heard of Borg or Bacharach. These are the days before Venus and Serena Williams: what inner-city Black kid watches tennis?!? Maybe they'll be able to figure things out by process of elimination, but I think that the best I can hope is that my team will be smart, play it safe, and not buzz in.

"Bzzzz."

"Walden Middle School. You have buzzed in first. Give the answer, please."

Benny's voice pipes up.[1] He's a great kid—incredibly smart, possessing a terrific sense of humor, intellectually and politically engaged, and, to his great frustration as an eighth grader, not yet five feet tall. I'm hoping against hope that he knows what he's doing. "Our answer is: a-4; b-2; c-1; d-5; e-3. Nixon resigned over Watergate. Bacharach wrote 'Smells Like Teen Spirit' for Nirvana. Borg composed 'Raindrops Keep Falling on My Head.' John Wayne acted in Westerns. And Kurt Cobain won Wimbledon."

A wave of laughter erupts from the other side of the room. The Sutton coach glares at her team, and they work hard to compose themselves, occasionally letting out a snort or a giggle, but doing a pretty good job for a bunch of middle schoolers. It's clear, though, that they remain amused by Benny's answer; they're not laughing just because we got it wrong.

"I'm sorry, that's incorrect. Sutton, you have one minute to buzz in."

Sutton buzzes in and misses the answer as well—they've confused Borg and Bacharach—but that does little to save our team. At the end of the game, we've been trounced 72 to 23. I'm not surprised; Sutton is the wealthiest and Whitest middle school in the district (meaning that one-third of its student body is White, and only about half qualify for free or reduced-price lunch), and its team is obviously drawn from the upper socioeconomic end of the school, which is statistically much more likely to do well on these kinds of tests than low-income kids of color. The students are almost entirely White, despite Sutton's large Black population, and they're clearly children of lefty (hence attending public school) Buckhead (hence wealthy) parents—children of doctors, lawyers, businessmen, and other professionals. I can see my students commenting about this among themselves, and craning their heads to look into other classrooms as we walk out to the bus. When I chastise Shaniqua for drifting too far from the group, she explains, "I want to see what a rich school looks like, Dr. Levinson."

After herding my thirty-five dejected team members onto the school bus to return to Walden, I conduct a post-game analysis with the students. As our school bus jounces down Peachtree Street, making its way from Buckhead back to the all-Black, historically significant but now impoverished Fourth Ward of Atlanta where our school is located, we discuss how our team could have worked more efficiently and effectively, what kinds of questions we need to prepare for, where our weak spots are academically. We strategize for next week's game and agree to focus on math and social studies during our semi-weekly practice sessions. Then, out of curiosity, I ask the students, "Do you know why the Sutton kids laughed when Benny gave his answer to that matching question?" No, they tell me; they were confused, because otherwise the Sutton team was pretty well-behaved and respectful.

"They laughed," I continue, "because we misidentified Kurt Cobain. How many of you have heard of Kurt Cobain?" Out of my thirty-five students, not a single hand goes up. Surprised, I ask, "How about the band Nirvana?" Nothing. "Grunge—you know, the music trend?" Blank stares. "Seattle?" I ask in desperation. A couple of kids may have heard of Seattle.

I explain to them who Kurt Cobain is, about Nirvana, grunge, and Cobain's suicide a few years before. "Probably 95 percent of White people under the age of thirty could tell you who Kurt Cobain is," I conclude. "That's why the Sutton kids laughed. Your not knowing who Kurt Cobain is seems as weird to them that was 99 percent Black and about 94 percent poor enough to qualify for free or reduced-price lunch. In response to these demographics, we taught what we described as an inclusive, multicultural curriculum, but in practice this meant that it was incredibly inclusive primarily of African Americans and of the African-American urban experience in particular. The only novel taught in seventh-grade English, for example, was Mildred Taylor's *Roll of Thunder, Hear My Cry;* it focuses on the life of an African-American family living in the South in the 1930s. Similarly, the major essay assignment in the second semester of eighth-grade U.S. History (covering Christopher Columbus through World War II) was a comparison of Booker T. Washington's and W. E. B. Du Bois's positions on the status of African Americans. Students learned about Faith Ringgold in art class, wrote reports on the Côte d'Ivoire and other Francophone African countries in French class, and assisted the librarian in creating elaborate Kwanzaa displays every December.

As one of six White teachers among a faculty and staff of about forty, I readily and enthusiastically followed my colleagues' lead. Of the 300 books I had bought for my classroom library, at least 100 were by African-American authors or were about African-American literature, history, poetry, scientists, inventors, musicians, athletes, or artists. I assigned a personal narrative as my first major assignment in eighth-grade English each year because I knew that teenagers tend to love writing about themselves; we used an excerpt from Maya Angelou's *I Know Why the Caged Bird Sings* as one of our primary models. We began the year reading Toni Cade Bambara, completed Black history projects in the middle of the year on Matthew Henson, Marian Anderson, and Lewis Latimer (I nixed projects on Martin Luther King, Jr., Malcolm X, Rosa Parks, and Harriet Tubman on the grounds that students could recite details of their lives in their sleep), and finished up the year reading poetry by Langston Hughes and Nikki Giovanni. This wasn't all we did, of course. We also read stories and poems by Gary Soto, a Latino writer of young adult poems and novels; we completed a unit on the Holocaust while reading the play version of *The Diary of Anne Frank,* and compared events then to the tragedy taking place at the time in Kosovo; and we wrote daily journal entries on topics such as "One goal I have for today is . . ." and "What did the period say to the exclamation point?" It was a varied class. But it, like the school and the district as a whole, drew much of its strength from its focus on African-American authors, themes, and history, and on the African-American urban experience in particular.

Until our pounding by Sutton and the conversation we had on the bus on the way home, I thought that was generally a good thing. Our school was entirely African American, after all, and teenagers are interested in nothing if not themselves. As a faculty, we thought that it was important to give students numerous role models—examples of African Americans from all walks of life succeeding in a whole range of professions. Most of our students came from single-parent homes, with a large percentage living with a grandmother or occasionally an aunt, and few had relatives who had attended, let alone graduated from, college. We wanted to give students a vision of what they could achieve if they worked hard and succeeded in school; frankly, we wanted to give them a vision of what life could be like beyond the blocks that defined the Fourth Ward. As my colleagues frequently emphasized to our classes, "You can't control where you came from, but you *can* control where you're going." From this perspective, it made absolute sense to grab students' attention and interest with people like them—African Americans from the inner-city—and to inspire them to aim for the same level of achievement. We were trying to reach students by connecting with their own lives, increasing their self-esteem, and making the historical and literary record more inclusive than it had been in the past.

In doing so, we were following the lead of Atlanta Public Schools as a whole, which overtly had as its aim the education of

African-American children. This explained the one professional development course required of all its teachers: "African and African-American Infusion in the Curriculum." At one "Atlanta Public Schools Middle School Mini-Conference" I attended, one school choir sang a spiritual, another school's double-dutch team performed, a group of girls gathered from a few middle schools performed a "step" routine, and another school choir sang "Lift Ev'ry Voice and Sing"—at which point our school librarian exhorted everybody to "stand up for the Black national anthem!" This focus on Black cultural forms and pride was typical for all districtwide events I attended over my three years of teaching in Atlanta.

Our objectives were honorable and thoughtfully chosen, and to some extent our methods were essential to the process of inspiring and empowering poor, young, African-American students. In another respect, however, it was clear that our teaching limited students' imaginations in certain directions as much as it expanded them in others. Students had learned an impressive amount about Black history, authors, explorers, inventors, artists, and so on, but they had little context in which to put these achievements. They could tell me about Marian Anderson's triumphant concert on the steps of the Lincoln Memorial and her debut at the Metropolitan Opera—but almost none of my students knew what an opera was, let alone had ever heard or attended one. My students created excellent presentations on Lewis Latimer, but they knew nothing about Thomas Edison's achievements over the same period. Although they were enthusiastic supporters of Martin Luther King, Jr.'s "dream" (King's boyhood home was about three blocks from the school, and Ebenezer Baptist Church was across the street), they had little knowledge of the civil rights movement as a whole; most had no idea, for example, who Lyndon Baines Johnson was. Most frustrating from my perspective, they weren't even aware of what they didn't know, since they lived entirely in a Black world in which their peers, relatives, neighbors, ministers, radio stations, and even television programs had identical cultural and historical referents.

My students were able to live in this world in part because Atlanta has such a large and thriving Black community, and in part because African Americans have collectively developed "a semiautonomous, rich, and robust information network (including newspapers, magazines, and artistic products), which provides news and analyses that often vary considerably from that which is found in the mainstream media."[2] My students uniformly listened to the three Black-oriented hip hop radio stations in Atlanta, watched Black Entertainment Television and UPN (which in 1999 showed five of the top ten primetime shows watched by African Americans but none of the top ten shows watched by non-African-American audiences), and started their Internet searches at blackplanet.com—this was in the days before Google's preeminence, before Facebook or YouTube.[3] Social life was also uniformly segregated. In my three years of attending my students' dance and orchestra recitals, church choir performances, basketball games, and other out-of-school activities, for example, I only once sat in an audience that was noticeably racially integrated.

It would be misleading to suggest that my students were unusual in their degree of racial isolation. Racial and other forms of segregation are equally characteristic of many communities across the United States. We tend to live in neighborhoods segregated by class and often by race and ethnicity; we talk and socialize only with people who share our religious and political convictions; we educate our children in economically and racially segregated schools, or in segregated classrooms within apparently diverse schools; we consume cultural products targeted to an ever-narrower demographic.[4] Walden and the Old Fourth Ward are therefore not particularly unusual in their isolation; they just represented my first experiential case study of the phenomenon from an outsider's perspective, as opposed to my living in social and cultural isolation as an insider within other communities.[5]

My Walden students were actually more advanced than many young people growing up oblivious to their racially, socially, economically, politically, and culturally homogeneous and isolated settings—including perhaps especially those growing up in middle-class, wealthy, White suburbs. My students knew they were isolated racially and socioeconomically; they commonly referred to the Fourth Ward disparagingly as "the ghetto," and they were continually surprised when they saw me in the neighborhood in the evening or on the weekends, because, as Jaquinn pointed out to me, "Nobody, you know, uh, White, ever comes down here." They also knew that the White world had different sets of cultural markers: LeKwaun, Benny, and Davonte would drive me nuts pretending to speak in British accents while answering questions in class; all of my students loved making fun of country music; and they were usually fascinated to examine what I had brought for lunch, because they knew it would be something exotic: hummus, say, or asparagus on pizza, or blueberries. But these, as they knew, were superficial differences. What they didn't know was the extent to which their own world was unknown in many other corners of American culture—and vice versa. After all, *everybody* knows Master P, don't they?

As I further puzzled over what my students at Walden *should* know about the world beyond their doorsteps, I turned in search of guidance to state and national curriculum standards in social studies and English, and to philosophical literature on diversity, civic membership and engagement, and multiculturalism. With disappointment, I discovered that there was almost nothing written either about or in response to the aims and implementation of civic or multicultural education specifically in minority classrooms and schools. State and national curricula invariably emphasized the *commonality* of what students are expected to learn in the name of establishing "high expectations" for "all children," while steadfastly ignoring the vast differences among students, schools, and communities across the state and nation. They presented a "one size fits all" model that I found deeply suspect as well as educationally impractical. Literature specifically on diversity and multiculturalism tended vaguely to parrot this goal of making the curriculum "inclusive" of "all people and perspectives," which hardly made for a coherent, let alone practical, curriculum. It was also usually implicitly assumed that the classroom was broadly diverse or was majority-White. The only literature I found at the time that explicitly addressed majority-minority schools advocated a totally separate, Afrocentric curriculum—similar to what we were teaching at Walden, but what I was trying to get away from.[6]

So what did I want instead? I knew I wanted my students to be able to exercise power and control over their own lives as they grew up. As a doctoral student in political theory just a couple of years earlier, I had written my dissertation about liberal democratic states' responsibility to help all children develop their capacities for autonomy.[7] I still believed that giving students the knowledge and skills to make meaningful choices about their own life course was a fundamental responsibility of schools. I also knew that I didn't care in any absolute sense that they had never heard of Kurt Cobain or grunge, or that they didn't know that Master P was relatively unknown among White youth (this was before Whites had thoroughly embraced hip hop). Kurt Cobain is frankly an insignificant figure outside of the history of late-twentieth-century American popular music. But I did care that they couldn't identify cultural references that might matter when they were trying to write a college entrance essay, apply for a scholarship, or get a job. I also wanted them to understand what kinds of knowledge *not* to assume that others had: for example, *not* to assume that nonurban youth or non–African Americans would necessarily have heard of Master P. In other words, I cared about their "mainstream" or "dominant" cultural capital.[8] What Sutton kids know about history and culture isn't necessarily better, deeper, or more important than what Walden kids know about history and culture, but Sutton students' knowledge is structurally more empowering given the unequal distribution of economic, political, cultural, and other power in the United States in the early twenty-first century.

In this respect, empowerment is a collective condition, not just an individual possession or state. Power is relational and contextual.[9] It wasn't enough to try to empower my students within their school and community, to give them confidence and capacities within the confines of Walden and the Old Fourth Ward, which is essentially what the Atlanta Public Schools were doing, and what much of the Afrocentrist literature advocates. This was an okay start, but it still left them in a profoundly subordinate position in the larger world. As our school bus carried us down Peachtree Street after the National Academic League match, leaving behind the office towers and luxury malls of Buckhead and heading toward the shotgun houses and funeral parlors of the Old Fourth Ward, we were literally being driven out of power. Students' pride in Marian Anderson's achievements wasn't going to change that. Nor, however, would knowledge of *The Magic Flute*. Even if they had a greater mastery of dominant cultural capital, they would still be mere visitors to the halls of power. Shaniqua had demonstrated this understanding as she wandered through the halls of Sutton to explore what a "rich school" looks like.

Instead, I have come to believe, Davonte, Shaniqua, and Benny needed to have the opportunity to make the United States a more just and equitable place on their own terms. They wouldn't be truly empowered until their own school was as "rich" as Sutton, until they and their quiz bowl coach couldn't look at a team and know immediately based on their color and class who was likely to win, and until their ignorance of Kurt Cobain was a matter of as much indifference as Sutton kids' probable ignorance of Master P. This kind of empowerment goes beyond individual students' mastery of mainstream cultural capital. It also goes beyond students' mastery of and pride in local, nondominant cultural capital. Furthermore, it goes beyond any individual student's mastery of academic, cultural, or social knowledge and skills, and beyond any educator's attempt to "fix things" for his or her own students. We can't transform American society—which is what it would take truly to empower my students from Walden—simply by transforming opportunities for one kid at a time. Instead, I am convinced, schools need to teach young people knowledge and skills to upend and reshape power relationships directly, through public, political, and civic action, not just private self-improvement.

What does this look like in practice—especially in urban public schools like Walden that are struggling to provide even the academic basics to young people growing up in historically marginalized communities? What principles can and should guide this work? How can one justify to a skeptical public this ideal of empowerment—an ideal that literally puts power in the hands of youth? These are the questions that I address. In so doing, I also ask and strive to answer a number of other questions: Why should we care about empowerment particularly within de facto segregated schools and communities? Does and should empowerment look different in these contexts than in others? When students are living in historically marginalized and disempowered communities, should schools focus on helping them gain the knowledge and skills to contribute to and build up their own communities, or to escape into more efficacious communities? How much can be achieved in settings such as Walden if we don't transform education at Sutton, too—not to mention transforming educational practices in wealthier and Whiter suburbs such as Marietta or Cobb County? In this respect, what are the implications of the choices we make in de facto segregated schools and communities for the nation as a whole?

Although these questions arise out of my specific teaching practice, they are of general interest because Walden's level of segregation is not unusual. Fully one-third of Black and Latino students in the United States, and over half of the Black students in the Northeast, attend schools that have a 90–100 percent minority student population.[10] The overwhelming majority of these schools are in urban areas, often central cities. Over half of all schools in the hundred largest school districts were 81–100 percent non-White in 2008–2009, and one-sixth of these districts had a non-White student population above 90 percent.[11] In practice, therefore, most schools in these latter districts had a virtually 100 percent minority population, often from a single race or ethnicity.

Even those school districts that have some diversity often contain a number of schools that are racially or ethnically homogeneous. There are Black schools and White schools. Over half of Washington, D.C., public schools have a 97 percent or higher Black student population, for example—but six schools are over 50 percent White. In Atlanta in 2010, similarly, although the student population is about 81 percent Black, half of the elementary and middle schools are at least 97 percent Black; this racial clustering is counterbalanced by seven elementary schools that are over two-thirds White, and one that is 40 percent Hispanic (and 59 percent Black).[12] The disparity between Walden's and Sutton's demographic profiles clearly illustrates these within-district segregation patterns. Thus, as dismal as the district data are with regard to racial and ethnic segregation, they often present a rosier picture of integration even than individual school data do. These trends are further exacerbated by urban charter schools, which tend to serve a more highly segregated minority population even than the districts in which they are embedded. Sixty percent of Boston-area charter schools have a non-White enrollment of over 90 percent, for example, in comparison to only one-third of Boston Public Schools with a similarly high non-White student body. The students in these schools and districts are also generally poor. Over half of all students in the 100 largest school districts are eligible for free or reduced-price lunch, and in nineteen of these districts, which together serve close to four million students, more than seven out of every ten students are eligible for free or reduced priced lunch.[13] Many of these students thus face "double segregation" both by race and ethnicity and by class, or even "triple segregation by race, class, and language."[14]

The number of these schools serving poor, urban, de facto segregated populations is likely to increase in upcoming decades, as schools and school districts in the United States are resegregating, not desegregating.[15] This trend will potentially accelerate thanks to the Supreme Court's decision in *Parents Involved v. Seattle,* which invalidated race-conscious school assignment policies designed to promote integrated schools in Louisville, Kentucky and Seattle, Washington. Furthermore, public pressure for integrated schools has diminished considerably. Integration is viewed by many as "yesterday's struggle," with greater importance being placed on students' obtaining an "equal opportunity to learn," whether in integrated or segregated settings.[16] The "No Excuses" charter school movement presents perhaps the most visible contemporary exemplar of this shift. These schools have been celebrated nationwide despite—in fact, because of—their serving student populations that are highly segregated by both race and class. Knowledge Is Power Program (KIPP) schools, for example, boast that "Every day, KIPP students across the nation are proving that demographics do not define destiny. Over 80 percent of our students are from low-income families and eligible for the federal free or reduced-price meals program, and 95 percent are African American or Latino." Hypersegregation is overtly rejected as a concern; if anything, KIPP schools' commitment to "clearly defined and measurable high expectations for academic achievement and conduct that make no excuses based on the students' backgrounds" subtly charges those who do express concern about segregation with low expectations and a culture of excuse-making.[17] Similar claims have been offered in Raleigh, North Carolina, where the Wake County school board voted in 2010 to end busing after twenty years of nationally recognized desegregation efforts.[18]

African American and Latino political leaders have similarly shifted their focus from integration to equality of opportunity. Leaders of the National Association for the Advancement of Colored Persons (NAACP), for instance, have held "a formal debate over the virtues of nonsegregated versus black-run schools for black students" and released statements minimizing desegregation concerns, although it did file an amicus brief in support of Seattle's and Louisville's school integration policies.[19] Black mayors in Seattle, Denver, St. Louis, and Cleveland have also led efforts to dismantle desegregation practices, while a leader of the Latino civil rights group La Raza recently asserted, "Having 100% of one ethnicity is not a bad thing."[20] As Justice Clarence Thomas wrote in his concurring opinion in the Seattle and Louisville cases, rejecting the constitutionality of school integration policies, "it is far from apparent that coerced racial mixing has any educational benefits, much less that integration is necessary to black achievement."[21] Some prominent scholars have also questioned the desirability of school integration; in Gloria Ladson-Billings's words, "it would be better to have a 'real *Plessy*' than to continue with a 'fake *Brown*.'"[22] Such scholarly, public, and Supreme Court opinions, combined with the United States' growing non-White population, will ensure that segregated schools remain a fact of twenty-first-century American life.[23]

De facto segregated schools thus pose meaty and important challenges in and of themselves, while also serving as proxies for even deeper conversations about who we are as a people and how we should deal with new forms of American diversity. If as a nation we are abandoning the ideal of integration in practice, what does that mean for our civic identity as Americans? Is there a collective, shared civic identity any longer—or was there ever?

What should students learn about themselves and one another, and what are the opportunities for crossing divides among these? Furthermore, what light do the struggles for membership, meaning, and power in historically disenfranchised communities and schools shed on U.S. politics and civic community as a whole? In confronting these questions, I delve into quandaries surrounding multiculturalism, the relationship between personal and political identity, political engagement, cynicism, diversity, and disenfranchisement—issues that are central to American life and American politics. *E pluribus unum* stands as America's perennial challenge. By looking at this challenge in part through the lens of de facto segregated schools and the communities in which they are embedded, we can learn more about the *pluribus* we are and the *unum* we strive to be.

Before continuing, I want to acknowledge that I am a White, upper-middle-class, highly educated woman writing about how we should educate poor youth of color. This likely, and appropriately, raises some red flags. Low-income students of color in the United States have in general been poorly served by the overwhelmingly White, middle-class men and women who have controlled and taught in public schools over the past century or two. These students have been condemned as "uneducable," pitied for suffering from a "culture of deprivation," asked by enthusiastic and well-meaning teachers to do work that often increased neither their achievement nor their opportunities, assigned schools and teachers that were vastly inferior to those enjoyed by wealthier and Whiter students, and told that their knowledge and skills were unimportant or even disreputable. The long history of White educators making declarations about how we should educate "other people's children" stands as a troubling reminder of the risks I take venturing down the same path.[24] Nor are good intentions sufficient. Misunderstandings, misinterpretations, and misapplications inevitably afflict attempts to reach out across multiple dimensions of difference. I have run ideas, arguments, and chapters by many readers and interlocutors in order to discover and get past some of these misperceptions, but I am sure I will make mistakes nonetheless.

I have hence tried to write this book in an unusually transparent fashion. Scholarly works are usually written in ways that ignore, obscure, or even deny the personal attitudes and biases of the author. Rather than treat my personal experiences and reactions to events or individuals as irrelevant background to the act of scholarship, however, I've built them into the text and analysis. In so doing, I hope to give you, my readers, tools that enable you to evaluate my arguments on your own terms. In honestly relating the events and interactions I found challenging as a teacher, and in giving experiential context for the intellectual choices I have made, I am trying to equip you with the means of identifying assumptions and biases that clouded my own judgment despite my best intentions. In this respect, I offer a personal intellectual history to accompany the normative, analytic, and empirical arguments that drive this book.

I reference normative, analytic, and empirical arguments because these various "ways of knowing" equally drive my work in this book. I am a normative political philosopher and a teacher by training. Neither of these groups learns research methods as such. Political philosophers are trained to think, hard. We look for logical inconsistencies (ways in which one claim does not follow from another), logical entailments (what must follow from a claim), explicit and implicit assumptions, and other characteristics of linear, logical argumentation. We also think about what seems reasonable, especially with respect to human behavior. What can we expect people to feel, think, or do under certain conditions? What would it be reasonable for people to feel, think, or do in these circumstances? And finally, we are trained to think about values. We reflect about what values seem to be embedded within a variety of institutional structures or relationships, and if necessary, how we might reform those structures and relationships to embody values we hold to be more desirable values. We argue in favor of some values and against others, propose hierarchies of values, and develop propositions for how to cope when values conflict. Political philosophers tend to care passionately about justice in particular, and about developing theories and principles that help people understand and enact what justice demands under a variety of circumstances. Oftentimes, although not always, this thinking occurs in the world of "ideal theory," where the moral and institutional pathologies of the world as it exists are assumed away in order to gain clarity about our ideal rights, obligations, and relationships.[25]

Teachers are trained to work, hard. We look for resources that can help us convey complex material to students with a mindboggling variety of desires, needs, and capacities. We reflect upon what happened in class one hour to make on-the-fly modifications to how we teach the next hour; we do the same at night, reflecting on one day to prepare for the next. We beg, borrow, and steal ideas as quickly as we can find them. When we face a challenge, we ask colleagues, friends, online communities of teachers: how can I do this better? What's going wrong? What's worked for you? We try out these ideas, evaluate them as we go, and try to separate the wheat from the chaff in real time. When we're lucky, we find time in the summers or on weekends to read, take classes and attend workshops, and modify our plans for next year. When we're really lucky, we create or join communities of practice, in which a group of teachers meets regularly throughout the year to read, discuss, and learn together. We think about subject matter, pedagogy, data, school and public policies, community contexts, the economy, values, learning theory, psychology, language development, special needs, the impact of politics on our work, and the mismatch between hopes and dreams and reality, all in a jumble. Teachers tend to care passionately about children in particular, and about applying professional knowledge in ways that serve each child's needs to the greatest possible extent. Oftentimes, although not always, all this work occurs in the world of concrete practice: what do I need to learn and do to help these particular students, at this particular time, in this particular place?

This book tries to draw upon the best of both "research" traditions—or more accurately, of both traditions of truth-finding. I draw as best as I can upon the analytic skills and normative commitments I have learned as a political philosopher. I evaluate arguments, defend and critique principles, and look for hidden assumptions and discuss what is entailed when these assumptions are brought to the light of day. I propose values that I think should guide our actions, and try to be reasonable about human behavior, psychology, and interests in making recommendations that follow from those values. I also draw as best as I can upon the synthetic skills and practical judgment I have learned as a teacher. I look for evidence of what works in concrete situations, steal promising ideas and practices wherever I can find them, and reflect about how theory, practice, and young people intersect in decidedly nonideal contexts.

But I also go beyond both of these traditions. Normative political theory's relative indifference to empirical data frustrates me. There's a lot of reliance on "common sense" that has been disproved by the social science literature, or has been shown to be more particular (to White, middle-class academics, say) than general. Theory that never leaves the world of the ideal also frustrates me. I care about people—especially young people—in the here and now. If normative political philosophy *could not* be relevant to the very nonideal facts on the ground, then maybe I would accept its self-satisfied confinement to ideal worlds. But I actually think that philosophy *can* be useful with respect to contemporary life in all its complex ugliness and beauty. It can help us better understand our current ways of life and potential options, and help us justify those choices that are hard (because they're resource-intensive, or challenge cherished preconceptions, or force us to give up enjoyable privileges) but morally necessary.

With respect to teaching, I go beyond typical teaching practices by stepping back from the world of the everyday to try to put ideas and actions in broader perspective. This isn't opposed to the tradition of teaching, by any means. But it's frankly a luxury that few teachers have. I have been profoundly grateful to have the time as a scholar and professor to read, reflect, and write about practice. I also go beyond some teaching traditions in taking academic research very seriously. I try not to assume reflexively, "They don't know my kids. That won't work for my class." More broadly, I have confidence that many ideas and practices can be generalized, even while acknowledging that they will always require some modifications for one's specific children, school, and community context.

As a means of moving beyond both political theory and teaching as pragmatic intellectual enterprises, I draw upon empirical literatures whenever I can. I am not a social scientist, but I am an enthusiastic *user* of political science, political and social psychology, and sociology, as well as of history.[26] High-quality social science research can unsettle philosophers' assumptions that their own reasons, values, and ways of being in the world are in some fundamental way universalizable to all "reasonable" people. Data are also useful for highlighting the profoundly nonideal and oppressive power relationships in which many children and adults find themselves. They can thus bring urgency to problems that theorists are otherwise inclined to set aside. Careful social science research can also help educators examine and refine their own practices, in part by subjecting them to the hard light of data, but also by provoking teachers to question their own assumptions and try out new ideas. I do not mean to advocate that we should uncritically embrace social science in theory or in practice. Given the nature of scientific research in general and the messiness of social science research in particular, we must assume that many of the "truths" of social science today will be overturned sometime in the future. I thus approach social science findings with a healthy level of skepticism, but also recognize their relevance to answering the kinds of questions I pose in this book, and to political theory and teaching more generally.

My background in these two different traditions of truth-finding, as well as my inclinations to go beyond both, result in a book that is methodologically eclectic, and intentionally so. I draw on personal experience a great deal—partly to illuminate questions that I think are worth asking, as well as to demonstrate the possibilities and consequences of taking the actions I propose. I don't claim that these anecdotes prove anything in and of themselves, but I do think that they can help us gain insight into the intellectual and pragmatic complexities of the issues I explore. In service of achieving these insights, I try to step back fairly frequently and analyze the normative principles at stake, as philosophers are wont to do. As noted above, I also draw upon rigorous empirical research as often as it is available, especially in political science, sociology, history, political and social psychology, and education. Civic and political education and participation research have both undergone exciting resurgences in the past twenty years, and I'm especially grateful to be able to draw upon significant new, rigorous, thought-provoking, and often interdisciplinary empirical work in these fields. Finally, I have supplemented my secondary readings with some original empirical research. Scattered throughout the book are quotations from and occasional statistics about youth and adults associated with four de facto segregated school communities: Walden Middle School in Atlanta; McCormack Middle in Dorchester, a neighborhood of Boston; Zavala Elementary School in Austin, Texas; and Fordson High School in Dearborn, Michigan. These data derive from focus groups, interviews, and surveys that I conducted with 125 parents, teachers, students, and adult and youth civic leaders in spring 2004. These schools and locations are real, as are the names of the adults (other than my colleagues) that I interviewed. I have assigned pseudonyms to all children, however, as well as to my colleagues, out of respect for their privacy.

"So why did the Articles of Confederation make it so hard for the states to work together and get anything done? Adam, what do you think?"

"Ummm—oh, Dr. Levinson, there's someone knocking at the door. Can I let them in?"

"No, I'll get it!"

"No, me, no, me!"

"I'm the closest!"

Josephine triumphantly makes it to the door first, and opens it to reveal my colleague Ms. Sanchez, who is visibly shaken. She teaches just two doors down from me, but we usually see each other in the teacher room, not in our classrooms. "Dr. Levinson, have you heard?"

"No, heard what?"

"The World Trade Center has been hit by two planes. There are rumors that the Pentagon has also been bombed, and maybe the Capitol Building. Do you have a TV in your classroom? No? Why don't you bring your students into my room; you all can watch the news with us."

Stunned, I line up my homeroom, nineteen eighth-grade students whom I first met only a week ago, and file them down the hall to Ms. Sanchez's room. We fill in the extra desks and perch on the radiators in the back of her Spanish bilingual classroom.

A thirteen-inch television is propped on a chair at the front of the room showing a wavy, often static-obscured image of Tom Brokaw and the World Trade Center towers pouring smoke and flames from gashes in their sides. Ms. Sanchez stands next to the TV, adjusting the rabbit ears on top every minute or two, trying to get a better picture. Some students call out recommendations to her in Spanish and English; most of us sit or stand silently, trying to assimilate the obscure images on the screen.

We watch for about forty-five minutes, long enough to see the first tower collapse, to learn that the Pentagon was indeed hit, and to hear more rumors about other missing, possibly hijacked planes. It's still unclear if other targets in Washington have been hit. My students start to get restless, and the news is admittedly repetitive: continued massive confusion with no new information. Also, we're due in the library in half an hour to check out textbooks for the year, and I want to have an opportunity first to discuss with them what we have seen. Quietly, I motion to my homeroom students to follow me back to our classroom.

After my students slip into their seats, I ask them if they have any questions or thoughts. I'm surprised to find myself hit with a barrage.

"I don't understand what's happening. Can you explain it, Dr. Levinson?"

"Are the World Trade Center towers in Manhattan or Washington?"

"Where's the Pentagon?"

"I couldn't see anything. Why were those buildings collapsing?"

I realize that I'm going to have to explain everything that we just saw on television. Whether it's because of the fuzzy picture or the difficulty my thirteen- and fourteen-year-old charges have interpreting the raw, undigested nature of breaking news, many of my students are totally confused about what's going on. I pull a student desk to the front of the classroom and sit on its top, resting my feet on the seat of the attached chair. "Well," I begin,

"I don't know more than you do, but it seems that some planes were hijacked and flown into buildings. Two were flown into the two towers of the World Trade Center, which is in Manhattan, and one was flown into the Pentagon, which is in Washington. We don't know yet if there are other places that have been attacked, and it seems that there are still some planes missing, which may also have been hijacked."

"Why would somebody attack the Pentagon?" DaQuin interrupts.

"Because it's the center of the American military. It's the symbol of America's military power," I answer.

"Oh." Upon some questioning, I find out that many of my students have never heard of the Pentagon, and most are confused about why it's named after a shape they learned about in math class. I go to the board and draw the building for them and explain its purpose; I can see understanding start to dawn.

"I saw the World Trade Center when I was in Manhattan last year," Anna volunteers.

"Yes, you can see it from many places in New York City," I answer.

"Wait," Yasmine asks. "Are Manhattan and New York City the same?"

I realize that I have to back up some more. As I will learn over the next few months, fewer than half of my students are native-born citizens. Although most have lived in the United States for many years, some since birth, few have traveled outside of Massachusetts within the continental United States; if they travel in the summer or over school holidays, it's to go "home" to Cape Verde, Puerto Rico, the Dominican Republic, Haiti, Jamaica, or Vietnam. Travel such as this is rare, too, as almost all of my students are poor, as measured by their qualification for free or occasionally reduced-price lunch. Except for the few students who have visited relatives in New York, none has heard of the World Trade Center before today, so I draw a crude map of southern Manhattan on the board. I fill in the twin towers, the Stock Exchange, and Wall Street, and show my students why the area symbolizes America's economic power.

Once my students assimilate the basic information, talk quickly turns to whether there will be more attacks, and if so, where they will be. My students are understandably scared. Our school is at most a couple of miles from Logan Airport. Adam looks out the window and points to the Prudential Building and John Hancock Tower, downtown Boston skyscrapers clearly visible from our classroom. "Maybe they'll hit those next," he offers. "Maybe that's where the next hijacked airplane is headed."

"Or what about our school?" Josephine asks. "We're so close to everything. They could kill 700 students at once."

"Look, I can't guarantee that we're safe, or that the Pru and Hancock Tower won't be hit," I respond, "but I'm pretty confident that nothing is going to happen here. First of all, whatever message the terrorists are trying to get across, they would lose the world's sympathy immediately if they attacked a bunch of innocent children. They're just not going to attack a school. And second, truthfully, we're just not important enough." Nineteen shocked faces look at me. Of course they're important!

"Think about it," I continue. "The terrorists, whoever they are, are attacking symbols of America's power: our military power, our economic power. What else symbolizes America's world domination? Our culture—in which case they'll attack Hollywood, or somewhere else in Los Angeles. Our politics—so maybe Washington, D.C. again. But Boston doesn't have anything that's a symbol to the world of America's might. We're a great city, sure, but we're not a great symbol of anything. The Freedom Trail? Yeah, but what would you attack—the Old North Church? Not exactly worth it. If you go to a foreign country and ask people to name great American cities, they'll mention New York, Washington, D.C., Los Angeles, maybe Chicago. Boston would be at best fifth or sixth on the list. We just don't matter enough."

I glance at the clock and realize that we're due to check out textbooks. We troop down the hall and spread out in the library, waiting for Mr. Bill to call out students' names and scan the bar codes on their textbooks into the computer. This is a new technology for the school, and some of my students gather around him, watching and complaining that now if they lose a book, they can't take somebody else's and write in their own names instead. "Dog, you ain't got nowhere to hide now," I hear Da-Quin comment to a friend.

There's a TV on in the back of the library; I tell students that I plan to watch the news and invite them to watch with me. Four or five join me as I stand, glued to the set, occasionally looking around to make sure that my kids aren't getting out of hand. By this time, both towers have collapsed, and all of the television stations are playing the footage of the collapse, along with the videos of the planes flying into the towers, over and over again. Despite the drama, most of my homeroom is content hanging out in the front of the library, gossiping about classmates, comparing teachers, speculating about whom the assistant principal is out to get this year. As students pass by with their books in hand, I try to corral them into watching with me, explaining that this is history in the making. "You see these images?" I ask. "These are going to be pictures in the back of the American history textbook next year. See these pictures of Clinton here in *Why We Remember*? After that, in the next edition, you're going to see these pictures of the planes and the towers." Some students are impressed and stay to watch, commenting to each other that they're watching history happen. Others talk about how it looks like a movie or a video game; it doesn't seem real to them yet, and they wander back to the front of the library to gossip some more.

I send my homeroom class off to science and then to lunch. When they return to me for the last period of the day, our conversation turns to who would have done this and why. "I bet George Bush is behind this," Laquita declares. "I bet he did this so he could have an excuse to go to war with Iraq."

"What?!?!" I respond. "We don't know who's done this, but I can promise you it's not George Bush."

"No, Dr. Levinson, I think you're wrong," says Travis. "Bush doesn't care about anybody except rich people, and he wants to go to war with Iraq to take revenge for what Saddam Hussein did to his dad. President Bush probably got somebody to do this for him, like Laquita said."

More voices chime in to back up Laquita. Bush has the power to do something like this because he's the president. You know that he doesn't care about the law because he stole the whole election. All he wants to do is go to war with Iraq, and this is the perfect excuse. People in power can do anything and get away with it; look how his brother managed to keep Black people from voting in Florida, and you don't see anything happening to him, do you? Bush is a horrible man—why *wouldn't* he do something like this?

I'm completely taken aback. Up until now, I've taken my students' questions in stride: their naiveté about the Pentagon, their confusion about the relationship between Manhattan and New York, their concern that terrorists might choose McCormack Middle School in Dorchester, Massachusetts, to attack next. But this vitriol against Bush, and their almost sanguine assumption that the president of the United States might choose to and be capable of killing 5,000, maybe 10,000, American citizens simply on a whim—I find it breathtaking in its combination of utter ignorance and absolute cynicism.

A few days after the September 11 attacks, when I started telling my mostly White, middle-class friends and family about my students' response, they generally shared my shocked reaction.[1] How could my students believe an American president could do this? And how could they never have heard of the Pentagon? After all, even though some of my students were recent immigrants, many had been born here or had lived here for years. A number of people asked me if my students had confused the current President Bush with his father, and I answered no; they clearly distinguished between the two, and knew that Hussein had been attacked by, and was alleged to have tried to assassinate, George H. W. Bush rather than George W. Bush. But nonetheless, I too felt as if my students had gotten confused somewhere along the way—and as if their mistrust of "the system" was almost pathetic in its casualness.

Nowadays when I tell this story, people comment on my students' prescience. Instead of questioning my students' understanding of the distinction between the two presidents, they question whether my students really could have made the claims I ascribe to them. Could they really have seen so far into the future, when none of the pundits in late 2001 and early 2002 had done so? How could they have known, on September 11, 2001, that President Bush would use these attacks to justify going to war in 2003 against Iraq and deposing Saddam Hussein? My students were brilliant! Also, people point out that although it is too bad that my students hadn't heard of the Pentagon and didn't know that Manhattan was a borough of New York City, there's little reason to think that the average White, middle-class, native-born eighth grader would have known this information either. Maybe the teachers in Arlington or Medford (two White, working- and middle-class suburbs of Boston) had to explain these things to their students as well.

The latter point is well taken. I am not yet convinced, however, of the former point, that my students were so brilliant. Despite President George W. Bush's use of the September 11 attacks to justify a profoundly misguided war in Iraq, his assault on due process, embrace of torture, cavalier dismissal of the Geneva Convention, shameless malingering, and patent war crimes,[2] I still disagree with my students' assessment. I don't believe that President George W. Bush planned and executed the September 11 attacks on New York City and Washington, D.C.

Why not? As far as I'm concerned, it's because I'm right—the facts don't bear out an alternative interpretation. But it's certainly plausible that I read the facts as I do in part because of my personal experience growing up and living as a White, middle-class, native-born American citizen. I have been well served by the United States: by its institutions, opportunities, freedoms, civil and public servants, class structure, and racial hierarchies. Thanks, too, to my social class and my educational experiences at Ivy League schools (these are heavily intertwined, of course), I know and am even related to a number of people who have been or are currently serving at high levels in various branches of federal government. I like and trust many of these people, and I find it hard to imagine how a conspiracy like September 11 would or could have originated and been carried out by their equivalents in the White House.

True, as an American history teacher I also taught for years about the horrors perpetrated by presidents of the United States: the eight men who owned slaves while president; Andrew Jackson's systematic slaughter of Native Americans before, during, and after his presidency; Lyndon Johnson's commitment to sending thousands of American men to die in a war he knew could not be won—to say nothing of the Vietnamese men, women, and children who also perished. But I don't interpret these events as revealing an essential injustice or inhumanity in the character of the American presidency, or of the United States more generally. I don't mean to say that I think these horrors are outliers in American history or culture. To the contrary, they both implicate and are implicated by some of the deepest strands within the American character, ones that we are still grappling with today.[3] Even so, I generally trust that public servants are well-intentioned, even if sometimes horribly misguided in their interpretation of the public good. At the very least, I trust that vast, murderous conspiracies against the American people are not circulating among top officials in the White House.

By contrast, why did so many of my students immediately assume that Bush could have planned and executed the attacks? Again, as far as they were concerned, it's because they were right. Facts such as the stolen 2000 election, presidents' slaveholding and other depredations, and White, wealthy politicians' history of holding ruthlessly onto power easily bore out their interpretation. It is also certainly plausible that my students read the facts as they did because of their experiences growing up as non-White, poor, first- and second-generation immigrants in de facto segregated neighborhoods and schools. When I taught at Mc-Cormack, close to 90 percent of the eighth graders qualified for free lunch; 90 percent were racial and ethnic minorities; and well over half were first or second-generation immigrants. The vast majority of my students lived in poverty, in apartment buildings or housing projects rife with violence and drugs. Many lived within blocks of the seven "hot spots" identified by the Boston Police Department as the most violent areas of town. They were used to having only negative interactions with representatives of governmental power such as the police, social workers, probation officers, and teachers. These interactions were often tinged with racism and mutual mistrust. They also attended school almost entirely with others living in the same situation. As I discuss in more detail in Chapters 2 and 3, these daily aggressions may have been further contextualized by family members and other adults in the community as being part of a lengthy history of mistreatment and oppression by the government. Small wonder they interpreted breaking news in such a way that implicated the president for complicity in the tragedy.

Whether my students were misguided or prescient, whether their life experiences blinded or exposed them to the true character of our political leaders, there is ample evidence that they are unlikely to become active participants in American civic and political life. As a result, they are unlikely to influence civic and political deliberation or decision making. This is because there is a profound *civic empowerment gap*—as large and as disturbing as the reading and math achievement gaps that have received

significant national attention in recent years—between ethnoracial minority, naturalized, and especially poor citizens, on the
one hand, and White, native-born, and especially middle-class
and wealthy citizens, on the other.

EVIDENCE OF THE CIVIC EMPOWERMENT GAP

African-American, Hispanic, nonnative-born, and poor students
perform significantly worse on standardized tests and surveys of
civic knowledge and skills than White, Asian, native-born, and
middle-class students do. These disparities appear as early as
fourth grade and remain consistent through middle and high
school. On the 2010 National Assessment of Educational Progress (NAEP) Civics Assessment, for example, White fourth and
eighth graders who were poor (defined as eligible for free or
reduced-price lunch) performed as well as nonpoor African-
American and Hispanic students—and significantly better than
students from those groups who were poor. Asian students' results were mixed. Within each ethnoracial group, poor students
earned significantly lower scores than middle-class and wealthier
students. Studies of adults confirm these patterns, which can
manifest themselves in startling ways. In 2004, for example,
none of my twenty-seven eighth-grade homeroom students at
McCormack Middle School knew that July 4 celebrates the sign-
ing and publication of the Declaration of Independence.[4]

These tests of political and civic knowledge and skills are
clearly limited and biased in a number of ways. They tend to focus on static governmental structures and institutions, usually at
the state and federal level. In this respect, these tests are unlikely
to capture the knowledge of contemporary political events that
my students demonstrably possessed, such as the contested 2000
election, the first Persian Gulf War, or Saddam Hussein's assassination attempt against George H. W. Bush. Tests and surveys
also tend to assess skills associated with conventional forms of
political participation, rather than young people's skills in avoiding altercations with the transit police or in negotiating with

public housing officials to fix chronically neglected public spaces.[5]

Nonetheless, both the sheer lack of knowledge as well as the consistency of the differences matter and should be troubling. People's capacities for civic empowerment are simply greater if they know about political structures and institutions as well as contemporary politics than if they don't. It is easy to imagine how people who don't know who their elected representatives are, what the White House's position is on various high-profile policy disputes, or how a bill becomes a law—or even what July 4 stands for—may find it harder to influence civic life than those who do.[6] These domains of knowledge aren't all that matter. But they are relevant to the distribution of power in society. Individuals' civic knowledge, skills, and attitudes profoundly influence their civic and political behavior, which are concomitantly central to the strength, stability, and legitimacy of democracy. Civic knowledge is clearly and directly correlated with higher levels of political participation, expression of democratic values including toleration, stable political attitudes, and adoption of "enlightened self-interest."[7] Individuals' mastery of civic skills is also tied to both their likelihood of civic participation and especially their effectiveness. "Those who possess civic skills, the set of specific competencies germane to citizen political activity, are more likely to feel confident about exercising those skills in politics and to be effective . . . when they do."[8] Thus, demographically predictable patterns in the distribution of these domains of knowledge presage a disturbing civic empowerment gap.

The civic empowerment gap also bleeds over into civic and political participation. Consider the 2008 presidential election, for instance. Despite widespread excitement about Barack Obama's candidacy and media coverage suggesting huge increases in youth and minority turnout, 2008 voting rates exhibited vast disparities that almost exactly replicated those seen in 2004. As the table shows, two-thirds of White and Black voting-age citizens voted in the 2008 presidential election, while half or barely half of Hispanic or Asian citizens did so. Since about one-third of Hispanic and Asian residents are noncitizens and hence ineligible to vote, these low voting rates among those who are citizens further depress Hispanic and Asian American's already relatively weak political voice at a national level.[9] These numbers are stubbornly unchanged from 2004. In both elections, citizens with less than a high school diploma likewise were only half as likely to have voted as citizens who possessed a bachelor's or advanced degree. Voting disparities by income and by citizenship source are also both significant and virtually unchanged. These voting rate disparities persisted despite the extreme competitiveness of the Democratic primary election and the historic nature of the 2008 presidential campaign.

Significant civic and political behavior disparities also persist beyond voting. Reliable analyses of political participation, as measured by membership in political parties, campaign donations, campaign volunteering, participation in protests, contacting an elected official, and so forth show vast disparities linked with class, education, and race. People who earn over $75,000 annually are politically active at up to *six times* the rate of people who earn under $15,000, whether measured by working for a campaign, serving on the board of an organization, participating in protests, or contacting officials. Broader measures of civic participation—belonging to any group or organization, working on a community problem, volunteering, attending a community meeting, or even just wearing a campaign button or putting a political bumper sticker on one's car—are also highly unequally distributed by educational attainment and ethnoracial group.[10] As the second table shows, for example, college graduates in 2009 reported participating in nonelectoral political activities, volunteering with an organization, and working with neighbors to fix a community problem at twice the rate of high school graduates, and four times the rate of high school dropouts.

Percentage of U.S. citizens over 18 who voted in the 2004 and 2008 presidential elections, by race and ethnicity, educational attainment, income, and citizenship source

	2004 election (percent)	2008 election (percent)
Race/ethnicity		
African American/Black	60	65
White (non-Hispanic)	67	66
Latino/Hispanic (any race)	47	50
Asian/Pacific Islander	44	48
Educational attainment		
Less than high school diploma	40	39
High school graduate	56	55
Some college or associate degree	69	68
Bachelor's degree	78	77
Advanced degree	84	83
Annual income		
Under $20,000	48	52
$20,000–$49,999	62	61
$50,000–$74,999	72	71
$75,000–$150,000	79	77
Over $150,000	81	82
Citizenship source		
Native born	65	64
Naturalized	54	54

Source: Calculated using data from U.S. Census Bureau (2010b), tables 4a, 5, 8, 13; U.S. Census Bureau (2010c), tables 4b, 5, 8, 13.

White and multiracial individuals are similarly involved in these activities at twice the rates of Latino and Asian individuals, with African Americans in the middle.

It's important to note that none of these rates of involvement is particularly high. The fact that 65–66 percent of White and Black citizens of voting age voted in the 2008 presidential elec-

Percentage of U.S. residents over 18 who participated in nonelectoral political and civic activities, by educational attainment and race/ethnicity

	Participates in one or more nonelectoral political activities (percent)*	Volunteers with an organization (percent)	Works with neighbors to fix a community problem (percent)
Educational attainment			
Less than high school diploma	9	9	3
High school graduate	18	19	6
Some college or AA degree	31	30	9
Bachelor's degree or higher	42	42	14
Race/ethnicity			
Latino	13	14	3
Asian	14	19	4
African American/Black	23	19	7
White alone (non-Hispanic)	28	28	8
Multiracial	32	27	9

Source: Corporation for National and Community Service and National Conference on Citizenship (2010b). See also Corporation for National and Community Service and National Conference on Citizenship (2010a) for more detailed data.
*These include: contacting an elected official; attending a public meeting; boycotting; attending a rally, protest, or march; or demonstrating support for a party or candidate in some way.

tion means that a full one-third of such citizens failed to do so. Over half of college graduates report *not* participating in non-electoral political activities; the same is true for volunteering. Although the wealthiest and best-educated Americans are most likely to protest or to work with neighbors to address a community problem, their rates of involvement in these activities are still well under 20 percent. In 2009, for example, about twice as many Whites as non-Whites contacted an elected official—but in practice this means that about 11 percent of Whites did so, as opposed to four to six percent of Hispanics, Asians, and Blacks.[11] I do not mean to suggest, therefore, that wealthy, highly educated, or White citizens set a norm to which others should aspire.[12] Nonetheless, to the extent that I am arguing that we should be concerned about disparities in group members' civic and political power, these general and persistent inequalities matter even when absolute levels of engagement are low for all groups.

The civic empowerment gap is also a matter of attitude. What struck me most forcefully during my conversation with students on September 11, 2001, was how fundamentally mistrustful and cynical they were. How on earth could I convince them to become civically and politically engaged—simply to vote, let alone to contact government officials, write letters, volunteer for campaigns, or even run for office themselves—if they believed that their elected officials might readily murder 10,000 Americans on a whim? This dilemma wasn't particular to one set of students in Dorchester. The gap between my students' thoughts and mine mirrored a nationwide racial civic attitude "chasm" in individuals' trust in government (political trust) and their trust in each other (social trust).[13] Social class and trust are also directly correlated, as Robert Putnam reports in *Bowling Alone*: "In virtually all societies 'have-nots' are less trusting than 'haves,' probably because haves are treated by others with more honesty and respect. In America blacks express less social trust than whites, the financially distressed less than the financially comfortable, people in big cities less than small-town dwellers, and people who have been victims of a crime or been through a divorce less than those who haven't had these experiences."[14] Insofar as my students lived many of these demographic characteristics at once—they were poor, non-White, living in inner-city Boston, predominantly living with only one parent (or grandparent), and with depressing frequency victims of both petty and serious crime—their cynicism and mistrust may have been overdetermined.

Research does show that political trust is not necessary to motivate participation, especially among African Americans. When mistrust in government is combined with a healthy sense of political efficacy, political participation may remain steady or even increase.[15] Al Sharpton's closing statement at the 2004 Democratic presidential debate in Detroit exemplifies this conversion of mistrust and marginalization into participation, even as it directly echoes some of my students' sentiments from three years before.

> But the problem we have is that in America many of us are not taken seriously. Most of us are not taken seriously. That's why we have a president that would send money to Iraq and not money to the schools in Detroit. That's why we have a president that wants to give people the right to vote in the capital of Iraq, Baghdad, and not respect the right of the voters in the capital of the U.S. in Washington, D.C. So the problem is that they don't take me seriously personally. They don't take us, collectively, seriously. And that's why we need to register and vote and come out in numbers like we never did before, so they will never ever marginalize and not take us seriously again.[16]

The yawning attitudinal gap in trust between my students and me (and more broadly, between people who are poor, non-White, and victims of personal and social upheaval and those who are not) hence may not stand in the way of political participation if it translates into action instead of paralysis.

The trust gap is problematic, however, insofar as it demonstrates a significant cultural incongruence that is often inimical to good teaching—and that I am positive led to my being a much less effective civic educator that year than I had intended.[17] My own motivation to be civically and politically involved stemmed in part from social and political trust—my trust that most of my neighbors are well-intentioned and honorable people, that if good people are elected to office then they can change society for the better, that my vote will be counted most of the time. I thought, therefore, that I needed to teach my students to become more trusting as a step toward their becoming more engaged— and in fact, most of the adults I talked to about this issue, including other teachers, agreed with me. Hence I worked that year to help my students develop trust, even though that is exactly the opposite of what may have more effectively motivated them to become civically and politically active. I would be doing this still if I had not read the literature on political motivation and participation while researching this book. I learned (to my utter surprise) about the negative statistical correlation between trust and political involvement, especially among African Americans. To the extent that the trust "chasm" between myself and my students led me—and I'm sure has led many other teachers like me—to approach civic education in a manner that was incongruent with their needs, it remains a significant piece of the civic empowerment gap.[18]

Furthermore, the sizable gap between my students' and my sense of *efficacy*—in other words, our belief that individuals can influence government (political efficacy) and especially that we ourselves can influence government (individual efficacy)—should be a cause of major concern. Efficacy is clearly correlated with engagement. The less efficacious one feels, the less likely one is to participate. It is also significantly correlated both with class and with race and ethnicity.[19] As one of my former students from Atlanta reiterated in an interview I conducted with her in the spring of 2004,

[N]o matter what you vote for, no matter how much you vote, it ain't gonna be in our hands. Whatever is going to happen is going to happen . . . I believe it's in God's hands. Or whatever . . . I just feel like there ain't nothing nobody can do . . . The other reason why I haven't voted is because, like he [another student in the group] was saying, when Bush wasn't supposed to win, it's like, well, why do people vote? Why? It ain't going to make no difference . . . [T]hey're going to pick whoever they want, they go with whoever they want to win anyway. And that's how it happened. It happened. Whenever whoever they say is going to win.

President Obama's election narrowed the efficacy gap in the short term, but certainly has not eliminated it, if for no other reason than that the efficacy gap remains utterly rational.[20] As a White, well-educated, middle-class woman with extensive political and social capital, for example, I undeniably *do* have more opportunities to influence government or public policy than did my non-White, educationally underserved, economically disadvantaged students who often spoke little English and lived in neighborhoods with limited social and political capital.[21] Although unjust, inegalitarian, and profoundly antidemocratic, this fact remains equally true no matter who is president. The problem, however, is that the efficacy gap may be viciously self-reinforcing, if those who view themselves as able to make a difference ever more involved while those who question their efficacy withdraw from public civic engagement.

The same may also be true for individuals' senses of civic identity and civic duty, which figure importantly in influencing the character and quality of civic engagement.[22] Michael Dawson has demonstrated in detail the ways in which African Americans' senses of civic membership and responsibility are distinct from those of non–African Americans in being focused on the "linked fate" of African Americans as a group; these considerations become especially important to poor African Americans.[23] Immigrant citizens' sense of civic identity is similarly ambiguous. Although their sense of patriotism tends to be as high as or higher than native-born citizens, their sense of themselves as Americans is more tenuous. In interviews I conducted in April 2004 with first- and second-generation Arab-American students, parents, teachers, and community leaders in Dearborn, MI, for example, my interlocutors (most of whom were citizens) consistently referred to "Americans" as "they":

> *Meira:* Three of you are American citizens, born in the United States. But you have consistently throughout the interview . . . used the term "Americans" not to refer to yourselves but to refer to others . . . [Y]ou talked about Americans as other people. So I'm curious why.
>
> *Hassan:* I see what you're trying to get us to say—like we were born here, like, why shouldn't we consider ourselves as regular American people. But I think that we're different because we have to fall back on our parents' background because our parents—that's what they teach us. That's what our culture is. Like our background from our old country and stuff like that.

Hassan's statement echoes other scholars' findings from New York City.

> [Second-generation Americans] used the term *American* in two different ways. One was to describe themselves as American compared to the culture, values, and behaviors of their parents . . . But they also used "American" to refer to the native white Americans that they encountered at school, the office, or in public places, but whom they knew far better from television and the movies. They saw those "Americans" as part of a different world that would never include them because of their race/ethnicity. Many respondents sidestepped this ambivalent understanding of the meaning of being American by describing themselves as "New Yorkers."[24]

Beth Rubin and Thea Abu El-Haj have documented similarly ambivalent attitudes and experiences of civic "disjuncture" among poor, non-White, and immigrant youth.[25]

WHAT MAKES A GOOD CITIZEN?

Does this ambivalence signal a deeper challenge to how we measure and hence define the "civic empowerment gap"? Why privilege traditional civic and political knowledge, skills, attitudes, and habits of participation in assessing the presence or absence of a gap? In essence, this challenge highlights the need to establish some common understanding of what "citizenship" means in the first place—normatively, as well as empirically. What does it mean to be a good citizen?

Interestingly (and unfortunately), my colleagues and I almost never talked about this question in my eight years of teaching middle school—even when citizenship, civic and political engagement, or civic education were explicitly on the agenda. At McCormack, for example, we gave out "citizenship" awards every term, alongside honor roll, perfect attendance, most improved, and homeroom awards. We tended to give the citizenship awards to students who were unusually helpful and compliant: to the student, say, who never complained about being assigned to work in a group with the kids nobody else likes and who refereed the flag football matches after school. Students who were troublemakers—who explicitly questioned the purpose or value of a class project, or who got into noisy arguments with teachers about "free speech" in school and claimed that their rights were being disrespected—did not generally win citizenship awards. On balance, this was probably appropriate. Because we did not recognize these latter behaviors at the school or classroom level as being acts of civic engagement (even as civil disobedience), they were experienced by most students and teachers as being merely disruptive and antisocial. Furthermore, many of the instigators themselves used the language of civil rights merely for effect, without actually intending to promote civic or school reform through their actions. They simply grabbed for the nearest rhetorical device that was likely to disrupt class. I'm not trying to argue, therefore, that we should have given citizenship awards to the troublemakers, but it should have been under discussion.

This lack of discussion about what we meant by "citizenship" at my school is representative of a larger, nationwide uncertainty about what it means to be a good citizen. Can you be a good citizen if you don't vote? What if you vote, but are uninformed about most of the issues and candidates, or vote solely on the basis of a single issue? How important is it to be law-abiding? Is being economically self-sufficient a hallmark (or even a precondition) of good citizenship? Is never being a burden on others enough to make one a good citizen? How should we judge the act of protesting injustice via civil disobedience against the act of sacrificing oneself on the battlefield for the good of the country? Depending on how you answer these questions, your judgment about what makes for good civic education may be radically different from mine.

For the purposes of this book, I adopt the definition of good civic education and citizenship set forth in an influential report, *The Civic Mission of Schools*. This definition integrates many disparate strands of belief and ideology about citizenship:

> Civic education should help young people acquire and learn to use the skills, knowledge, and attitudes that will prepare them to be competent and responsible citizens throughout their lives. Competent and responsible citizens:
>
> 1. are informed and thoughtful; have a grasp and an appreciation of history and the fundamental processes of American democracy; have an understanding and awareness of public and community issues; and have the ability to obtain information, think critically, and enter into dialogue among others with different perspectives.
> 2. participate in their communities through membership in or contributions to organizations working to address an array of cultural, social, political, and religious interests and beliefs.

3. act politically by having the skills, knowledge, and commitment needed to accomplish public purposes, such as group problem solving, public speaking, petitioning and protesting, and voting.
4. have moral and civic virtues such as concern for the rights and welfare of others, social responsibility, tolerance and respect, and belief in the capacity to make a difference.[26]

It is notable that this definition says nothing about the legal status of citizens. Similarly, when I use the terms "citizen," "citizenship," or "civic education" in this book, I am also setting aside young people's legal status. Public schools are appropriately required to educate all students who walk through their doors, whether they are citizens, green card holders, temporary residents, refugees, or undocumented aliens. Educators may not distinguish among their students by their legal citizenship status.[27] Neither shall I.

One other virtue of this characterization of good citizenship, and hence of good civic education, is that it is capacious without being simplistic. Within this definition, good citizens may be those who vote, protest, boycott, run for office, join political parties, join civic organizations, commit acts of civil disobedience, circulate e-mail petitions, write influential political blogs, tweet or text about political events being kept under a news blackout, and attend neighborhood council meetings. Good citizens may not, however, merely keep to themselves; simply not being a burden to others is not sufficient for good citizenship. In this respect, this definition rejects the ideal of the "personally responsible citizen" while encompassing the ideals of both "participatory" and "justice-oriented" citizens. Participatory citizens believe that "to solve social problems and improve society, citizens must actively participate and take leadership positions within established systems and community structures," while justice-oriented citizens believe that one must "question, debate, and change established systems and structures that reproduce patterns of injustice over time."[28] Participatory and justice-oriented citizens may thus frequently disagree about the most fruitful acts to take as citizens—and so also would disagree about the best approaches to citizenship education—but they both embrace the importance of knowledgeable, skillful, active involvement in order to improve society.

On the downside, this definition arguably privileges traditional modes of civic action that are both increasingly outdated and unrepresentative of a range of actions and behaviors that have historically been important civic tools for members of disadvantaged, oppressed, and marginalized groups. For example, while intentional organizing via social media—such as that which facilitated the Arab Spring of 2011—clearly satisfies the definition above, many other internet-based activities occupy an ambiguous intermediate territory. It's hard to categorize virally spread videos such as will.i.am's 2008 pro-Obama music video "Yes We Can" or the video of Neda Agha-Soltan's 2009 shooting death during a previously peaceful protest in Iran. Facebook "fan" groups and other forms of social networking also blur the lines between private and public speech and action, despite their increasing and undeniable civic importance.[29] The above definition also seems to exclude artistic production and expression, including hip-hop music and video, poetry slams, and graffiti—all of which have been used especially by young, often poor, people of color in the United States and elsewhere to critique contemporary power structures and civic institutions.[30] Furthermore, it fails to credit the civic intentionality and implications of "everyday . . . forms of resistance" by "relatively powerless groups: foot dragging, dissimulation, desertion, false compliance, pilfering, feigned ignorance, slander, arson, sabotage, and so on."[31] Finally, emphasis on public and collective forms of engagement likely overlooks the ways in which especially members of historically disadvantaged groups may be "pillars of their community" without participating collectively in public activities. A well-known community elder, for example, may exert considerable civic influence by modeling rectitude, advising youngsters about how to behave and "do right," and serving as an informal but final arbiter of community disputes, even though he or she takes part in no obvious "public" activities. These are all arguably significant civic roles, actions, and dimensions of influence that are not obviously included in the definition above.

Even so, traditional forms of engagement still matter with respect to empowerment. People who vote regularly, contact politicians and other government officials, speak up in public meetings, join civic organizations, and donate money to both candidates and civic causes invariably have more civic and political power in the United States in the early twenty-first century than those who do not. We therefore need to take these traditional measures of civic engagement into account, even at the cost of privileging them over other modes that are more accessible to and more frequently employed by members of historically disadvantaged groups. I realize that this risks creating a circular and apparently deficit-oriented argument in which I place certain groups at the "bottom" of a civic empowerment gap precisely because I discount forms of civic engagement in which they are particularly involved. But gaps need not imply deficits— and it does no one any good to ignore the specific harms suffered by those who cannot or do not deploy traditional levers of civic and political power.

WHY THE CIVIC EMPOWERMENT GAP MATTERS

As the numerous sources of data themselves attest, it is no secret that civic and political knowledge, skill, efficacy, sense of membership, and participation are distributed in vastly unequal ways among U.S. residents and citizens. There is, however, shockingly little concern about this; rather, it's accepted as the natural state of affairs. Demographic differences in participation rates are rationalized in the same way differences in reading or math achievement were discounted by many a decade ago: "But of course poor people [or Hispanics, or another group] participate less. They don't have the time or financial resources [or education, or knowledge, or . . .] to participate as wealthier people do." This argument just doesn't make sense when one compares civic participation patterns in the United States to other developed and even many less-developed democracies. European, North and South American, and Asian voter turnout rates in the 1980s, 1990s, and 2000s reveal about a 10 percentage point difference in voter turnout between the most- and least-educated citizens and between the wealthiest and poorest citizens. This is far eclipsed by the United States' 25–35 percentage point gap.[32]

Poverty, ethnoracial minority status, and education level also don't necessarily impede participation. It is difficult to determine the demographic characteristics of the millions of courageous protesters who have participated in the "Arab Spring" uprisings. But the news from Al Jazeera and Jadaliyya.com do not seem to suggest that these are battles merely between elite groups. One early analysis even suggests that in several countries, including Syria and Yemen, protesters are from lower-class communities.[33] Other relatively recent events demonstrate that political participation needn't be the sole privilege of elites. Consider, for example, protests in Argentina in the 2000s, when hundreds of thousands of poor and middle-class Argentines alike took to the streets banging pots and pans and ended up forcing the resignations of their political leaders. They were actually following the example set by *piqueteros* (picketers)—unemployed workers who started a nationwide movement for social change in the 1990s and have sustained it for over a decade. If unemployed and uneducated citizens in Argentina (as well as other South American democracies such as Brazil and Venezuela) can demonstrate high levels of civic and political engagement, certainly poor people in the United States could do the same. Furthermore, it is worth remembering that the participation gap has not always been a major feature of American civic and political life. In the late nineteenth and early twentieth centuries, immigrant

zens—as exemplified by the Black Panthers, the riots after the Rodney King incident, and recent domestic terrorism threats—is an extreme but real possibility in a democracy, as such violence is tightly linked to feelings of disaffection and alienation.[36]

Furthermore, democratic deliberations and decisions are likely to be of lower quality if people representing only a fairly narrow range of experiences, interests, and backgrounds are involved. Part of the beauty of democracy, when it functions effectively and inclusively, is its ability to create aggregate wisdom and good judgment from individual citizens' necessarily limited knowledge, skills, and viewpoints.[37] To exclude citizens from this process is to diminish the wisdom that the collectivity may create. People who praise my students' "brilliant" political analysis in the wake of 9/11, for example, may wish that my students' voices had been heard within the national conversation from the start, from September 12, 2001, rather than only after mainstream commentators and politicians started voicing suspicions of the Bush administration's motives in 2003.

Above all else, the gaps in knowledge, skills, attitudes, and participation matter because they profoundly diminish the democratic character and quality of the United States. Larry Bartels has recently demonstrated that "political influence seems to be limited entirely to affluent and middle-class people. The opinions of millions of ordinary citizens in the bottom third of the income distribution have *no* discernible impact on the behavior of their elected representatives."[38] This follows on the conclusions of the American Political Science Association's Task Force on Inequality and American Democracy:

> Generations of Americans have worked to equalize citizen voice across lines of income, race, and gender. Today, however, the voices of American citizens are raised and heard unequally. The privileged participate more than others and are increasingly well organized to press their demands on government. Public officials, in turn, are much more responsive to the privileged than to average citizens and the less affluent. The voices of citizens with lower or moderate in-

comes are lost on the ears of inattentive government officials, while the advantaged roar with the clarity and consistency that policymakers readily hear and routinely follow.[39]

Not all of these unequal levels of influence can be attributed to differences in individual levels of knowledge, skills, attitudes, or participation, of course. There are powerful institutional, political, and other factors at work that would likely contribute to the persistence of inegalitarian and undemocratic outcomes even if the gaps explored above were eliminated. The exploding cost of political campaigns and politicians' corresponding dependence upon and attention to wealthy donors provide only one obvious example of the multiple barriers to equal civic empowerment. But it is clear that the civic empowerment gap among individuals is a significant and documentable threat to democratic ideals and practice. I suggest that it is important for both the civic and political empowerment of poor, minority, and immigrant individuals, and for the health of the polity as a whole, that we develop means for closing the gap.

CLOSING THE GAP

One important battleground for attacking the civic empowerment gap is the network of mostly urban schools serving a de facto segregated, poor, and minority student population. There is incontrovertible evidence that poor and non-White students are receiving demonstrably less and worse civic education than middle-class and wealthy White students, and that school-level differences are partly to blame. The civic learning opportunity gap suffered by poor and non-White students, especially those attending de facto segregated urban schools, also compounds the civic opportunity gaps they face outside of school. Considerable evidence demonstrates that people living in areas of concentrated poverty are significantly less likely to be engaged civically, and to have opportunities for such civic engagement, than those living in more mixed or affluent communities. Youth in particular face significant impediments in developing civic identities or acquiring civic knowledge and skills when they grow up in high-poverty urban communities. Since youth who are being educated in de facto segregated, non-White, and poor urban schools are also almost surely living in de facto segregated, poor urban neighborhoods, this means that students attending these schools are facing a civic opportunity gap in their neighborhoods as well as in their schools.[40]

If we care about political stability, democratic legitimacy, and civic equality, then we must care about what is taught and what is learned in these schools—not just for the students' sakes but for our own. This is consistent with condemning the phenomenon of de facto segregated schooling as harmful to the students who attend these schools, to the students who don't attend these schools (and who are thus often educated in relatively segregated settings themselves), and to the nation as a whole. There is substantial evidence that the best education for students in a liberal democratic society requires schools that are integrated—integrated ethnically and racially, but also by class, religion, immigration status, and other aspects of family background.[41] De facto segregated minority schools, however, are not only widespread but expanding. These schools pose challenges to American democratic politics today, and the students who attend them merit attention and support now, including an appropriate civic education.

This is not to say that schools can overcome the civic empowerment gap entirely on their own. There are numerous changes that need to be made across multiple sectors of society: consistent, same-day voter registration laws; early and expanded voting opportunities; nonpartisan redistricting boards to increase the number of contested elections; political and economic policies that reduce as opposed to increase economic inequality; increased investment in low-income communities; massive reform of the school-to-prison pipeline in poor and minority communities; improved and expanded social service provision; greater challenges to institutional racism; immigration reform; the list could go on indefinitely.[42] But schools should not be left out of the picture, as they also have an important role to play. De facto segregated minority schools in particular can help reduce the civic empowerment gap and help promote true civic and political equality for all Americans.

Schools can help close the gap in a number of ways. To start with, we need to commit to improving urban schools and reducing the dropout rate, which reaches nearly 50 percent in some urban districts. Calls for urban school reform may seem simultaneously banal and absurdly idealistic: who doesn't support the massive overhaul and improvement of urban schools in the United States in the early twenty-first century? At the same time, who has robust confidence in such an overhaul's bearing significant fruit in the near term? Yet it is a need that bears repeating. Both the civic empowerment gap and the quality gap between many impoverished urban versus wealthier suburban schools remind us that our society is inegalitarian and antidemocratic in some fundamental ways.[43] If urban schools were better, and if more students stayed in higher-quality schools and graduated, then the demographic divide in this country would narrow, and the civic empowerment gap would narrow along with it. Furthermore, higher-quality urban education resulting in higher educational attainment among students who attended those schools would likely have a direct effect on these students' civic empowerment, since education is the single most highly correlated variable with civic knowledge, civic skills, democratic civic attitudes, and active civic engagement.[44]

We also need to restore civic education to the curriculum. The decline in the number, range, and frequency of civics courses offered in U.S. elementary and high schools must be reversed. There is ample evidence that civic education improves civic outcomes, but resources devoted to it have dropped markedly over the past thirty or forty years—especially in schools serving minority students. In the 1960s, students regularly took as many as three civics courses in high school, including civics, democracy, and government; now students tend to take only one—government—and that only in the twelfth grade, by which point many poor and minority students have already dropped out.[45] If civic education is offered to students only in twelfth grade, therefore, then in effect it is disproportionately provided to wealthier, Whiter, and native-born citizens.

Furthermore, it is absurd to think that by offering civic education only a few times over the course of a child's education, we will reliably enable and encourage students to become active, engaged citizens. There is a reason that we require students to take English and math every semester of every year of elementary and secondary school: mastery takes time and practice. Hence we expect students to engage in ongoing, consistently reinforced learning and coaching with regard to these essential disciplines and practices. If we want students to become masterful citizens, then the same expectations should apply. If we want to narrow the civic empowerment gap, especially by increasing poor, minority, and immigrant students' civic knowledge and skills, then civic education must begin in elementary schools and be a regular part of education through twelfth grade and beyond.

Old-school "civics," however, isn't going to shrink the civic empowerment gap on its own. "Civics" usually covers the three branches of government, how a bill becomes a law, and other formal institutional structures demonstrating how government works. My students and others at the "bottom" of the civic empowerment gap, however, think that government *doesn't* work— at least for them or anyone they know—and they may well be justified in this belief. Civics classes that emphasize the mechanisms of a functional and essentially fair and democratic system will thus be rejected as irrelevant or worse by these students. So we need to take another approach. Schools need to take seriously the knowledge and experiences of low-income youth and adults of color—to teach in ways that are consonant with and that even build upon their knowledge and experience, in ways that are engaging and empowering rather than disaffecting and disempowering.

In other words, McCormack needs to figure out how to help Travis, Laquita, and their classmates build upon their passion and their insights to get involved rather than to withdraw. Traditional "civics" classes, I submit, will not accomplish this. Instead, we need to rethink civic education from the ground up. We need to rethink how we teach civic knowledge, skills, attitudes, and actions through history classes, multicultural curricula, interdisciplinary experiential programs, and even the very rules, procedures, and physical layout of the school itself. Once we figure this out, we need to consider how assessment and accountability mechanisms can be used to ensure that educators, schools, and communities teach this "new civics"—in other words, that they take an approach that reduces rather than exacerbates the civic empowerment gap.

At the same time, we must remain attuned to how our answers to these apparently merely "practical" questions about educational matters—how should we teach history? What interdisciplinary experiences should we encourage?—pose deep and provocative challenges to our very self-conception as a democratic nation. Public schools have always been charged with the responsibility of making Americans and (re)making America. Decisions about how to educate our and others' children are at their heart decisions about how we conceive of the world we live in now and how to create the world we want to inhabit in the future. I argue that solving the civic empowerment gap is a central responsibility of schools (and other public institutions); it is a necessary precondition of our claim to be a democratic nation. But the task is not without danger. It risks exposing fissures in our national identity and democracy that many people would rather keep under wraps. It also risks upending our collective understanding of who we are and who we hope to be, even potentially revealing that no such collective understanding exists. We must confront these risks with clear heads and honest hearts if schools are to tackle the civic empowerment gap in a meaningful way.

CHARTING A NEW VISION

I begin to sketch a picture of what a truly empowering education might look like—and what such an education would reveal about American democracy and nationhood as a whole—by focusing on how schools can help students confront, address, and begin to overcome the deeply inequitable ethnoracialized structures and outcomes of American civic and political life. In Chapter 2, I argue that schools should teach all students to assume a kind of "double consciousness" that enables perspective-taking and power analysis.[46] I also argue that students from historically marginalized communities should be taught both codeswitching and solidaristic collective action as means of exercising civic and political power both within and outside the system. On a practical as well as a conceptual level, this means that civic identity is not a "neutral," shared space in which all can participate equally and in the same way. Even if we are all equally citizens in theory, our other identities intersect with our civic identity in such profound ways that they cannot be disentangled.

In Chapter 3, I examine the implications of some of these ideas for how we teach, learn, and co-construct American historical narratives. Solidarity, collective action, inclusion versus exclusion, and the significance of ethnoracial identities for American civic membership are not plucked from thin air, after all. Rather, they are rooted in long traditions of effective and even transformative civic engagement by minority groups, especially African Americans. I argue that the traditional, moderately triumphalist narrative about U.S. history taught in most schools reinforces many students' alienation and disempowerment. U.S. history education must be reformed to help students construct and engage with a multiplicity of historically accurate and empowering civic counternarratives—many of which may shock the conscience of those of us who were raised on stories of American exceptionalism. We should stop searching for or assuming the truth of one unified American story. A corollary of this is that there is no unified American national identity.

Surely there are some unifying American heroes, though? What about such "great Americans" as Abraham Lincoln or Martin Luther King, those who symbolize what is best and most noble about the United States and who provide a common vision around which we can organize and strive to emulate? Such figures may be inspiring in the abstract, I argue in Chapter 4, but they do not move us forward as a democratic nation. To the extent that students learn to gaze upon others' heroic visages, they fail to learn and be moved to engage civically themselves. Elimination of the civic empowerment gap, and education for civic empowerment more generally, necessitates a shift in focus from distant heroes and their accomplishments to more ordinary role models and their specific techniques of civic engagement, especially of collective action. Civic heroes may continue to play some role in helping us embrace national civic ideals, and even in unifying us through a common civic religion. But civic empowerment is again found in the particular and the contextual, not in the general or abstract.

The most concrete and pervasive context in which most young people interact is in fact school. Schools are themselves civil societies, for good and ill. They exert a profound effect on students' and adults' civic experiences, identities, and opportunities—even when they have no intention of doing so. In recognition of this fact, in Chapter 5, I shift from investigating how students learn *about* citizenship in settings such as history class to arguing that we must change students' opportunities to learn *through* citizenship in the school as a whole.[47] If we want young people to develop the knowledge, skills, attitudes, and habits of empowered citizens, they must be given the opportunity on a regular basis to practice being citizens. I demonstrate how this plays out across the school, in hallways, classrooms, and even bathrooms and the schoolhouse steps. I also develop a set of criteria by which we can evaluate the civic experiences students are afforded in schools, and toward which we might aspire. As schools become more civically engaged and empowering communities, however, they also are forced to confront issues that trouble the wider polity, such as political partisanship and diversity of conscience. Through exploring one student's proposed citizenship project opposing same-sex marriage on religious grounds, I argue that the demands of "public reason" fail to satisfy egalitarian democratic norms either in the classroom or in civic discourse more broadly.[48]

These arguments remind us how porous the boundaries are between schools and the "real world" beyond. In Chapter 6, I assert that we should do more to knock down the walls between schools and their surrounding communities. If we want adults, other elites, and youth themselves to recognize and value the civic contributions that young people—especially low-income youth of color—can make, then these young people must be given the opportunities to make a visible and effective difference in the world beyond the school. I argue that guided experiential civic education offers students such opportunities, whether through mock trials, community organizing, voter registration drives, internships, or other initiatives. These stand in contrast to community service learning programs, in which students often engage in and reflect about short-term ameliorative acts like cleaning up a park or raising money for a charity. To close the civic empowerment gap, young people must be given a chance to engage in policy-oriented, collective action about potentially contentious issues; service learning usually fails to do this. There are many examples of programs that work; most promising among these are action civics initiatives, some of which I highlight.

To offer high-quality guided experiential civic education and especially action civics to students, however, requires significant time, training, and community support. It also entails risk for educators, students, and the polity alike: risk that students will push too far, that educators will find themselves in uncharted and politically uncertain territory, that communities will find themselves vocally and persistently challenged by youth whose perspectives raise uncomfortable truths. How can anyone be encouraged, let alone enabled, to take such risks? In the contemporary United States, almost all public education policy comes down to standards and accountability metrics. Should civic education be any different? In Chapter 7, I discuss the roles that standards, assessment, and accountability mechanisms play in promoting or hindering high-quality civic education reforms. I argue that these mechanisms are salutary for enabling adults to exercise control over education *within* a democracy, but they tend to undercut young people's legitimate claims to receive an education that equips them *for* democracy. Because the latter should trump the former when they are in tension, I claim that standards, assessments, and accountability systems should play only a limited role in democratic education reform that selects, trains, and provides ongoing support to civically engaged and thoughtful educators. Under such circumstances, it is possible that they will promote a virtuous circle that builds capacity, motivation, and public support for strong and effective civic education practices, while still offering the adult public a strong democratic voice in public schools.

Notwithstanding the challenges and the dangers, the pursuit of democratic equality and legitimacy is a laudable and necessary goal. As schools put these reforms into place, they will provide students and teachers with a set of powerful civic experiences that are likely to increase their efficacy and engagement, and hence to inspire their acquisition of civic knowledge and skills as well as continued productive participation. In doing so, schools will also help strengthen local communities and the nation as a whole, both via the direct work that students accomplish and by building a new generation of mobilized, empowered adults. Reducing the civic empowerment gap also strengthens democracy. It broadens government's representativeness, increases its responsiveness to diverse individuals and communities, and thereby also reinforces its political legitimacy in the eyes of historically disenfranchised community members. It strengthens schools, as students turn their attention to solving problems collaboratively as opposed to fighting against the system or just checking out. And finally, it promotes civic and political equality and fairness—ideals that are central to our American democracy. These are goals that all schools—and all citizens—can and should embrace.

Race Talk and Civic Empowerment

2

It's October 1999, a month into my first year teaching at Mc-Cormack Middle School in Boston. I'm feeling okay about the curriculum, but discipline has been fairly rough. I have four boys with me after school for detention today; I'm hoping that forty minutes of silent work time plus cleaning desks will provide an incentive for them to be a little less disruptive tomorrow. Of course, as soon as detention begins they all *have* to go to the bathroom. Immediately. I write their names up on the board and tell them they can go one at a time in the order I've recorded.

Noah immediately protests, "That ain't right! You're racist, Dr. Levinson. Why did you make the two Black kids go last, huh? You just discriminating against African Americans."

I'm baffled. All four boys have dark skin. All four seem "Black" to me! What on earth could Noah be talking about? I ponder for a moment whether to ask; will this help me understand my students a bit better, or make me look foolish and ignorant in front of them? I decide I need to know whether Noah's just trying to get my goat—which certainly wouldn't be the first time, even in only twenty days of school—or if there really is some distinction of which I'm unaware.

Thanks to Noah and his friends' enthusiastic tutelage (after all, every minute they can discuss this is a minute they don't have to suffer through silent work time), I learn that the first two students on my list do not identify as "Black" at all. Danny is Cape Verdean. Jose is Dominican. They both are astounded that I couldn't tell that from the start.

As I take attendance the next day, I notice for the first time patterns in the spellings and pronunciations of students' names. Yesenia pronounced with a "J" at the beginning—she's Dominican. So is Yulia. Kids whose names seem Spanish but have "s" where I'd expect a "z"—Peres, Lopes: they're Cape Verdean. The names are Portuguese, not Spanish. That explains the "s/z" switch, which I had until now found totally perplexing.

The Asian kids' names, by contrast, require no decoding on my part: they're all Vietnamese. I can also tell who is Haitian by their French-origin names. I can't keep track of some of the other kids from the islands, though. I have a hard time remembering who is from Puerto Rico as opposed to the Dominican Republic when there's not a handy "Y" in the name. I also forget whose families hail from Jamaica or Trinidad versus who identifies as African American. I'm learning that these distinctions matter deeply to my students, and I need to remember them for my students to feel I really know them. But it's a challenge these first few months. At least I know that Mohammed is from Somalia and that Sadiq is from Guyana, although I can't figure out how either of them identifies beyond that.

I realize that knowing the official demographics of our school—50 percent Black, 30 percent Hispanic, 15 percent White, and 5 percent Asian—is actually worse than knowing nothing at all. I had the illusion of understanding, but these broad statistics are misrepresentations of a much more complex reality on the ground. What amazes me is that my students seem to be able to keep track of every peer's race, ethnicity, and national origin. There are over 200 eighth graders. Many of them don't know each other's names. But they know where they're from, and how they identify. "You know, that Spanish girl. From Puerto Rico. The one with the pouf and light skin."

Their fluency with each other's ethnoracial backgrounds

places my own mistakes in sharp relief. One day, I spontaneously ask Charize to stand in for a nineteenth-century African-
American historical figure during a role play in history class. Her
classmates ridicule this suggestion. Everybody knows Charize's
family is from Trinidad. She's Black, but she's not African American! The pedagogical purpose of the role play gets lost in the
ensuing scrum.

This is not to say that my students are attuned to ethnoracial
differences beyond those directly represented at McCormack.
During a conversation about push-pull factors in immigration,
for example, Julio makes a comment about all the families in
Dorchester who are "Vietnamese, Chinese, Japanese, whatever."
Thu and Tran nearly fly out of their chairs in protest. Julio
doesn't understand why they're making such a big deal about
the elision. "Hey, you're all Asian! Why does it matter if I call
you Vietnamese or Chinese? You all ain't that different."

While Thu splutters in frustration, I interject, "Yeah, Dominican, Puerto Rican, whatever."

The class swivels toward me, shocked into silence. Then a
dozen voices call out in protest. "You're whack, Dr. Levinson!
There ain't nothing the same about Dominicans and Puerto Ri-
cans! How could you even say that? That's nothing like Chinese
and Japanese people! They're all Asian! But we're different!"

I spend the next twenty minutes teaching an impromptu lesson about the Sino-Japanese War.

In April, the disparity between Boston's official racial classification systems and students' own ethnoracial identifications
comes to a head. Boston Public Schools has asked homeroom
teachers to distribute a personalized form to each student listing
his or her racial (White, Black, Asian or Pacific Islander, Native
American) and ethnic (non-Hispanic/Hispanic) group membership. Students are requested to verify the information on the
form and return it to me—a supposedly quick and simple process. But my Cape Verdean students are outraged that they are
classified as Black—and they hate all the other options, too.

They spend their time crossing out the official designations and writing "Cape Verde" under both race and ethnicity. My Puerto Rican and many other Latino kids are incensed that their "race" is officially White, and only their "ethnicity" is Latino. They certainly aren't White, not under any circumstances! They want simply one designation of being Latino—or in their terms, "Spanish." Some Dominican kids who are classified as "Black" and Latino are also frustrated. Although they aren't as appalled as those who were classified as White, they also profoundly disagree with the idea that they are Black, no matter what their skin color.

In response to these assaults on their ethnoracial identities, a diverse group of students joins together—two Vietnamese, one Puerto Rican, and one Haitian—and decide with my encouragement to write a letter to Superintendent Thomas Payzant requesting an overhaul of the system. To my surprise and gratitude, Superintendent Payzant writes back. He explains that Boston is required to follow federal racial designation guidelines. Later that week, therefore, I help my students research the Census, which is about to conduct the 2000 count. They're pleased to discover that individuals can designate themselves as multiracial for the first time, but wish they had started their project earlier enough to change the Census categories, too. I nod sympathetically, and then turn our conversation back to the day's lesson on the Missouri Compromise.

We must grapple with both ethnoracial politics and the politics of race if we are to have any hope of ever achieving a civically inclusive, egalitarian, and hence truly legitimate democratic society in the United States. By ethnoracial politics, I mean the ways in which individuals have in the past, do currently, and can in the future use ethnoracial group membership as the basis for political organizing and collective action. By the politics of race, I

mean the myriad ways in which race and ethnicity both explicitly and covertly influence politics and public policy, as well as
the ethnoracial patterning of public policy and political outcomes.[1] We stunt civic life when we don't talk about race, especially across racial lines. Furthermore, race itself is the subject of
many difficult civic and political issues having to do with resource distribution, school assignments and busing, affirmative
action, immigration, policing policies, sentencing guidelines, and
issues of enfranchisement, such as denying felons the vote.[2] If
we cannot grapple directly with race across racial lines, if we
cannot navigate racial divisions thoughtfully, analytically, and
effectively, and if we cannot individually and collectively use racial awareness to overcome racial inequities, then we cannot fulfill the intrinsic promises—nor combat the engrained deficien-
cies—of American democracy.

In a certain way, writing about race is like teaching Black History Month. Black History Month is self-defeating if February
becomes the only time that Black history is taught or discussed,
and if it thus further segregates a history that is as a matter of
fact woven throughout American and world history as a whole.
But even if history is taught, correctly, in such a way as to take
thorough account of Blacks' roles as agents and objects throughout history, Black History Month would still be necessary. It is
the case both that Blacks are intrinsically part of American history—it would be nonsensical to try to tell or understand American history without Blacks as central figures at every stage—and
that "Black history" deserves attention and can be explored on
its own terms. Similarly, this book would defeat its own purposes if it failed to weave considerations of race and ethnicity
throughout its chapters and not only because I've said that I'm
especially concerned about de facto segregated minority schools.
It is impossible truly to understand civic identity, political power,
or public education itself in the United States without race and
ethnicity serving as central concepts every step of the way. But
they also deserve a chapter of their own.

Race and ethnicity are identifiable features of the civic empowerment gap, distinguishable from other demographic characteristics such as income or educational level. Number of years of education trumps all other measures as the most significant single predictor of people's civic knowledge, skills, attitudes, and behaviors. But other demographic characteristics, including ethnoracial ones, are also significant in their own right. Asian Americans are more civically disengaged than other ethnoracial groups both in absolute terms and especially once one takes socioeconomic predictors into account.[3] Hispanics are similarly underengaged in a comparative context, even when one restricts measures to Hispanic citizens (an important distinction, since over one-quarter of American Hispanics are not citizens), and even when one controls for income and education level.[4] African Americans are more civically engaged than members of other racial groups, including Whites, when other demographic characteristics are held constant—but of course, the interaction between race and socioeconomic status runs so deep that making these distinctions runs the risk of overlooking the real-world forest for the statistical trees.[5] The facts and the causes of these ethnoracial differences matter if we are to address the civic empowerment gap effectively.

Furthermore, race and ethnicity have been powerful tools historically for mobilizing African-American civic engagement and other ethnoracial groups. Civil rights movements throughout U.S. history provide the most obvious examples of this process; African-American civic institutions such as churches and schools have played a crucial role in constructing and promoting empowering historical civic narratives. But it is not only at the institutional level that ethnoracial mobilization makes a difference. Individuals' racial consciousness also facilitates mobilization. African Americans with higher levels of "racial salience," meaning that they view being Black as an important part of who they are, combined with "group consciousness," understood as "a conviction that the group can make a difference if it acts together—in short, group efficacy—and dissatisfaction with the status of the group," are significantly more likely to be civically and politically empowered than others.[6] It's unclear whether these same mechanisms come into play with other ethnoracial groups. But given what we do know, engaging schools in students' development of their racial identities potentially has significant consequences for reducing the civic empowerment gap— although this is also admittedly a delicate and potentially dangerous enterprise.

Finally, ethnoracial differences are embedded within American civic and political life and structures. In the U.S. system of "aggregative democracy," whether one is in the minority or majority matters.[7] Majorities win; minorities lose. If ethnoracial minority status were disconnected from political priorities, then numerical differences wouldn't matter. But racial demographics strongly track political beliefs, preferences, and priorities.[8] Hence, ethnoracial minorities suffer unequal civic and political outcomes in a system that structurally favors ethnoracial majority group members (i.e., Whites). Reformed political structures that favor deliberative approaches or structure voting in ways that give minorities strategic advantages could do some good.[9] But I'm not holding my breath in anticipation of state and federal voting reform anytime soon, especially since these practices favor those who currently possess most of the power. So instead we need to think about how these ethnoracially structured civic inequalities can and should be overcome.

TALKING ABOUT TALKING ABOUT RACE

It's hard to talk directly about race. Race does not exist in the physical world, and as a cultural construction it is rooted in some of the most inimical practices ever devised in the history of humankind. Race as we understand it today was invented a half-millennium ago as a means of justifying the slave trade. It is a pseudoscientific system of classification generated to justify temporary or lifetime subjugation, deportation, and even extermination of some people by others.[10] Given this sordid history, some scholars have understandably advocated for eliminating from our vocabularies both "race" as an overall term and "Black" and "White" as racial categories on the grounds that "they reinforce and legitimize precisely that biological notion of 'race' that we claim we want to be rid of."[11]

Talking about ethnoracial groups also poses challenges because of the way in which it ignores vast differences among individuals. There are hundreds of ways to signify and live as an "African American" or a "Latino," for example. African-American and Latino identities are multivarious, complex, and fluid. They also intersect with individuals' other identities: age, gender, religion, sexuality, class, geographical region, vocation, and so forth. No one is defined by race or ethnicity alone. Panethnic terms also obscure more specific variation. Vietnamese, Laotian, and Chinese American youth, for example, all face quite distinct sets of challenges and opportunities thanks in part to their particular ethnoracial identities and histories, their "Asian" designation notwithstanding. Moreover, panethnoracial categories are applied to new arrivals who have never thought of themselves as such, and whose similarity to one another may go no further than hailing from the same continent. My students made this clear in their responses to my "Dominican, Puerto Rican, whatever" comment in class—a comment that was intentionally designed to provoke, but that itself faltered on the grounds that the government did officially classify them as one large, panethnic group. There is a special bitterness in teaching immigrants and their children that they should classify themselves ethnoracially when these categorizations are wholly and maliciously invented in the first place.[12] Such categorizing also belies the creative ways in which many immigrants construct new *mestizo* identities that reflect no single nation or political entity. Immigrant youth culture in particular, informed by rapid globalization and boundary-crossing experiences, may be quickly outstripping the clumsy panethnoracial categories reflective of a more simple (and simplistic) construction of identity and difference.[13]

The vast differences between the racial acculturation, oppression, and resistance of Black people versus other ethnoracial minorities in the United States raise additional questions about focusing on race and ethnicity in general. African Americans' civic and political histories, identities, and actions are arguably so unique that it confuses the issue to discuss African Americans in the same breath as members of other ethnoracial minority groups such as Latinos and Asians.[14] Likewise, there's a danger in unthinkingly applying research findings from the rich literature on African Americans and Whites to other groups, where the research literature is much thinner and more tentative.

In spite of these concerns, I choose both to use standard U.S. ethnoracial terms—"White," "Black," "African American," "Latina" and "Latino," "Hispanic," "Asian," and so on—and to address race and ethnicity as general constructs, rather than looking at each group independently. These terms define the landscape in which the majority of Americans live, think, act, make decisions, learn, educate, exercise power, and respond to others. adopting different language would obscure more than it would clarify.[15] Whenever possible, we should engage with others using language they recognize and use themselves, rather than hoping that they will recognize the relevance of ideas and arguments expressed in unfamiliar terms. For better or worse, these are the terms that most Americans of all ethnoracial backgrounds use to refer to themselves and others.

Furthermore, because Americans do live and act in response to these broad ethnoracial frames, adopting these frames is likely descriptively useful in helping us gain insight into aspects of individuals' experiences and lives. The life paths and civic and political opportunities in particular of low-income youth of color, for example, in many ways cross specific ethnoracial lines. For this reason I choose to risk over-generality in service of our seeing and thinking about broader racial and ethnic patterns. Finally, the abandonment of even broad-brush ethnoracial language risks reinforcing the fallacious notion that we live in a colorblind and postracial world. We do not. It is hard to keep track of and illuminate the pervasiveness of ethnoracialized experiences within and for civic life, however, without using ethnoracial language. I therefore use *White, Black, Hispanic,* and so on, as imperfect and ill-defined as they are.

Educators in particular confront treacherous pedagogical and political waters when they use ethnoracial language and explicitly discuss ethnoracial categories in the school context.[16] How adolescents hear, understand, and use these terms may be very different from adults' intentions, and this mismatch may result in harmful misunderstandings. Also, because ethnoracial identity is not determined by visible physical characteristics, educators may also often misinterpret or misidentify their students' ethnoracial group memberships—just as I did when I assumed that my four students in detention were "Black," or when I spontaneously selected Charize to play an "African American" in our historical role play. Such misattributions can lead students and families to feel misunderstood and even disrespected, which in turn undercuts the foundations for good teaching.

Mismatches between families' and teachers' beliefs about the meaning and significance of ethnoracial identification can also place everyone at risk. As public employees within a low-status profession, educators are vulnerable to parental complaint and public outcry. As youngsters under the tutelage of powerful adults, students are vulnerable to educators' claims and decisions. As private citizens and residents subject to the powerful bureaucratic arm of the state education system, families are vulnerable to schools' authoritative status as gatekeepers to the worlds of college and career. Students and families may be anxious, baffled, or angry when their teachers' ethnoracial language and analysis contradicts that which they learn or teach at home.

On the other hand, it is neither easy nor even desirable to ensure that such mismatches never take place. Consider my Cape

Verdean students' rejection of their racial designation as "Black." In one way, it was easy for me to affirm students' desires to reject federal racial categories and to construct their own ethnoracial identities as they saw fit. Racial categories are cultural constructions grounded in a history of evil; they have no "natural" or biological existence; so individuals and group members should be able to define their own ethnoracial identities. On the other hand, many Cape Verdeans reject the "Black" label because they value their Portuguese ancestry—they essentially take the opposite approach to the U.S. "one drop of blood" theory. Portuguese ancestry "saves" them from being Black. This is the same approach taken by most Dominicans, who essentially elevate their Spanish over their African ancestry, and who further differentiate themselves from "Black" Haitians specifically on the grounds that Dominicans were never enslaved—thereby enmeshing slavery into their construction of Black identity. Anti-Black racism thus infects not only Americans' designations of those with any African ancestry as Black, but also Dominicans' and Cape Verdeans' rejections of Black identity in preference for their Spanish or Portuguese ancestry. To complicate matters further, Dominican, Cape Verdean, West Indian, and other islanders' rejection of the "Black" label may also serve as a crucial tool of self-preservation in a racist American society. By refusing to identify as Black, these immigrants attempt to avoid the "downward mobility" that tends to result from being so classified.[17] Given these complexities, educators' responsibilities for affirming or challenging students' ethnoracial identities are hard to sort out. We should challenge racism—but is this possible without either reifying other arbitrary ethnoracial categories or subverting non-White families' very strategies for surviving in a racist society? Neither is an attractive option.

It is not only students' ethnoracial identifications that pose pedagogical and political challenges. Teachers' own ethnoracial identities also play into the student-teacher relationship in powerful and sometimes unpredictable ways. I was always aware that my students accurately saw me as White and middle class—which to them meant wealthy—and that this led them to make other assumptions that were sometimes less accurate. Many of my students assumed, for example, that I was a Republican. This may in part have resulted from my unwillingness to tell them my political views; since my students in both Atlanta and Boston were overwhelmingly Democrats, they may have reasonably extrapolated that I was reticent because I didn't want to subject myself to their scathing attacks. But I think it also simply resulted from their associating Republicans with wealthy White people, and Democrats with poor people of color.

Although I almost never broke my silence about my political partisanship, I did try to make common cause with my students across ethnoracial lines in other ways.[18] I used my anticipated absences for Rosh Hashanah and Yom Kippur as a vehicle to tell my students early in the year that I am Jewish and to discuss my family's history. Every September, I would explain that my great grandparents came over to the United States in the late 1800s and early 1900s—well after slavery and the Civil War, in other words—and that they immigrated in part to flee pogroms or their equivalent. In doing so, I intentionally encouraged my students to draw connections between both their immigrant roots and my own, and their contemporary ghetto-ization and my ancestors' life in the Jewish ghettos. I wasn't trying to create a moral or experiential equivalence by any means, but I was trying to create a sense of moral and experiential solidarity that crossed ethnoracial boundaries. The influence of these personal revelations on my students—their willingness to place trust in me as their teacher, to believe that we really could work together in an atmosphere of mutual trust and respect—was palpable. At the most basic level, my students were visibly relieved to know that my ancestors did not own, colonize, or otherwise oppress their ancestors. More generally, they were more willing to suspend judgment, less likely to assume that as a White, middle-class woman, I couldn't understand their experiences, desires, or needs. They would hang out in my classroom and seek advice about problems they were facing, pull me aside to ask me to help friends or even family members, and share their experiences in class discussions and homework assignments. I was able to be a better teacher as a result, and they were able to learn more.

At the same time as I tried to foster a sense of cross-racial solidarity by distancing myself from some historical dimensions of Whiteness, I also openly discussed the ways in which I benefited from "White privilege," although I never used that exact term.[19] I commiserated with my eighth graders about their experiences of being followed in stores or being harassed by the transit police on the subway, and readily acknowledged that I never had such experiences and expected my children wouldn't either. We discussed these injustices openly. I intended these discussions to empower students, insofar as it's unfortunately still rare for a White person in authority to acknowledge publicly the racial injustices that youth of color face in their daily lives. But it wasn't and isn't clear how these discussions are heard and interpreted by students.[20] This was brought home to me most recently after a conference session I mis-facilitated about racism and racial identity among an ethnoracially diverse set of graduate students. When I talked during the session about racism in the academy, it turned out that I was heard by many in the audience as accepting it, as essentially saying "that's just the way it is." I was stunned. I think of "racism" as an inherently morally condemnatory term, but that's not how it was heard, probably in part because I am White. I was far too cavalier as a professor about assuming that my visible race wouldn't pose a barrier to solidaristic conversation with graduate students, and I likely made similar mistakes as an eighth-grade teacher.

Given these obstacles, educators are often tempted to avoid race-talk altogether. The demands of standardized curricula and tests are so great that we can zoom through these as fast as possible and still not reach the end in time; also, state standards are virtually certain not to ask teachers to engage in explicit, tough conversations about race. Nonetheless, I argue that there are good pedagogical reasons to discuss race in the context of empowering civic education. Because ethnoracial patterns exist, and ethnoracial resources exist as well, we should name them and help students to reflect critically upon them. Furthermore, leaving something out of the curriculum doesn't mean it gets left out of students' lives and ideas. Students learn about race, through race, in spite of and because of race, by simply growing up in the United States. Unfortunately, learning how to think about race is a fundamental part of learning how to think as an American. Schools don't need to teach that; others will. What schools can do is help students reflect critically on what they're learning and consider how to fight against some of the more inimical features of life in a race-influenced society. This sort of critical thinking is a key feature of civic education. American civic life will be better for it.

SIGNIFYING RACE IN CIVIC AND POLITICAL LIFE

In an era of "postracial" rhetoric spurred by Barack Obama's presidency, it is especially important to clarify how individuals' ethnoracial identities affect their daily experiences of and abilities to exercise power in American civic and political life. In part, historical ethnoracial discrimination is built into present-day civic structures and institutions. Redlining by banks, which was required by the federal government, created patterns of residential, political, and economic segregation that continue to infuse every aspect of U.S. civic life. Vast wealth gaps, whereby the average White family has ten times the savings as the average Black family, may have historical roots but inescapable present-day consequences for the distribution of economic and hence political power in the United States. Tax laws, criminal statutes, and social policies have vastly different effects on White, native-born, middle-class homeowners than on non-White, non–native-born, and poor Americans without property—often intentionally so. These and many similar injustices are central to any account of the ethnoracial dimensions of American civic and political life.[21]

Furthermore, racism, classism (which interacts with racism), religious prejudice (which in the case of anti-Islamic sentiment also interacts with ethnoracism), and anti-immigrant fervor are still potent political factors in the United States in the second decade of the twenty-first century. These prejudices impede minority group members' capacities to participate effectively in civic life in a whole range of ways. In part, minority group members face outright blocks placed by others, such as reduced access to the ballot box or fear that contacting public authorities about illegal working conditions or other injustices may result in one's own arrest or deportation.[22] Ethnoracial minority group members also have to bend over backward to prove their democratic bona fides, as then-presidential candidate Barack Obama was reminded when his bare lapel—missing the expected American flag pin—caused some to question his patriotism. Non-Whites find their fundamental citizenship status repeatedly challenged, as the "Birther" movement questioning Obama's origin exemplifies, and as countless especially Hispanic and Asian Americans encounter daily. Implicit attitude test data reveals that the majority of U.S. citizens and residents see Asians as inherently non-American, as "perpetual foreigners,"[23] despite many Chinese and Japanese Americans' roots going back to the mid-1800s—and despite Congress's own responsibility for denying Asian Americans citizenship throughout much of the late nineteenth through mid-twentieth centuries. Similarly, Latinos are often assumed to be recent, even illegal, immigrants even though many Latino families have lived in territory that is now the United States for a dozen generations or more, well before the land was captured by, purchased by, or ceded to the United States. These prejudices may even become self-reinforcing, as the psychology of system justification leads minority group members themselves to treat their own second-class status as acceptable and even justified.[24]

Even in the absence of outright prejudice and discrimination, there is a widespread cultural and hence civic and political bias toward White middle-class norms—norms of speech, dress, personal appearance, body language, and cultural and historical references. There is no inherent superiority in wearing pants that have narrow, straight legs rather than legs that bag and bunch. Making eye contact is not inherently more demonstrative of attentive deference than averting one's eyes is. No more information is conveyed by explaining "I did that already" in Standard American English than by explaining "I been done that" in Black English, assuming the listener understands both. Nonetheless, there is a strong bias in favor of the former expressions of "dominant" cultural capital as against the latter, "nondominant" cultural expressions.[25] Ethnoracial minority group members who try to engage in civic and political action therefore often find themselves marginalized, disrespected, or ignored if they present themselves in culturally nondominant ways. This racialized cultural bias is further exacerbated to the extent that power in the civic and political sphere is exercised in large part by talking with diverse others and trying to convince them of one's own point of view. Arguing, reasoning, and presenting universals are valued in mainstream political settings; forms of discourse such as witnessing, testifying, storytelling, and presenting particulars—all of which have strong roots in Black churches and African-American political settings—are not.[26]

Even if there were no ethnoracial prejudice or cultural bias that reduced minorities' opportunities to influence American civic and political life, sheer numbers combined with racially patterned policy preferences put ethnoracial minorities at a distinct political disadvantage in a democracy. These differences of opinion and priorities in part reflect differences in life experience that lead members of different ethnoracial groups to "read" the world in different ways.[27] The problem, however, is that majority group members often judge minority perspectives as totally unreasonable, even irrational. Because Blacks and Whites live in "historically different worlds" as characterized by culture, history, income, education, residence, and employment, "few whites see the world through the lens that most Black Americans use for understanding their world."[28] As a result, Blacks may put forth arguments within a political debate that rest on premises about the world that are generally accepted by most other Blacks but are rejected as bizarre or crazy by Whites or other non-Blacks.

At a micro scale, this is essentially what occurred on September 11, 2001, when I thought that my students were crazy to believe that President Bush was behind the 9/11 attacks and my students thought that I was crazy to be so confident that he wasn't. (I should note that the situation was not quite so straightforward, as there were many students who likewise dismissed the idea that President Bush had ordered or at least had known of the impending attacks. Furthermore, I agreed with my students' utter mistrust of and dislike for Bush; I just didn't believe that he would choose to fly airplanes into the World Trade Center and the Pentagon.) As I pointed out in the first chapter, people with views like mine were in power, and people with views like my students' were not. Their perspectives therefore did not get a full hearing in the civic sphere.

Perhaps the most potent contemporary example of how Blacks' and Whites' experiences of life and specifically citizenship in the United States can lead them to mutually incomprehensible conclusions is Hurricane Katrina. Blacks and Whites saw the same events unfold before, during, and after the hurricane. Their access to the facts on the ground—what happened, when, and where—was virtually identical. But they reached radically different conclusions with respect to *why* these happened; their interpretations of the facts, especially of governments' actions during and after Hurricane Katrina, diverged quite sharply.

In one representative survey, for example, only 20 percent of Whites, versus 84 percent of Blacks, agreed that "the government response to Hurricane Katrina would have been faster if the victims had been white"; similarly, 38 percent of Whites as compared to 90 percent of Blacks agreed that the "Hurricane Katrina disaster showed that racial inequality remains a major problem."[29]

This disparity reflects racial differences not just in perceptions of racism, but specifically in perceptions of Blacks' citizenship status: in the relationship between the state and a group of its citizens. Such concerns came to the fore in response to the mainstream media's adoption of the term "refugees" to refer to Hurricane Katrina survivors in the days immediately following the storm; many African Americans saw this as an implicit denial of their American citizenship. Refugees are outsiders, people whom a country may generously take in and help out, but not members of the community to whom the country bears an essential obligation.[30] Melissa Harris-Lacewell quotes a Katrina survivor who testified in front of Mayor Ray Nagin's Bring Back New Orleans Commission two months after the devastation hit: "When the next African-American man spoke, he pleaded for a moment 'to pause and recognize the loss of thousands of people. The nation paused on 9–11, but not now. No one cares about our losses. I am a homeowner who is homeless. I am a taxpayer and a voter. I placed my trust in the elected officials to do what is right but instead we got nothing. We are not refugees, we are Americans.'"

Harris-Lacewell cites examples like these to demonstrate "the nearly universal agreement among African-American survivors that their suffering was related to their status as second class citizens"; their "racialized understandings of themselves" were specifically "as disposable members of the American populace."[31]

Such perceptions can only be reinforced when representatives of state power like the police kill in cold blood Black children and families who were merely trying to cross a bridge to reach safer ground in Katrina's aftermath.[32] In this context, it makes sense that many Lower Ninth Ward residents believe that the government intentionally allowed the levees to fail, just as it is "taken as a given that, during Hurricane Betsy in 1965, the city blew up a levee and intentionally flooded the ward in order to save the mostly white and tourist-friendly French Quarter."[33] But that doesn't mean that claims of intentional state destruction of vast swathes of poor Black New Orleans will be countenanced by the White majority—only 20 percent of whom, remember, even believe that the government responded more slowly to the disaster because the majority of the victims weren't White.

Hurricane Katrina is representative of the myriad ways in which Whites and Blacks—and more generally, ethnoracial majority versus minority group members—may experience and interpret the world entirely differently, and in ways that lead Whites (and the mainstream media that they essentially control) to reject non-Whites' views as "extreme" or conspiracy-ridden. Thanks to the government-sponsored Tuskegee syphilis study, in which government researchers spent decades studying the effects of untreated syphilis on Black men, many African Americans have been deeply suspicious of state-mandated childhood immunizations, antiretroviral drug treatments against AIDS, and even of the source of AIDS in inner cities and Africa, which has been attributed to the CIA as an attempted genocide against Blacks. These are ideas that most Whites tend to reject out of hand, if they bother to pay attention at all.[34] When attention is paid, Whites' reactions are usually ones of disbelief exacerbated by a short attention span. Examples include the furor over the O. J. Simpson case in the 1990s, when "the compass of race went haywire," and the sermons of Reverend Jeremiah Wright during the 2008 election.[35] Wright preaches a fairly mainstream version of Black liberation theology, but that fact failed to hit home to White audiences, and was seen as evidence of Blacks' extremism when it did. There was certainly no attempt on the part of the mainstream media to engage seriously with the ideas Wright was presenting.

Finally, even when Whites do come to understand Blacks' experiences and perspectives, unification may be brief. African Americans protested for years, for example, against the phenomenon of "Driving While Black." It finally received mainstream attention in the late 1990s with concerns about "racial profiling," but these gains were short-lived when in the response to the 9/11 attacks, racial profiling became publicly acceptable again almost overnight.[36] As Lawrence Bobo explains, "Minorities not only perceive more discrimination, they also see it as more 'institutional' in character. Many Whites tend to think of discrimination as either mainly a historical legacy of the past or as the idiosyncratic behavior of the isolated bigot. In short, to Whites, the officers who tortured Abner Louima constitute a few bad apples. To Blacks, these officers represent only the tip of the iceberg."[37]

Another source of ethnoracial inequality lies in the fact that members of the majority group may live by certain norms, or benefit from experiences of the world, that they deny when these are articulated by members of minority communities. Studies of "White privilege" have illuminated this with regard to race. Whites usually normalize their own race, seeing themselves as raceless and as a result failing to see race as being relevant to their or others' lives.[38] It is clearly a White privilege to see oneself as not having a race, or as not being even partially defined by race. But this differential experience of race—the experience of its not seeming to matter because it is taken as a default assumption—is very hard for Whites to acknowledge. For many Whites, being White is "normal" in a way that being anything else is not. Thus, in response to a Black person's invocation of race in a political debate, Whites will often complain, privately at least, "Why do Blacks talk about race all the time?" They have listened to the Black person's reason or idea, but they do not "hear" it or allow it to influence them appropriately because of their inability to acknowledge that their own experiences have been shaped by race—but in their case by the privilege of White race. Similar selective race-blindness occurs when Whites accuse minorities of self-segregating while remaining indifferent to their own racial clustering.[39]

Finally, in well-meaning response to the previous two problems, majority group members may unintentionally but pervasively reinterpret what minorities say in order to make minorities' claims make sense to them. This may be done unconsciously, or it may be done as a misguided extension of respect—they may think that by saying or thinking, "What you're really trying to say is . . . ," they are doing a service to the minority group. This restatement usually brings the minority group member's claim into alignment with what the majority group member already knows or believes. In this respect, efforts to rephrase a person's position ("What she's really trying to say is . . .") often have the outcome of neutralizing her claims. Her claims are shifted to fit comfortably into the other discussants' already-present understanding of the matter at hand, rather than forcing people to grapple with an idea that is new or challenging. As a result, dissenting individuals, especially if they come to an issue as outsiders whose views and experiences are different from the mainstream, run the risk of having their positions seemingly assimilated into the deliberations without their actually exerting influence in the appropriate way. For an individual's claims really to count in and appropriately influence deliberation, the *differences* between his position and others' must be recognized and taken into account; otherwise, he might as well not participate.[40]

This is not to say that achievement of mutual respect, or of deliberative democratic equality, is guaranteed when a group's apparent "otherness" or "difference" is embraced by the majority. It's a fine—and frankly often baffling—line between respecting appropriate authentic cultural difference and abandoning appropriately universalized standards.[41] My first year teaching eighth-grade English in Atlanta, I asked a parent to come in after school to discuss her daughter DeShauna's misbehavior in my class. We spoke for ten minutes, during which time she was extremely apologetic and promised me, "It won't happen again, Dr. Levinson, you can be sure of that!" I thanked her profusely for coming in. I felt good about our working as a team on DeShauna's behalf; together, her mom and I would help DeShauna improve her behavior and focus on learning. As they left my classroom, however, DeShauna's mom pulled her into the empty room right next door to mine. She started beating DeShauna with a belt, yelling in between beatings, "You will never disrespect a teacher again! don't make me come up into this school again because of your foolishness! Do you understand?" DeShauna sobbed her assent. I sat in my classroom, paralyzed with shock and confusion.

Later, I sought advice from a number of my colleagues—all African American, as were DeShauna and her mom. Some sympathized with my horror. Others told me this reveals why we struggled with discipline at Walden. The parents have recourse to corporal punishment, so kids don't act the fool at home. Instead, they cut up at school, especially since they know we can't paddle them ourselves. If we could only "whup them upside the head" once or twice, too, then we'd have a much easier time getting our students to behave. As I listened to these explanations, I realized that I was confronting a profound cultural difference about the acceptability of corporal punishment in middle-class White versus African-American child-rearing practices.[42] I understood where they were coming from. But this recognition didn't alter my judgment that beating a child with a belt was wrong. Nor did it help me figure out how to work across the cultural divide. I wanted to partner with DeShauna's mom. I fully believe that she wanted to partner with me. Nonetheless, I was stymied. I never called DeShauna's mom for anything negative again—and this wasn't because DeShauna was an angel for the rest of the year. I just didn't want DeShauna to be beaten. I still don't know what I should have done.

PERSPECTIVE-TAKING AND POWER ANALYSIS

Given the many ways in which mainstream political power and ethnoracial identity unjustly interact, some people have proposed that the interaction itself must be eliminated, either by eliminating minority race identity within mainstream politics, or by eliminating mainstream politics from the activities of minority raced individuals. The first approach is assimilationist.[43] From the assimilationist perspective, ethnoracial minorities are most likely to achieve equality by competing as equal individuals in the political and economic playing field. "The issues are honor, dignity, respect, and self-respect, all of which are preconditions for true equality between any peoples. The classic interplay between the aggrieved black and the guilty white, in which the former demands (and the latter conveys) a recognition of the historical injustice is, quite simply, not an exchange among equals."[44] Rather than making claims as a raced person or on behalf of a ethnoracial group, individuals are exhorted to "cast down your bucket where you are" and master the knowledge and skills necessary for success within society as it currently exists.[45] This approach may be seen in many of the "no excuses" schools like KIPP, where they explicitly teach kids to adopt White, middle-class cultural norms and language. Success in these schools is likewise measured by students' capacities to gain entry into and succeed in traditional high-status, usually majority-White secondary and higher education institutions.

The second approach is separatist; in African-American thought, where it has been most developed, it takes the form of Black nationalism in political thought and Afrocentrism in educational practice. From this perspective, ethnoracial minority group members should create their own autonomous political and economic institutions rather than try to integrate into those mainstream institutions controlled by Whites, since integration is inevitably doomed to failure. As Eugene Rivers put it,

> For more than forty years the integrationist conception of racial equality has dominated the nationalist alternative. But skin color still determines life chances; millions of blacks continue to be excluded from American life: segregated residentially, educationally, and politically. Moreover, racial barriers show no signs of falling, and affirmative action is all but dead. Committed to racial equality, but faced with a segregated existence, we need to rethink our identification of racial equality with integration, and reopen debate about a sensible nationalist conception for racial equality . . . Blacks constitute a "nation within a nation."[46]

This philosophy—or really, constellation of philosophies, since there are many strands both of Black nationalism and of other racial separatist movements inspired by Black nationalist movements—tends to be reflected in schools that teach an Afrocentric or other ethnoracially or culturally specific curriculum. Afrocentrism takes nearly as many forms as Black nationalism.[47] In general, however, students learn that Blacks have historically been a great and self-sustaining people and they can and should continue this legacy of collective achievement and self-determination. Collaboration and coalition-building across ethnoracial lines is usually discouraged in favor of ethnoracially separate empowerment.

I propose that public schools pursue neither of these approaches. Rather, I would encourage us to take on the description of the problem—and the proposed solution—that W. E. B. Du Bois provides in the opening essay of *The Souls of Black Folk*. It is worth quoting at length:

> [T]he Negro is a sort of seventh son, born with a veil, and gifted with second-sight in this American world,—a world which yields him no true self-consciousness, but only lets him see himself through the revelation of the other world. It is a peculiar sensation, this

double-consciousness, this sense of always looking at one's self through the eyes of others, of measuring one's soul by the tape of a world that looks on in amused contempt and pity. One ever feels his twoness,—an American, a Negro; two souls, two thoughts, two un-reconciled strivings; two warring ideals in one dark body, whose dogged strength alone keeps it from being torn asunder.

The history of the American Negro is the history of this strife,—this longing to attain self-conscious manhood, to merge his double self into a better and truer self. In this merging he wishes nei-ther of the older selves to be lost. He would not Africanize America, for America has too much to teach the world and Africa. He would not bleach his Negro soul in a flood of white Americanism, for he knows that Negro blood has a message for the world. He simply wishes to make it possible for a man to be both a Negro and an American, without being cursed and spit upon by his fellows, with-out having the doors of Opportunity closed roughly in his face.

This, then, is the end of his striving: to be a co-worker in the kingdom of culture, to escape both death and isolation, to husband and use his best powers and his latent genius.[48]

Full-scale assimilation is the death that Du Bois rejects. Political separatism is the isolation that he also rejects. In their stead, he pleads for the achievement of a "better and truer self" that rep-resents a true merger—or perhaps simultaneity—of individuals' ethnoracial and civic identities. Neither need dominate or elimi-nate the other. Rather, they can coexist and even inform one an-other. It is possible to be truly American as an ethnoracialized being, and to be truly an ethnoracialized group member in part through one's political and even patriotic engagement.

What does this mean in pedagogical practice? Although trans-lating principles into pedagogies is never a simple one-to-one correspondence, some educational implications stand out. First, young people should be taught to recognize the particularity of their own perspective, including the ways in which their ethno-racial and cultural identities help shape those perspectives. This is an important lesson for all young people to learn, including majority group members, as they are most likely to be unaware of diverse perspectives and to view their own identities and experiences as the unquestioned norm. They do not suffer the "double consciousness" of which Du Bois speaks. In Du Bois's eyes, of course, this is basically a good thing; double consciousness is a hardship that could ideally be overcome in a reformed, egalitarian society. But even in a society that permitted the achievement of a "better and truer self," Du Bois "wishes neither of the older selves to be lost." There is a value in recognizing that one's identity has *both* ethnoracial and civic components (and many other elements besides), and that how one both "measures one's [own] soul" and takes the measure of the world will likely be different from how others make the same assessments. These are reasons for majority and minority group members alike to learn how to take multiple perspectives and to develop the inclination to do so. Ideally, this will reduce the need for minority double consciousness, as "American" will no longer be taken as synonymous with "White." It will also potentially spread such consciousness to Whites, insofar as they become conscious of their own limitations of perspective, and their own subjection to the gaze and judgment of others.[49]

The skill and habit of viewing the world from multiple perspectives serves many salutary civic functions. In addition to helping students recognize that their own civic identity isn't any more "normal" or "natural" than others'—in other words, that there's not just one way to be American or to be patriotic, say—students' capacities and inclination to take multiple perspectives also equip them to recognize and fight against ethnocultural bias. They may be more willing and able to hear testimonies that conflict with or shed new light on their own experiences. They may also be more willing and able to listen for the content of individuals' claims, rather than being distracted by the clothing their fellow citizens are wearing, the colloquialisms they use, or the color of their skin. Majority group members, and all citizens for that matter, who are skilled at taking multiple perspectives may find it easier to recognize, comprehend, and take seriously the beliefs and norms espoused by minority group members—both when their context makes common norms seem unfamiliar (such as when Muslim headscarves inspire anxiety while nuns' habits do not), and when truly different norms are asserted that majority group members would prefer to reinterpret into something more familiar.

One important additional way in which these skills and habits of perspective-taking can be taught in a civic and political context is to teach power analysis. Power is often invisible to those who have it; it is so naturally woven into the fabric of their existence that those with power are able to exercise it unintentionally and even unconsciously. Consider the powers that derive from being well-dressed, exuding a confident air, speaking English fluently, being a member of the majority group, knowing professionals who have unpaid summer internships to offer, having the financial security to take a promising unpaid internship instead of a job bagging groceries, being contacted by political campaigns looking to secure votes among a powerful demographic, having one's views represented on local and national media outlets, or living in a community that is producing rather than bleeding jobs. These sources of power and opportunity are usually invisible to those who wield them, while they are painfully evident to those without similar access. Many also have a significant ethnoracial component. If students are taught to recognize and analyze these kinds and sources of power, therefore, they may similarly come to understand and respect how and why others' interpretations of the world differ meaningfully from their own.

This is not to say that any of this is easy. On the contrary, these skills and habits are hard to teach and hard to learn. Hearing the claims made by people who seem very different requires a real exercise of thoughtful imagination combined with complex historical knowledge and understanding. It is extremely difficult to help students reach this point. Throughout my teaching career, I was frankly thrilled if once or twice per term students really seemed to grasp a complex set of ideas from the inside and were able to rethink and reimagine their own experience in that historical or cultural context. It is possible that I set my goals too low, but I doubt that was the problem. Although I strongly advocate these pedagogical goals, therefore, we cannot trust that this type of civic education will on its own equip citizens to reduce ethnoracialized inequities in civic and political life. Furthermore, while this vision of civic education is strongly worth pursuing and would be transformative in the long run, there also continue to be at least short- and medium-term ethnoracial inequities and experiences of differential citizenship. Hence, I argue in the next section, we also need to equip minority youth with specific skills to combat current obstacles to civic equality and civic empowerment.

CODESWITCHING

If civic empowerment is our goal, then educators need to teach minority students to "codeswitch": to represent and express themselves in ways that members of the majority group—those with political privilege and power—will naturally understand and respect. Students should learn that in every community there is a language and culture of power. If one wants to be effective through political dialogue, as opposed to solely through direct action, boycotts, or radical street theater, say, one must master and use that language and those cultural expressions.[50] As we saw in the last section, these include specific grammatical constructions, rhetorical devices, vocabulary, narrative or expository forms, clothing, body language, and other aspects of personal appearance. They also include substantive cultural, political, and experiential referents: hearkening back to this book's introduction, those who occupy the halls of power even today are more likely to recognize Kurt Cobain than Master P. "[E]ducation is as much about being inculcated with the ways of the 'culture of power' as much as it is about learning to read, count, and think critically."[51]

Teachers have always tried to teach kids to "speak right" and "act right," of course. The point here, though, is that instead of teaching kids that they do things wrong, or that they and their families have nothing to offer in the world of school or the wider public, educators should teach codeswitching as a powerful tool that kids can use in addition to their "home languages" and their cultural forms and knowledge.[52] It is taught *in addition to,* not *in place of,* students' nondominant cultural capital. This is most frequently and effectively achieved via "translation" exercises, in which students not only translate Black English (or whatever the local language or dialect is) into Standard American English (SAE), but also translate SAE texts into their home dialect. In this technique, known as *contrastive analysis,* students discuss when different languages or cultural expressions are appropriate and why. In doing so they become "strategic movers across the cultural spheres."[53] One teacher explains, "We make up our own tests that speakers of Standard English would find difficult. We read articles, stories, poems written in Standard English and those written in home language. We listen to videotapes of people speaking. Most kids like the sound of their home language better. They like the energy, the poetry, and the rhythm of the language. We determine when and why people shift. We talk about why it might be necessary to learn Standard English."[54] Students are similarly instructed in nonverbal communication.

> Standing at the front of the room, Ms. Heinemann demonstrated various nonverbal gestures. Staring at one student, she asked, "What does staring mean?" A student responded by saying that staring is rude, and Ms. Heinemann nodded . . . Next, she averted her eyes and asked, "Is it negative or positive for student-teacher and teacher-student interactions if a student does not make eye contact?" She explained that while eye contact is considered inappropriate in some cultures, teachers in the United States appreciate eye contact . . . She then asked students to compare nonverbal communication patterns in the United States with patterns in their own countries.[55]

At the same time, codeswitching is about more than just rhetorical self-presentation. It is also about selecting cultural, historical, and political touchstones that are recognizable by and comprehensible to a mainstream or even elite audience. When I taught Martin Luther King, Jr.'s "I Have a Dream" speech, for example, we focused on how many of King's allusions were to Shakespeare, the Bible, Abraham Lincoln—not to Langston Hughes, Phyllis Wheatley, Frederick Douglass, or Sojourner Truth, as important as those Black Americans are to American history and culture. For students to be able to emulate King's rhetorical prowess in this regard, they need to know what "counts" as compelling to the majority and be able to draw upon those references. Again, this is ideally additive; it is a means of ensuring that students gain the tools to exercise power within a variety of ethnoracially and culturally constructed spaces.

Codeswitching is thus explicitly taught as a tool to be used when appropriate. It is something over which young people can feel they have control, rather than something that requires a wholesale abandonment of their own ways of being in the world.[56] It's not that they're trying to guess how to behave or sound; rather, they should feel like masters of the situation, able to adopt the cultural formats appropriate to the time and place. Young people (and adults) do this all the time, ideally taking pride in their cultural "bilingualism." Two of my former eighth-grade students—one Guyanese, one Vietnamese—demonstrated this when I interviewed them in the spring of their sophomore year of high school. As Sadiq first explained, "Wherever I go I adjust. I go down here and I'll speak proper, and I know not to be like, "Oh, yeah, whatever," and "Y'all," and then, but when I get to my home and I'm with my friends, I know that's the way they talk, and I know that's how they act, so I'll readjust to those . . ." Lien immediately concurred. "I do that too. When I talk with my sister, I talk really ghetto. And at school I talk straight."

Codeswitching isn't costless, though. It takes time, which impinges on teaching other knowledge or skills. This is a real consideration in classrooms and schools already struggling to find the time and resources to teach the basic curriculum. It is also hard to teach codeswitching well. From both a pedagogical and a more broadly civic standpoint, it is dicey to teach citizens (or future citizens) that they are "outsiders" of a civic community. We want all children to learn that they are civic beings who can and should function like insiders in democratic settings: they should join, speak up, vote, and take action. In order to teach them to function effectively as insiders in the deliberative process, however, the school must simultaneously reinforce to minority students that they are outsiders in the sense of having to learn and use a "language of power" that is initially not their own. Despite educators' best efforts, students may feel as if they're being told to assimilate to dominant cultural norms on the grounds that their own cultural capital has to be abandoned if they want to achieve success. Lien's distinction between talking "really ghetto" and talking "straight" suggests this conclusion. Related to this, students may also feel as if they're being taught one more way in which they are deficient and will never gain power; they may see these lessons as reasons to disengage. It's especially hard and risky for White, middle-class teachers to do this kind of work with low-income students of color. One long-term way to address this problem is to attract more highly qualified minority teachers into the system—exactly those kinds of teachers who were fired en masse during desegregation in the 1950s–1970s.[57] But in the meantime, we're going to have to teach White teachers how to do this the best they can.

Furthermore, codeswitching does not solve all ills of ethnoracial civic inequality no matter how well it is taught. One problem is that of translation. Merely learning the language of power does not mean that every good idea can necessarily be expressed within it. This may be especially clear if we consider the cultural, political, and social referents implicit within majority dialogue.

Let me give an example drawn from religious, rather than racial difference. A religious conservative, for example, may be against pornography for religious reasons but may know that these reasons will not be heard by a secular majority. She may choose, therefore, to translate her arguments into secular terms—arguing not that pornography desecrates God's sacred vessel, for example, but that it promotes violence against women. Although this act of translation may allow her to promote her ultimate goal of banning pornography, it distorts her position in the meantime. Pornography's potential for violence is not the reason that she opposes it. She may in fact be more convinced by research showing that soft-core pornography reduces violence against women by giving men another outlet. Furthermore, in contrast to the notion that deliberative democracy promotes mutual communication and understanding, this woman is reduced virtually to lying to her fellow citizens; she is promoting an action based on reasons to which she does not necessarily subscribe, and cannot give the reasons that she truly believes in. Members of other minority groups—including ethnoracial groups—may feel the same way in other situations. Thus, teaching students to translate their ideas, thoughts, and concerns into language that members of mainstream groups will understand does not guarantee that they will feel able to express themselves honestly and openly, free of distortion.

Second, learning the language of power may in some, even many, cases extract the ultimate cost of permanently altering students' personal identities. Short-term accommodations, made over and over again, can have transformative long-term consequences in the form of assimilation and loss of original language. This is essentially the risk Du Bois warned against in his plea for Black civic equality without invisibility. This approach to democratic empowerment in many ways demands that students "fit in," seem reasonable rather than radical, and position themselves as insiders rather than as outsiders. To what extent can we expect individuals to fit themselves into mainstream dialogue, repeatedly and completely, without expecting that they will eventually fit permanently into the mainstream—that they will assimilate? Closing the civic empowerment gap should not require young people to shed their own languages, their own experiences, and their own cultural or social referents at the door of the polis.

COLLECTIVE ACTION, RACIAL SOLIDARITY, AND GROUP CONSCIOUSNESS

Minority civic empowerment must be about more than individuals' mastering the language of power and gaining internal access to the halls of power as they are currently structured. Groups also need to master strategies for amassing and deploying collective power—including building alliances, gaining media exposure, lobbying effectively, voting strategically in blocs, and disrupting traditional political and civic institutions via protests and other techniques—so as to change the political opportunity structures themselves. These are very specific techniques that youth who are members of historically marginalized groups can and should learn in order to increase their collective political power, and also to avoid having to make individual accommodations that require self-misrepresentation and identity loss as described above. Political struggle will always impose costs as well as benefits. By exercising collective action techniques that subvert existing power dynamics, however, minority group members can conduct an end-run around some of the ethnoracial political inequalities that make traditional, "insider" political engagement such a difficult and often demoralizing affair.

Hispanics or Muslims or gays, for example, may exert influence and power not by convincing politicians of the reasonableness of their positions, but by convincing those politicians that their positions must be *treated* as reasonable if they want to earn the Hispanic, Muslim, or gay vote in their (re)election bid. Thus, for example, few in mainstream American society in 1999 thought that six-year-old Cuban refugee Elián Gonzáles should be forcibly kept in the United States or that his Cuban father's custody claims should be rejected. But because of the strategic voting power of Miami Cuban Americans, many mainstream media outlets and politicians—including Al Gore, who was even then acutely aware of Florida's potential importance in the 2000 presidential election—treated these claims seriously. Cuban Americans in Miami did not have to convince anyone of their position; rather, they used their power as a voting bloc to compel people to treat their position as reasonable despite their apparent extremity. Other collective action techniques such as boycotts, marches, and overwhelming the local jails via arrests for civil disobedience played an enormous role in forcing policy changes during the height of the civil rights movement—again, even though many of those making the changes were not yet intellectually or morally convinced it was the right thing to do. Adversarial power may be less morally attractive than deliberative power, but it is also a crucial tool for rectifying the civic empowerment gap.[58]

Collective action does not spring out of the air—or more pertinently, out of thin identity. Rather, empirical research demonstrates that collective action is rooted in individuals' sense of group consciousness plus group solidarity. As in most research about ethnoracial aspects of political behavior, the data is richest with respect to African Americans, for whom racial consciousness clearly heightens individuals' awareness of the racial injustices they and others face and also motivates associated action. Jane Junn describes this as "consciousness with political kick."[59] More broadly, "group consciousness" during the civil rights movement

> helped galvanize thousands of disadvantaged African Americans to engage in collective action and demand the equal rights that would pave the way for their political incorporation. The classic literature on early immigrants to the United States also emphasized group identification as a resource for political engagement. Group identifi-

cation was believed to motivate participation among newcomers who might otherwise find American politics confusing or daunting, owing to their lack of knowledge and resources. Among the triumvirate of factors that promote participation—civic skills and resources, psychological engagement, and political mobilization—group consciousness was another psychological resource that made politics relevant to people's lives and supplied them with reasons to become active.[60]

This association between group consciousness and political action seems to be true of youth, as well.[61]

Mere consciousness, however, is not always sufficient to motivate political action. Especially with regard to collective mobilization, consciousness is usefully supplemented by a sense of solidarity. Consciousness raises awareness of the hardships the group faces, while solidarity motivates individuals to commit to working together to overturn these hardships.[62] Community organizers frequently enact these insights by reaching out to people from a single ethnoracial group and using ethnoracial consciousness plus solidarity to unify and mobilize their members.[63] Historically, too, private associations that were built around ethnocultural identification and solidarity were often the primary drivers of immigrant political incorporation in the United States. Although such groups are much weaker nowadays in the United States, they still make a significant difference in promoting immigrants' civic and political empowerment in places like Canada, whose government supports these ethnic organizations for precisely this reason.[64]

CHALLENGES FACING EDUCATORS

It is hard to imagine walking into any statehouse and getting legislators or school board members to sign on to a civic curriculum that teaches ethnoracial "double" consciousness, group solidarity, collective action, multiple perspective–taking, power analysis, and codeswitching. As a practical matter, this is because these recommendations sound radically race-conscious and divisive—far more so than I believe they are. With some rhetorical tweaking, I think most people could come to agree with the basic ideas behind many of these approaches. But they also risk rejection because they explicitly put the lie to the idea that citizenship is an equalizing status and experience. Almost all contemporary discussions of citizenship among political philosophers emphasize the common heritage of citizenship. To be a citizen, almost by definition, is to have the same bundle of rights and obligations, legal status, and even civic identity as all other citizens. "Citizenship is supposed to provide [a common] reference point. Our personal lives and commitments may be very different, but we are all equally citizens, and it is as citizens that we advance claims in the public realm and assess the claims made by others."[65] In essence, I have been arguing throughout this chapter that this isn't true. Even if we are all equally citizens as a theoretical matter, our other identities—ethnoracial as well as gendered, sexual, or religious—intersect with our civic identity in such profound ways that they cannot be disentangled. We do not "advance claims" merely "as citizens" but as raced people, if for no other reason than that our "personal lives and commitments" are also themselves subject to ethnoracial identity.

To take this insight seriously, however, significantly complicates public schools' roles as civic educational institutions. The model of civic education I propose implicates the public school, and hence the state, in partially interpreting the relationship between personal identity and civic identity. In some sense, the school at least temporarily "fixes" what a minority student's identity means in the civic context by stressing the knowledge and skills particular to minority membership in a majoritarian democracy. Black students, say, are thus consciously and intentionally introduced to a civic education curriculum different from that taught to White students, and within that curriculum they are explicitly taught that *as Blacks,* they must develop particular skills in order to be successful as citizens. This is extremely problematic. From an empirical standpoint, little good

civic context would simply leave current ethnoracial and educational injustices untouched. When the status quo is itself anti-democratic, as I claim the civic empowerment gap proves it to be, state inaction has no greater claim than state action, the demonstrable dangers of the latter notwithstanding.

In what I therefore admit is at best a partial response to these concerns, I suggest that education for and about group solidarity needs to be conjoined with teaching ethical and moral responsibility. Civic education is not solely about learning how to access power, but also how to use it wisely and justly. In this respect, too, we want students not only to learn the values of and reasons for group solidarity, but also to develop the habits of and capacities for forming cross-group alliances. There is immense value in diverse, cross-racial groups that form precisely because group members can think across group lines, take alternative perspectives, and commit to ethical action that combats injustice regardless of identity.

To accomplish this requires exquisite developmental awareness and pedagogical finesse, of course. It is intensely challenging to convey to students an open-eyed awareness of ethnoracial civic inequality, outrage over injustices that demand both solidaristic and collaborative engagement, and simultaneous optimism that one can succeed.[67] There is ideally a sweet spot of critical awareness in the middle between complacency on one side and despair on the other. How one reaches that sweet spot, however, will vary from one community, classroom, and even student to the next. Cynicism and lack of trust fuel Black political action, for example, but depress White political action.[68] In line with this, one researcher has found that a social justice curriculum designed to teach privileged White students about injustice actually hardened their attitudes and makes things worse.[69]

Where does this leave us? Teachers are challenged to teach *through* race, *about* race, and even *for* race: (a) without defining what race means for the students (who may well have different opinions); (b) without naturalizing race—after all, it's a cultural construction, and a fairly toxic one; (c) while navigating students' various opinions about their and others' racial identifications; and (d) in full awareness that their own racial identities—most commonly, as White middle-class women—are constantly themselves in play and under scrutiny by their students. These challenges admit no easy answers. They will arise in various ways throughout the rest of this book. But I do suggest that if we work to combat the civic empowerment gap honestly and clear-headedly, acknowledging rather than eliding over the ethnoracial dimensions of our work, and in collaboration with our students as co-learners rather than experts, then we are more likely to be successful. In this respect, I recommend a constructivist approach that helps students construct their own empowering means of engaging in this work, rather than telling them how to do it. As important as it is for students to learn to take multiple perspectives, educators, too, need to be open to students' diverse perspectives and experiences. I demonstrate how this constructivist approach can work with regard to civically empowering, racially aware history education in the next chapter.

It's November 1996, and Walden is four months into its first year of "reconstitution"—a radical response by the Atlanta Board of Education to years of academic failure.[1] Although the physical school building and the seventh- and eighth-grade students remain the same, almost everything else at Walden has changed. There's a new curriculum: the International Baccalaureate Middle Years Programme, the implementation of which I've been hired to coordinate. We also have a bunch of new computers, which most teachers don't know how to use, an almost entirely new faculty and administration, a sixth-grade class of which about 20 percent are bused or driven in from elsewhere in the city (until now, Walden had been a solely neighborhood school), and school uniforms for students and staff.

It is this last change—school uniforms—that most rankles students. No, "rankles" isn't the right word. The students hate the uniforms. Despise them. This is especially true of the eighth graders, since they had known the school for two years before reconstitution, before uniforms, and came in expecting to own the place this year. But now almost all of their old teachers are gone. Their old principal is gone. Their status is gone. Their traditions are gone. And in their place? Uniforms.

When the opportunity arises for me to advise a student group for the social science fair, which is like a science fair but with projects focusing on geography, history, economics, sociology, psychology, or government, it's easy to think of a topic that would excite students' passions. Soon I have a group of three eighth graders, James, Krystal, and Albert, researching the historical question: "Why were school uniforms imposed at Austin T. Walden Middle School?" My students intend to use this information to change the uniform policy, of course, but they understand they first need to figure out the causes for their misery by researching the history behind the policy. A couple of teachers raise objections to the project, believing that investigating the issue is tantamount to insubordination; they don't understand why I'm "encouraging the children" in this way. But most teachers view our project with benign amusement—they're also pleased that Walden will have an entry in the fair—and wish us luck as we borrow their computers during lunchtime and after school to conduct our initial research.

A week or two into our meetings, the group is reading newspaper articles about the surging national popularity of public school uniforms when James raises his head and comments, "You know why the school board imposed uniforms, don't you? They don't want us to be in the 'hood, but they stuck with the school where it's at, so they gave us uniforms to make us look different."

"He right," Krystal concurs. "They want us to look clean, get the ghetto out of us. We look dumb walking down the street in them yellow shirts and blue pants. But they be trippin' if they think they can keep us from the neighborhood that easy."

"Why would you think the school board doesn't like your neighborhood?" I ask. "Sweet Auburn has an amazing history: music, art, politics, Martin Luther King, Ebenezer Baptist . . . It's a place to be proud of!"

"Sweet Auburn history, maybe," Krystal clarifies. "But not the Old Fourth Ward now."

"Let's keep focused on gathering evidence," I respond. "I really don't think the school board was trying to diss the Fourth

Ward! Look at all the schools across the country that are adopting uniforms. They're really popular now. Anyway, we'll find out for sure when we go to the Atlanta Board of Education offices next week. Their meeting minutes will explain what they were thinking."

The following Thursday, James, Albert, and Krystal hop in my car for the quick drive downtown to the Atlanta Public Schools central administration building. Our school is barely five minutes from downtown Atlanta. But Walden and the "Old Fourth Ward," as my students call the neighborhood, or "Sweet Auburn" (named after historic Auburn Avenue that runs through it), as neighborhood boosters and city officials term it, might as well be on the other side of the state for how accessible it feels. This is thanks to I75/85, the "Downtown Connector" highway that irreparably separates the neighborhood from downtown Atlanta, and whose entrance and exit ramps define the perimeter of our school grounds and playing field.

As we turn out of the school driveway and head immediately under the I75/85 overpass, I grimace yet again at the proximity of the highway to our school. I've been thinking of encouraging some other students to conduct a science project testing our soil's lead levels, but I'm concerned that if the lead content is determined to be too high, we'll be banned from using the playing field without getting another place to play or cleaned-up fields, so I haven't done anything yet. I decide I should encourage student activism about one contentious issue at a time; after all, this is only my fourth month of employment here. So I don't say anything as we drive downtown, except to joke with the students that my car radio may break from playing hip hop in place of its usual classical music or public radio news. Krystal and James each hold folders filled with articles about the history of school uniforms in the United States, as well as research on the benefits and drawbacks of school uniforms, and drafts of questions for interviewing teachers and school board members next week. Albert has forgotten his folder at home, as usual, but does have some blank pieces of notebook paper stuffed into his pocket for taking notes. Krystal is the only one who has remembered to bring a pen; after pulling into the parking lot, I scrounge a few extra pencils from the floor of my car before we head inside.

Albert, James, Krystal, and I are ushered into a room with a large table in the center and bookshelves along one wall. The shelves are filled with binders. Pointing out where minutes from the 1994–1996 meetings are stored, the school board secretary explains that we'll find records of committee meetings and full school board meetings there; students will need to read both if they want to figure out why the school board decided to impose school uniforms on Walden.

Within minutes of starting to read, my students' eyes start to glaze over. They're bored to tears and making little progress. "Let's learn some skimming skills!" I suggest. "Then you won't have to read all of this; you can just look for what's important." We make a list of promising words to look for—reconstitution, Walden, uniforms—and then practice skimming a page in ten to fifteen seconds, looking just for the target words. After some warm-up practice, Krystal and Albert are zooming through pages, and James is helpfully marking with stickies all pages with the relevant committee meetings to go back and skim later. I'm pleased; I wanted to facilitate this project in large part to teach students research skills such as how to skim texts, find primary documents in government archives, conduct interviews, develop a thesis and back it up with evidence from their research, and so forth. Today's visit, plus their other research and the interviews they're scheduled to conduct next week, should collectively help them master most of these skills. This project couldn't be going better, I think.

Two hours later, my students are ready to call it quits—not just for today, but for the project as a whole. They've skimmed through two years' worth of documents and found no discussion about uniforms. None. Uniforms show up in the final reconstitution plans, but as far as we can tell, members of the board never actually had a conversation about why or whether to impose uniforms on Walden students. They just did it.

"I can't believe it!" James exclaims. "They make us wear this crap and didn't even discuss it?"

"That just not right," Albert agrees.

"Well, maybe they talked about it, but didn't write it down," I counter, weakly. "Let's see what you learn when you interview people next week. Krystal, you have an interview set up with Midge Sweet, right?" Midge is a White woman known to be a fairly progressive force on the school board, and she had readily agreed to an interview when we called her the week before. I'm sure it doesn't hurt that my mother-in-law and she are acquaintances, and so I had been in touch with her earlier this year when I was looking for a teaching job. But she seemed genuinely enthusiastic about helping out my students, and she had been involved in the reconstitution planning. "I bet Ms. Sweet can explain what their thinking was."

"I sure hope so, Dr. Levinson," Krystal glumly replies.

At my urging, students spend their next meeting summarizing what they have learned so far. They create a T-chart listing arguments in favor of uniforms on one side and against uniforms on the other. The list is surprisingly balanced, although my students predictably find the antiuniform arguments far more compelling. Albert and Krystal create a sketchy timeline of Walden's reconstitution, while James writes up a summary of the history of school uniforms in the United States, grudgingly including at my insistence the information that school uniforms are the norm in most other countries. "But we're not most other countries, Dr. Levinson!" James protests. "We supposed to be the land of freedom and liberty. What about our rights??"

The following Saturday, I meet Krystal at her place to drive her to Midge's house for the interview. It's less than a mile door to door, but the change in the neighborhood landscape is stunning. Krystal lives in a small housing project with her grandmother in the heart of the Old Fourth Ward. The door to her

apartment opens directly into the parking lot; their kitchen window looks out on an overflowing dumpster. The blocks surrounding her place are filled with other subsidized housing projects, poorly maintained apartment buildings, and vacant lots. A
few of the historic Queen Anne and shotgun homes near Martin
Luther King's boyhood home and Ebenezer Baptist Church have
been restored by a neighborhood development group and purchased by middle-class and professional families. But they are
confined to a block or two on Auburn Avenue, close to the King
Center and the National Park Service's King Visitor's Center,
which is under construction. As Krystal and I drive down Edge-
wood, a commercial street paralleling Auburn, we instead pass
Popeye's, a couple barber shops and hair parlors, a funeral home,
some more vacant lots, and too many liquor stores.

After five blocks, we cross over the old railroad tracks into
the Inman Park neighborhood. The landscape alters radically.
Large clapboard Victorian homes and smaller brick bungalows,
almost all meticulously maintained, sit on grassy, landscaped
lots with swing sets and jungle gyms peeking out from back-
yards. The few remaining industrial buildings near the tracks
house a small experimental theater company, a funky home-
decorating store, and a couple nonprofits. Although we're barely
half a mile from her house, Krystal looks around in wonder-
ment; she has never seen Inman Park before today. "Wow, Dr.
Levinson," she comments. "These houses are like palaces!"

As we pull in front of Midge's house to park, Krystal checks
herself anxiously in the car mirror, fussing with her hair and tug-
ging on her dress. Krystal is dressed to the nines for this interview; she looks gorgeous. I say some encouraging words to her,
then we climb the steps and ring the bell.

The interview mostly goes well. Midge is extremely welcom-
ing and kind, and she answers Krystal's questions forthrightly.
Krystal is clearly nervous, but she conducts a terrific interview,
asking appropriate initial and follow-up questions, listening
carefully to Midge's answers, taking notes, and generally dis-

playing the intelligence, knowledge, and seriousness of purpose for which I have come to admire her over the past few months. There are only two problems: first, Midge has to keep asking Krystal to repeat herself because Krystal both has a mild speech impediment and speaks solely Black English—she doesn't know how to switch into Standard American English at all.[2] Second, Midge can't explain why the school board imposed uniforms at Walden. My students are zero for the count in answering their question.

At our next meeting, therefore, the students agree that it's pointless to keep trying to find out why uniforms were imposed on Walden; the social science fair is just two weeks away and they're eager to type up their research and start decorating their project board. They decide, therefore, to write up their findings such as they are and in their conclusion to speculate about what the lack of apparent reflection and debate about uniforms might signify.

I'm curious to see what the students come up with. I expect they'll take the prouniform arguments they've found through their research—reduces fashion competition among kids, focuses students on academics, reduces gang affiliation, improves discipline—and impute them to the board members. My own assumption is that the uniform policy was set for these plus other more-or-less inchoate reasons: to seem forward-thinking by jumping on the national prouniform bandwagon; to appeal to middle-class parents, a critical mass of whom have been convinced to send their sixth graders to Walden (these are the kids coming in from outside the neighborhood); to reduce costs for poor parents; or maybe just to make school look spiffy. Although I'm not convinced that uniforms necessarily further these aims, I'm also not strongly opposed to uniforms, so these reasons strike me as relatively inoffensive.

Krystal's, Albert's, and James's conclusions about the unstated assumptions that led the board to impose uniforms on Walden, however, turn out to be much less benign. By their lights, as they explain in their results section, the board has done everything possible to separate Walden and its students from the surrounding neighborhood, and by extension, from their families, friends, and culture. The school board clearly thought Walden teachers and students were bad—hence the reconstitution. They adopted the International Baccalaureate Middle Years Programme because students aren't supposed to think of themselves as part of the neighborhood anymore; they are supposed to be "international," not local. All these new "rich" kids in sixth grade are from outside the Fourth Ward; the new curriculum and uniforms are meant to appeal to them and change Walden's status as a "ghetto school." By making local students wear their school uniforms walking to or from school, the school board is trying to make them look "clean" and different from the rest of the neighborhood. They're no longer supposed to be or feel part of the hood. The board's apparent lack of conversation about uniforms itself constitutes proof of its deep disrespect for Walden students; if they actually respected the students, then the school board would have taken the time to talk about the policy and think about whether it was a good one or not.

"But what about all the other reasons they might have imposed uniforms, that you found in your research?" I ask when I finish reading through their arguments.

"Oh, Dr. Levinson, that may be why some schools have uniforms. But that don't apply to us," James replies.

What happened here? I knew that my students were starting out with opinions about uniforms. That's why we had picked the topic; they were already invested in it. But I failed to recognize that students didn't have only *emotions* about the uniforms; they also had *knowledge* about the context of their imposition, *attitudes* about the political and social status of the "ghetto" and of their place within it, and quite advanced interpretive *skills* in connecting apparently unrelated data points—the influx of middle-class sixth graders, the adoption of the new curriculum—in order to generate a sophisticated narrative about endemic disrespect for their community, their families, and themselves. I also failed to understand except in retrospect that my students' interpretation of what I viewed as a purely historical question (why were the uniforms imposed) both was shaped by and reinforced their attitudes about contemporary political relationships between Fourth Ward residents and local political elites such as the Atlanta Board of Education. Because my students were bringing more to the table than I realized or was able to engage with, at least as a first-year teacher, they ended their project more convinced than ever of the veracity of their civic narrative of personal, familial, and communal marginalization, disempowerment, and disrespect, even though that was not my intent as their teacher at all. They may well have been right, of course; the evidence, or lack thereof, certainly doesn't prove otherwise. But my failure to engage with students' entering assumptions meant that they never seriously challenged their own beliefs either; despite our collective good will and considerable hard work, we mutually failed to change our own or others' minds, and therefore also failed to empower ourselves or others.[3]

When we think about how to eliminate the civic empowerment gap, we need to take seriously what students bring with them into the classroom from "outside": from their lived experience, from the stories and messages they hear from family members, friends, and neighbors, from various media sources, and so forth. Students aren't empty vessels waiting to be filled with appropriate civic attitudes and knowledge; rather, they come into the classroom having already at least partially constructed their own understandings of their civic identity, of their membership in or exclusion from the polity, and even of history's significance and meaning for their own lives. This was evident from James's, Krystal's, and Albert's analysis of the uniform policy; it was also evident in my students' responses five years later to the events of September 11, 2001, as I discussed in Chapter 1. Travis and Laquita readily drew upon a narrative about the uses and abuses of political power in the United States—grounded both in their personal experiences and in their understanding of historical events including the 2000 Florida election controversy, Saddam Hussein's attempt on the first President Bush's life, and the Persian Gulf War (which ended before most of them had turned four)—to contextualize and interpret the events of that day. In both cases, these interpretations were not reliant on what they had learned in school, or even particularly responsive to what school-based "authorities" such as myself had to say. My students didn't necessarily treat the information that I offered, such as the articles we read about the school uniform debates, as being wrong; it was just of limited value, and to the extent that it conflicted with or failed to take into account other things that they already knew to be true, they reasonably discounted it. As James told me, "That don't apply to us."[4]

When teachers and schools attempt to address the civic empowerment gap, therefore, they need to engage with students' constructions of history, civic membership, political legitimacy, and power relations. They need to recognize that students construct meaning independent of—and therefore often in conflict with—the meanings specified by curricula, textbooks, teachers, or other educational "authorities."[5] Educators must therefore overtly and intentionally engage with students' beliefs, attitudes, and narrative schema—which means adjusting instruction from school to school, class to class, and student to student. At the same time, educators must maintain a vision of desirable civic and political knowledge, skills, attitudes, and behaviors that goes beyond what students enter with. Engagement with students' constructed narratives, in other words, does not mean straightforwardly validating them, since the civic empowerment gap cannot be solved simply by reinforcing students' beliefs, attitudes, and differences. Rather, educators need to help students to construct more empowering civic narratives: ones that are truthful but not self-defeating, that incorporate individuals' and communities' lived experiences while simultaneously justifying and reinforcing a sense of personal and political efficacy, of civic membership, and of civic duty.

This is admittedly a tall order. In the spirit of the task itself, however, I suggest that truthful, empowering histories already exist that demonstrate how schools have accomplished this in the past and can still do so today. We have both historical and contemporary examples of how schools, in particular segregated Black schools, have helped students construct empowering civic narratives. De jure segregated schools pre–*Brown v. Board of Education,* Freedom Schools from the 1960s through today, and contemporary de facto segregated schools, especially those that serve African-American students, all provide potential models of helping students construct civically empowering historical counternarratives centered on themes of struggle, obligation, and opportunity. With some imagination and flexibility, I suggest, teachers and students in other settings could expand upon and incorporate these historical narratives in ways that promote their own civic and political engagement.

WHY HISTORY MATTERS

History teachers are vital to reducing the civic empowerment gap. The way students understand the present, including the opportunities available to them, is to a significant extent shaped by their understanding of the past. In addition, history has long been recognized as crucial for grounding effective, reflective, and productive civic and political participation. Reasons that a "serious engagement with history is essential to the nurturing of the democratic citizen" may include: giving students "an appreciation for how long and hard and tangled the road to liberty and equality has been," placing them at the "center of the battles . . . that have determined our fate," helping them "recognize antidemocratic ideas," grounding students in reality and tempering self-righteousness, shielding them from despair, and valuing the truth.[6]

The assumption that "an understanding and appreciation of history makes every American a more engaged citizen,"[7] as then–First Lady Laura Bush put it, however, is misguided. Historical knowledge makes every American a more *informed* citizen, but not necessarily a more *engaged* citizen. Here is how one of my former eighth graders at McCormack related history and civic engagement in a poem she wrote and e-mailed to me in 2005, a few months after she completed my civics class (in which she earned an A+, incidentally):

I Love America

I love the country that made us slaves
I love the country that segregates
I love this country
I love how we are old enough to go to war and risk our lives
But we're not old enough to drink or drive
I love how we had to FIGHT to receive equal rights
I love the government that doesn't care
The richest country that isn't aware,
Of the youth living amongst poverty
I love Mr. President who doesn't see what I can see
I love this country for going to war and killing our fellow
    "Americans"
They live for America and DIE for America
Now they died as strong soldiers and troops
One day you'll realize how much you love this country too . . .

It would be hard to argue that Carmen's knowledge of history has inspired her to feel greater identification with, loyalty to, or belief in the United States.

Many people have responded to sentiments such as Carmen's with a protest against the kind of history and civic education that students expressing such sentiments must have received. As the American Textbook Council concludes in its analysis of twenty U.S. history textbooks, "faith in progress and patriotic pride have vanished . . . What has replaced them is too often a nation that has repeatedly fallen short of its ideals, led by a patriarchy that deserves censure . . . Young readers . . . may learn about a nation's shameful past . . . in such a way as to undercut civic confidence and trust . . . The new history textbooks are helping to erase—if not national memory—then juvenile appreciation of the nation's achievements."[8] Sandra Stotsky similarly charges in her critique of supplemental curricula and professional development programs for history teachers, "In the guise of providing teachers with ideas for a more engaging pedagogy and deeper understanding of a historical phenomenon, frequently one involving instances of prejudice, they recruit unwitting teachers as their agents in cultivating hostility toward America as a country, toward Western culture, and toward Americans of European descent. The poisonous effects of these supplemental resources on teachers' thinking and pedagogical practices can spread throughout the entire school curriculum in the moral and civic vacuum created by neutered textbooks and a host of competing 'multiple perspectives.'"[9] This critique itself has a long history, as the educational historian David Tyack relates: "In the 1920s a number of states prohibited American history textbooks that criticized the heroes celebrated in real history. Oregon, for example, made it illegal to use any textbook that 'speaks slightingly of the founders of the republic, or of the men who preserved the union, or which belittles or undervalues their work.' History could not be, in this scheme of things, both critical and patriotic."[10]

Critics of such "hostile" history texts generally recommend that history education return instead to what Peter Gibbon lauds as its "moderately triumphalist" roots: a story of a country founded on universally admirable ideals of freedom and equality, admittedly tempered in practice by egregious violations of the ideals (slavery, sexism, racism, and so on), but always striving for and achieving progress in realizing those ideals more fully.[11] "The great drama of American history, as traditionally told," Diane Ravitch approvingly explains, "was the conflict between the nation's ideals and its practices; over time, that conflict was increasingly resolved by elections, court decisions, legislative changes, a bloody civil war, heroic individuals, reform movements, and other advances in the realization of democratic institutions. Even when they were violated, the ideals were a constant set of goals toward which Americans continued to strive."[12] Not only is this a more accurate depiction of American history, Ravitch and others argue, but it also is more engaging and motivating, and hence more likely to reduce the civic empowerment gap. Students should learn about "the genius of democracy," for example, "not only because it is true, but also because they will realize that change is possible and that the future is indeed in their hands."[13] An inspiring historical narrative centered on the achievements and progress of American democracy will thus increase students' political and personal efficacy, and presumably also their civic and political involvement. If Carmen had just received such a history education, these authors would argue, then her poetry might not have been infected with the poisonous critique of American history and policy, and her "love" for the United States might not be so sneering.

I think there is some justification for this historical narrative. To tell a story of the United States as a redeemably flawed instantiation and a symbol of a number of inspiring ideals is both historically legitimate and potentially inspiring for many people. The problem is the assumption that this is the *only* or even *most* historically legitimate interpretation of American and world history, as well as the assumption that this narrative could be an inspiring and unifying force for all Americans if only schools would teach it right. Both of these beliefs, I contend, are wrong. In an important way, they represent the same misapprehensions that I labored under while advising Krystal, Albert, and James on their social science fair project. I assumed that as their teacher, I knew what they knew (and more, of course): in other words, that I knew the contours of their knowledge and their ignorance, and that anything they were knowledgeable about, so was I. Furthermore, I unthinkingly assumed that once my students had thought about what they knew and had learned, they would reach the same conclusions I did. Common data would lead to common conclusions. But I was wrong, both because I didn't know what they knew, and because we understood what we knew differently. I didn't know enough to understand their stories about how the uniforms visibly and symbolically separated them from their neighborhood. I also didn't have the perspective to see that my analysis relied on weighting the data differently— privileging published accounts over personal experience, for example—than my students would or did. The story I constructed about the history of uniforms at Walden, therefore, was different from that which my students constructed, and they were legitimately indifferent to my construction of history.

Similarly, many of the critics I cite above seem to labor under the misapprehension that schools are the major purveyors of historical understanding and civic identity. If schools would just teach the right national narrative, they claim, all would be fixed. In other words, a common narrative would lead to common civic and political outcomes.[14] Just as what I taught Krystal, Albert, and James about the history of school uniform policy, however, was only part—and not even the most significant part— of what they knew and believed about school uniforms, what schools teach about the history of the United States and the world is only part—and not necessarily the most significant part —of what students know and believe about American history and identity.[15] Students learn civic and historical narratives from their families, neighbors, pastors, peers, and media. These sources vary widely in what they teach, especially as different ethnoracial, cultural, religious, and other communities hold and teach quite contrasting views about their place in history, what historical sources to trust, and the veracity or mendacity of "official" history, such as that taught in schools.[16]

Students hence demonstrate similarly significant race-based differences in their experiences and constructions of school-based history. In her comparison of African-American and White high school students' responses to their American history classes, for example, Terrie Epstein found that

> the sociocultural contexts in which the students had been raised profoundly shaped their perspectives on U.S. history and the credibility of secondary sources. The African-American students not only objected to the absence of African Americans in history textbooks and classes, they also were suspicious of the absence of a perspective on the American past that took into account those which they had learned about at home and through African American–oriented media. Conversely, most of the European-American students saw little if any discontinuity between the history that they had learned about at home or through the media and that which they learned about at school.

Furthermore, "[b]ecause textbooks and teachers rarely presented historical events from perspectives framed by [their] assumptions, the African-American students perceived school-based historical accounts as 'white people's history.'"[17] If students reject what they are taught in school as being someone else's history—in this case, being both *about* other people and *for* other people—then any hope for history education's being civically empowering is lost. "School knowledge" will stay in school, being trotted out for homework and tests and then promptly forgotten, while "home" or "street knowledge" remains unchallenged and unchanged.

One doesn't actually need to go to academic studies, of course, to see potent evidence of how the lessons of history are understood differently by different groups in different contexts. The controversy over Reverend Jeremiah Wright's sermons during the 2008 presidential campaign exemplified this nation's divisions about what we should learn from American history both in terms of understanding the past and in terms of charting our course into the future. Wright was excoriated in the mainstream media for his infamous "God damn America" sermon, thirty-second clips of which were played incessantly on the nightly news and cable talk shows. If one examines the entirety of his 2003 sermon, which was entitled "Confusing God and Government," however, we can see more than reflexive, unthinking anti-Americanism; rather, he sets forth a careful and transparent—although still enormously contentious—critical narrative of American history. During the sermon, Wright proclaims:

> Governments fail . . . [T]he British failed. The Russian government failed. The Japanese government failed. The German government failed. And the United States of America government, when it came to treating her citizens of Indian descent fairly, she failed. She put them on reservations. When it came to treating her citizens of Japanese descent fairly, she failed. She put them in internment prison camps. When it came to treating her citizens of African descent fairly, America failed. She put them in chains. The government put them in slave quarters, put them on auction blocks, put them in cotton fields, put them in inferior schools, put them in substandard housing, put them in scientific experiments, put them in the lowest paying jobs, put them outside the equal protection of the law, kept them out of their racist bastions of higher education and locked them into positions of hopelessness and helplessness. The government gives them the drugs, builds bigger prisons, passes a three-strike law, and then wants us to sing "God Bless America." No, no, no! Not "God Bless America." God damn America! That's in the Bible, for killing innocent people. God damn America for treating her citizens as less than human![18]

The narrative that Wright tells here is clearly linked to the narrative set forth in Carmen's poem above. Although Carmen, a Boston native, never sat in Wright's Chicago church and had not heard his sermons when she wrote her poem in 2005, she nonetheless is drawing on similar conceptions of the civic lessons of American history.

To teach the same material to all students, therefore, fails to take into account their diverse and critical construction of what is being taught. Schools can't just feed students a carefully calibrated combination of historical *mea culpas* and inspiring tales of progress and success and expect them all to embrace the wonders of American citizenship and civic and political engagement. This approach simply won't work with students growing up in communities that convey a counternarrative rejecting the traditional story of the triumph of the American experiment. Furthermore, insofar as history is in dialogue with the present, not confined to the past, students whose present experiences are radically different from each other are likely to have different historical interpretations as well. Students are critical consumers of knowledge, and educators—especially history teachers—must take this into account.

MODELS OF HISTORICAL COUNTERNARRATIVE

One important model of the efficacy and power of teaching an empowering civic narrative that does not follow the moderately triumphalist or progressive story line can be found in historically segregated African-American primary and secondary schools, historically Black colleges and universities, and other historically segregated African-American institutions such as churches and fraternal organizations.[19] For over a century, they have taught—and continue to teach—American history as a story of ongoing struggle against inherent oppression and injustice, accompanied by an obligation to use one's opportunities to continue the struggle through civic and political engagement. Empowerment doesn't derive from satisfaction at the current state of affairs. The lesson is not "what a great country—wouldn't you like to get involved?" Rather, it emphasizes that continued fighting by others was necessary to achieve even this currently unjust state of affairs, and for this reason continued individual and collective struggle is necessary to continue moving toward justice.

The struggle to survive, let alone to thrive, to be recognized as equals, to "be at the table/When company comes,"[20] is necessary in part because of the United States' intrinsic racism and injustice. America was founded in a state of "original sin," committed to slavery from the founding of the first surviving colony at Jamestown through slavery's enshrinement in the Constitution and beyond.[21] Given this, the notion of an almost "inevitable" historical progression toward increased equality and justice is risible; African Americans (and others) had to—and will continue to have to—fight for every right and opportunity they have gained. As President Barack Obama put it in his famous speech on race when he was still a candidate,

> And yet words on a parchment would not be enough to deliver slaves from bondage, or provide men and women of every color and creed their full rights and obligations as citizens of the United States. What would be needed were Americans in successive generations who were willing to do their part—through protests and struggles, on the streets and in the courts, through a civil war and civil disobedience, and always at great risk—to narrow that gap between the promise of our ideals and the reality of their time.[22]

This narrative is in certain ways a mirror inversion of the traditional progressivist perfectibility narrative. Both stories see the United States as instantiating a promise of something better. But the inspiration that constitutes the "usable past" in this narrative is provided not by the promise itself, but by African Americans' history of struggling to realize that promise.[23] Rather than seeing the struggle as demoralizing, this narrative teaches African Americans' struggle as an ennobling history, as one that reveals African Americans' collective power and resilience. Children learn that by working together and *demanding* justice, equal rights, and equal opportunities, their ancestors forced those in power to cede to them the rights they were due. As James Baldwin puts it, "To accept one's past—one's history—is not the same thing as drowning in it; it is learning how to use it."[24] As a result, they are taught that they too should commit themselves to American democracy and learn about and participate in its civic institutions as a matter of justice, and as a matter of agency—of controlling one's own destiny, rather than counting on a spurious historical inevitability. They must demonstrate the same resilience and commitment to fight for what they are rightfully due; they should not and cannot let the United States off the hook.

The narrative of struggle also leads one to the narrative of obligation and opportunity. It is one's duty to become politically aware and involved, this narrative goes, because it is the obligation of young people to take advantage of opportunities that were not afforded one's ancestors. It is disrespectful, even shameful, on this account, to squander the opportunities that those who came before had to fight so hard to achieve—to achieve for those who came after, often, and not for themselves. Carol Mosley-Braun implicitly invoked this narrative in her closing statement at one of the early Democratic presidential debates in the autumn of 2003. "I hope everyone here commits themselves to register voters and to let people know that every vote counts, in spite of the 2000 election. We have a responsibility to our children to make sure that we leave them no less opportunity, no less hope, no less freedom than our ancestors left us. And if we are to do honor to our ancestors and justice to our children, we have to come together to make certain that these people do not continue to bait and switch and take our country and take the promise of our country away from us."[25]

My colleagues at Walden Middle School similarly subscribed to and fostered this understanding of African Americans' historical struggle in the past as entailing obligations for our students in the present to make the most of their educational opportunities. As one former Walden teacher explained, "You tell our children to take education for granted. Uh-uh . . . My forefathers worked too hard for children to have what they have today and not want it!" My colleagues emphasized time and time again that because enslaved and even free Blacks were often denied the most basic of freedoms, because Blacks were forbidden to learn to read and write, and could be harshly disciplined or even killed for daring to do so, and because the only way African Americans survived during slavery was by looking out for one another, it is the obligation of every Black man, woman, and child to make use of these rights, freedoms, and skills now. It is the obligation of every Black child to learn to read, to stand up for his rights, and to make her voice heard because not to do so is the equivalent of spitting in the face of those who longed and fought for these opportunities.[26] Another colleague talked about putting it to our students this way: "What's stopping you? You don't have to read by candlelight and in caves and be beaten and all of that for learning. Look at what your ancestors went through just so you could sit here. I used to tell the kids, *'Just so you could sit here.'*" Local pastors and ministers promoted similar teachings from the pulpit on Sundays and during weekday Bible classes. Reverend Gerald Durley, the pastor of Providence Missionary Baptist Church in Atlanta, volunteered when I interviewed him in 2004, "You have to take them where they are today and show them that they have an obligation and responsibility to improve the piece of ground that they're on . . . People bled and were hung and were lynched so that you could have this opportunity. don't throw that away . . . Each of us, we have an obligation to build a bridge. And you are part of the bridge building to the future for those that are coming behind you."

This message is reinforced in some elite historically Black colleges and universities such as Morehouse and Spelman. In an interview in 2003, Jeffrey, a recent graduate of Morehouse College, framed its take on the obligation narrative succinctly: "Do not drop the baton!" Morehouse uses both history and identity to promote this message, inducting incoming freshmen into

Morehouse's history and traditions and teaching them what it means to be a "Morehouse man" through an intense week of freshman orientation that is then extended throughout the year via a two-semester "Freshman Orientation" course required for graduation.[27] Freshmen attend the chapel Martin Luther King, Jr., attended as a student, watch a film on Morehouse history, memorize the school song, learn about the "great graduates" of Morehouse, discuss the accomplishments of Morehouse's "towering" former president Benjamin E. Mays, and feverishly study a booklet about Morehouse history and traditions. Upperclassmen regularly stop freshmen (identifiable by their required white shirts and ties during Freshman Week) and ask them to recite key events in Morehouse's history, sing the school song, discuss the qualities of a Morehouse man, and so on. The consequences for demonstrating ignorance about these can be "severe," Jeffrey explained. Freshmen Week ends with a torch-led march from the college through the surrounding African American historic neighborhood and back to the drum- and music-filled chapel where students commit themselves to fulfilling their historic and contemporary obligations as Morehouse men. History and identity thus combine to create a powerful narrative of membership and obligation, one that both echoes and reinforces the African-American civic counternarrative of struggle, duty, and opportunity.[28]

These lessons about the nobility of struggle and the obligation to take advantage of opportunities have strong roots in segregated Black primary and secondary schools as well, with such education taking place through both formal and informal means. As one veteran African-American teacher invoked the "purpose and dignity" she and her colleagues tried to instill in their students in segregated Black schools in "earlier times," she explained, "I tell the children that they have to push and struggle for what they want . . . I also remind them that they have a responsibility to use their talent to benefit someone other than themselves, and that they have a responsibility to give something back to the community."[29] Another African-American teacher described the all-Black school she herself attended seventy-five years ago, "Even though the schools were segregated, the teachers did quite a few things with the curriculum that did not coincide with the white school and were not sanctioned by the school board. The teachers taught us a lot about our own race even though the school board prescribed a curriculum that didn't include anything much about black people. We sang the Negro National Anthem, 'Lift Ev'ry Voice and Sing,' before every class and assembly."[30]

Singing this anthem—a practice which was continued at Walden and many Atlanta public schools during my years teaching there—was a political act of communal and historical self-definition. The very notion of a "Negro national anthem" explicitly frames African-American civic identity as different from—and in some ways in contrast to—a generic U.S. identity as defined by "The Star-Spangled Banner" and other symbols of American political identity and membership. The story recounted by "Lift Ev'ry Voice and Sing" is also a stirring paean to African-Americans' collective struggles, obligations, and opportunities, as the second verse demonstrates:

> Stony the road we trod, bitter the chastening rod,
> Felt in the days when hope unborn had died;
> Yet with a steady beat, have not our weary feet
> Come to the place for which our fathers sighed?
> We have come over a way that with tears has been watered,
> We have come, treading our path through the blood of the
>   slaughtered;
> Out from the gloomy past, till now we stand at last
> Where the white gleam of our bright star is cast.[31]

Furthermore, "Lift Ev'ry Voice and Sing" is but one of many "rituals of remembrance" beyond the formal curriculum that historically contributed to the maintenance of the community narrative. These included Emancipation Day, "a celebration once ubiquitous in the black communities of the late 19th and early 20th centuries," as well as "Lincoln-Douglas Day, Fifteenth Amendment Day, Decoration Day," and assorted community pageants, all of which were taught and celebrated in segregated Black schools and other sites including NAACP Youth Councils, Black colleges, and Freedom Schools.[32] De jure and de facto segregated African-American schools and communities thus used formal and informal means to combine struggle and obligation into a seamless story of both individual opportunity and civic responsibility.

Freedom Schools, for example, were designed in 1964 to help students draw upon their personal experiences of struggle and oppression as a means of motivating civic and political action designed to transform power relations in their communities. "What they must see is the link between a rotting shack and a rotting America," explained Charles Cobb, the twenty-year-old field secretary of the Student Nonviolent Coordinating Committee who initiated the Freedom Schools. The answer to the "rotting America" was not depression, disengagement, or violent rebellion—rather it was civic and political activism.[33] Contemporary Freedom Schools continue to embrace a similar vision.[34] Chris Myers, a young White man who founded the Sunflower County Freedom Project in Sunflower County, Mississippi, explained to me in a 2004 interview, "We paint the picture very clearly for them. We don't shy away from the racism and the inequalities of power that exist, not just in Mississippi but all over the place. But we also don't shy away from saying that if you have the guts, if you have the determination, you can and you will overcome those odds. Because there are a lot of opportunities in this country if you . . . engage [them]." He went on to link these opportunities to the history of struggle and the civic narrative of obligation: "Part of the reason that it is the land of opportunity is precisely because of Fannie Lou Hamer and the civil rights movement and the things that they did to open up opportunities like ours. And to deny that, is not only wrong, not only a denial of reality but it's also a slap in the face to the people who did sacrifice so much."

A LIVING NARRATIVE

It is worth noting that this narrative is not just a construct of educators spinning out radical countercultural narratives that have no traction in the real world. Stories about struggle, opportunity, and obligation—and identification with the struggle, rather than with the success—came up frequently in interviews I conducted in 2004 with people who have "beaten" the civic empowerment gap. These are young people and adults who are non-White, for the most part grew up poor, are in some cases first- or second-generation immigrants, and live or work predominantly in de facto segregated minority environments. Nonetheless, they became civic and political leaders and activists.

One of the most eloquent expositors of the motivational power of this antitriumphalist civic identity is probably Aaron Watson, an African-American lawyer and former member and president of the Atlanta Board of Education. In response to my question, "What makes somebody American and what makes America, America?" he explains,

> Well, I would say that as an African American—in America I probably don't define myself without that caveat—that is, what does it mean to be an African American in America? . . . I probably might extend it to other minorities in America, I think it means that you have the right to struggle . . . [You have] the right and opportunity to struggle against all the various oppression, and the right and the opportunity, I would add, to succeed to the extent that you're willing to pay the price of that success . . . I'm one of the people that doesn't think that struggling is a bad thing.[35]

Later in the interview, Watson explicitly frames his civic and political identity and engagement in these terms: "I would not define myself as patriotic. I'm proud to be an American, but I'm proud to be an 'Aaron Watson American.' An American who's here for the struggle, for the struggle for me, and for the struggle for a whole bunch of other people. I'm happy to be a part of that . . . So I choose my own picture and in that picture I'm proud to be one of them." Watson almost willfully constructs an empowering American history and identity from the building blocks of struggle—not from the building blocks of success, as the "moderate triumphalists" would have it. Watson realizes that there are many possible Americas to feel a part of: "[I'm] not necessarily proud to be an American in George Bush's America, so to speak." This America is in certain ways more concrete, and certainly more visible, than the "right to struggle America" Watson refers to and identifies with. But it's his conscious choice to attach himself to the other, more metaphorical America, and to feel proud of and connected to that: "So I choose my own picture and in that picture I'm proud to be one of them."

At the same time, it's worth noting that the narrative of struggle, opportunity, and obligation is not necessarily politically partisan; it's not confined to radical activists or even Democrats. Michael Steele, the first African-American chair of the Republican National Committee, commented soon after his election, "Who would think in 2009, you'd have two black men at the pinnacle of political power in this country? That fact is a testament to struggle, perseverance, and opportunity."[36]

This empowering narrative of and identification with struggle is also not confined to African-American civic and political activists. Joel, a Latino youth activist with the Hyde Square Task Force in Boston, answered the same question I posed to Watson by explaining, "America—I don't know. The first two words I think of are freedom and struggle . . . Like there's so many opportunities, but also struggle to get there." Abed Hammoud, a Lebanese-American county prosecutor, civic and political activist, and two-time mayoral candidate in Dearborn, Michigan, provided an immigrant gloss on the story as he explained his own activism to me:

So that's what drives me, is to pave the way to a new generation of Arab-Americans. I think I'm the transitional generation . . . I'm half/ half. Ask me. I want to be as American as the Italian, Irish, French, everybody. And I think it will happen. Maybe in my lifetime I'll sit here and tell stories to my grandkids how hard it was in my days . . . So, but to do that, some of us have to suffer. My dad even said to me one time, he said, "If you wait ten more years to get involved, it'll be a lot easier for you." He said because the initial time people suffer a lot, and there'll be lots of pain. I said to him, my answer was, "If everybody waits, then the transition will never happen."

Hammoud is motivated by the ideal of progress, I acknowledge. He anticipates "transition" in the long run from his "half/ half" generation to a "new generation" of full Americans. But he also sees honor in the struggle in the present day, and he clearly both identifies more with and is inspired more by those who engage in the struggle than by those who reap the rewards. "[W]e need to tell these people that not only the peaceful not-rocking-the-boat Arab will make it. Not only the peaceful not-rocking-the-boat African-American will make it. Everybody will. And that's why there should be movies about Malcolm X and all sides of his life. And about Martin Luther King. But also about Dearborn and AAPAC [Arab American Political Action Committee]." Themes of struggle, opportunity, and obligation suffuse many immigrant stories about why they came to America, what life and citizenship in America mean, and how children are expected to respond. Immigrant communities frequently emphasize the sacrifice made by the immigrant generation in order to generate opportunities for their children; these are opportunities the children are obliged to take advantage of in order to justify their parents' or ancestors' sacrifice.

Immigrants and other minority group members may also be moved by this narrative insofar as it does not require the same kind of active, personal identification with the nation as traditional civic narratives often seem to demand. Under the moderately triumphalist narrative, civic engagement is presented as a way of expressing one's identification with a country defined by laudable ideals. American civic identity is something to feel and be proud of, and civic and political involvement are ways of expressing and embracing this identity. Many transnational and migrant youth and adults, however, may not feel this strong sense of identification with the United States. They may have multiple national affiliations, harbor ambivalent feelings about a country that has oppressed as well as embraced them, or feel that their cultural, religious, or other identities are more significant than their identity as American citizens. By rooting civic engagement in a tradition of action, rather than identification, the counternarrative I've described overcomes these difficulties. This is obviously also a benefit for other young people who may not consider U.S. citizenship as a salient or even desirable part of their identities.

Thus, we can see that although the antitriumphalist counternarratives of struggle, opportunity, and obligation are historically grounded in the African-American community, they can potentially be effectively implemented in African-American and non–African-American schools alike. In schools without a significant African-American student body, students may draw on different historical examples and contemporary contexts than those highlighted here. The struggles that people went through simply to make it to the United States, and then to find a place within it, may be more meaningful to students in a predominantly immigrant neighborhood than the struggles taken on by those who were already considered to be Americans.[37] Furthermore, teachers may need to do additional work in helping students expand their conceptions of their families' struggles, and the opportunities and obligations that are attendant upon them as children of immigrants, from the purely economic realm to the civic and political realms. Even if the benefits of such engagement are posed in purely self-interested terms—that immigrant children, their families, and their ethnoracial communities will directly and personally benefit from their civic and political participation—without reference to the broader civic and political health of the democracy, this may be enough to help shrink the civic empowerment gap and set patterns of participation that will replicate themselves through future generations.[38]

In predominantly African-American schools, too, it is important to recapture and teach these empowering counternarratives of struggle, opportunity, and obligation. The loss of segregated Black schools, Freedom Schools, and even churches and other institutions that taught a collective narrative of struggle and obligation may be partially responsible for the declining levels of Black political and civic participation in the United States, which used to be the highest in the country.[39] Bringing these narratives back into schools can potentially help slow or even reverse the decline in African Americans' civic and political participation, as well as shrink the civic empowerment gap for other groups.

CONSTRUCTING AND ENGAGING MULTIPLE NARRATIVES

Is one "answer" to the civic empowerment gap, then, to nationalize this construction of history—to replace the moderately triumphalist narrative with a common historical narrative of struggle, opportunity, and obligation that all students would learn? There are some powerful arguments in favor of this approach. First, to the extent that this narrative is true (which I've at least implicitly argued it is), it is not only young people from historically marginalized groups and those who attend de facto segregated schools serving students from poor, minority, and immigrant communities who should learn this construction of American history. All young people in the United States, in all schools, should learn historical truth.

Second, it is quite possible that this counternarrative could be easily mainstreamed insofar as it parallels many elements of the moderately triumphalist narrative by emphasizing both the ideals of liberty, justice, equality and the possibility of progress in achieving these ideals. As the first verse of "Lift Ev'ry Voice and Sing" exhorts us,

> Lift every voice and sing, till earth and Heaven ring
> Ring with the harmonies of liberty . . .
> Sing a song full of the faith that the dark past has taught us
> Sing a song full of the hope that the present has brought us.[40]

This emphasis on both liberty and progress is fully compatible with the triumphalist narrative. James's response when I stressed other countries' embrace of school uniforms is also relevant here: "But we're not most other countries, Dr. Levinson! We supposed to be the land of freedom and liberty. What about our rights?" Both narratives draw deeply upon and reinforce American values of equal rights and liberties, that progress is possible, and that progress has been achieved—with the crucial exception that the counternarrative emphasizes that this progress is not inevitable or historically deterministic. Rather, it depends on constant vigilance and struggle, both by those who lived and struggled in the "dark past" and those still living who must "march on till victory is won."[41] Even this emphasis on "original sin," however, need not be seen as totally undermining the American civic narrative; thus, it may be fairly easy to replace the one with the other.[42]

Third, a shared American narrative of struggle, obligation, and opportunity could break down the misunderstanding (and worse!) that tends to result when Whites who have learned the moderately triumphalist narrative encounter the counternarrative for the first time, and often respond to it as seeming foreign, ungrateful, or flat-out wrong. I noted above that the triumphalist narrative can be potentially inspiring for many people, and even has some historical legitimacy insofar as there has been a fairly steady increase in rights and liberties for most American citizens over the past few hundred years. But if young people who are privileged and White learn that narrative, while young people who are not privileged and not White learn the counternarrative, the meeting of these worldviews may result in mutual mistrust, misunderstanding, and resentment. Charles Payne comments wryly in response to a conference titled "Education for Liberation" that "one of the least well-attended workshops was titled 'Freedom Schools for White Youth.' Even people who are thinking about more powerful forms of social education for children of color do not necessarily see the point of it for young people in the majority group. White children are presumed to be whole. In fact, racial privilege and class privilege bring their own ways of not seeing."[43] Certainly one means of counterbalancing this racial blindness would be the replacement of the triumphalist narrative with one of struggle, obligation, and opportunity. Introducing a counternarrative would better educate White students, offering them an education more aligned with the education in double consciousness that I argued for in the last chapter. James Baldwin explains that African Americans have "the great advantage of having never believed that collection of myths to which white Americans cling: that they were born in the greatest country the world has ever seen."[44] Why disadvantage White Americans by denying them access to a more truthful and yet still empowering story of American struggle and opportunity, and why disadvantage other Americans by forcing them to contend with White students who "cling" to a false and ultimately destructive myth?

This leads me to the fourth potential argument for teaching a common, standardized narrative of struggle, opportunity, and obligation: namely, that multiple civic narratives are civically divisive, whereas a unified civic narrative functions as "a kind of civic glue."[45] In line with this idea, Congress resolved in 2002 that "without a common civic memory and common understanding of the remarkable individuals, events, and ideals that have shaped the Nation, people in the United States risk losing much of what it means to be an American, as well as the ability to fulfill the fundamental responsibilities of citizens in a democracy."[46] The Shanker Institute's *Education for Democracy* concurs: "the mastery of a common core of history binds us together, creates a common civic identity based on a patriotism of principles, and unites us in the shared undertaking that is both our past and our future." With regard to 9/11, the Shanker Institute adds, "We were attacked for being American. We should at least know what being American means."[47]

These arguments are all plausible to at least some extent, and some of these arguments are even deeply compelling. Ultimately, however, it would be wrong to conclude that we can or should try to beat the civic empowerment gap by replacing one monolithic civic narrative of moderate triumphalism with another monolithic narrative of struggle, obligation, and opportunity. First, to replace the former with the latter risks homogenization and cooptation of the counternarrative, thus converting it into uninspiring pabulum, at best. Promoting any monolithic narrative also ignores students' own active construction of civic narratives. This approach assumes that a single unified narrative is possible, which is at best implausible. Ultimately, we must equip our students to recognize, respect, and engage with ambiguity and difference, including with different people's constructions of the civic lessons of history, rather than continuing to promote the idea that there is one "right" way to understand history. Taken together, I think these reasons point us away from the uniform nationalization of the particular "counternarrative" I have been discussing in favor of an approach that encourages teachers and students both to co-construct truthful, empowering civic narratives and to engage with multiple civic narratives in their telling and analysis of history. Let me expand on these in turn.

First, it is frankly frighteningly easy to imagine what textbook authors and curriculum writers could do to defang the narrative of struggle, opportunity, and obligation *en route* to universalizing it. One can imagine the transformation of "struggle" into a purely uplifting enterprise, with the misery and the injustice leached out in favor of a packaged vision of an ennobling sacrifice. Struggle could also well become confined to the past in this telling: "Let us be thankful for the struggles of those who came before so we can appreciate the opportunities we have now." One of the main strengths of the particular counternarrative we have been exploring in potentially combating the civic empowerment gap is its extension of struggle to the present. It teaches that the struggle must continue. But it's all too easy to imagine the struggle becoming mythologized in the past, and the obligation to continue the struggle being lopped off in the present. Similarly, the recognition of "original sin"—that incidents of racism and injustice are not incidental, superficial stains on the essentially pure core of American ideals and values, but rather are central and inescapable elements of America's foundation and ongoing history—may easily be submerged and ultimately sidelined. At this point, textbooks would be back to telling a story simply of struggle leading to opportunity, a ready morph back into the moderately triumphalist narrative. It is worth noting that this transformation is likely even in the absence of malign intent. In his book on the culture wars, Jonathan Zimmerman points out that many people who would seem to have had an interest in overturning the moderately triumphalist narrative—including many representatives of groups which have historically experienced discrimination—in fact were complicit in supporting it, so long as their own group was equally represented or included as heroes in the American pantheon.[48]

Second, to the extent that the first half of this chapter was an extended argument about the need for constructivist history education, straight replacement of one official narrative with another does little good. Helen Haste reminds us in this regard, "Rather than being regarded as passively 'socialized,' the individual actively constructs—and co-constructs with others—explanations and stories that make sense of experience, to develop an identity that locates her or him in a social, cultural, and historical context. Self and group identity, negotiated through narrative and dialogue as well as through trying to make sense of social structures and representations, are crucial to understanding the construction of the citizen."[49] These active constructions, dialogues, and negotiations occur no matter what schools do. But if schools end up selecting an "official" narrative, regardless of what that narrative is, then they effectively write themselves out of the process. Schools cannot and will not help students construct personally empowering civic understandings if they see their purpose as the transmission of a predefined story. Valorization and calcification of a narrative of struggle, obligation, and opportunity would thus be unfortunate, and end up feeling to young people of many backgrounds as sterile and irrelevant as the triumphalist narrative does to many now.

Third, we need to recognize that it's impossible in practice to have a single national narrative. There's just too much variation in people's lived experiences, in their knowledge and conceptions of history, and in their construction of the relationship between these. No civic narrative will work for all students, or adults, or communities.[50] History teachers may draw upon some guiding principles, but ultimately they will need to teach American history in such a way as to enable students to construct their own empowering civic narratives and sense of American identity, whether that is modeled on the narratives described above or on something entirely different. In other words, a truly "common civic memory" and especially "common understanding" of American history are impossible, no matter what Congress has to say about the matter.

Although I have focused on one narrative exemplar in this chapter, there are others that are also well articulated. One such narrative is that of "public work": the idea that "practical public effort by ordinary people in everyday environments" has created what is of greatest value in our communities, and so is also the key to understanding both the nature of historical progress and the joys and obligations of citizenship. By understanding "politics" as "the everyday activity of problem solving and building our environments," Harry Boyte argues, we come to understand U.S. history and citizenship very differently. These understandings are firmly in line with narratives promoted by many social and labor historians, on the one hand, and also with many poor and non-White communities who take pride in the fruits of their labor, on the other.[51] Howard Zinn's popular *A People's History* series of high school history books also builds on these ideas. Other potential narratives reject a perspective that puts the United States at the center, embedding both U.S. history and civic engagement within a more global context of interdependence necessitating urgent action in response to environmental threat, neocolonial oppression, or global market forces (depending on one's politics).[52] Still other narratives may be confined to a particular, self-defined ethnoracial group, cultural or religious community, or geographic location. Histories may be told, and tales of self and nation constructed, that are intensely specific to a small group of people. In any case, no matter how narrow or inclusive the civic historical narrative may be, it can be counted on to be challenged elsewhere—and hence to challenge teachers who encounter these alternatives, as well.

In these respects, it may be good that some American history textbooks have lost their sense of narrative altogether, that the narrative has "unraveled."[53] As a matter of practice, unfortunately, textbooks' newfound abandonment of a coherent story hasn't generally led to constructivist teaching on teachers' parts. Rather, it's led in many cases to a mere absence of direction or purpose, except maybe the "motivation" of the standardized test. But this isn't a necessary response to the storyless textbook. If teachers used textbooks "only [as] reference works," as Diane Ravitch correctly recommends, then they could really start teaching constructively instead.[54]

Fourth and last, it is crucial for the purposes of civic empowerment and democracy that we equip students to take multiple perspectives and to engage constructively with ambiguity, not just that we inculcate in them a single civic narrative—no matter how empowering and truthful—that is so deeply rooted from their perspective as to brook no dissent. History teachers, who are necessarily civic educators, need to keep this dual purpose in mind. They should see themselves as co-constructing empowering civic narratives with their students when they teach history. But they also need to help their students engage imaginatively and thoughtfully with difference: different perspectives, different times and places, different experiences, different ways of viewing and living in the world. In order to be responsible citizens, students need to learn that other people legitimately see and experience the world differently from them, that there are legitimate and reasonable other historical and civic narratives. We don't want students—our youngest citizens—to grow up thinking there is only one way to understand the world or U.S. history, regardless of how compelling that interpretation may seem. "Reading or listening to someone else's story, no less than telling one's own, belongs to the work of a citizen."[55] The compatibility of these two claims is admittedly more achievable in theory than in practice. From developmental and pedagogical perspectives, teachers face a daunting task in attempting simultaneously to help students develop an engaging, truthful, and empowering historical narrative about which they become passionate and to help students recognize the reasonableness of others' experiences, perspectives, and narratives even when they are radically unlike one's own. But from a civic perspective, this task is absolutely essential, no matter how hard, and so we cannot and should not push merely for one standardized civic narrative to overthrow another.

A TOOL FOR CIVIC EMPOWERMENT

Where does this leave us? To begin with, students—all of us—are surrounded by stories of, about, and that shape history. They—and we—learn history from all sorts of places, of which school is only one among many. Thus, it is not the case that if schools don't teach history, students won't know any history. Rather, students will draw judgments about and from history that they will have learned or picked up elsewhere. It is also not the case that if schools do teach history, then this is necessarily the history students will learn. Students will draw judgments about and from the history they are taught in school with respect to the history they learn elsewhere. Given this, it's important for schools to become engaged in a *conversation* about history with students. They should not and cannot leave the transmission and interpretation of history solely to others, but they also cannot and should not position themselves as the sole arbiters of historical transmission and interpretation. Like it or not, school-based history educators are in a dialogue with students about history and about citizenship, and they need to take their responsibilities as civic educators seriously as a result. I have proposed that one way to do so—especially insofar as schools have a responsibility to help close the civic empowerment gap—is to help students construct truthful and empowering civic historical narratives.

One partially truthful narrative that has been empowering for some students is the traditional, "moderately triumphalist" narrative. Moderately triumphalist history teaches that the United States was founded on the basis of ideals such as liberty, equality, freedom, and so on. Although the United States did not realize these ideals fully at the beginning of its history or even necessarily now, American history has moved inexorably, even inevitably, in the direction of these ideals because they represent who we are as a people. This narrative has proved to be empowering by motivating people to be civically active in order to be part of the wonderful "experiment" that is America. Action here is an expression of identity: "I'm proud to be an American," and civic engagement follows from this pride. Insofar as this narrative blinds students (and adults) to the perspectives of others whose experiences of the United States have not been so benign, and insofar as this narrative is patently unable to inspire all Americans to become civically engaged and empowered, other civic narratives are also necessary.

Drawing upon a wide variety of historical and contemporary evidence, especially from African-American schools and civic institutions, I propose one counternarrative that could be considered to be both historically true and civically empowering: one that teaches that the United States was founded in the "original sin" of racism and discrimination, but that holds out the hope of redemption via struggle because of its accompanying founding ideals of equality and liberty. According to this historical civic narrative, civic action is crucial both because of the need to push the United States toward its better self by fighting against the inherent flaws at its core, and because of the obligation one has to those who came before who helped secure the rights and opportunities we currently have. Inaction is dangerous, because of the risk that the United States could revert to its racist, discriminatory, inegalitarian roots; inaction is also profoundly disrespectful to previous fighters in the struggle for freedom. Action here is an expression of agency—"I can and need to make a difference"—rather than an expression of identity: as Aaron Watson explained, "I don't think of myself as American."

Although I think this narrative has the potential to be both truthfully constructed and civically empowering in a fairly wide variety of settings, it too should not be considered the "new" American civic narrative. Unreflective acceptance of this story would also blind students to the legitimate experiences and perspectives of others. Some students and some communities will be unable to see this narrative as appropriately reflecting and describing their own experiences; as a result, it will not be civically empowering for all students. Furthermore, no civic narrative should become entrenched as "official" history and thus insulated from critique. One of the crucial lessons both of the study of history and of democracy is that our perspectives are always partial, our understandings are always flawed, and our need for dialogue and communal problem-solving are always great.

Furthermore, it is worth noting that no historical narrative on its own—no matter how collaboratively constructed or civically inspiring in its telling—will solve the civic empowerment gap. Narratives rarely offer sufficient motivation on their own. When told in terms of the broad sweep of history, rather than as examinations of specific means of achieving power or change, they provide little guidance for how to translate aims into action. It is also hard to construct an empowering civic narrative if one has never had a positive civic experience. Subsequent chapters take up these challenges.

The Texas Education Agency in July 2009 is in the process of drafting new social studies curriculum standards to guide teaching, testing, and textbook selection for the next decade. Although the standards themselves are being written by a team of educators and community members, the Texas State Board of Education has appointed an additional six "experts" to guide the writing team. These experts include four university professors, as well as two founders and presidents of Christian organizations.[1] Each has been asked to start by reviewing the current Texas Essential Knowledge and Skills (TEKS) curriculum in social studies, which was written in the 1990s. In their reviews, the two heads of Christian organizations take an emphatic stand on many of the historical figures included and excluded from the curriculum. Anne Hutchinson, Cesar Chavez, and Thurgood Marshall, among others, come under challenge.

Peter Marshall, founder and president of Peter Marshall Ministries in Massachusetts, explains that "Anne Hutchinson does not belong in the company of" such "significant colonial leaders" as William Penn, John Smith, or Roger Williams. "She was certainly not a significant colonial leader, and didn't accomplish anything except getting herself exiled from the Massachusetts Bay Colony for making trouble." Similarly, he challenges the curriculum standard asking students to "'Identify significant individuals such as Cesar Chavez and Benjamin Franklin who modeled active participation in the democratic process.' To have Cesar Chavez listed next to Ben Franklin is ludicrous," Marshall explains. "Chavez is hardly the kind of role model that ought to be held up to our children as someone worthy of emulation." In his curriculum review, Marshall also opposes the inclusion of Thurgood Marshall as not a "strong enough example" of someone who has "impacted American history."[2] *Brown v. Board of Education*, argued and won by Thurgood Marshall in front of the U.S. Supreme Court he would later join as an associate justice, seems not to count as historically significant in Peter Marshall's worldview.

David Barton, founder and president of WallBuilders, an organization dedicated to "Presenting America's forgotten history and heroes with an emphasis on our moral, religious, and constitutional heritage,"[3] concurs with Marshall's assessment of both Hutchinson and Chavez. In his written assessment under the section heading "Heroes of History," Barton acknowledges that Hutchinson, who co-founded Rhode Island and argued on behalf of women's equality and against Native American slavery, is a "historic figure." But he also challenges her status as a "significant colonial leader." He is more directly incensed about Chavez's inclusion: "Cesar Chavez may be a choice representing diversity but he certainly lacks the stature, impact, and overall contributions of so many others; and his open affiliation with Saul Alinsky's movements certainly makes dubious that he is a praiseworthy to be heralded to students as someone 'who modeled active participation in the democratic process.'"[4] Barton is clearly challenging the democratic character of Chavez's union organizing via the United Farm Workers and of *Rules for Radicals* author Saul Alinsky's community organizing.[5]

I start following the controversy because of my interest in civic education, of course. But I'm also curious because of a more personal connection. I grew up and attended public schools in Texas from fourth grade through the end of high school. During that time, my mother worked for the Texas Education Agency and spearheaded the development of the first TEKS. I was in high school when she organized community forums in English and Spanish that involved over 25,000 Texas citizens and residents. They discussed what they thought children growing up in Texas should know and be able to do. I remember her working with educators, business leaders, parents, and others to revise and specify the first statewide curriculum in all content areas. I also remember listening to her describe her frustration with the State Board of Education, which was an early target of religious conservatives' entry into electoral politics in the 1980s.

I know that these controversies still haven't diminished in Texas. If anything, they have gotten worse, as members of the religious Right have been elected to the majority of the seats and been appointed president of the state board. There are frequent fights over sex education, phonics, evolution, and environmental education, among other topics. One board member recently celebrated the success of the State Board of Education in stopping "environmentalists from using high school environmental science classes to bash the Texas oil and gas industry."[6] But I'm curious to see what's going on specifically in social studies.

Mostly, as I read first the newspaper article and then the specific social studies reports submitted by each of the six "experts," I'm appalled by David Barton's and Peter Marshall's positions. How could one deny that Thurgood Marshall is a "strong . . . example" of someone who has influenced American history—and clearly for the better? As for Cesar Chavez, the very reason that Barton wants to exclude him from the curriculum is why I want to make sure he remains in the state standards. Chavez exemplifies exactly the kind of "active participation in the democratic process" via collective struggle and action that I want students to learn about and to emulate. Cesar Chavez and Thurgood Marshall, I think, are the American heroes that we should be teaching about in history and social studies classes. They refused to give in to the apparent limitations of their own social,

economic, and political circumstances; they committed themselves to the struggle against injustice; and they organized collectively with others to create a better country for us all. Who
better to inspire and empower students—especially those at the
bottom of the civic empowerment gap—than such heroes as
these? At the same time, I sense that it is exactly these characteristics—in addition to the fact that Chavez and Marshall tend to
be heroes of the American Left, not of the religious Right—that
makes them unappealing to Barton and Peter Marshall. Sitting
at my computer, I get increasingly agitated at these men's influence on the Texas State Board of Education, and by extension on
the schools, teachers, and students throughout my home state.

This particular battle is now over. Chavez, Marshall, and
Hutchinson all squeaked through in the end, accompanied by
some newly added conservative icons including James Baker,
Friedrich Hayek, and Phyllis Schlafly. National press coverage,
which peaked with a 2010 *New York Times Magazine* cover
story about the controversy, has disappeared.[7] Teachers are busy
trying to adapt their lesson plans to the new TEKS, and state officials have moved on to other concerns. This may be the right
time to ask if the outcomes of this battle matter. Are students'
lives likely to unfold differently because they're learning about
both Chavez and Schlafly rather than one or neither? Is the character of students' civic engagement, or their capacity for civic
empowerment, likely to be affected in any way? Frankly, I doubt
it. I spent time every year talking with my middle schoolers
about Martin Luther King, Jr.—a hero of collective democratic
action if there ever is one. Almost all of my 1,000 or so students
expressed fervent admiration for Martin Luther King, as do virtually all Americans. King, for example, polls second only to
Mother Teresa as the most admired person from the twentieth
century.[8] But virtually none of my students—and seemingly

equally few Americans—ever thought to try to put his techniques into action. My students would speak generally of King's perseverance, his standing up for what he believed in, his willingness to sacrifice himself to the cause, and other such platitudes. But they rarely if ever referenced his broader civic leadership or his empowerment of others to advance the causes for which he and they stood.

The techniques used by King and his colleagues in the civil rights movement are arguably moribund, despite the fact that our country faces a multitude of ills, and commits a multitude of sins, that threaten justice, equality, and liberty as much now as fifty years ago. Civil disobedience, collective action among thousands of citizens for a sustained period of time, nonviolent protest—these are evident neither in school curricula, which tend to treat King as a towering figure who single-handedly led Americans into "the promised land," nor in American civic or political practice in the early twenty-first century—Tea Partiers notwithstanding. Young people (and probably adults, too) fail to recognize even that they could carry forward King's work in any but the most anodyne ways. Furthermore, even the sanitized and "antiseptic" personal characteristics my students did identify each year did not motivate them to act in a different way on a day-to-day basis.[9] They admired King, but they did not emulate him.

If young people don't emulate Martin Luther King—one of only two nonpresidents to have a national holiday designated in his honor, a man celebrated in every U.S. history and civics textbook as well as in literally thousands of trade books for children and adults, a civic leader in whose "dream" the whole nation can seemingly find itself—then why think that they would be inspired to emulate other historic figures? Barton and Peter Marshall opposed Thurgood Marshall, Chavez, and Hutchinson because they represent "radical" forces who deeply opposed the status quo and used a variety of democratic techniques to promote far-reaching changes.[10] They were deeply worried that students who learn about such people will be inspired to follow their examples as opposed to being inspired to "restore America to its Bible-based foundations."[11] I want students to learn about these civic heroes for the same reasons, so that students will be inspired to follow their examples. In this respect (and probably solely in this respect), Barton, Marshall, and I seem to agree: it matters what "heroes" are included in the state social studies curriculum. But does it? Is there any reason to think this is true?

CIVIC FUNCTIONS OF HEROES

Let's start by taking a look backward at why adults have taught children about civic heroes.[12] One of the most basic functions that the public elevation of heroes has served is that of providing models for emulation. A typical nineteenth-century school recitation taught, for example:

> Perhaps the reason little folks
> Are sometimes great when they grow taller,
> Is just because, like Washington,
> They do their best when they are smaller.[13]

In other words, as our greatest citizens such as Washington did, so should we try to do in our own small ways. Through such emulation, it is thought, young people will develop into virtuous citizens themselves. Furthermore, they will presumably imbibe the civic values that are intended to tie the nation or *civitas* together. A nation's heroes are often thought to provide a window into understanding its soul: what the nation values and emulates, and how it conceives of itself—what it believes it stands for. Thus in his landmark work on American heroes, Dixon Wecter lauds Washington, Franklin, Jefferson, Andrew Jackson, Lincoln, Robert E. Lee, Theodore Roosevelt, and others as those "from whom we have hewn our symbols of government, our ideas of what is most prizeworthy as 'American,'" linking them as tangible symbols of American values with "touchstones like the Declaration of Independence and the Constitution."[14] As many authors have noted, this is in large part a constructed, even artificial process. Jackson is in that list because he symbolizes democratization and populism, not Native American genocide or anti-intellectualism, even though these may equally accurately capture both the man and some foundational American values. On the other side, the "heroification" process has similarly turned Martin Luther King into a symbol of America's ongoing "dream" of equality and diversity, rather than a reminder of its persistent racism or militarism, against which King protested so mightily.[15]

This process of national civic self-conceptualization and self-actualization through hero identification is made transparent when one looks at the treatment of national heroes in civics textbooks. Youth are explicitly instructed in the meaning they should ascribe to such heroes, and thus in the values they should ascribe to their country. Thus, *Civics for Citizens* (1974) instructs students that Mount Rushmore honors "four great Americans who were dedicated to the American ideal of freedom."[16] In the same vein, *Magruders American Government* (1953) shows a picture of students literally dwarfed by the statue of Thomas Jefferson at the Jefferson Memorial. The caption reads, "These students in the Jefferson Memorial, Washington, D.C., find inspiration from one of our greatest patriots. Jefferson believed that all men were created equal, that men should make their governments, and that men should enjoy freedom of speech, of the press, and of religion. In his sixty years of public service, Jefferson stamped his personality and ideals indelibly upon our country."[17]

In addition to imparting the values that define the country in general, the identification and elevation of civic heroes can also serve to teach citizens the characteristics that ideally define democratic civic leaders in particular. In this respect, civic heroes may not necessarily be models of emulation for all citizens. Rather, the implication is that such heroes are the kind of people who should be running the country. Thus, the elevation of military heroes may serve to teach citizens that their elected leaders should also have served in the military, or at least demonstrate the virtues of strength, fearlessness, and discipline that military heroes often possess. Conversely, if young people are taught about heroes who fought injustice, bucked the system, worked to incorporate the disenfranchised, and so forth, they may learn to look for civic leaders who embody these ideals.

A corollary of this approach is the potential demeaning or civic exclusion of those who are not elevated as heroes. If certain kinds of people—women or non-Whites, say—are *not* elevated as heroes, then the message is that such people are also not appropriate civic leaders. In response to a vast array of pressure groups, contemporary textbook publishers are now exquisitely sensitive to this concern about the exclusionary power of symbolism, and thus focus intensely on making sure that the heroes that students learn about are visibly diverse and multicultural. White men are now almost never featured consecutively in sidebars or photos in civics (or any other) textbooks; rather, every White man or other apparent "mainstream" hero is followed by a visible ethnic or racial minority, woman, naturalized citizen, disabled person, or other "multicultural" hero.[18] In this case, the aim is to provide multiple touchstones in order to inspire an inclusive conception of desirable civic leaders.

Another purpose of teaching about heroes has always been to inspire patriotism. As Noah Webster argued, "[E]very child in America should be acquainted with his own country . . . As soon as he opens his lips, he should rehearse the history of his own country; he should lisp the praise of liberty and of those illustrious heroes and statesmen who have wrought a revolution in her favor."[19] This patriotism may sometimes require some historical reconstruction or even deception: "Although he had not admired Washington's leadership during the war, [Benjamin] Rush thought it wise to tell less than the full truth about the founding fathers: 'Let the world admire our patriots and heroes. Their *supposed* talents and virtues . . . will serve the cause of patriotism and of our country.'"[20] Similarly, the real and mythic accomplishments of such icons as Lewis and Clark, Douglas MacArthur, Harry Truman, Theodore Roosevelt, and the American cowboy are used to reinforce America's can-do spirit as a means of imparting common civic values and inspiring love of the country that exemplifies such a characteristic. Students are also taught that "only in America" could heroic entrepreneurs such as Andrew Carnegie or Bill Gates achieve their dreams—and thus achieve the American dream more broadly—or could heroes such as Helen Keller and Colin Powell rise from obscurity to greatness.

At the same time, "mere" patriotism is just one stage along the continuum of civic unity. Further along, civic heroes can be turned into "demigods," used to establish or burnish a civil religion that unites the country in a shared reverence of their deified patriots.[21] This process has been especially apparent with George Washington, Abraham Lincoln, and Martin Luther King. "[H]ero-worship of the living Washington," for example, started as early as the 1770s and has continued virtually every decade since.[22] Consider *Legends of the American Revolution*, published in 1847, which "told of a mystic who had heard the voice of God, 'I will send a deliverer to this land of the New World, who shall save my people from physical bondage, even as my Son saved them from the bondage of spiritual death!' This mystic came from Germany to the New World and one midnight consecrated Washington with holy oil, a crown of laurel, and a sword."[23] Seventy-five years later, the civic impact of such deification can be seen in the report of a young immigrant girl: "'Never had I prayed . . . in such utter reverence and worship as I repeated the simple sentences of my child's story of the patriot. I gazed with adoration at the portraits of George and Martha Washington, till I could see them with my eyes shut.'"[24] Similarly, although it took longer for Lincoln to achieve demigod status, "In the twentieth century . . . Americans began to refashion the man of the people [Lincoln] along epic lines. Increasingly, they saw the Christ-like Man of Sorrows. They saw the Savior of the union who takes upon himself the pain of his people. They saw the great moralist, the prophet of democracy, the Great Emancipator, the giant who changes the course of history. They saw the man that can never be reached: a man, for sure, but too good, and too big, to be treated as a man."[25]

Martin Luther King, Jr., too, has attained an almost Christ-like stature in the United States. The standard narrative could be summarized, only a little facetiously, as: "King lived and died for our sins. He wanted all people to live as brothers and to love each other. For some reason there was a lot of racism when King was alive. Through his work and especially his 'I have a dream' speech, he taught people to love each other and not be racist anymore. A racist person then killed him. But his dream lives on and now everybody gets along." This myth was carried to a logi-cal extreme a few years ago by the four-year-old son of a friend of mine. A week or two after Martin Luther King Day, Jeremiah asked his teacher, "Who gave us nature?" Before his teacher could respond, Jeremiah burst out, "Martin Luther King gave us nature! Since he wanted us all to be kind and nice to each other he gave us nature to help us remember how to be nice." As his teacher wryly remarked in an e-mail to his mom, "I thought this was wonderful, but reminded Jeremiah that while MLK did want all those things, nature was here before him."

In all of these cases, Washington, Lincoln, and King are con-structed as Christlike heroes used to center a civic religion. As Wecter puts it without irony (and probably appropriately so), "these heroes are . . . men who stand somehow for the essence of our faith, whose birthplaces and graves we make into shrines, and whose faces we carve upon mountains as our American way of writing poetry."[26]

Another way to unify the country is by establishing and rein-forcing an inclusive narrative in which all the nation's peoples (however defined) play a variety of heroic roles. I discussed above how the definition of a civic leader may be constrained by a limited set of virtues—say, being White, a military veteran, or male—and I noted contemporary textbook authors' attempts in response to expand these often literal images of civic leadership in order to establish more inclusive ideals. A similarly self-conscious, symbolically inclusive approach to establishing and teaching civic heroes can also be deployed for the purposes of promoting a common national story in which all citizens are encouraged to see themselves and of which they are encouraged to feel a part.[27] The 2005 edition of *Civics: Government and Economics in Action,* a fairly typical contemporary middle and high school civics textbook, demonstrates this logic. Although it doesn't feature "heroes" as such, it does feature fifteen "Citizen Profiles" ranging from Mickey Leland, James Madison, Carol Moseley-Braun, and Louis Brandeis to Andrea Jung, Alice Rivlin, Thurgood Marshall, and Madeleine Albright. Each paragraph-long profile—which invariably highlights the subject's non-White, non-Christian, or female status—is accompanied by a photo and followed by a question that reinforces the civic contribution made by that person to the country.[28]

Public identification and elevation of heroes serve an entirely different set of civic purposes when they are used to demonstrate the importance of individual agency to civil society. If citizens can be taught to recognize heroes' power to redirect history, for example, then they will realize that historical fatalism is foolish. History is not inevitable. Thus, citizens must assume some responsibility for shaping the future, too.[29] An even more ambitious goal is to inspire citizens to reach for the same level of greatness in assuming that responsibility as their heroes have achieved. "Great men enable us to rise to our own highest potentialities. They nerve lesser men to disregard the world and trust to their own deepest instinct."[30] In a certain way, this takes us back to the very first civic function of heroes: to provide models for emulation. But that first goal was fairly modest. Citizens were expected to emulate their heroes only in specific ways, and to a limited degree. Citizens might be honest, for example, because George Washington was honest, and their endeavours would be human rather than heroic. Yet one may teach about the heroes of the past in order to inspire and even create the heroes of tomorrow. This function of teaching about heroes is to inspire citizens to seek out and achieve their own heroism, not necessarily in the same domain or emulating the same virtues as the hero studied, but in some way that enables "the higher self to prevail."[31] Thus, someone who learns about Washington's heroic bravery may be inspired to reach for greatness inside of herself and become a great teacher, a remarkable sportswoman, or attain some other heroic standing, even if her achievement has nothing to do with bravery or politics (or honesty) as such. The Giraffe Heroes Project, which works extensively with young people and adults to "find new heroes, to tell their stories, and to help more people be heroic," clearly attempts to promote this civic function of identifying and elevating heroes. As they put it, "*Everyone* has what it takes to be a Giraffe"—their term for heroes who "stick their neck out for the common good."[32]

Finally, heroes can be used to expand our sense of what is possible for all of humanity. I discussed heroes' use in establishing touchstones for elected or other civic leaders; in this case, heroes are used to help citizens envision possibilities beyond those represented in their own lives or experiences. "Public heroes—or imperfect people of extraordinary achievement, courage, and greatness of soul whose reach is wider than our own—teach us to push beyond ourselves and our neighborhoods in our search for models of excellence. They enlarge our imagination, teach us to think big, and expand our sense of the possible."[33] This is obviously related to the previous two functions, but its purpose is not necessarily to inspire citizens to emulate particular heroes; rather, it is to inspire citizens to develop civic aspirations that go beyond the realm of the apparently possible and even realistic in order to set society on a better, more uplifting path.

THE FALL OF HEROES AND RISE OF ROLE MODELS

It is no accident that most examples I have given of civic education about heroes came from previous centuries. There is strong evidence that heroes' salience is severely limited in the contemporary United States, and thus that they no longer fulfill the functions they once did. In an October 2000 Gallup Youth Survey, for example, young people were asked, "Do you have any heroes or heroines in the world today—men or women whom you personally greatly admire for their achievements and for their strong moral character?" Over a third of respondents (36 percent) answered no; they were unable to identify any hero or heroine whatsoever. The next largest group, comprising almost a quarter of young people (23 percent), selected a family member. After that, selection slowed to a relative trickle. In other words, barely 40 percent of young people were able to identify anyone beyond their own family whom they greatly admired for their achievements and character.[34]

Furthermore, even those nonfamiliars whom youth do claim to admire are diminishingly likely to be viewed as true heroes. Between 1979 and 1996, young people ages 13–17 were asked annually, "What one man/woman that you have heard or read about, living today in any part of the world, do you admire the most—not including relatives or personal friends?"[35] The table lists the top ten admired men from 1979, 1986, and 1996. In contrast to those on the list from 1979, it is hard to imagine that many teens in 1996 would define most of the men they listed as *heroes,* despite their potentially fervent admiration for them. Perhaps even more to the point, if they did in fact view these celebrities as heroes, that would suggest as much about the diminishment of the contemporary conception of heroism as about teens' propensity for selecting heroes in the first place.

Young people aren't operating in a vacuum, of course. Their contemporary disavowal of heroism arguably reflects a more general cultural shift. As I was researching the literature on he-

Gallup Poll results for the man respondents "admire the most," from most popular to least popular

1979	1986	1996
Jimmy Carter	Ronald Reagan	Michael Jordan
Anwar Sadat	Jesse Jackson	Bill Clinton
Gerald Ford	Don Johnson	Brad Pitt
Menachem Begin	Pope John Paul II	Jesse Jackson
Richard Nixon	Desmond Tutu	Anfernee Hardaway
Muhammad Ali	Lee Iacocca	Emmitt Smith
Jerry Lewis	Bob Geldof/Prince (tie)	Ken Griffey, Jr.
Pope John Paul II/Gov. Jerry Brown (tie)	Tom Selleck	Cal Ripken, Jr.
John Travolta	Rob Lowe/Bruce Springsteen (tie)	Michael Jackson
		Jim Carrey/Shaquille O'Neal (tie)

roes for this chapter, I was taken aback by the rash of articles starting in the late 1970s specifically titled "Where have all of the heroes gone?" Book titles have undergone a similar transformation. Consider the ambivalent *The Hero in Transition* (published in 1983) and despairing *Everybody Is Sitting on the Curb: How and Why America's Heroes Disappeared* (1996) in comparison to such previous studies of heroism as *The Hero, American Style* (1969) or Dixon Wecter's 1941 classic *The Hero in America: A Chronicle of Hero-Worship*. Along the same lines, in "Hero Worship in America," published in 1949, sociologist Orrin E. Klapp grapples with the challenge of explaining why there is so *much* hero worship. It is hard to imagine a sociologist identifying such a challenge today.[36]

Admittedly, every age bemoans loss of great heroes of previous ages and their replacement by apparently transient and superficial stars of the present. "[T]oday seems always less heroic than yesterday."[37] Winston Churchill himself regretfully noted in 1925, "The great emancipated nations seem to have become largely independent of famous guides and guardians. They no longer rely upon the Hero, the Commander, or the Teacher as they did in bygone rugged ages, or as the less advanced peoples do today." After asking, "Can modern communities do without great men? Can they dispense with hero-worship?" he commented in sorrow, "We miss our giants. We are sorry that their age is past."[38]

Churchill's regret, however, was rooted in heroes' replacement by measures, machines, and "'the common sense of most.'"[39] He didn't bemoan generalized indifference or even antipathy toward heroes and heroism in general, the way many do today. "The modern image of a leader is not Theodore Roosevelt charging up a hill, but rather Jimmy Carter fighting off a rabbit with a canoe paddle, Gerald Ford stumbling and bumping his head, or George Bush vomiting in the lap of the Japanese prime minister. Bill Clinton will be defined forever by his handling of the Monica Lewinsky affair. These images demystify power and produce a culture of disillusionment with politics and moral leadership."[40] In recent decades, the conception of heroism—especially to the extent that it has historically been tied to leadership—has become diminished and even potentially debased. Heroes are no longer "great men" and women straddling the world like a colossus. "Today," by contrast, "many Americans define heroes as decent people who sacrifice or try to make a difference. They name streets after local World War II veterans, parks after teachers, bridges after local politicians and philanthropists . . . [T]hey democratize the word *hero* and jettison the Greek notion of the hero as superhuman and godlike."[41]

One potent contemporary example of this trend may be found in CNN Heroes, a "global initiative" that intentionally "showcase[s] examples of ordinary people who have accomplished extraordinary deeds."[42] When I randomly checked CNN's links to "Heroes in the News" one afternoon (August 16, 2008, 4:19 P.M.), every single link highlighted a person who had intervened in a crisis to save someone's life: "Missing toddler found safe," "Wheelchair-bound woman pulled from train's path," "Baby pulled from burning car," "Boy, 8, saves pal choking on rock," and so forth. This vision of heroism is totally divorced from any notion of societal change, greatness of character, or even intentionality. Perhaps even more to the point, this list hardly presents a model for civic emulation, unless we want young people to seek out disaster at every turn.

None of this evidence suggests that admiration and even emulation of others are impossible or even unusual in contemporary American society—just that heroes are not the means by which such admiration and emulation are likely fostered. In place of outsized heroes, I believe that Americans have come to value life-sized *role models*. "Role models," as the concept was first defined in the 1950s—interestingly, just as conceptions of "hero-worship" seem to have been drawing to a close—and continues to be used today, are people whom we admire and attempt to emulate.[43] Heroes could in theory thus also be role models. But as an empirical psychological matter, at least in contemporary times, heroes do *not* serve as role models. Instead, role models are almost inevitably "ordinary": people who seem generally similar to ourselves and whose differences from us tend to be along one particular dimension, rather than those who are truly extraordinary, especially across multiple dimensions.[44] It is their very ordinariness that inspires us to act differently and emulate their achievements, not any overarching greatness of character, stature, or even impact.

Americans' shift from emulating (at least admiring) extraordinary heroes to emulating ordinary role models may help explain recent survey results in which family members and friends have come to trump others in meriting mention as heroes or role models. Among adults, for example, the percentage of Gallup poll respondents identifying a family member or friend as their "most admired" living man has sextupled over the past sixty years; it has likewise doubled for most admired living woman.[45] Youth over the past thirty years have similarly embraced their close friends and especially their parents as being among the most admirable people.[46]

Maria, a neighborhood council youth representative whom I interviewed in Boston when she was a senior in high school, exemplifies this rejection of the distant, extraordinary hero in favor of the intimate, ordinary role model. In response to my questions, "Who do people try to teach you to take as role models? And who are your actual role models?" her reply speaks volumes:

> Of course, famous leaders. Martin Luther King, Malcolm X, people who have brought changes in our culture. But . . . the one role model . . . that's like my hero or whatever you may call it, is my father. I didn't have the privilege for him to raise me as a child, as a baby or whatever . . . My father was in jail. He served his time. He got out and the first thing he did was move from New York to Boston to start life. So I kind of got my father like 10 or 11 years old. And from then we've been growing as father and daughter . . . You see

my father now and you don't think that he had a hard life and that he did that stuff or whatever. Because he's left that behind and he started something new. And through his trial and error he succeeded through everything.

Maria is well aware of whom she is supposed to view as a hero. But she is equally aware that these "famous leaders" do not directly inspire her in the way her father does. To some extent, it is her father's very weaknesses and struggles—matched by his slow but steady success "through everything"—that makes him a hero. Maria's attitude in this regard is absolutely typical of the young civic leaders whom I interviewed in 2004 as a means of determining how and why some youth from historically disenfranchised backgrounds beat the civic empowerment gap. Well over half of the youth civic leaders I talked with selected a formerly incarcerated family member as a role model or hero. Again, this was not because they were unaware of more traditional heroes.[47] Rather, the personal relationship was key, as Joel, a seventeen-year-old high school student in Boston, explained.

> Like all my teachers want me to look at Martin Luther King and Cesar Chavez. Martin Luther King. And I look at them and I don't see them as role models. You know? . . . I mean, they were great leaders and all of that, but I don't mean, like, "Wow, that's a fine role model." You know, my role model is Jésus [the youth organizing leader at the nonprofit where Joel worked]. He has helped me so much. He's talked to me, you know. He's done things for me that I don't know if anybody would have ever done for me. And I'm so grateful for him. That's my role model right there. I look up to him.

DO DEMOCRACIES NEED HEROES?

What are the civic implications in a democracy of this contemporary disavowal of extraordinary heroes in favor of ordinary role models? Perhaps heroes' fall from grace, and role models' concomitant upswing, is actively good for a democracy. After all, democracies are founded on a notion of equality—especially civic equality—that seems profoundly at odds with the public recognition and elevation of heroes. All citizens should be capable of democratic deliberation and participation—of ruling by the people. Citizens may well learn from and be inspired by fellow-citizen role models in this process, since role models are in essence equal to oneself except for in defined particulars. It is antithetical to democratic egalitarianism, on the other hand, to identify heroes whose achievements and strength of character ordinary citizens could never hope to match.[48] In this respect, if democratic structures are designed correctly, citizens will almost automatically be enabled to contribute to the collective good through their ordinary actions. No extraordinary efforts of will would be required, or even be desired, since democratic institutions should have been structured so as to anticipate and provide for a nation's needs through the everyday acts of its citizens, all of whom have the capacity to so contribute.[49]

Furthermore, it is profoundly dangerous for a country to put its faith in individuals' greatness with regard to civic leadership. Such an approach makes "human welfare contingent on the exceptional intervention, often unreliable and always arbitrary, of these unique individuals. The successful resolution of crises then depends essentially on luck—on the chance that extraordinary people will be found to meet a crisis or that some person will undergo an ennobling transformation at the critical moment."[50] In this respect, critics of historical fatalism have gotten it backward. It's true that history's direction and outcomes are not inevitable, and that heroes can make a profound difference in shaping the history of a nation. But it would be rashly fatalistic to hope that such a hero will emerge in times of crisis.

Furthermore, it is antidemocratic for individual actors to act as legislators unto themselves and reshape the destiny of a democracy. The point of democratic governance is that all citizens should be empowered to work in concert to shape the nation's history. In this respect, the presentation especially of those in power as heroic can discourage citizens from exercising the level of scrutiny that is necessary for a well-functioning and just democracy. James Loewen argues, for example, that history textbooks which heroize the state are essentially "anticitizenship manuals—handbooks for acquiescence."[51] Citizens in a democratic society should maintain a healthy skepticism about their leaders and the claims made on behalf of the state. If they do not, then they are effectively abandoning their governance and oversight role. But one does not treat heroes with healthy skepticism; to do so is effectively to deny their heroism. Thus, democracies may be better off without heroes—or at least, without the heroification of those in power.

Even if all of the above arguments are true, however, there may well be other reasons to identify and honor heroes within contemporary democracies. Democratic nations still need to foster some form of civic unity as a tool for self-preservation. I argued in the last chapter that historical civic narratives are not reliable and empowering sources of civic unity. But normative principles exemplified by civic heroes, or even a civil religion centered on leaders such as Lincoln and King, could potentially foster a sense of common purpose and combat fragmentation. Also, as a practical matter, democratic leaders both need and deserve respect for doing their jobs well. The diminishment or even negation of the heroic aspect of leadership arguably weakens those who have committed themselves to public service, as well as discourages other good men and women from assuming the mantle of leadership when they know they will be granted little honor or respect for doing so.[52]

Relatedly, democracies as much as any system of governance—and possibly more than most—need to hold high expectations for their elected leaders and representatives. There was much talk in the 2000 and 2004 presidential elections about George W. Bush's appeal to the electorate as a "regular guy" with whom they would enjoy sitting down and sharing a beer—unlike Al Gore and John Kerry, who few people at the time saw even as beer drinking types, let alone as enjoyable bar stool company. In this context, Bush's poor grades in college, drunk driving arrest, verbal miscues, and other peccadilloes made him more attractive to the electorate rather than less. But democracies are not well served by mediocrity (nor was ours well served by Bush, as even most Republicans would agree), and they do not have to foster it.

By 2008, in fact, the American electorate had overcome its infatuation with electing someone who seemed ordinary, recognizing perhaps that the country is better served by presidents who have extraordinary rather than merely run-of-the-mill capacities. This recognition was arguably reflected in, even encouraged by, the candidates' emphasis on their own heroic qualities. John McCain's entire general election campaign emphasized his status as a war hero and his heroism as a "maverick." Although Barack Obama's campaign did not argue directly that Obama himself was a hero, he was certainly treated as—and invested with the expectations of—a hero by a significant portion of the American electorate. It is encouraging to think that these appeals to and invocations of heroism raised the electorate's expectations for their future president and led them to demand more rather than less from each candidate. These inflated expectations, however, have come at a cost: namely, disillusionment and even a sense of betrayal any time Obama fails to live up to his heroic billing.

Obama's inevitable failings in the eyes of even—perhaps especially—his most ardent supporters serve to remind us that democracies depend on virtuous and vigorous citizens to remain healthy, legitimate, and effective. As I discussed above, heroes can be used to promote qualities of civic virtue, active civic engagement, and belief in and pursuit of excellence. Obama, for instance, quite transparently reflected his ascribed heroism back onto his acolytes, repeatedly claiming, "We are the ones we've been waiting for," and featuring at the top of every page of his website, "I'm asking you to believe. Not just in my ability to bring about real change in Washington . . . I'm asking you to believe in yours."[53] The tenor of these messages was to draw upon the implicit greatness ascribed to him by his followers (even the language of "acolytes" and "followers," which came so much more naturally in Obama's case than merely "supporters" or "voters," emphasizes his heroic stature in some circles)—and to try to expand that attribution of greatness to include heretofore "ordinary" citizens.

At the same time, one reason that people have been both suspicious of Obama himself and concerned about his message of citizens' being their own salvation (or at least their own change agents) is that this salvation and change have been perceived as self-satisfied in a way that undercuts another potential civic function of heroes in a democracy: namely, to promote a healthy skepticism of oneself, and a recognition of one's own fallibility. As George W. Bush's presidency demonstrated as well as any, implacable self-confidence and refusal to doubt one's actions or judgments may have profoundly antidemocratic consequences. Recognition of others' greatness—including others' superiority even to ourselves—may be necessary to combat such hubristic self-satisfaction.[54] This is not to disavow the egalitarian concerns raised above; teaching citizens their (lowered) place in contrast to others' heroism is clearly problematic from an egalitarian democratic perspective. But there is a democratic version of this attitude, by which the encouragement of humility, skepticism, and self-doubt can actually contribute to such democratic virtues as tolerance and willingness to deliberate with others.

HEROES IN CONTEMPORARY CIVIC EDUCATION

Although heroes may no longer speak much to young people, there is little evidence to suggest that the majority of young people are actively *opposed* to heroes. In other words, there's no reason to think that teaching about heroes for a particular purpose would inevitably backfire. Many extraordinary individuals are still known to young people, as the example of Martin Luther King, Jr., demonstrates. Furthermore, many of the goals historically served by society's elevation and recognition of heroes remain desirable in a democratic society, at least when pursued in moderate fashion and with aims that do not overreach. All could be pursued tyrannically, but none except for the unreconstructed version of "teaching citizens their place" need be so. It is worth raising expectations for our leaders and elected officials, for example, even though at the same time we do want young people, and citizens in general, in a democratic society to feel as if they have the capacity and opportunity to become civic leaders.

Given this, I think that examples of extraordinary individuals, whether defined explicitly as "heroes" or not, could effectively be used to promote civic aims that are based upon passive admiration and identity formation as opposed to active emulation. Specifically, it is possible that civic education about heroes could: impart and reinforce common civic values and norms; establish touchstones for the qualities citizens should expect of elected officials and other civic leaders; inspire patriotism; unify the country via establishment and reinforcement of symbolic, inclusive membership; and symbolize human possibility. I do not think that any of these would come about easily, nor even that education about heroes is necessarily the best way to achieve these goals. But I also see no reason that teaching about heroes would be actively detrimental to these aims.

To the extent that we aim to inspire active *emulation*, however, then I think the evidence is quite clear that ordinary role models instead of extraordinary heroes should lie at the heart of civic education.[55] To guide this process, educators need to select civically efficacious people who share some range of characteristics (ethnicity or race, culture, religion, national origin, residence, or class) with students in order to increase the chance that students will see them as role models—people mostly like themselves who inspire emulation. Students need to have the opportunity truly to get to know and feel a connection with these people, just as they feel intimately connected with the family members and friends they most often identify as their role models. They also need to learn *how* the ordinary, everyday acts taken by these people make significant differences to their communities. Educators can help students identify and practice the key skills deployed by these ordinary role models. In doing so, students are more likely to become efficacious, engaged civic and political actors themselves.

One year when I was teaching eighth grade at McCormack, for example, we hosted Sam Yoon as a guest speaker. Yoon was then working for the Asian Community Development Corporation and running to be Boston's first Asian-American city councilor, an office he won a few months later. After his presentation, students easily picked out such generic attributes as getting an education, caring about others, and working hard as keys to his success. But students' mouthing of these platitudes is hardly civically empowering—nor even a proof of learning, since students could equally easily have lauded such attributes before Yoon's presentation. Instead, therefore, I goaded students to examine the specifics of his efforts for social change: for example, how he tried to use the media's interest in his personal story as the first Asian-American candidate for citywide office in order to focus attention on issues he cared about. Students were inspired to learn about how to communicate with the media, present themselves publicly, and use their own personal stories to direct others' attention to issues such as neighborhood violence and lack of job opportunities for youth. They developed valuable communication and presentation skills while incorporating their own backgrounds, interests, and concerns. The fact that students actually met and talked with Yoon—one student saw him in a neighborhood diner a few days later, and another ran into him on the bus—helped keep them energized and fostered their sense that learning these skills might enable them to make a difference.

This active, relationship-oriented, and experiential approach contrasts significantly with the well-intentioned but fatally flawed approach to ordinary role models promoted in contemporary civics textbooks. These texts do an admirable job of gesturing toward the importance of ordinary role models under such headings as "Teens in Action," "American Biographies," "The Power of One," "Young Citizens in Action," "Students Make a Difference: The Active Citizen," "Citizen Profiles," and "You Can Make a Difference."[56] Each of these textbooks promotes a much more active, engaged, and "ordinary" vision of effective citizenship than do comparable civics books from the 1950s—including 1950s editions of some of these same textbooks—none of which feature such profiles or resources.

Despite publishers' evident good intentions, however, textbook-based paragraphs about "young citizens in action" suffer three fatal flaws. First, given standardized curriculum and especially standardized testing mandates, teachers have no incentive—actually, a negative incentive—to use these textbook resources. By definition, "ordinary," unknown people will not be included in state curriculum frameworks or national content standards. When I taught eighth grade, therefore, I skipped over almost every one of the sidebars, insets, and pages emphasizing active citizenship because they did not fit into my curriculum calendar. It is hard to see how and why other teachers might be led to make a different choice. The same disincentives apply as well, of course, to teachers' more significant incorporation of visits from ordinary role models to their classrooms. But paradoxically, the greater effort and resources needed to incorporate meaningful role models through experiential education may actually increase the odds of its implementation in comparison to the relatively minor cost of reading a paragraph about "teens in action." No one in charge of developing state curriculum frameworks or finalizing the district pacing guide will explicitly allot time to read textbook sidebars. The assumption may be that teachers will naturally weave them in, but the inevitably overstuffed curriculum and high-stake assessments required make their addition unlikely.[57] In the case of experiential learning in partnership with class visitors, by contrast, no one could plausibly assume that teachers will simply "find the time." If it is agreed that students should be learning about, developing relationships with, and practicing the skills or strategies of local, ordinary role models, then it will also be agreed that time must be set aside in the curriculum for teachers to help facilitate this. If time is not set aside, then it is clear to everyone that this is not a priority. If time is set aside, then teachers get the clear message that this is a priority and, with appropriate professional support, are more likely to implement it.

Another problem with textbooks' single-paragraph snapshots of "young people making a difference" is that they are inevitably superficial, even *pro forma*. How much are students going to learn from—let alone be inspired by—reading a paragraph about what some other teenager did? A single paragraph cannot teach students actual techniques or strategies for civic empowerment. In fact, four to five sentences cannot actually achieve *any* of the civic purposes discussed above. They may be nicely symbolic of the importance of individual citizens' contributions to public life, but a snippet of this length cannot be anything more than symbolic.

Third, these references in textbooks to ordinary but unfamiliar people misunderstand the source and nature of role models. Role models are people with whom students feel a direct connection, usually because they know them personally. Four or five, even ten, sentences about a random teenager in a textbook are not going to promote the kind of personal identification and change in behavior that we hope for from young people who are inspired to emulate actual role models. Thus, the "ordinary role model" approach when mediated by textbooks may end up being the worst of both worlds. Young people neither learn about extraordinary heroes who help them envision the expanse of human possibility, nor do they identify true role models (usually people they know personally, not just teenagers in a textbook) in order to learn to emulate them.

What can be done, then, in the context of a traditional, textbook-oriented, even coverage-driven civic education class that cannot or will not take on the more ambitious agenda I outlined above? In this case—and in fact, in every case, I believe—students should learn about collective action as an essential lever of power in civic life. Ordinary role models and even extraordinary heroes are rarely lone actors. Collective action by scores, hundreds, thousands, even millions of people frequently underlie the success of an apparently individual civic actor. Julian Bond makes this point in a compelling way with respect to Martin Luther King:

> Americans long for single, heroic leadership, the lone figure delivering salvation. King became that figure, but he came from a movement that was group-centered, representing democracy at its best. He did not march from Selma to Montgomery by himself. He did not speak to an empty field at the March on Washington. There were thousands marching with him and before him, and thousands more who one by one and two by two did the work that preceded the triumphal march. Black Americans did not just march to freedom; we worked our way to civil rights through the difficult business of organizing. Registering voters one by one. Building a solid organization, block by block. Building interracial coalitions, state by state.[58]

In this respect, teaching about Martin Luther King *requires* that one simultaneously teach about the thousands of ordinary Americans who sustained the civil rights movement and ensured its victories. It is simply factually inaccurate—and civically disempowering—to teach in any other way.

This kind of curricular change could at least in theory be made fairly easily by reframing history and civics textbooks' civic narratives along the lines I discussed in the last chapter. Right now, they tend to focus relentlessly on the individual, neglecting the collective action lying at the heart of individuals' achievements. Sam Wineburg and Chauncey Monte-Sano thus complain with respect to Rosa Parks,

> Instead of a story about a mass-organizing movement—a narrative of empowerment and agency among ordinary people who in a single weekend printed 52,500 leaflets (enough, and then some, for every member of Montgomery's black community) and distributed them to churches while organizing phone trees and Monday morning car pools so that no one would have to walk to work—we meet the singular figure of Mrs. Parks. Together with King, she sets out on her civil rights walkabout, only to return to lead a passive and faceless people in their struggle for racial equality.[59]

This is a tragedy, but it is totally unnecessary. Textbooks could tell Rosa Parks's story as clearly, in the same amount of space, and much more accurately by framing her actions as part of a "mass-organizing movement" of essentially ordinary people. Good examples of such approaches are readily available.[60]

In this respect, extraordinary heroes and ordinary role models are not opposed figures but actually complementary tools for promoting civic purposes. Educators can draw upon both in tandem to help young people come to understand that even the most profound civic changes, led by the greatest and most extraordinary of human beings, are usually brought about by the collective work of ordinary people working together: of "men and women obscure in their labor," as Obama put it in his Inaugural Address.[61] Such lessons pick up on the grand ideals of solidarity, efficacy, and collective struggle, and bring them into the "here and now" of the classroom.

But it would also be a mistake to think that these lessons should or even can be learned solely within the classroom or through studying other people's achievements. Over the past few chapters, I have argued that we should change how students learn about citizenship by changing how they learn about American history and how they learn about civic and social actors (such as heroes and role models) within historical and contemporary life. I turn now to arguing that we should also change students' opportunities to learn *through* citizenship.[62] If we want young people to develop the knowledge, skills, attitudes, and habits of empowered citizens, they must be given the opportunity on a regular basis to *practice* being citizens. Furthermore, if we want adults and other elites to recognize and value the civic contributions that young people—especially low-income youth of color—can make, then these young people must be given the opportunities to make a visible and effective difference in the world beyond the school. How schools can give young people these opportunities constitutes the focus of the next two chapters.

Making Citizenship Visible in Schools

5

Every morning as they enter Walden Middle School, students line up in front of our assistant principal. Holding a metal-detecting wand in his right hand, he sweeps it in front and back of each child before he allows them to proceed down to the cafeteria. A number of the sixth graders are tiny—barely four-and-a-half feet tall—and are still obsessed by trading cards and bathroom jokes. What do they think about as they're screened for weapons each day? What do my eighth graders—many still on the cusp of puberty themselves—think? In the three academic years I teach at Walden, from 1996 to 1999, it never occurs to me to ask them.

September 1998. Deyana—smart, mature, high-achieving, and very sociable—is running for eighth-grade class president at Walden. She's popular among students and teachers alike, and as our eighth-grade teaching team counts up the votes after school, we can see she's won easily. But there's one hitch: Deyana is pregnant. We are roiled with doubts about how to proceed.

What would it mean for us to honor a pregnant fourteen-year-old as eighth-grade president—essentially the leader of the entire student body? On the other hand, what would it mean for us to overturn a free and fair election? Deyana is committed to remaining a school leader and graduating with honors. If she isn't treating her pregnancy as a reason to turn her back on Walden, why should we turn our backs on her? Still, there's a big difference between turning our backs on her and celebrating her as eighth-grade president. We will certainly continue to support, educate, and even love her. But that doesn't mean we should honor her, nor hold her up as a role model for the rest of our student body, many of whom are at risk of becoming pregnant or fathering a child themselves.

Our conversation goes late into the afternoon as we debate what to do. We have to announce the results of the election in the morning. But right now, about the only thing we all agree upon is that there is no easy decision.

December 1998. I'm hanging out with Mrs. Farmer and Mr. Beeza on the Walden steps before school. "Good morning, Keesha," Mr. Beeza says with a smile. "Good morning, DeQuin," Mrs. Farmer smiles to another. "Good morning, Extravrious," Mr. Beeza greets a third. "Glad to see you—but take off your hat, please," he instructs pleasantly. Most students respond with a grunt, if they reply at all. But Mrs. Farmer and Mr. Beeza are undaunted. They stand there morning and afternoon, greeting every student with their name and a smile, every single day.

1998–1999. Three teachers at Walden are pregnant this year. Mrs. Henshaw, the bubbly, popular, and rigorous art teacher, is honored with a baby shower after school one day. We buy her a huge basket of baby items through our Sunshine Fund. Ms. Clark and Ms. Nelson, by contrast, are less celebrated. Unmarried, they receive smaller baskets thanks to donations made by individual teachers. We host no baby shower. Including Deyana, four of our middle schoolers also become parents this year.

May 1999. Our eighth-grade team at Walden is consumed by doubts again, this time about eighth-grade graduation ceremonies. We're trying to figure out what to do in memory of Bobby Welch, who was murdered in January. A pipsqueak of a kid, he had been involved in what was initially a relatively trivial altercation with an older, stronger, tougher kid. From what we heard afterward, Bobby had left that fight with a bruised ego but otherwise fairly intact. Forty-five minutes later, though, he returned with a gun. Nobody who knew him thinks Bobby would have shot anyone; he just wanted to flash it around to prove he was "hard." But his "fronting" got him killed. So here we are in May, choking up as we try to figure out how to memorialize Bobby. There's a tree planted outside the school in his memory. But that doesn't address his absence from graduation.

Ms. Norris suggests we leave an empty chair, draped in black, among the graduates. It can serve as silent testimonial to his death, and to our collective loss. Ms. Leon, though, is troubled by this suggestion. Our kids might interpret the memorial as glorifying violence, heaping attention on a kid who chose to return to the scene of a confrontation with a gun. Many of our eighth graders will be missing from graduation thanks to academic failure. Had he lived, Bobby frankly might have been in that number. Why "seat" Bobby among the graduates in death when we were already excluding so many students in life? On the other hand, Mr. Graham points out, we have to think about what our students and their families would think if we failed to acknowledge Bobby's tragic absence. Lots of fourteen-year-olds make foolish, impulsive choices. None deserve to die for them. We certainly don't want to seem to be accepting a student's murder—particularly a Black male's murder—as par for the course.

October 2000. "Ms. Grant, your children are not filing appropriately!" Ms. Bishop, our former gym teacher and new assistant principal at McCormack, bellows down the hall. Ms. Grant's English class, who were a moment before sauntering rather casually toward the library, suddenly press themselves up against the lockers on the righthand side and fall silent. Two boys, though, entertain each other by making farting noises with their armpits.

Ms. Bishop draws closer. "Jamie and Eddie, come with me right now. You may not make that kind of noise in the hallways. Ms. Grant, take your kids back to class and get them to line up right. I will not tolerate this kind of behavior in our school."

The kids glance covertly at each other as Ms. Bishop dresses down their teacher. Will Ms. Grant stand up for herself? They shift nervously from foot to foot.

Ms. Grant replies, "Ms. Bishop, we're heading to the library. My students have only a half-hour left to finish their research projects because of the fire drill. Jamie and Eddie need to stay with their group to complete their research. I need to have them in class."

"They'll come to class, Ms. Grant, after I discipline them for their disrespect. And I know you don't have much time, but we cannot have this kind of behavior from the eighth grade, the leaders of the school. If they can't walk down the hall properly, then they don't deserve the privilege of going to the library." Ms. Bishop moves away, propelling Jamie and Eddie in front of her as they head toward her office.

Humiliated and seething, Ms. Grant grimly turns her class around to return to their classroom and try walking to the library again.

February 2001. Kids love student government this year at McCormack. It's being advised by our new eighth-grade science teacher, Ms. Antonio. Each classroom has two elected representatives, and there are leaders from each grade level. They meet once a month during the school day—allowing kids to skip class—and once a month after school. Student council members are excited by their biggest initiative yet: a Valentine's Day carnation fundraiser.

October 2004. Each student takes a turn sitting in the "author chair" in English class, reading aloud his or her memoir. They've been working on memoirs for over a month, writing multiple drafts, and they're excited to share during this publishing party. Ms. Sleeper and Ms. Grant, their English teachers, have carefully instructed the students what to expect and how to behave. Some kids dress up for the occasion. They all listen attentively and applaud at the end. For some students, it is the first time they have ever shared their work aloud. Later in the year, rotating casts of Ms. Sleeper's eighth graders perform scenes from Romeo and Juliet around the school. We give them standing ovations.

December 2005. My students are working on their "citizenship projects," in which they research and try to address problems in their community. As usual, a bunch of students have decided to try to address the disgusting state of the student bathrooms at McCormack. They take pictures of overflowing toilets, stalls with no doors, soapless dispensers, and empty toilet paper and paper towel holders. A couple of students interview the school nurse to document the physical harm of "holding it" all day long. Although they are too self-conscious to put this in their presentations, some girls testify privately about their unwillingness ever to defecate in school, and how challenging it is when they have their periods.

One enterprising group schedules a meeting with our school principal to advocate for bathroom renovations. The principal cancels her meeting with them a couple of times. But finally they meet in her office and present the problem to her.

She's dismissive. "The boys' toilets overflow because students plug them up with paper towels and toilet paper rolls. Brian [the custodian] spent an hour unclogging a toilet just last week. It was stuffed with toilet paper—which is why there's no paper this week." She turns to look at each of the students in turn. "It's your classmates who cause the problem. Why do the stalls have no doors? Because students rip them off their hinges."

"We've thought of this," my students respond. "If the bathrooms look nice, kids won't tear them up. And what about having automatic hand driers, autoflush toilets, and lockable toilet paper dispensers? That would solve a lot of the problems." They are proud of their proposal and curious how our principal will react.

"No," she replies. "Fixing up the bathrooms is a waste of money we don't have. They'll just be vandalized again anyway."

January 2008. My husband and I are touring Shady Hill School, a private K–8 school nestled atop a hill in Cambridge, Massachusetts. We are led from one mini-building to another, each housing just a couple of classrooms. Each grade basically gets its own home, often with an outside porch and other indoor and outdoor nooks in which students can settle down to work alone or with others. I'm struck by how freely and frequently students move around, both within the classroom and among different areas of the school. At McCormack, we were constantly striving to minimize "transition time": time lost to instruction due to students moving from one activity to another or one classroom to another. The faster they could move, the sooner they could get to work and start learning again. We also organized and monitored every transition, lining up students and walking them from class to class, supervising locker time, escorting kids to the cafeteria. But at Shady Hill, transitions seem both ubiquitous and comparatively unmonitored, as students move from their home classroom to the art studios, science labs, cafeteria, and multiple playgrounds on their own. It is clear where our mischievous and autonomy-loving older daughter for whom we're looking for a school would be happier. Frankly, it's clear where virtually any kid would be happier.

November 2009. For a session on "classroom management" in the Fall 2009 class I teach to aspiring urban history teachers at Harvard, I invite five veteran urban middle and high school teachers to visit the class and share their "tricks of the trade." All of the teachers agree that good relationships are one key to classroom management success. They discuss how they try to build respectful relationships with the class as a whole and with individual students, and they emphasize the need to persist with kids who seem resistant and defiant. They also agree that clear routines and predictable procedures are key to smooth class-room management. Most of the concrete tips they suggest reflect this respectful stance toward students.

But things also break down a bit between theory and practice. A teacher talks about giving crayons to high schoolers who come to class without a pen on the grounds that it's so humiliating they'll come to class prepared in the future. Another teacher shares her bathroom tip with a giggle: "My bathroom pass is an old toilet seat. The kids have to carry it, or wear it around their necks. If they ask to go to the bathroom in my class, I know they really need to go!" My heart sinks. These really are terrific teach-ers. I know that they adore and respect their students, and that their students generally know this. But the panel also reminds me of how challenging it is to remain humane and respectful, especially in large, urban schools. Competing pressures are just so great.

I think guiltily back to my own missteps in this regard: the time I emptied a girl's purse in front of the whole class because I was sure she had stolen an item from a classmate; my policy one semester disallowing students from purchasing snacks if they were with me for silent lunch even though I knew the school-provided lunch was virtually inedible; other random acts of hu-

miliation and disregard that I have forgotten but I'm sure still
live on in students' hearts.

Schools inherently shape young people's civic experiences. Both
students and adults learn "their place" and what's expected of
them in the broader public sphere by observing and participating in the limited public space we call schools. Schools also
give—or deny—students and teachers opportunities to practice a variety of civic skills and behaviors via classroom procedures and routines, curricula and pedagogies, interactions in the
hallways and cafeteria, and cocurricular and extracurricular activities. This need not be intentional. Rather, *all* schools teach
experiential lessons about civic identity, expectations, and opportunities—even when they have no intention of doing so.

In Chapter 4, I discussed the importance of introducing students to "ordinary role models" from the community. I suggested that these local role models might inspire students to take
their own civic action, and that with teachers' help, students
could learn effective and empowering civic skills, attitudes, and
practices by studying and emulating these community models.
But not all role models come from outside the school walls.
Teachers themselves, and all adults in the school with whom students have frequent contact, inevitably model for students a variety of civic-relevant habits, attitudes, and skills, for good or ill.
They model fair or unfair treatment of diverse others; respect or
disrespect for presumptive inferiors (youth), equals (colleagues),
and superiors (school and central office administrators, school
board members); respectful and equitable treatment (or not) for
students and families with different strengths, needs, and backgrounds; commitment versus indifference or outright rejection
in word and deed for the mission and goals of the school community; and many other similarly civic or anticivic approaches.
Students learn a lot from these models and encounters. As one

study shows, for example, "Regardless of their racial/ethnic background, adolescents were more likely to believe that America is a just society and to endorse civic goals if they felt that their teachers were fair to and respected students"; this was especially true for ethnic minority adolescents.[1]

Schools are also inevitably models of civic community and civic institutions. As civic communities, they model whether individuals matter or are seen as being interchangeable, one of a mass. They model inclusivity or exclusivity: whether diverse people are included and diverse voices are heard. They model trust and respect. As civic institutions, schools model fairness or lack thereof, equity or its opposite, transparency or Kafkaesque obscurity, humaneness and flexibility or rigid, bureaucratic indifference. These models significantly influence students' civic attitudes and beliefs.[2]

As young people directly experience the positive or negative civic norms, relationships, and practices modeled by adults in their schools, they respond by developing and enacting skills and behaviors that enable them to navigate these experiences. They learn when to stay quiet and how to fly under the radar, and they learn when—and with whom—they can speak up. Depending on the norms modeled by the school, they may practice the skills of assimilation, fitting into the mainstream and emulating high-status students, or they may practice skills of accommodation or even self-assertion, navigating among diverse groups without assimilating to any one. Students develop attitudes and habits of collaboration in schools that model these norms and practices; students in other schools learn to think individualistically and focus their efforts on self-preservation. In addition to providing models of civic engagement, therefore, schools also provide students opportunities to practice empowering (or disempowering) relationships, norms, and behaviors.[3]

Let's take a look at how these models and opportunities play out in practice, drawing upon some of the anecdotes above. They are obviously a fairly random and truncated assortment:

drive-by snapshots of undeniably complex events and practices. Taken together, however, I suggest that they offer a window into the inescapably civic life of schools, and into the vast array of ways in which students' experiences in schools are educative— or miseducative—with respect to their civic identities or opportunities. Furthermore, on a more demoralizing note, I suggest that the anecdotes I present reveal how low-income, predominantly minority schools such as Walden and McCormack enact a continuous series of civic microaggressions against their students. I borrow the term *microaggression* from scholars who use it to emphasize the daily unrecognized and often unacknowledged insults and invalidations of individuals that occur as a result of their ethnoracial identity. "Racial microaggressions are brief and commonplace daily verbal, behavioral, or environmental indignities, whether intentional or unintentional, that communicate hostile, derogatory, or negative racial slights and insults toward people of color."[4] These scholars suggest that although each microaggression is barely noticeable to its victim—and is usually totally invisible to its perpetrator—they may cumulatively cause those at the receiving end to experience "feelings of degradation, and erosion of self-confidence and self-image." Students' experiences of these civic microassaults may profoundly influence their civic skills and identity development in ways that further exacerbate the civic empowerment gap.[5]

Consider the lessons kids learn at the school door itself. On the one hand, teachers like Mrs. Farmer and Mr. Beeza teach them that they are welcome and valued members of the school community. On the other hand, when children as young as eleven are routinely screened for weapons before they are allowed to enter the school building, they are also implicitly being taught how they are viewed within the public sphere: namely, as a potential threat to public safety and security. These are not lessons that most middle-class and White students are learning in their schools, since they are four to ten times less likely to be subject to such policies. But they are civic identities imposed upon a significant percentage of poor youth of color growing up and at-tending de facto segregated schools in urban areas.[6]

The regulation of students' movement through space once they get into the school building has equally strong civic conse-quences. When at Shady Hill students move from one area of the classroom to another in order to find a more comfortable spot to work without being challenged by the teacher for doing so, when they are permitted to leave class on their own initiative to go to the bathroom, and when they choose whether to eat in the cafe-teria or to wander outside to eat with friends, they are learning both that they are trusted and responsible members of the com-munity, and how to exercise their responsibility appropriately and live up to the trust placed in them. This learning process in-volves some mistakes for many kids. They take the opportunity to move around in the classroom as a license to whisper to friends along the way, or they wander off too far at lunchtime and show up late to their next class. In facing the consequences for such misdeeds, students learn to exercise better judgment in the future, and then practice doing so in subsequent days and weeks.

Other schools regulate students' movements quite differently. At many urban schools—especially some of the most celebrated, such as KIPP schools—students are instructed to walk through the halls silently, in straight lines, with their hands to their sides so as to minimize risk of disruption or the possibility of a fight breaking out. A similar policy was the source of the confronta-tion between Ms. Bishop and Ms. Grant in my opening anec-dotes. Regulation extends into other domains as well. Students must wait for permission (and a hall pass) to exit the classroom for any reason. Bathroom privileges are particularly tightly con-trolled: no going the first or last period of the day, nor the first or last ten minutes of each period—and if a student's bathroom patterns have raised suspicions in the past, permission may be refused altogether throughout the day. Or, as in my opening ac-count above, students may simply be discouraged from exiting the class to go to the bathroom by having it turned into a humiliating public experience. Schools also regulate movement within the classroom itself ("Stay in your seat!") and in other gathering spaces such as the cafeteria. Students at both Walden and McCormack were required to stay with their class during lunchtime, and shifting seats was not permitted. If a student's best friend was in a class seated on the other side of the cafeteria, too bad; these eleven- to fifteen-year-olds were not empowered to choose on their own where and with whom they ate.

These rules were rational. Lunch at McCormack was an extraordinarily rushed affair in which students had to go to their lockers, get to the cafeteria, wait in line for food, eat, clean up, and be prepared to line up for their next class all within a twenty-minute time span. The cafeteria held 250 students at a time, and since the vast majority qualified for free meals, almost all had to be herded through the lunch line in a way that reduced potential for adolescent hormones and hijinks to kick in. The school bathrooms were prone to vandalism; the doors had all been torn off the stalls and there was frequent flooding, especially in the boys' bathrooms because students blocked the toilets with paper and other debris. At both Walden and McCormack, there was always the risk that an unsupervised student might pull the fire alarm without cause, and although both schools were relatively safe and orderly, enough fights broke out each year that it made sense to guard against the possibility of untoward contact by lining up and supervising students in the halls.

But although the rules were rational, they were not reasonable. In controlling students' movements and even their physical bodies in these ways, we were teaching them our poor opinion of their potential for responsible and self-regulating behavior. Thus we denied all students, including the vast majority who were not inclined toward vandalism or other serious misbehavior, opportunities to demonstrate or develop these self-regulating capacities. Unlike the students at Shady Hill, our students had no opportunities to learn from their mistakes because they were denied the opportunity to make such mistakes. Our students also had no opportunities to practice and model success because they were denied the freedom to make choices that could enable success. We were caught in a vicious cycle. Our mistrust of students led us to deny them opportunities to demonstrate responsible behavior and gain our trust. Their lack of opportunities to practice responsible school-based behavior led some of them to behave irresponsibly when they did grab freedom, which reinforced our mistrust and led us to clamp down even more. We unintentionally exacerbated rather than eliminated the skill, attitude, and behavior disparities that lie at the heart of the civic empowerment gap.

In this respect, we replicated in the civic sphere what some Marxist and functionalist scholars have charged schools with doing in the economic sphere. These scholars argue that low-income schools have in practice generally been structured to prepare students experientially for low-income jobs.[7] Whether intentionally or not—and I would like to think not, although that's no excuse—de facto segregated urban schools are similarly structured to prepare students experientially for de facto segregated citizenship. We can see this with respect to civic skills, as I have argued already, as well as civic attitudes and behaviors. There is good evidence that "children's concepts of political authority are constructed from their proximate experiences with adult authorities"; the most proximate of these authorities, other than parents, are teachers and other school personnel.

[A]dolescents' perceptions that people who wield authority over their lives are fair and responsive to them and that fellow citizens in their community are committed to a common good are the bases on which young people come to believe that America is fundamentally a fair society and the bases on which they develop an allegiance to the principles that make democracy work. We know from research with adults that confidence in the political system is associated with perceptions that institutional processes (not outcomes) are fair. In a similar vein, we argue that young people's confidence in the system

occurs via the accumulated experiences of fair (due) process and responsive interactions with adult authorities . . . The kinds of public
spaces our schools and communities provide and the behaviors of
adults in those settings communicate to the younger generation what
it means to be part of the body politic and to what extent principles
of inclusion, fairness, and justice figure in that process.[8]

To the extent that we modeled relationships and structured students' civic experiences in ways that reified hierarchical structures and authoritarian control, emphasized their lack of efficacy, and aggravated mutual mistrust, we likely exacerbated the
civic attitudinal gap by reinforcing our students' sense of civic
disengagement and disempowerment.

We may have deepened the behavioral gap as well. Public
schools in the United States have always been justified as places
that instill civic "virtue" through experience, not just through
didactic instruction.[9] Participatory experiences in schools are
among the most important predictors of future civic engagement.[10] Again, therefore, our neglect or even prohibition of such
informal but powerful opportunities may have intensified the
civic empowerment gap for our students. When our student
council found its greatest purpose in organizing a Valentine's
Day fundraiser, rather than in any form of collective governance,
they lost the opportunity to practice democracy. When my students' advocacy for bathroom renovations was peremptorily
dismissed by their school principal, they experienced hands-on
training in rejection and disempowerment.

Furthermore, we unintentionally magnified the empowerment
gap by reinforcing the idea that our students' demonstrated
knowledge, skills, and capacities outside of school were irrelevant inside the school building. Outside of school, many of our
students readily cared for younger siblings and cousins. They
traveled to school using public transportation, took responsibility for family chores such as shopping and cleaning, and worked
summer jobs. They helped non-English-speaking relatives fill out
government forms and translated for them at doctor's offices.

These were capable young people—yet we wouldn't even trust them to go to the bathroom or choose where to sit in the cafeteria without strict monitoring. Again, to the extent that the public school serves as a stand-in to youth for public institutions as a whole, students' experiences at McCormack and Walden merely reinforced their sense of being powerless half-members of an unwelcoming and mistrustful civic community.

Students' precarious status both in and outside of school, combined with the school's precarious status both within the community and as a community, also leads to paradoxical, almost self-defeating complexities. Consider the practice of screening children for weapons as a matter of course before allowing them to enter school. I suggested that this experience—which is confined almost exclusively to low-income urban schools serving large numbers of students of color—teaches students that they are viewed by authorities as potential criminals.[11] Alternatively, it is possible that youth infer a different civic lesson from undergoing weapons screening every morning: namely, that their own safety and security are valued by school officials. In this respect, they may feel valued and even validated by this process. When youth gang violence was heating up on the streets of Dorchester around 2005, resulting in the highest murder rate in the city for a decade, my principal at McCormack (which did not use metal detectors or wands) made impassioned pleas to both teachers and students to keep the school a safe zone in which students could concentrate on learning without fear for their safety. She talked about the school as a haven from the uncertainty and dangers of the outside world. In this respect, we implicitly aimed to become a model civic community within our four walls, despite the seventy-five people—thirty of them youth—killed on the streets of Boston that year.[12]

On the other hand, even this approach posed some civic complications. A few students complained to me that they were at risk of getting jumped on their way to and from school each day, and they were terrified of making the journey unarmed, and hence defenseless, as they saw it. They approved of the school's serving as neutral and safe territory. But they were perplexed by the school's insistence that they eschew carrying a "blade" to and from school; did we want them to be open targets for getting jumped, or worse? Did the teachers and administrators even understand the circumstances under which they were trying to survive? Some students thought not. School stood as just one more example of a public institution that ignored their needs and concerns, imposing policy "solutions" that were out of touch with reality. Let me be clear that I don't necessarily agree with students' reasoning. There shouldn't be weapons in the school building. And I'm dubious that carrying a knife with them to and from school kept them any safer, although I readily admit I know little about surviving the streets of Dorchester. Violence likely begets violence. But none of this means they were wrong to feel frustrated at their lack of safety to and from school, or more broadly at the failure of public institutions to protect them in even the most basic ways.[13]

In this respect, I was struck reading a 2010 *New York Times* article about the supposedly costly, $15 million "turnaround" of Locke High School in Los Angeles. School reformers were concerned because this sum includes significant support from private philanthropies, whose contributions inherently cannot be taken to scale for all schools needing comprehensive turnaround services. Locke's extra costs include hiring "bus companies to transport 500 students who previously walked dangerous streets to school" as well as "the salaries of two psychologists and two social workers who help students endure hardships like losing a sibling to gang warfare, or being evicted." When called on to justify why these expenditures should be taken to scale, one expert quoted in the article explains, "We're wasting billions every year by not fixing these schools because the students they're not educating end up filling our prisons." This is one way to analyze the problem. Another would be to say that the most basic obligation of the state is to ensure residents' physical safety. If the state can't even do that for children, and if it further begrudges the money to attempt to do so—Senator Al Franken, Democrat from Minnesota, is quoted asking dubiously, "I'm thinking, how scalable is this?"—then it has lost all civic legitimacy. These children literally risk their lives to attend school, and yet their (and our) elected officials debate whether the predicted future cost of incarcerating these youth justifies spending money on school buses and counseling today. Poor children of color attending de facto segregated urban schools don't live just in struggling communities. In some cases, they live in a failed state.[14]

I want to dwell a little longer on students' experiences of their schools as apparently willfully detached from the civic norms and expectations of the surrounding community. In Chapter 3, I discussed my students' beliefs that the uniform policy at Walden was intended to alienate them from their home communities. Denied the opportunity to wear clothes that would help them fit in on the street, students felt exposed on their walks to and from school. They experienced the daily transition from neighborhood to school and back again as tense, distancing, and symbolically fraught.[15] With over half of high-poverty schools and almost half of majority-minority schools requiring uniforms, as opposed to under 5 percent of schools that are less than a quarter non-White or poor requiring uniforms, this experience is again overwhelmingly more likely for low-income youth of color attending de facto segregated schools.[16] This sense of alienation may also be replicated inside schools, as when a student asks, "Why do we have to learn this?" and receives the answer, "Because that's what I'm required to teach you," or "Because it's on the test." A similar alienation may be felt when students and teachers alike confront what Deborah Meier calls schools' "scale of virtues," in which "the worst sins involved talking out of turn or not standing properly in line, while generosity was barely noticed."[17]

Nonetheless, it is not acceptable simply to advocate for making schools fully consonant or civically "congruent" with the surrounding community. My principal was right to strive to make McCormack a visibly safe space that was positively different from the dangers of the surrounding neighborhood. Many teachers rightly try to make their own classrooms "havens" from the broader social threats and stresses over which they and their students feel little control. Educators are right to try to help their students envision worlds beyond that which they directly experience. Janie, a former colleague of mine from Walden, expounded on this challenge in an interview that captured much of my own ambivalence. She started speaking as if she was talking to her own students: "You [Walden students] have your long-term vision and you start seeing where you're going to be 10 years from now . . . Your mom might be in jail and your brothers and all your sisters have babies and brothers in jail. You might have to look beyond your family." She transitioned later to first person:

> I tell my children all the time I would never tell you to leave your community or to leave your family because that's not a situation where you can help them. And that's a lot of weight for a 13-year-old and sometimes I'm uncomfortable with it myself. But I don't know another way. I guess many teachers feel like, "If I don't do this, suppose they don't get anybody else to come their way that will help them see their way out of this": out of Fourth Ward [the "ghetto" in which Walden was located and our students lived] or out of the situation that they're in now. So every year we spend a long time and we talk about it . . . I want them to understand that there's such a thing called upward mobility . . . I know they're young but they have to be told now. They must be told now.

At the end of the interview, she summarized her concerns by returning to the kind of community we created at Walden, a school in which we tried hard to be nurturing and attentive but also imposed sometimes harsh discipline and that frankly looked like a prison from the outside, with the merest slits for windows: "I was always concerned that to me how conveniently those kids were locked in over there [at Walden]. I was always concerned about that. And getting them to grow wings and know that they can soar was very, very difficult. Very difficult. How are you going to soar into a world you've never seen—you don't know anything about?"[18]

Schools need to exemplify the civic world that students have "never seen." They need to create model civic spaces for young people, and give students opportunities to develop and practice empowering civic skills, habits, attitudes. By doing so, schools promote and encourage students' identities as efficacious, engaged youth. This is crucial especially for the many low-income youth of color who, outside of school, rarely have the opportunity to practice such skills and are often treated not as future productive citizens but as likely criminals. Their experiences are of being followed by security guards in stores, watching others cross the street to avoid passing by them on the sidewalk, and being asked for proof of citizenship in Arizona and Alabama based on their appearance. Many of these young people have had few if any positive interactions with public officials. They receive substandard services (public housing, health care, education), describe their neighborhoods as being tantamount to living in a "war zone," and see the government as unwilling to ensure even their basic safety let alone establish the conditions for pursuing the "American dream." Reconstructing history so as to create simultaneously more accurate and more empowering civic narratives, as I advocate in earlier chapters, may help to some degree. But it's also the case that schools need to help change young people's lived experiences. Youth at the bottom of the civic empowerment gap have no reason to embrace civic engagement in the absence of proof that it makes a difference, or that they are respected as citizens, as valued contributors to and rights-bearing members of society. Schools can and must help students experience empowered citizenship in order to enable young people to build the knowledge, skills, procivic attitudes, and habits of civic participation for the future. These experiences can and should be built into the everyday practices of school.[19]

A DEMOCRATIC THEORY OF CHANGE

The question is thus not whether schools should model and promote experiential civic education, but how they should do so. I
suggest that every school must be intentional, transparent, and
reflective in how it both models and enables students to practice
authentically empowering civic relationships, norms, and behaviors. By doing so, schools will help students acquire essential
civic skills, empowered civic attitudes, and habits of civic participation that are collectively necessary for combating the civic
empowerment gap. *Intentionality* is necessary because otherwise
schools will fall back into the inadvertent mélange of sometimes
empowering but at least as often demoralizing practices sketched
in the stories that open this chapter. *Transparency* is necessary so
the "sorting out" that both students and adults do to make sense
of their experiences becomes a shared activity, and ideally therefore also comes to reflect shared judgments. I discussed the ambiguity of our checking students for weapons: did students see
this as an implicit accusation of incipient criminality, a welcome
commitment to ensuring their safety, a misguided demonstra-
tion of our cluelessness about the risks they took just getting to
school, or something else entirely? We didn't know, and we had
no way of knowing, because we never discussed the practice.
Hence, we lost the opportunity to explain our intentions to students and to help them see things our way. They also lost the opportunity to explain their perspectives to us, and to help us improve our practices. Similar second-guessing characterizes many
of the decisions and experiences I mentioned in the opening to
this chapter, from how we treated out-of-wedlock parenthood to
where we placed the "author chair" in English class. We were
usually very intentional in what we did. It's just that we didn't
reveal our intentions to our students, and so we lost the opportunity for a conversation about the effectiveness of our decisions.

Reflection forces educators and students alike to continue this process of checking themselves and seeking feedback over time. The fact that a procedure worked well or was justified at one time does not justify it in perpetuity. Furthermore, reflection combined with transparency enables "teaching for transfer": i.e., enabling students to apply knowledge, skills, attitudes, and behaviors that they learn in one context to a new or different situation. This is based on learning theory and research, which has shown quite definitively that when learners are able to name, identify, practice, and reflect upon specific techniques of effective practice, then they are empowered to transfer their understanding to novel contexts.[20] Finally, *authenticity* matters because only authentic experiences will fully convince students that they can and should "soar into" this new world of empowering civic engagement. Every generation of young people reaffirms Holden Caulfield's rejection of "phoniness"; mere pretences to empowering civic experiences will not convince young people that they are truly efficacious and responsible civic actors. Simulated experiences may help students develop the civic skills needed to reduce the civic empowerment gap. But authentic experiences are necessary to help them develop the engaged and efficacious identities, as well as the habits of action, that predict civic engagement and empowerment.

Intentionality, transparency, reflection, and *authenticity* are essentially pedagogical characteristics of schools. If schools exhibit these characteristics, then the civic relationships, norms, and habits that they model and that students experience have a good chance of sticking. Students will learn from these models, and from navigating, practicing, and enacting these civic experiences, in service of becoming more skillful and engaged civic actors themselves. The question remains, however, what skills, attitudes, and habits we actually want students to learn. In other words, I've argued that schools should model and give students opportunities to practice civic relationships, norms, and behaviors—but what should those be?

Put simply, and at the risk of being circular, these skills, atti-

tudes, and habits should be ones that reduce the civic empowerment gap, meaning that they promote *civic equality in practice.*
In essence, I have been arguing over the course of this book that
civic equality on the ground—in practice, not just in theory—is
necessary for democratic quality, stability, and legitimacy. This
argument lay at the root of my analysis of the civic empowerment gap in Chapter 1. It also lies at the heart of my advocacy of
empowering civic education. Achieving civic equality in practice
is an arduous task; I have no illusions that changing civic education practices in de facto segregated schools serving low-income
youth of color will do the trick on its own. But doing so can
make a significant difference. To achieve civic equality on the
ground, young members of historically marginalized groups
need to speak up and speak out—to make themselves heard.
Furthermore, they need to develop the skills and the self-confidence to make themselves heard about issues that matter to
them, and about which they may have knowledge and understanding that others (adults, members of more privileged groups)
often do not have.

It is therefore incumbent upon schools to teach youth to value
and exercise their voices, knowledge, capacities, and understandings of the world—more minimally, but crucially, it is incumbent upon schools not to *undermine* youths' confidence in their
voices, knowledge, and capacities. Efficacy matters, as do such
skills as codeswitching and taking multiple perspectives.[21] In addition, young people from historically marginalized minority
groups need to learn how to magnify their voices through collective action. Numbers will rarely be on their side, and marginalized individuals who are trying to change the system are easily
suppressed (and oppressed). But collectives can succeed where
individuals falter. Schools should therefore also give students opportunities to collaborate, and to practice collective action, not
merely individual action. And finally, insofar as civic identity
and civic responsibility are also crucial correlates of engaged
civic action, schools should model and create civic communi-

ties with which students positively identify and to and through which they develop a sense of duty. In sum, students' civic experiences in schools should reinforce the value of (via modeling) and their capacities to (via opportunities to practice) speak up in their own voices, assert the relevance and value of their understanding of the world, and magnify their voices through collaboration, effective leadership, and collective action.

It may be useful to think of these school characteristics as existing along a set of continua of achievement from minimal to maximal, as shown here. It would be unrealistic to expect every experience to fall on the maximal end of every continuum. The minimal end is frankly quite ambitious for many schools, especially many de facto segregated schools serving low-income youth of color. But they nonetheless may provide a set of ideals

Continua of civic experiences in schools

How schools construct civic experiences (pedagogies)

minimal ⎯⎯⎯⎯⎯⎯⎯⎯⎯⎯⎯⎯⎯⎯⎯⎯⎯⎯⎯⎯➤ *maximal*

reactive and sporadic	intentional, consistent, comprehensive
invisible, under the radar	transparent; visible to students and adults alike
simulated	authentic
specific, isolated, unreflective	generalizable, with explicit teaching for transfer

What students learn through civic experiences (aims)

minimal ⎯⎯⎯⎯⎯⎯⎯⎯⎯⎯⎯⎯⎯⎯⎯⎯⎯⎯⎯⎯➤ *maximal*

power of individual	power of collective action
value of participation	value of creating change through leadership
they have remediable deficits	they can leverage their capacities and build on their strengths to become able contributors

to which educators and students may aspire. They may also provide a set of criteria by which we may evaluate various activities in schools, and also evaluate the qualities of students' daily experiences.

These expectations may seem overwhelming, but it's irresponsible in a democracy to demand anything less. We consider it perfectly appropriate to expect schools to model and help young people practice being readers, writers, and mathematicians every day of every year. Without such practice, we reason, how will they ever master the complex knowledge, skills, efficacious attitudes, or habits such enterprises require?[22] We make similar judgments even about athletics. We take it virtually as a given that youth who want to become good baseball players, say, will practice for hours every week throughout the season—to say nothing of the pre- and post-season practices now becoming standard even for quite young children. They may play multiple games every week, all under the guidance of attentive and disciplined coaches. But what coaching, practice, and "Little League" games do young people get for citizenship? Is it truly unreasonable to ask that schools and other public institutions provide students as much coaching in the rules, skills, and norms of citizenship as in baseball?

Furthermore, a school without a baseball team simply teaches nothing about the game, except perhaps that it's not as valued as other sports for which the school does have teams. All schools, however, are engaged in experiential civic education. Students are inevitably practicing *something* with respect to civic skills, norms, and habits: how to navigate relationships with authorities, how to treat similar and diverse others, whether to speak up or keep one's head down, whether to work with others or go it alone, whether to treat others as collaborators or as competitors. A school that doesn't have a baseball team doesn't teach students to play baseball *badly;* rather, it doesn't teach them to play it at all. A school that doesn't structure empowering civic experiences, however, is structuring disempowering or at least disengaging civic experiences.

The old-fashioned notion of apprenticeship clarifies this relationship between schools' serving as models of civic community and engagement and their providing students opportunities to practice such engagement themselves. "Just as young people need models who show what it means to be a historian, mathematician, musician, or soccer player, so too do they need models of adults who engage in the arts of democratic life . . . By inviting young people into their circle, the adults act much like a religious community or tribe, offering the young ways to gradually assume more and more of the privileges and responsibilities of full membership."[23] Young civic apprentices thus learn through a mutually reinforcing cycle of both observation and practice. Role models, after all, aren't just static symbols of civic virtue or vice. They are also potential spurs to emulation. Models demonstrate, inspire, and encourage similar behavior in others. By enabling young people to assume an apprenticeship in the norms and practices of citizenship, such models ideally thrust them into a virtuous cycle of identity, skill, action, efficacy, and empowerment.[24] To accomplish such goals, though, apprenticeship also requires intentionality, transparency, and reflection. These are essential to schools' civic responsibility.

CREATING A CIVIC CULTURE IN THE CLASSROOM

These ideas can play out in the classroom in a variety of ways. Something as simple as "wait time"—how long a teacher waits between asking a question and either calling on someone to answer it or answering it herself—can open students up or shut them down. Teachers who extend wait time can model inclusion and collaboration by giving space to students who are slower, more reflective, and less prone to waving their hands wildly to get the teacher's attention the moment the question is phrased. Teachers who shrink wait time, on the other hand, answering their own questions in a demoralizing echo of the economics teacher in *Ferris Bueller's Day Off* ("Anyone, anyone?"), can quickly teach students that their thoughts and perspectives are not valued. Virtually every aspect of pedagogy has similar civic implications.[25]

I want to focus here on what may be the most basic—but also unfortunately rare—aspect of civically empowering pedagogy: namely, that which encourages and enables student voice. Even more specifically, I want to look at pedagogies that support an "open classroom climate" for real, engaging discussions in which students feel comfortable and supported taking on controversial points of view and listening to others' perspectives. The positive association between an open classroom climate and desirable civic outcomes is probably the most robust finding in the civic education research literature. Research over the past forty years, across dozens of countries, has conclusively demonstrated that students' belief that they are "encouraged to speak openly in class" is "a powerful predictor of their knowledge of and support for democratic values, and their participation in political discussion inside and outside school."[26] Students' experiences of an open classroom climate are also positively associated with overall civic and political knowledge, intent to vote, likelihood of being an informed voter, expectation of engaging in other political and civic actions, expression of political efficacy and civic duty, comfort with civic and political conflict, interest in politics and attentiveness to current events, and critical thinking and communications skills. These findings are consistent and strong across a wide variety of schools both within the United States and around the world.[27]

It makes sense that an open classroom climate for discussion would have positive effects since it essentially replicates within the school context the value and habits of political discussion within the family context. Political discussion within the family has been demonstrated to have a significant impact on young people's political knowledge and engagement. The frequency of these discussions has been shown to correspond to parents' educational and socioeconomic levels. Hence, by creating open classroom climates for discussion, schools can help remediate these sociodemographic differences—especially if the school serves predominantly low-income students.[28]

Given the uniformly positive effects of an open classroom climate, and the extent to which history, social studies, and English classes naturally lend themselves to civically empowering pedagogies that create such a climate for student voice, one might expect student discussion, exercises in perspective-taking, formal and informal debate, and other means of encouraging student voice to be widespread. The majority of social studies teachers both in the United States and worldwide, however, rarely use these teaching techniques. Textbooks, lectures, and worksheets reign supreme. Role playing, debates, and discussions do not.[29]

Even when something called discussion does take place, it most frequently follows a hub-and-spoke pattern, radiating out from and then quickly back to the teacher, rather than fostering a truly inclusive and mutually engaged discussion among students about the issue at hand. Courtney Cazden terms this the "IRE" model of classroom interaction, in which teachers initiate a conversational interaction (I) (usually by asking a question), a student replies (R), and then the teacher evaluates the student's reply (E) before then starting the process again, usually with another question.[30] This may occasionally be an effective mode of delivering instruction, but it hardly promotes a classroom culture in which students truly explore their own ideas and practice exercising voice and listening actively to others' ideas. Teachers and students often report this as discussion nonetheless, most likely because student expression of any sort is so relatively rare.[31] But calling it that does not make it so.

Sadly but unsurprisingly, evidence consistently shows that low-income students of color and immigrant students are less likely to experience rich discussions within an open classroom climate than wealthier, White, and native-born students—even though the benefits of such experiences for their civic knowledge and engagement are disproportionately positive when they do. One study, for example, examined 135 separate lessons in thirty-five high school classrooms across the Chicago Public Schools, which serves an overwhelmingly low-income and non-White student population. In *none* of the observed lessons were the majority of the students engaging in deep inquiry or discussion for a significant length of time. This is especially unfortunate since other research in Chicago public high schools shows that *if* civic engagement opportunities including an open classroom climate were provided in classrooms, they would likely more than offset the civic empowerment gap caused by other factors.[32]

If we are serious about using schools to close the civic empowerment gap, then it is essential we change classrooms' culture and climate so they become more open to and inclusive of students' own voices. Students need to experience their thoughts and opinions being treated as relevant rather than as beside the point, as worthy of careful discussion and examination—including being worthy of serious disagreement and challenge—rather than as pesky, inappropriate distractions from or even intrusions upon real "learning." Minimally, this means that actual discussions, where students express and defend opinions, listen to others do the same, and do so in a context of mutual respect and engagement, should be a relatively common feature of classroom life. If we were to listen in on such discussions, we would hear students knowingly expressing views that contradicted other students' and the teacher's expressed views. If we tracked the order of speakers, we would see students responding to one another, not just the teacher. Their responses would also indicate that they had listened to and mostly understood what the other students were saying, and that they were actually engaging with one another, not just talking in sequence. Students would attempt to provide evidence to support their statements, and they would challenge one another for evidence. Most of the students would participate; the discussion—and the classroom as a whole—wouldn't be dominated by a few strong or loud voices. A teacher in Austin whom I interviewed summed up this vision nicely. "My classroom is not quiet during our conversations because I expect everybody to be participating, everybody up, ask me questions, challenge me. My kids are good at challenging me. They'll say, 'Wait a minute, Mr. Estrada, what about this?' They'll come up and they'll say this, and that's what I expect from them. I don't want them to just be lumps on the log. They know that phrase already; don't be a lump on the log. If you're a lump on the log, we don't need you in here. You need to be an active participant." If all teachers—especially those in de facto segregated schools serving primarily low-income students of color, as is the case for Mr. Estrada's school—conveyed to students that active participation was required and respectful and justified challenges to their authority were expected, then students' classroom experiences and consequent civic empowerment would be significantly altered. No, more than this: young people's experiences in classrooms would be radically transformed.[33]

Nonetheless, the shift to a more open classroom climate is the *minimal* level of change required to help combat the civic empowerment gap. Consider the continua of students' civic experiences. Discussion in the classroom as I describe may be a fairly invisible pedagogy—"a teaching method"—rather than something that is directly taught for transfer—"a curriculum objective." In other words, teachers may teach "with discussion" but neglect to teach "for discussion"; they fail to teach students how to engage in effective discussions on their own in the future.[34] Furthermore, discussions may be simulated rather than authentic. If discussions occur only with respect to matters the teacher claims are important rather than matters the students have embraced (or introduced) as being meaningful to them, then these are not authentic discussions.

It is important to note that one cannot tell from the topic itself whether a discussion is authentic or not. Thanks to good teaching, students may well become passionate about investigating very focused and curriculum-based questions: Who benefited more from slavery: the North or the South? Should Andrew Jackson be inducted into the Presidential Hall of Fame? Was John Brown a terrorist? Did World War II end the Great Depression? Students may well embrace each of these essential questions and become passionately invested in discovering, and debating, the answer.[35] On the flip side, although students usually love discussing local issues and current events—areas of focus which are sadly neglected in today's classrooms due to the relentless demands of curriculum coverage—students may shrug off discussions about contemporary issues for which they feel little affinity, or about which they feel their teacher is patronizing. Five minutes of talk about a recent neighborhood shooting or whether they support the war in Afghanistan may be worse than none at all. What students need to experience and see modeled is having their cares, concerns, and ideas taken seriously, and doing the same with others. So one cannot tell from the topic alone whether students feel they are engaging in a simulation of a discussion or whether they are fully invested in an authentic mutual engagement of ideas. But in any case, the minimal end of the continuum does not entail authenticity.

Also, the classroom I describe as exhibiting a minimal level of open climate rewards participation, but does not necessarily help students develop communicative leadership skills. Students may participate effectively in a discussion initiated and led by others. But they don't learn how to lead and direct discussions themselves, nor how to transform conversations so they more inclusively address issues or recognize perspectives that may be invisible to the majority. Finally, an open classroom climate such as I describe may do little to foster students' sense of *collective* comprehension and learning. Students may view discussions as opportunities to express their individual opinions, and even to hone their own thinking and communication skills, but not as opportunities to collectively reach an understanding that they could not have achieved individually.

Again, this is not to say that a minimally open classroom climate is undesirable or not worth bothering with. In such classrooms, students feel comfortable expressing potentially unpopular views, hear others doing the same, and experience and see modeled a climate of mutual respect and engagement. These opportunities are rare, especially in urban schools serving predominantly low-income children of color. I would be thrilled if all young people consistently experienced such classrooms throughout their school careers. Not only would the civic empowerment gap be reduced, but I imagine the dropout rate and school discipline problems would decrease as well, and academic achievement and emotional and social development would improve.

Nonetheless, I want to indulge for a moment in describing maximally open classroom climates. These are classrooms in which students would have the opportunities to see modeled, to experience, and to learn how to lead free exchanges of ideas in ways that are respectful, inclusive, collective, and empowering. Discussions would be a regular, possibly even daily, component of class. They would be authentically engaging and about topics that matter to students, including addressing controversial public issues. Again, this doesn't mean they all have to be about contemporary issues or "real life." As I emphasized above, students who are guided by a good teacher can come to care deeply about events and eras that are remote in time and space. But they would engage with dilemmas that truly matter to young people, sparking rich and meaningful discussions and investigations in which students were driven to express themselves, challenge one another, revise their understandings without embarrassment, and learn collectively through their inquiry. These would clearly not be perfunctory, solely teacher-driven affairs.

Students would also learn how to conduct, lead, and take

ownership of their collective inquiry. This is a hard set of skills to learn. When I was teaching eighth grade, I had to teach students how to restate classmates' claims in their own words, how to build on others' ideas, how to express respectful disagreement, and how to ask for clarification. Students referred to a sheet of "sentence stems" during discussion, and in the first few months of the year I required them to begin with one of the stems when they wanted to talk. These included:

I agree with her because . . .
One question I have is . . .
I don't understand why/how . . .
This example may help . . .
In order to make your argument, you are assuming that . . .
What I hear you saying is . . .
To answer this question, we need to know . . .
The main issue seems to be . . .
Something that people haven't brought up yet is . . .

The same sheet included "active listening questions" that my thirteen- and fourteen-year-old students used to help themselves keep track of and engage in the discussion:

Is this person making an argument, or just talking for the sake of talking?
What is the main point of disagreement?
Are people supporting their arguments with facts, opinions, or assertions?
Could this question be answered if we did some research? What would we have to learn?
Why do people care about this topic?
How does this issue affect my own life, or how might it affect my own life?
Have I experienced anything personally that relates to this issue?

Diana Hess's research into teachers who successfully teach both
with and for discussion reveals similar pedagogical techniques.
Hess describes one teacher, for example, who taught his students "each of the elements of the discussion scoring checklist
so that students understood what it meant to engage in the forms
of discourse it valued." Another teacher shows her students a
videotape of a successful student discussion from the previous
year; the students and teacher use a grading sheet that describes
the qualities of a good discussion to help them collectively analyze and evaluate what they're seeing. Students then watch a videotape of a poor discussion among adults and use the grading sheet to guide their critique, and then they finally are
equipped to have a controversial public issues discussion of their
own.[36]

The explicit scaffolding, or stepwise teaching, for how to hold
a discussion makes the process transparent and comprehensible
to students. It enables participation among students who might
otherwise feel shy, incapable, or overwhelmed ("I can't sound
smart like he does!" "I don't know what I think!") because
the expectations, guidelines, and procedures for contributing are
clear. Such procedures enable all students to contribute something valuable, whether or not they have totally mastered the
material; they also enable all students, even those who are most
informed, to learn something from others. It gives students the
experience of both contributing to and learning from shared inquiry; and it accords them respect as both individual and collective thinkers and learners. Individual contributions and learning
are valued; but even more valued is the collective transformation
in understanding that occurs when diverse people with a range
of beliefs and understandings investigate a question together.
Students also learn from this kind of process how to insist (respectfully) that they have contributions to make and that their
points of view be heard. They learn how to facilitate discussions
in an inclusive and constructive manner, and why they would

want to—why mutual inquiry is more rewarding than a shouting match. After a while, they don't need the teacher constantly to monitor the conversation, inject probing questions, coax students into speaking, or introduce opposing points of view. They can use their communicative leadership skills to do these tasks themselves. This is not to say the teacher has no role; she does, especially insofar as she is often, though not always, the most knowledgeable participant in the room, and she also knows the most about each individual student's learning needs. But students need not rely on her. Finally, by seeing discussions "unwrapped," students can transfer these skills and techniques to novel situations: discussions and public debates outside of school, for example.

Establishing an open classroom climate can nonetheless be perilous, to the point of threatening teachers' livelihoods. Consider elementary school teacher Deborah Mayer, who

> said her class of fourth- through sixth-graders was discussing an article in the children's edition of *Time* magazine, part of the school-approved curriculum, on protests against U.S. preparations for an invasion of Iraq in January 2003. When a student asked her whether she took part in demonstrations, Mayer said, she replied that she blew her horn whenever she saw a "Honk for Peace" sign, and that peaceful solutions should be sought before going to war. After a parent complained, the principal ordered Mayer never to discuss the war or her political views in class. Her contract was not renewed at the end of the school year.[37]

When the 7th Circuit Court of Appeals ruled that her dismissal was permissible on the grounds that her speech is "the commodity she sells to an employer in exchange for her salary," teaching about controversial public issues became that much riskier.[38] Teachers need greater legal protections if they are to feel confident teaching students the skills and habits of open, democratic discourse.

WHAT BOUNDARIES SHOULD BE PLACED ON STUDENT CIVIL DISCOURSE?

It's not just teachers' expressions of their own views that pose challenges. The permissible boundaries of students' expression pose complexities for teachers, too. In Spring 2006, my student teacher Kirsten was meeting with her students to discuss what problem they wanted to address via their "citizenship projects." Some chose the dire state of school bathrooms, as I described above. Another group focused on second graders' poor reading test scores in the elementary school next door. Other kids chose to tackle drunk driving, teen suicide, violence in Dorchester—the usual stuff. Jonah, an Orthodox Jewish kid who had enrolled in McCormack just a few months before, had a different problem in mind, one we had never encountered before. He wanted to tackle the problem of legalized same-sex marriage in Massachusetts. More specifically, he wanted to protest it on Talmudic grounds.

Jonah's proposal occasioned hours of anguished conversation after school between Kirsten and me. Gay marriage was clearly a controversial public issue on which well-intentioned people disagreed. The Massachusetts Supreme Judicial Court had delivered a verdict legalizing same-sex marriage in Massachusetts as of May 2004. In response, conservative activists organized a state ballot initiative to outlaw same-sex marriages; legal tussles over this initiative were in the news frequently throughout 2005 and 2006. In these respects, same-sex marriage was a legitimate topic for debate and political action. Both Kirsten and I, however, supported the legalization of gay marriage on human rights grounds. From our perspectives, it should have been no more legitimate as a topic for debate, even in 2006, than interracial marriage is considered to be now. In this respect, we thought of gay rights much as we thought of abolitionism or anti-Nazi activism, not like "ordinary" contested issues like war, economic policy, or social services provision. We might feel passionately about a particular stance on these latter issues, but we could easily agree that students should have the opportunity to support positions opposed to our own. Such tolerance lies at the heart of having an open classroom climate, and frankly also at the heart of educating as opposed to indoctrinating. But not all positions are permissible, even in a public school classroom: we don't need to entertain pro-Nazi ideology, or wistfulness about the days of Jim Crow. So where did opposition to same-sex marriage fall? If gay rights are human rights, was it really appropriate to allow their civil, even human, rights to be married in the eyes of the state to be challenged in our classroom? Kirsten thought no. I felt torn, but ultimately thought yes. Same-sex marriage was being discussed, and debated, across Massachusetts and the United States. Who were we, in a civics class no less, to declare this extremely timely and salient political issue off-limits?[39]

The status of the issue itself, though, was only one of many considerations. Our antihomophobic opinions might not in themselves be reasons to forbid Jonah to tackle this issue. But the human rights of other students in the class might. We were committed to establishing our classroom as a safe and respectful environment for all of our students—including students who had gay family or friends, or who were themselves gay. I have always made it clear to students that they may be personally opposed to homosexuality on moral or religious grounds, but that in my classroom, I view all students as having equal standing and expect them to be treated as such. Jonah's proposal to fight against same-sex marriage as an abomination in front of God, however, put in jeopardy our effort to create an open classroom culture in which all students felt welcome, respected, and empowered. Ironically, the openness of our classroom created a situation in which one student's exercise of voice risked disempowering, driving into the closet, and fundamentally alienating other students in the same class. Since homophobia was overt and unapologetic at McCormack, we had no students who were out;

we weren't even aware of any same-sex families in a school of 750 kids. But one student in Jonah's class was clearly gay, and of course we had no idea if other students might be questioning their sexual identity, have same-sex parents, or otherwise feel personally attacked by Jonah's proposed project. So it seemed clear that some students would be directly harmed by Jonah's presentation.

But was the potential for social and psychological harm to others enough of a reason to censor a student's civic engagement? Let's say a group wanted to protest the Iraq War while another student's parent was in the military and was deployed to Iraq. If this group presented a project opposing the war in Iraq, emphasizing civilian casualties and declaring the war unwinnable, then this student might be angry, hurt, or even emotionally traumatized. Arguably, the harm suffered by this student is no less real than the harm suffered by a closeted gay student or child of same-sex parents. If we would nonetheless allow the antiwar group to move ahead with their plans, as I assumed we would, then why not allow Jonah the opportunity to move ahead with his chosen project?

As we discussed this scenario, we realized that as responsible teachers, we would approach those potentially affected in advance. We would sit down with the student whose parent was in Iraq and prepare her for what to expect; we would probably also talk to her family or guardians. Reaching out to the affected parties would clearly be necessary. But how would we identify such affected parties in the same-sex marriage case? The whole point was that we didn't know who was in the closet or struggling with sexual identity issues, nor who had gay family members or friends. Issuing an open invitation to kids—"You're about to hear one of your classmates mount a frontal attack on a core element of your identity, so please come talk to us if you're closeted or questioning"—did not seem like a recipe for success.

How much was the issue one of religion versus the topic itself? Kirsten thought this was key. First of all, by attacking same-sex marriage as sinful, not just as a policy mistake (because it weakened traditional marriage or something of that sort), Jonah would be challenging other people's fundamental sexuality. This was more than a policy dispute. Furthermore, Kirsten argued, religious arguments didn't have a place in "citizenship projects." Jonah was missing the whole point of the separation of church and state in the United States. As civics teachers, we needed to help him understand and adopt this separation. Maybe, in fact, this would be the value of allowing Jonah to go ahead with his project. If he was willing to get rid of the religious element and pursue his argument on data-driven, empirical grounds, then not only would the project itself pose less of a threat to other students, but also Jonah would learn an important principle of American constitutionalism. Kirsten could see herself supporting his project on these grounds—although then she'd have to figure out what reputable social science literature she could point him to that would support his position.

I disagreed with Kirsten's insistence on eliminating religious argument from the citizenship project, although I was ambivalent. As I discussed in Chapter 2, I think it harms public discourse when citizens are forced to express reasons for a policy stand that obscure or even misrepresent their true beliefs. If Jonah's opposition to same-sex marriage was based on religious grounds, why force him to talk about social science instead? It is true that Jonah *might* learn about the virtues of separation of church and state from this exercise. Or he might come to feel as if he himself is being treated as a second-class citizen, prohibited from talking about the true reasons for his policy stand while secularists face no such restrictions; he might thus reject church-state barriers altogether, come to see political debate as a form of lying, or become personally alienated from political and civic engagement. None of these would be desirable civic outcomes. Furthermore, religious language and even religious reasoning have always been part of American political discourse—perhaps most obviously in the case of civil rights movements, of which the fight for same-sex marriage rights is part. Could one imagine the civil rights movement of the 1950s–1970s, for example, without the religious language of the Reverends Martin Luther King, Jr., Fred Shuttlesworth, Joseph Lowery, or the other members of the Southern Christian Leadership Conference? It isn't a historical accident that religious leaders and language played such a crucial role then, and religious beliefs would necessarily be part of the debate now.[40]

What Kirsten and I were essentially wrestling with at this stage of our discussion was John Rawls's account of and justification for the limits on "public reason." Rawls argues that in discussing and deciding constitutional essentials and questions of basic justice, citizens must rely solely on public reason, which among other characteristics should be "independent of the opposing and conflicting philosophical and religious doctrines that citizens affirm."[41] Only in this way will all citizens in a deeply pluralistic society recognize and affirm the justice of the state's political and social institutions. Same-sex marriage is clearly a question of basic justice, so public reason must apply. It is fine for members of a religious organization to talk to one another about the religious reasons for or against a particular public policy, Rawls asserts. But these nonpublic religious reasons are irrelevant in the public sphere because they are not public reasons—meaning that not only should they not enter the public political discourse, but they also should not sway citizens' decisions in the voting booth.[42] In Jonah's case, according to Rawls's framework, we should teach him not only why and how to frame and present his anti–same-sex marriage citizenship project on nonreligious grounds in the public sphere, but also why he should bracket his deeply held religious beliefs in reflecting on his own upon this policy question. Talmudic considerations would be simply irrelevant to the public debate, for non-Jews and Jews alike.

I am frankly not convinced by Rawls's arguments about the character or boundaries of public reason. I am suspicious of the hegemonic character of public reason, which too easily tends to elevate majoritarian cultural norms and perspectives into the "public" category and reject minority norms and perspectives as "nonpublic." But even if Rawls's claims are justified as a matter of ideal theory, meaning that in an ideally just state only public reason truly would hold sway both in public discourse and in legislators' and voters' actual decision making, the pedagogical questions with which Kirsten and I were wrestling were rooted in a decidedly nonideal context. Furthermore, we were also confronted by developmental considerations. Our eighth graders were just learning how to identify and use evidence effectively. We were trying to help them answer such basic questions as: When you read a bunch of statistics, how do you figure out which ones are relevant? How do you select a quotation from an interview? Who counts as an authority? How do you evaluate and cite sources you find on the web? In this context, teaching Jonah or his classmates about the boundaries of public reason seemed daunting, to say the least.

In the end, Kirsten decided to propose to Jonah that he focus on nonreligious arguments in favor of his position. Adolescents being who they are, Jonah immediately responded that he had actually been thinking about a different topic since he and Kirsten had talked last: he thought he'd work on teen smoking instead. With that, our practical dilemma was over. The principled dilemmas of course remain. Furthermore, the pedagogical, political, and even job-security risks inherent in shifting power from teachers to students within classrooms also remain. Creating and maintaining an open classroom climate will always be challenging at many levels. Doing so maximally may be beyond many teachers' or schools' reach thanks to time, legal or cultural restraints, lack of training, and other challenges. But these practices are also essential for giving students empowering classroom-based experiences that reinforce the value of their participation and leadership, build their skills, and help them develop habits of public engagement.

BEYOND THE CLASSROOM

I want to end this chapter with a reminder that these goals challenge educators along every dimension of school practice, outside the classroom as much as within its walls. Consider school
discipline, for example. I spend time wistfully imagining disciplinary policies that exemplify the maximal criteria for civic experiences: policies that are intentional, consistent, transparent,
authentic, and generalizable, and that prepare students to work
collectively to exercise change-oriented leadership thanks to
their understanding of themselves as able and valued contributors to the group. Such policies would have to include some form
of student voice and involvement, through peer mediation programs, honor councils, youth courts, restorative justice circles,
or other models in which youth themselves are involved in setting expectations, intervening when conflict arises or expectations aren't met, and recommending consequences for transgressions. No longer would Ms. Bishop either need or want to dress
down students and their teacher in the hallway. Eighth graders
would continue to make farting noises with their armpits, of
course—honor councils can't eliminate juvenile humor—but the
consequences would be both reflective and internal to the student community. There are many exciting examples of such programs, but they remain rare, especially in urban public schools.
Instead, many of the latter impose "zero tolerance" policies that
impose extraordinarily harsh punishments—including long-term
suspension, expulsion, and criminal charges—for an ever-
growing list of transgressions. Poor children of color, especially
Black boys, are subjected to these policies and the harshest punishments at vastly disproportionate rates.[43]

Or consider how schools design and provide access to cocurricular and extracurricular activities. Participation in all forms
of extracurricular activities, aside from sports, is strongly correlated with increased voting, volunteering, and other forms of
civic participation, even controlling for prior civic interest and

involvement; civically oriented activities such as student government, school newspaper, service organizations, and leadership clubs are especially effective in promoting students' civic identity and engagement.[44] Low-income urban schools tend to have a small fraction of the extracurriculars available to students from higher-income, suburban schools. Those that are offered are often highly structured, with adults running the show; they also often focus on academic remediation rather than expansive, experiential exploration. Students should have opportunities to work collectively with peers, cofacilitate activities, and build on their strengths to contribute to the common good. As students lead meetings, run for office, and organize events, they would develop public speaking and collective organizing skills. They would also learn to work together, negotiate, and even establish friendships across boundaries of difference. These "twenty-first-century skills" are both necessary and empowering across students' lives.[45]

Through their participation, students would also be introduced to worlds beyond their own immediate school and neighborhood. They would get the opportunity to "see what a rich school looks like," as Shaniqua did when our quiz bowl team visited Sutton, or enter a school board member's house both half a mile and a world away, as Krystal did during our uniform project. Finally, students involved particularly in governance would actually have the opportunity to govern. Students might be voting members of the school's or district's governing committee, or participate in a youth council that has advisory power. These ideas are not outlandish. They can be found in action in schools across the nation and even around the world. But again, they are in sad contrast to most schools today—and especially most urban schools serving historically disenfranchised populations.[46]

None of these practices are any more straightforward to implement than are class discussions, cafeteria policies, or even weapons screenings. Consider Deyana, our pregnant fourteen-year-old who had won the election at Walden. We ultimately decided to honor her peers' votes and install her as eighth-grade class president. To no one's surprise, she did an outstanding job. But frankly, we'll never know whether our honoring her encouraged some of her schoolmates to view pregnancy as normal, or even as a potential source of pride. What did it mean to our sixth graders to see Deyana—smart, beautiful, popular, and swollen with pregnancy—representing our school? Students' voices and leadership are challenging. On the other hand, silence is not the answer.

THE CASE FOR ACTION CIVICS

6

In January 2000 I'm in the midst of trying to organize a field trip for my eighth-grade American history students. They will serve as jurors in mock trials argued by second- and third-year students from Harvard Law School. Although McCormack is on the same subway line as Harvard, most of my students haven't ever met a Harvard student. They don't believe me when I tell them that if they work hard and achieve at a consistently high level—which many of them would be capable of doing, given the right supports—they could attend a competitive college or university on a full scholarship one day. So I decide to try to demystify things a bit by organizing this trip. Also, lots of my students say they want to be lawyers; as is typical of eighth graders, they like to debate. If nothing else, they'll enjoy taking part in a professional-feeling mock trial.

I manage to corral about thirty students to go on the trip. Although I don't find any parents who are able to chaperone, I do convince a friend of mine to join us on the grounds that she is thinking of becoming a teacher, and this would be good experience. (Marcella subsequently decides to pursue a master's degree in the much quieter and calmer field of library science—I like to think not in response to this trip and the other few she chaperones.) The day of the trial, we pack all of the students into my classroom after lunch to go over ground rules: we expect students to demonstrate respectful behavior, pay attention to all directions from adults, act maturely, keep up with the group, spit out their gum and take off their do-rags and wave caps upon arrival, resist the urge to throw snowballs, and represent the school well—the usual stuff. I spout lots of dire threats for the consequences of misbehavior while Marcella does her best to look fierce.

After laying down the law and checking permission slips one last time, we head out to the T, as the subway is called in Boston. Normally a seven- to ten-minute walk from the school, it easily takes fifteen minutes thanks to eighth graders' remarkable ability to dawdle, straggle, and drag. "It's so far, Dr. Levinson!" they start whining about a block from the school door. As soon as we arrive at the station, however, whining gives way to excited chatter and yells to friends to come buy a pretzel or a soft drink. Marcella and I hang out on the platform waiting for the train, while I keep up a nervous count of how many students we have and try to come up with a plan to ratchet down the decibel level once we actually get on the T. For many of these young adults, it is no big deal to ride the T downtown, but for a substantial minority, this is the first time they've taken the T without a parent or other relative. They are really wound up.

Upon our arrival at South Station, I perform yet another head count and remind students of my expectations, and we head off to walk across the massive construction project known as the "Big Dig." Although the Big Dig has been underway for almost a decade by now and is one of Boston's defining features—it slices through much of the city as engineers attempt to bury a major highway downtown and build tunnels under water while not disrupting the subways, trains, and utilities that cut through the city—a surprising number of my students have never seen it before. We stop and peer through the viewing holes cut into the walls surrounding the project, impressed at the depth of the tunnels being constructed nearly 200 feet below us.

In response to agitated prodding from me and Marcella, we

finally move on. As soon as we reach the Fort Point Channel bridge leading to the courthouse, we are hit with icy January winds coming off the water. Some students start making their now-predictable complaints: "It's so cold, Dr. Levinson!"

"You didn't tell us we would have to walk so far! This is bogus!"

"Why couldn't we do this in May?"

Marcella and I ignore the whining and trudge on, urging the students to hurry up. "The faster we walk, the sooner we'll be back inside where it's warm! Come on, we're going to be late!"

In contrast to my students' reflexive whining, however, I hear a squeak from the back of the group that sounds like an authentic cry for help. Wending my way back, I join a group of girls circling around two of their friends. "What's the matter?" I ask.

"I can't cross the bridge, Dr. Levinson!" Tameka replies. "What if I fall over? I can't swim!"

Anna echoes her concerns. "Yeah, you didn't tell us we'd have to walk across a bridge! I'm scared of the water. What if the bridge collapses while we're on it?"

"Wait, you live in *Boston*. Water's everywhere. You have to cross bridges to get to Cambridge, Eastie, Charlestown, Castle Island, the waterfront. What do you mean, you're scared of crossing a bridge?" Tameka and Anna look at me uncomprehendingly. Sure, water divides a lot of places in Boston from one another, but that doesn't mean they have been most of those places. They are from Dorchester. Why do I think they ever would have gone to a tourist destination like the waterfront or to a neighborhood like Charlestown, known as unwelcoming to non-Whites? Anyway, even though they have been around Boston by T, they certainly have never walked from one part of town to another.

Realizing that trying to reason my students out of their fears is going to be ineffectual, Marcella and I each take charge of one of the girls. Draping an arm around their shoulders, and holding their hands to give them extra comfort, we slowly start walking across the bridge, encouraging them gently every step of the way. With effort, Tameka and Anna force themselves to keep on moving, looking straight ahead of them or down at their feet—anywhere except the water—until we reach the other side. "Congratulations!" I declare as we reach solid ground again.

"Thanks!" Anna responds, when she stops holding her breath from nervousness and feels able to speak again. "I can't believe I did it!" She and Tameka are both so proud of having crossed over a bridge; I don't have the heart to ask them what they plan to do when we have to walk back over the bridge to get home after the trial.

A few minutes later, we reach the federal courthouse. It is a huge, beautiful building, covered in marble and glass inside and out, commanding an impressive view of the Boston Harbor in one direction and downtown Boston in another. Marcella, many of my students, and I fall into a kind of hushed awe. As we join the line to go through the metal detectors, I quietly point to the trash cans where students can spit out their gum, and remind them in pantomime about taking off their headgear.

After we all make it through security, we gather in a clump in the main lobby, joining the other schools that have come to serve on the juries. With do-rags stuffed in their back pockets and accents that clearly do not originate in the tony Boston suburbs of Wellesley or Milton, my students stand out, both in the grand federal courthouse and among the gaggle of other middle- and high school jurors. We are the only racially diverse group, as far as I can tell. Mirroring McCormack as a whole, our group includes students from the Dominican Republic, Vietnam, Puerto Rico, Cape Verde, Haiti, and Jamaica, as well as native-born White, African-American, and Latino students. We also contrast with the other schools in manner of dress. Their students are generally dressed up for the occasion: the boys in coats and ties or even suits; the girls in skirts, dresses, hose, and heels. By comparison, my students are quite a rag-tag bunch, sporting mostly baggy blue jeans, hoodies, sneakers, and huge, puffy jackets. I can't tell if my students feel out of place, but I feel defiantly conspicuous on their and my behalf: "You may look like you belong here more than we do," I think, glancing around at the students and teachers from the other schools, "but just wait until you see what we can do!"

After a few minutes of milling around, we're approached by one of the Harvard organizers for the event, who asks me to divide my students into groups. As I split my kids into juries, I try to make sure every group includes someone who's articulate, a good leader, a quirky or creative thinker, and a facilitator. I avoid as best I can putting either close friends or dire enemies together. Once the students are divided up, they head out to their various courtrooms, each led by a Harvard student.

I follow Anna's group into one of the courtrooms and observe as they're officially empanelled, which they think is great, and then shown to their chairs in the jury box. "Hey, this is mad dope [cool]—they swivel!" Juan-Carlos exclaims as he sits down. I take a seat in the observer's section, positioning myself just behind the law students who will be arguing the case. From what I can tell, the two prosecuting and two defense attorneys all look a little nervous when they see who's on their jury. While my students sit and joke with each other, waiting for the trial to begin, the law students take out their opening and closing statements, working on modifying and simplifying the language. As they admit with chagrin to me and my students after the trial is over, they are concerned right now about whether my students will pay attention to and understand the details of the case.

In contrast to the law students' ongoing discomfort, however, my students settle enthusiastically into their role as jurors when the case begins, feeling proud and excited about having the opportunity to affect the outcome of the trial. They gravely introduce themselves to the judge when asked their names, and then sit attentively as the attorneys-in-training make their opening statements. As the trials progress, I wander from courtroom to courtroom, checking in on my charges and trying to glean enough information about the cases to be able to discuss them with my students afterward. I am gratified to see each group ask, unprompted, for paper and pencil with which to take notes during the trial. They seem to listen carefully throughout the proceedings, despite the cases' taking over two hours to argue. Each side has three witnesses, in addition to the two attorneys, and the attorneys conducting the cross-examinations are vigilant, to say the least. This can be a long time for eighth graders to stay focused and engaged without a break, but all the groups do so without complaint.

I turn down one of the judge's invitations to serve as foreman of the jury, pointing out that not only was I not empanelled, but my students will do a fine job on their own. I can't resist eavesdropping on three groups' deliberations, however, and I'm extremely impressed by their work. In all three cases, their deliberations are vociferous, with each student contributing something to the discussion. All of the groups take at least twenty minutes—and in one case, forty minutes—to review the evidence, develop a group consensus, and ensure that everyone is on board before they notify the judge of their verdict.

After they deliver their verdict and the trial has ended, each judge asks them to give feedback to the law students. As my students start to explain the reasons for their verdict, their analysis of the evidence, and their assessment of each lawyer's strengths and weaknesses, it is clear that the Harvard Law School students and the judges are initially taken aback and then awed by the depth of my students' thoughtful and sophisticated analysis. The law students admit to having been nervous about whether my students would understand what was going on, and to wondering whether they were really paying attention. At the end, they acknowledge that their fears were totally unfounded, and thank my students for their helpful advice. The judges commend them, too, for their sagacity and insight. My students and I all grin widely—well, except for the ones who are trying to appear too cool for that; they just sit back and project an "I told you so" look. After we rejoin Marcella and her charges downstairs in the lobby, all of my students find their friends and start talking a mile a minute comparing their trials, boasting about what the law students and judges had said about them, declaring that they want to become lawyers, and dishing out gossip about who got the hottest-looking law students.

By the time we are sitting around at McDonald's, marveling at Hank's ability to put away three Big Macs plus fries and apple pie, the conversation has generally turned to other matters. But it's clear that we all emerge from the experience feeling excited and empowered. Back at school, the students use the mock trial as a touchstone throughout the rest of the year. They insist we conduct a mock trial of our own, in fact, so in March we put Andrew Jackson on trial in order to determine whether he should be inducted into the Presidential Hall of Fame. This turns out to be such a successful activity that I repeat it in subsequent years, also in response to requests from my students who participate in the field trip each year I teach. In the end, despite (or maybe in part because of) the initial sense of dislocation and unease, the mock trial turns out to be a powerful lesson in civic engagement and multicultural understanding for all students involved, from my eighth graders, on the one hand, to the Harvard law students, on the other.

Guided experiential civic education—whether it be serving on a mock trial jury, engaging in community organizing, participating in Model United Nations, or interning with a nonprofit—has the potential to promote a huge range of extremely important civic (and other) outcomes, ones that can be difficult for teachers and schools to help students achieve in any other way. In this particular case, one of the most important of these civic outcomes was students' embracing the right and the obligation of jury service. Before I even told my students about the mock trial opportunity, we had briefly studied the constitutional guarantee of trial by a jury of one's peers. We discussed why this political right, as well as its unspoken attendant civic obligation to serve on juries when called upon to do so, might be so important as to be enshrined in the constitution. My students were hardly fired up by the discussion; I feel confident in admitting that our in-class review did little to convince a new generation of (potential) American citizens to embrace jury duty as an important obligation. By contrast, the students who participated in the mock trial *loved* serving on the jury, and affirmed that they would do so in the future if given the opportunity. After all, they discovered that they had power—they were deciding people's fate! What's not to love about that, at least if one is fourteen years old and not yet afflicted by existential angst?

The experience also empowered my students in other ways. Noel, for example, signed up for the trip because she really wanted to earn the 100 bonus points I had promised I would award to all participants. Her grades were low, and although she thought the whole trip would probably be boring, especially if she was assigned to a civil rather than a criminal case, she knew she'd get to ride the subway with her friends, go out to McDonald's after the trial, and earn some extra credit in the process. So why not? During the deliberations, however, Noel surprised her classmates and herself by taking a strong stand on the merits of the plaintiff's case, ultimately persuading the rest of the jurors to reach a different verdict than that toward which they were originally tending. Noel emerged from the experience with an enhanced sense of self-efficacy; for the first time in the five months I had known her, she started believing in—and acting upon—her ability to develop and communicate good ideas effectively to others. Many of the students whom I took on this trip over five years had similarly empowering experiences, whether as a result of discovering their ability to follow complex arguments during the trial, to convince others in the deliberation room, to explain to the law students (*Harvard* law students, no less!) how they could have improved their presentation of the case—or to walk over bridges without panicking.

The mock trials also exposed my students to positive role models; each year, some students commented to me afterward about how excited and surprised they were to see female, Black, and occasionally Latino judges and Harvard law students. In addition, they acquired knowledge—the difference between a civil and a criminal trial, how a cross-examination works, where the federal and district courthouses are in Boston, or how the Big Dig changed Boston's landscape both above and below ground. This knowledge was important, but either wasn't in the prescribed curriculum and hence was not something I made the time for in class, or was hard to teach in the classroom setting in a way that felt meaningful to kids. Finally, participation in this civic experience helped my students to apply some of the knowledge and skills they were learning in school; whether or not they realized it, in the process of serving on the jury my students had to assimilate knowledge through listening to the lawyers and witnesses, weigh conflicting evidence, apply previously acquired knowledge to judge the plausibility of each side's arguments, support their own judgments by making organized, reason-based arguments that took opposing viewpoints into account, listen sympathetically to others' concerns, and communicate respectfully and effectively with adults in a public setting. These are hard skills to learn and apply, but because the experience was meaningful to them, each year almost all of my students were eager to make the effort to do so.[1]

In addition to the benefits accrued by my students, various adults also benefited from the process. The Harvard law students were able to argue their case in front of a jury similar in composition to one they might face in a real trial and then receive honest, critical feedback—a specialty of eighth graders—from the same group. Both they and the judges hearing the cases were reminded not to prejudge those who are subordinate in power according such superficial attributes as race, ethnicity, age, style of dress, or accent. My own thinking as an educator was similarly expanded. I had thoroughgoing confidence in my students' capabilities, of course, since otherwise I would not have scheduled the field trip. But my students also exceeded my expectations in ways that forced me to grow as a teacher. Their overwhelming success also challenged my vestigial assumptions about who "belongs" in civic spaces such as marble-lined courthouses. At a conscious level, I already believed passionately in my students' potential to be active and empowered citizens. But subconsciously, in some way I must have still bought into class- and race-conscious norms about who was qualified to participate: "You may look like you belong here more than we do . . ." This experience thus nudged my thinking closer to a truly egalitarian conception of democratic participation.

We can see here how the mock trial fostered transparent, authentic, and transferable experiences that enabled participants to realize young people's power as collective actors and recognize their capacities for effective, active citizenship. Many other guided experiential civic learning opportunities can achieve similar "maximal" results. For example, students may serve on the leadership team, governing board, or diversity committee of the school. Students may work together as a class to conduct a "constituent survey" of their peers and then develop and implement a strategy to improve an aspect of their school. They may debate current events and then write a letter expressing their opinions to an elected representative or government official. They can conduct a voter registration drive in the school parking lot or create a WebQuest about a policy issue that matters to them. As a senior project, students might volunteer with a nonprofit social services agency or an advocacy organization and prepare a presentation about what makes it an effective (or ineffective) organization. Students may research a public policy issue and then make a presentation to local officials, or attend a city council meeting as advocates for their position. Closer to home, they can elect class officers who will collaborate with the teacher on planning field trips and other special activities; or, they may as a class deliberate about and vote on issues including due dates for major projects, the order in which to read class novels, or the consequences for minor disciplinary infractions. Students can participate in online simulations of a global public policy challenge with other youth from around the world; they could also participate in a technology-free, classroom-based simulation.[2]

These examples all strive to replicate the features I listed in the continua of civic experiences in the last chapter. They also all intentionally build on collective and policy-oriented action. None represent such piecemeal approaches as donating cans to a homeless shelter or spending a morning visiting elderly people in a nursing home. Although both of these activities are noble and may be worthwhile, they don't foster the kind of attention to systemic issues that is important. Nor do they help students recognize the power of their community and of joining together to effect change.

SERVICE LEARNING IS NOT GUIDED EXPERIENTIAL CIVIC EDUCATION

The guided experiential civic education I advocate differs substantially from its seemingly close neighbor: service learning. Service learning is "a teaching and learning strategy that integrates meaningful community service with instruction and reflection to enrich the learning experience, teach civic responsibility, and strengthen communities."[3] It departs from community service insofar as it is explicitly tied to the curriculum and it leads students in a cycle of learning, action, and reflection rather than focusing solely on the service action as such. Service learning has enjoyed popular and financial support at local, state, and federal levels.[4] Both Maryland and the Chicago Public Schools require forty hours of service learning in high school for graduation; nine other states allow for service learning to be applied toward graduation. Participation has dropped off somewhat in recent years, most likely in response to the testing pressures imposed by state and federal education policies such as No Child Left Behind. Nonetheless, service learning is still common among public schools that serve higher income and White students, which are almost a third more likely to offer service-learning programs than those in low-income areas. Furthermore, given how rare any forms of experiential civic education are in the United States, service learning probably remains the most prevalent such opportunity available to all students, including to low-income students of color.[5]

There are several reasons that service learning has caught on in ways that other forms of guided experiential civic education have not. Most service learning is justified on intentionally apolitical and hence also apparently nonpartisan grounds. The motivations for service-oriented civic action usually include expressing a sense of caring for others, promoting a self-identity as a kind or caring person, and expressing a generalized moral concern, rather than a driving political sensibility or commitment. Although service projects such as helping out at a homeless shelter, tutoring younger children, or volunteering with Second Harvest may also be motivated by a sense of injustice and opposition to inequality, the conception of justice is vague enough, insofar as it is generally unconnected to any policy agenda or systemic approach to reform, that it is usually not thought to have a partisan bias. This approach is quite intentional. Because service learning does not engage with or tread upon political controversy, it can safely be embraced and promoted by people from across the political spectrum.[6]

Also, because service often does not tackle systemic or structural concerns, students more readily experience immediate or short-term success. Insofar as service-oriented programs rarely encourage students to try to "change the system" via political action but instead encourage direct service to aid a single individual or organization, participants are likely to feel they have helped others, and they are less likely to experience the frustration that can result from trying to tackle larger, systemic, or organizational problems.[7] Under this model, students can volunteer, reflect on their achievements, feel positive about their accomplishments, and move on. This is important because in the absence of success, students may decide that civic and political engagement are demoralizing and not worth one's energy.[8]

These very qualities that ensure widespread bipartisan support for service learning also make service learning an inadequate tool for addressing the civic empowerment gap. As I have shown, most service-oriented experiential education is driven by—and hence teaches—a conception of citizenship that is voluntary, based on individual rather than communal action, and independent of government involvement. At its best (which isn't very good), this vision of citizenship promotes an apolitical motivation for civic engagement, "a vision of citizenship devoid of politics."[9] In their effort to avoid partisan causes, teachers and districts often direct students into not just nonpartisan but also nonpolitical service. Whether intentionally or not, this approach can subtly guide students away from confronting political issues and the controversy that can result. It can also reinforce students' distaste for and even fear of controversy.[10] Meta-analyses of service-learning research support these concerns; no rigorously designed study has shown a significant or long-term relationship between participation in service-learning and political participation.[11] Avoidance of conflict is inimical to effective civic education, insofar as controversy, politics, and yes, even polarization lie at the heart of many of our most important political dilemmas. If students are taught to shun controversy and seek out ways of "making a difference" that are free from complexity, politics, and frustration, then I fear they will learn a weak, even eviscerated, conception of civic engagement.[12]

At its worst, this vision of citizenship can reinforce students' opposition to governmental involvement and their sense of powerlessness to make a difference via political action. Young people develop "confidence in personalized acts with consequences they can see for themselves; they have no confidence in collective acts, especially those undertaken through public institutions whose operations they regard as remote, opaque, and virtually impossible to control."[13] Young people are vocal about this. Youth volunteers pointedly characterize their work of "helping others" as *unrelated* to the work others may do to address social or political problems. They disavow the latter, rejecting the ideas both that their service might be connected to problems that the government should also address and that they might contact government officials in service of their cause.[14]

This individually oriented approach may be especially disempowering for low-income and immigrant youth of color at the "bottom" of the civic empowerment gap. Many of the tasks that youth do for free in these settings—raking and bagging leaves as part of a park clean-up, scrubbing graffiti off the school walls, or packing boxes and serving food at a soup kitchen—are ones that they or their parents would normally get paid to do in low-skill service jobs. Young people in this situation may come to feel they are being exploited rather than doing valuable service for the community. Service learning can also be alienating to these young people and their parents when they themselves are turned into objects of charity. On the flip side, service learning experiences that put affluent and White students in positions of authority over historically marginalized groups or position them as one-way deliverers of service to these groups may also exacerbate the civic empowerment gap.[15]

Furthermore, although service learning motivated by an ethic of care and mutual assistance is apparently nonpartisan, its merely participatory and ameliorative rather than activist and change-oriented approach has an inherently conservative effect. By centering responsibility on individual citizens and exempting social, economic, and civic structures and institutions—government, corporations, legislation, economic regulations, and so forth—service learning implicitly fosters a political ethic that favors the status quo and reduces activism for social change. This is not a new critique. But it is one that we should take seriously in considering how schools can use experiential education to help shrink the civic empowerment gap.

Service learning done well exemplifies many "best practices" of guided experiential education listed above. In particular, it provides authentic experiences that build on youths' capacities to improve society in tangible and visible ways through a cycle of research, action, and reflection. It also may promote other moral and ethical virtues in a developmentally appropriate way. But service learning as it is currently implemented in most settings should not be confused with the kind of civically empowering guided experiential civic education that I have advocated above. Individual acts of service are no replacement for comprehensive, collective, policy-oriented action that teaches transferable principles for achieving long-term civic and political change.

ACTION CIVICS AS THE GOLD STANDARD

Instead, schools should foster action civics as the gold standard of guided experiential civic education. As defined by the National Action Civics Collaborative, *action civics* is designed to create "an engaged citizenry capable of effective participation in the political process, in their communities and in the larger society."[16] Through this model, students *do* civics and *behave as citizens* by engaging in a cycle of research, action, and reflection about problems they care about personally while learning about deeper principles of effective civic and especially political action. A small but inspiring group of organizations and individual educators promote this approach both within and beyond schools, including in urban schools serving predominantly low-income students of color. Exemplar organizations include Public Achievement, Earth Force, Hyde Square Task Force, University Community Collaborative of Philadelphia at Temple University, and the Mikva Challenge.[17] In each case, they help guide young people through the process of taking informed and empowered action on behalf of issues youth themselves care about, with the aim of helping them master knowledge, skills, beliefs, and habits of civic action that they can apply in the future as well. The organizations differ somewhat in their focus and approach: Earth Force focuses on environmental justice issues, for example, and works in communities around the United States and abroad; Hyde Square Task Force, on the other hand, focuses solely on Boston and applies such youth organizing principles as teaching power analysis as part of its regular curriculum. But they also share some very similar "best practices."

All employ virtually the same six stages of civic action. The Mikva Challenge's "Issues to Action" program, for example, teaches students to: "examine your community; choose an issue; research the issue and set a goal; analyze power; develop strategies; take action to affect policy."[18] These steps clearly encourage students to take ownership of a civic challenge that they care about, support their acquisition of the knowledge and skills needed to take meaningful action, expect students to take that action—to learn *through* citizenship and not just *about* citizenship—and then challenge students to reflect upon the experience as a means of consolidating their learning and empowering them to take effective action in the future.

These organizations, and others like them, also take a purposefully political or policy-oriented stance. They discourage short-term ameliorative approaches—one-shot park cleanups or other forms of short-term volunteerism—in favor of longer term, institutionalized reforms via engagement with public policy, coalition-building, public awareness–raising, political engagement, and other change-oriented work. Youth organizers from the Hyde Square Task Force, for example, have successfully organized to get a youth center constructed next to a notoriously unsafe housing project, implement a pilot civics curriculum in

Boston public high schools, and develop an action plan to improve relations between Boston's transit police and youths.[19] Furthermore, as these examples demonstrate, these organizations and the civic engagement they foster build on students' strengths. Students are positioned as knowledgeable insiders whose insights enable them to make a positive contribution as effective and powerful agents of change. This approach stands in stark contrast—especially for low-income youth of color—to their traditional positioning as bundles of deficits who traumatize the community via academic failure, idleness, and even criminal delinquency.

Finally, the best organizations and individual educators who take this action civics approach help students make sense of their experiences—in this case, both their daily lived experiences and their experiences of guided civic engagement—within a critical frame.[20] They challenge students to take on a social justice orientation in reflecting upon their lived experiences and the actions they propose to take. They teach media literacy, power analysis, feminist perspectives, and similar critical stances to help young people rethink what is "normal" or acceptable about both the lives they lead and the changes they would like to bring about. Action civics–inspired educators are not content to let students' unexamined assumptions—that Blacks are poor because they're lazy, say, as many of my own Black and non-Black students felt perfectly unabashed about asserting in class—structure and limit students' analyses of the problems they face or of the range of solutions they consider.[21] By changing how youth understand the world in which they live, therefore, these programs empower young people not only with respect to the particular problem they are concerned about, but more broadly with respect to rethinking social and political possibilities as a whole. This is another way in which short-term amelioration is rejected in favor of more transformative approaches.

These more critical approaches incorporating both power

analysis and social justice frameworks are most evident in programs and educators inspired by community organizing, like the Mikva Challenge and Hyde Square Task Force, and by traditions of youth participatory action research (YPAR), which are often inspired and led by university researchers and students. In YPAR, students "study social problems affecting their lives and then determine actions to rectify these problems," but they do so usually using the techniques of critical theory and analysis. Students research current and historical power dynamics and systems of oppression, investigate their own realities through a newly developed critical lens based on their research, and then formulate collective action plans to create social change.[22] As the noted YPAR researcher and activist Michelle Fine explains, "YPAR is not just about collecting stories and voices. It's about attaching those . . . to local conditions and the history of those conditions so young people can interrogate: how did we get here and how else might it be?" In so doing, students potentially learn to see not only current conditions but also knowledge itself as fallible and susceptible to reconstruction. In this respect, YPAR may function not only as a direct tool to promote civic empowerment, but also as a way of thinking about knowledge and the world that is itself civically transformative beyond the application of YPAR techniques themselves.

YPAR also intentionally builds on students' strengths rather than solely remediating their perceived deficits. For example, YPAR "takes really seriously critical local knowledge"—knowledge that young people in the community are often best positioned to possess.[23] Jeffrey Duncan-Andrade explains how YPAR pulls together youths' capacities both for social critique and privileged knowledge.

Urban youth bring unique and important insight to the dialogue about social justice. They experience the material conditions of urban poverty in visceral ways that cannot be captured through adult lenses. Sadly, schools and the larger society have failed to create avenues with which youth can discuss their understandings of the problems and conditions facing urban centers. The absence of these narratives has not only meant the increasing marginalization of urban youth, but also that insight into solutions to these problems have been overlooked.[24]

As his comments suggest, although YPAR is still fairly rare, it is most often implemented in urban settings with students of color as a means to help young people combat injustice. This makes YPAR one of the few approaches to guided experiential civic education that can be found more often in schools serving predominantly low-income youth of color than in schools serving more affluent and White youth.[25]

Advocates of these approaches debate whether they can be implemented within schools, or whether external organizations and pressures are needed to do this kind of work. Adults themselves often need to develop new skills and ways of doing things in order to empower youth. "It has enormous power when adults play a facilitative, respectful, liberating role rather than a controlling, limiting, disciplinary role. This role is one that takes concentration, practice, and often times, training. It is opposite to the most typical adult role."[26] It is also extremely time-consuming. Schools' internal capacities to promote action civics are limited by time constraints such as 45–60 minute periods and a relatively short school day, their focus on mandated curriculum coverage, and prioritization of tested subjects and skills.

Furthermore, schools are thought to be unlikely locations of this kind of education because student-generated action civics projects often focus on reforming schools themselves. Consider the Philadelphia Student union's vision statement, for instance:

> We have a right to decision making power in and out of our
>   schools.
> The community has the right to control their schools.

We have the right to learn from people who like us, who are like us, and who we trust.

We believe schools must be based on hands on learning and real life experiences.

Everyone has the right to an equal opportunity/education that engages us in questioning and changing the world around us.

Students have a right to an education that liberates, not domesticates!

We believe that the school to prison pipeline is unacceptable and must be ended.

We have been denied a quality education and we must reclaim it.[27]

It is hard to imagine most schools' independently promoting the kind of research, collective activism, and reflection that this vision statement—by a youth-run, independent organization of Philadelphia Public Schools students—demands. Institutions are inherently self-protective. Especially insofar as low-income, urban, public schools are frequently on edge about maintaining control over a youth population that vastly outnumbers adults, they are unlikely venues for opening themselves up to critique and potential civic action.

These are compelling reasons for external organizations such as youth community organizers, university professors and students, and other nonprofits to facilitate action civics with young people. But they do not prove that schools cannot be part of the picture. Brian Schultz, for example, has vividly described work he conducted as a teacher with fifth graders at a public school next to Chicago's Cabrini Green housing project, in which they used action civics techniques to try to replace their crumbling, bullet-hole pockmarked building. Students at Cesar Chavez Public Charter Schools for Public Policy in Washington, D.C., complete interdisciplinary freshman and sophomore "capstone projects," a three-week junior year public policy internship, and a year-long senior project focused on making "this world a better place by influencing the public policies that affect their communities." First Amendment Schools, the Democracy Prep charter network, and schools that support youth participatory action research also demonstrate the potential for school-based action civics.[28]

Promising districtwide initiatives also exist, including in urban districts serving predominantly low-income youth of color. In Chicago in 2010–11, for example, more than 1,500 students at forty high schools worked with Mikva Challenge to implement "Issues to Action" projects. In these projects, students "identify issues in their communities and learn about local government and the political process through research, analysis and the creation of action plans that tackle these issues" by advocating for policy change. They also "attend a Youth Activism Conference to gain essential advocacy skills" and present their final action projects at Mikva Challenge's Annual Civics Fair. Even more comprehensively, forty Chicago public high schools taught a "Democracy in Action" course in 2010–11, also in partnership with the Mikva Challenge, that aims to help students to acquire the "skills, knowledge and dispositions to be 'superstar' citizens. At the core is the idea that students explore their communities from an asset-based perspective, identify issues that are important to them and important in their community, research the issue, analyze power, and ultimately develop an action plan and take action."[29]

EIGHTH-GRADE CITIZENSHIP PROJECTS IN BOSTON

Boston Public Schools similarly gives some space for action civics in the aptly named Civics in Action, a required eighth-grade class across the district, as well as in a range of pilot high schools and in a pilot high school civics course.[30] I taught Civics in Action during my final two years at McCormack, and students' "citizenship projects," as we called them, were clearly one of the highlights of the course. Students began by interviewing family members and other adults in the community, examining the newspaper and other news sources, and brainstorming together to identify a wide range of public problems that they thought needed to be addressed. Individuals or small groups of students then selected a problem that felt important to them. Representative problems included: teen suicide; gun violence in their neighborhood (a perennial choice; every semester at least eight or ten students out of eighty selected this problem); inequities between urban and suburban schools; the abysmal quality of school lunches (another perennial favorite); Boston Housing Authority's poor maintenance of two housing projects in the neighborhood; the lack of after-school and out-of-school opportunities for youth; gang violence; the gruesome condition of school bathrooms (another top choice every semester not just by my students but also around the world);[31] drunk driving; the need for new band instruments for our school; pollution in the Boston Harbor Islands; orphanage conditions in Ghana. Identifying civic and social problems can sometimes be difficult for adolescents growing up and attending schools in socioeconomically privileged communities.[32] This was most definitely *not* a problem for my students; with project titles like "Guns or Parks: What's Better for Dorchester?," they often demonstrated a kind of gallows humor that made the personal nature of the problems they were tackling all too evident. If my students had difficulties, it was in selecting just one problem and then making it small enough to tackle.

After selecting a problem, students conducted research to document and determine what was known about the scope, causes, and effects of the problem. This research usually combined web-based searches and library visits along with original data collection via in-person and telephone interviews and surveys. I also required students to identify both current and potential allies. In so doing, they discovered—often to their immense surprise—they were not the only ones who cared about their problem. They also found out what others were doing to address the problem, were prompted to analyze the current allies' approaches and discuss why the problem was not yet solved, and were able to identify potential collaborators with and targets of their civic action. We did not fully follow the model promoted by YPAR and community organizing advocates insofar as we did not engage in formal power analysis or other forms of critical social literacy. This lacuna is largely because I was making things up as I went along; like many educators trying to construct civically empowering experiences for my students, I felt relatively isolated in my work and was unaware of others' efforts in these areas.

Students then moved to researching and evaluating potential solutions for which they could advocate in a set of persuasive letters. Each member of the group had to identify a different target for their persuasive letter, which they wrote in English class. Recipients included elected and appointed officials, parents, directors of nonprofits, teachers, media outlets, and corporations, among others. For extra credit, students could take an additional civic action such as volunteering, lobbying, fundraising, organizing, circulating a petition, and so forth. (Again, because this was an organically developing curriculum, some of these approaches are less oriented toward public policy or other kinds of collective action than I would currently advocate.) The persuasive letter was the only required civic action, however, because arranging opportunities for eighth graders to volunteer with an organization or even travel to a site unsupervised by a teacher or a parent often turned out to be impossible. Students wrapped up their citizenship projects by creating and delivering presentations about their projects in front of a group of judges from outside my classroom, and often outside the school.[33] Finally, we debriefed in class and students wrote a reflective essay as part of their final exam.

By selecting problems they were personally committed to, including evidence from their own or friends' and family members' experiences in their presentations, and developing a level of expertise that enabled them to teach others, including adults from outside the school building, about the problems and their proposed solutions, students asserted and built upon their own knowledge and capacities rather than focusing on their ignorance or deficits. In contrast to the majority of their experiences in school, therefore, this project was not overtly structured around what they did *not* know; rather, it built on what they *did* know and positioned them as potential experts capable of following through on an important agenda of their own.[34]

Furthermore, thanks to the students' public presentations, adults in the school and the surrounding community came to recognize and respect young people's expertise. One group of four boys gave such a compelling presentation about the need for a "Violence Prevention League" of sports teams for city kids that they secured summer jobs with the city to develop the initiative. Other students' projects led variously to City Year's volunteering a day to fix up the locker rooms in the gym, the head of Boston's antigang unit making a series of presentations to seventh and eighth graders throughout the school, students' organizing a high school and college fair in the cafeteria with representatives from over twenty area schools, dissemination to local libraries and schools of a student-produced brochure about domestic violence, and other concrete actions. In retrospect, I wish some of these actions had been more oriented toward long-term change rather than one-off events. But these were nonetheless authentic civic contributions by thirteen-, fourteen-, and fifteen-year-old youth of color growing up in some of Boston's most economically impoverished neighborhoods. As with the mock trial and other examples of guided experiential civic education, these youths' contributions demonstrate how much young people have to offer if given the opportunity, and how much it serves everyone's interest to eliminate the civic empowerment gap.

In addition to building upon students' local knowledge and expertise, the citizenship projects enabled and even forced students to acquire a wide array of new knowledge and skills. Some of these skills were consistent among all of the students, including how to conduct both online and offline research, cite a source, write a persuasive letter, create a chart or graph, conduct an interview, and make a formal presentation while looking at the audience instead of at the screen. Other skills and most knowledge acquisition varied among groups and even students. One pair of students learned who runs the Boston Housing Authority, that the authority is a public entity rather than a private corporation, and that hence it was at least in theory answerable to them as citizen "owners." A group of girls learned to read a compass and a nautical map as part of their Boston Harbor Islands cleanup project. Other groups learned how to record survey data in a spreadsheet and do very basic statistical analysis of their results. Many students learned the identity of their city councilor and how to contact him or her. All students learned something about each others' areas of expertise by listening to one another's public presentations.

One semester, my entire group of eighth graders learned why it's better to write a division employee rather than the mayor. Not only did the division employees respond faster and more usefully to their letters, but when Mayor Thomas Menino came to listen to students' final presentations—at his instigation, not ours, I hasten to note!—he turned purple with fury and eventually, in a heated conversation outside the school building with me and my principal, castigated my students and me as "liars" for claiming they had written him with suggestions or requests for assistance but received no response. A week or two later, his neighborhood representative e-mailed to acknowledge that indeed, they had received the letters my students had written and that the mayor had not in fact responded. But our triumph was short-lived when she then excoriated us for "flooding" his office with over twenty letters (!!) and accused us of conducting something like a guerilla war on his mailbox rather than directing letters to appropriate officials. My students and I were all disappointed that the mayor did not take responsibility for responding to their quite legitimate concerns. At the same time, however, my students also recognized—and even reveled in—the power of their pen and of their voices thanks to this experience. They were frankly tickled to have ticked off the mayor, as they felt it demonstrated that he did care what they had to say, at least to the extent that he was concerned about the implications of appearing to ignore their appeals. This is itself useful civic knowledge, that the capacity to embarrass an elected public official can constitute a lever of power. And they learned an important lesson, too, about identifying officials who have direct responsibility for the problem they want addressed, as opposed simply to writing the most prominent person.

This interaction serves both as a caution and an encouragement for urban school districts embarking on guided experiential civic education, especially if it follows an action civics model. On the one hand, Mayor Menino's vitriolic opposition was frightening: I worried that our citizenship projects might be discouraged or even forbidden in the future by my principal or by our district deputy superintendent. Had I not had tenure and a supportive principal, I probably would have also been worried about losing my job. But on the other hand, we came through just fine. My students were thrilled to have had the experience of calling the mayor to account. My principal had my back. I wrote long explanatory, sometimes defensive e-mails to Sid Smith, the district deputy superintendent in charge of Civics in Action, and he waved them aside, totally unconcerned. As I mentioned above, four of my students ended up getting summer jobs with the city to develop their citizenship project proposal. Succumbing to fear in this particular case clearly would have been the wrong approach. I suggest, as well, that succumbing to fear and mistrust in the more general case is similarly the wrong approach in thinking about how schools must help shrink the civic empowerment gap. Although it is true that schools are difficult places in which to do guided experiential civic education, especially along action civics lines, we should treat this difficulty as a challenge to be overcome rather than an insurmountable obstacle to progress.

THE POWER OF GUIDED EXPERIENTIAL CIVIC EDUCATION

Guided experiential civic education approaches, and action civics in particular, motivate students to learn civically empowering knowledge, skills, attitudes, and behaviors because they are necessary to complete meaningful and demanding projects. The knowledge, skill, and behavior demands are intrinsic to the task, rather than extrinsically imposed by apparently arbitrary curriculum guides, standardized tests, or even teacher whim. In this respect, guided experiential civic education replicates the virtues of other forms of "authentic" education, in which students consistently demonstrate greater learning, motivation, retention, and transfer than they do in more artificial, school-based contexts. It also replicates the "stickiness" of authentic learning; when young people (or adults) master knowledge, skills, or practices to accomplish real world tasks about which they care personally, they are much more likely to retain what they have learned and apply it to other contexts than when they merely try to memorize facts or the steps of a skill for a school-based test.[35]

Guided experiential civic education also creates a virtuous circle or feedback loop, as represented in the figure, where effective learning and practice improve outcomes in a way that motivates further learning and engagement. As a youth participant in one action civics program explains, "I never really had to make any decisions like this before this kind of experience . . . Whereas, in school you work with a group to finish a project and do it the best you can, [here] you work in a group to make a good decision that will benefit other people and go farther and constantly expand."[36] Similarly, Maria, an eighteen-year-old youth community leader from Hyde Square Task Force, commented to me in an interview, "I wasn't even thinking about voting when I turned

18. But, I mean, through organizations like this who really give youth a voice and pushes them and gives them self-esteem and responsibilities, I think it changes your whole way of thinking. You become more open minded. And through that, I mean, you get to learn. Like I got to learn about politics. And not all are corrupted the way people say. I mean, you've got to stop complaining at times and start making a difference." Maria makes clear the self-reinforcing relationship among the tasks she was asked to take on such as exercising voice and responsibility, her attitudes about politics ("not all are corrupted"), and her desire to learn more about the system.

My eighth-grade students formally followed the exterior, clockwise cycle in completing their citizenship projects. Students acquired and used knowledge both to select and to learn further about a problem they cared about. In so doing, and in order to make a case to others, they practiced and applied a variety of extant and new skills. As they developed expertise both about their problem and in how to deploy the levers of power to address their problem, they developed empowered and public-spirited attitudes. Instead of being overwhelmed by the challenges they saw in their communities, they developed efficacious and engaged civic identities that pushed them to try to make a real civic difference. Their celebration and reflection about their achievements, and about obstacles they still faced, helped them acquire new understandings about both themselves and their problem in particular, and about civic action and the political process in general, which in turn set them up for another cycle.

But the backward-facing arrows, along with the internal arrows connecting each stage of the process with the others, demonstrate the more iterative and dynamic nature of the enterprise. As students improved their research skills, for example, they were able to access new knowledge. Some kinds of new knowledge—who their city councilor is and what he or she does, for example—directly impacted students' capacities to make a difference. Guided experiential civic education does not follow one

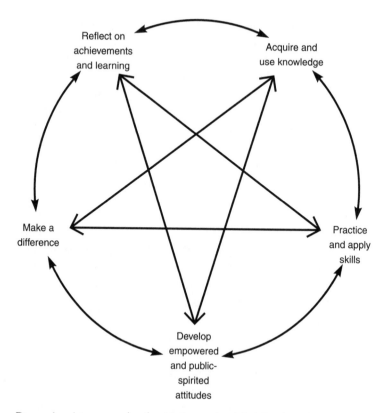

Dynamic, virtuous cycle of guided experiential civic education

neat path from conception to completion, just as its impact cannot be limited solely to one kind of capacity. Studies of other, similar programs illuminate these varieties of impacts and outcomes, including significantly higher levels of personal and political efficacy; communication, collaboration, and decision-making skills; knowledge of and interest in politics; expectation of participating in civic and political life, and sense of civic obligation.[37]

It makes sense that guided experiential civic education has such effects. There are three basic causal components of individuals' civic engagement: ability/resources, motivation/engagement, and opportunity/recruitment.[38] Guided experiential civic education addresses all three of these causal components. In enhancing students' acquisition of civic knowledge and skills, for example, guided experiential civic education increases youths' cognitive resources and abilities to participate effectively in civic and political life. Guided experiential civic education gives students direct civic engagement opportunities, and also facilitates future recruitment by introducing youth to networks of civically engaged peers and adults who get to know one another and encourage each others' participation, often across boundaries of race, class, immigration status, education level, and other traditional sources of social segregation.[39]

Furthermore, guided experiential civic education is especially promising and effective with respect to increasing motivation, which is often the forgotten middle child of political socialization and mobilization practices. By providing opportunities for civic involvement via personally meaningful experiences and projects that reflect students' own interests, guided experiential civic education builds motivation to participate that can then overcome diminished resources or opportunities in the future. As Gian, a Latino student involved in the Hyde Square Task Force whom I interviewed in 2004, explained with a quiet elegance: "Sometimes like working here makes me think that I have like the key to a door we can open. So it gives you a ray of hope." Other youth civic leaders I interviewed made similar comments. What excites these young people, at least initially, is not the civic engagement itself; rather, it is the achievement of goals that are personally important to them, for which civic engagement turns out to be the means. By achieving their goals through civic action, however, these youth remain civically engaged and are motivated to continue participating.[40]

Also, by giving young people experiences of actually making a difference in the world, including of being listened to by peers and adults, guided experiential civic education further reinforces youths' commitment and motivation. Consider the enthusiasm expressed by this community youth organization member: "I was like, 'Oh, are they listening to me? . . . I'm not even going to shut up.' You know? That's how I was. I was like, 'I'm finally being listened to. I might as well say everything I've got to say and not hide no words.'"[41] Although Gian describes himself as much more "quiet" and a "listener" rather than a talker, he was similarly excited by the importance of his role as one of two youth representatives on the neighborhood council.

> It's a good experience to be, to have that power, to being one of the people who vote on what goes on in the neighborhood, having your voice heard. It's like you could do an impact if you don't, like if you want . . . if somebody wants to build something and you don't think it's the right place or the right thing to build there, you have like the power to say, "No, I don't want that there." And you're on the seat so somebody's going to have to listen to you and listen to your opinion and why. You have to bring up a good point. So that's like an honor to have that kind of power.

The "honor" inherent in this status is as or more motivating than the exercise of power itself, which Gian rarely availed himself of given the mundane nature of most of the problems that the neighborhood council faced.

> *Meira:* Given that most of the meetings are boring, and given that you agree with the rest of the council members almost all of the time, why do you keep on going? Why do you stay there? What's the use of your continuing to be a member?
>
> *Gian:* Because it's . . . that is pretty hard. You have to know these things. It's like everything doesn't have to be fun. Like I know that now—that everything you do isn't always going to be fun. You don't always want to do everything. But in order for you to have that knowledge and for you to understand and be more aware of what's going on in your community, even if it's boring, you've got to stick there. You've got to know these things for you to build your knowledge about what you're talking about. You don't want

> to go somewhere and have no knowledge of what you're talking
> about and sound stupid. So . . . I think there's some sacrifices peo-
> ple have to make to do almost anything.[42]

In this response, Gian makes clear that he remains motivated
now by a sense of duty, and an awareness of his own civic identity—"You don't want to go somewhere and have no knowledge
of what you're talking about"—rather than by the specific benefits of the position itself. The experience is empowering, and
likely to remain motivating in the future, regardless of specific
self-interest.

These findings are consonant with evidence from other political socialization scholarship. In her Study of Political Pathways,
for example, which also focused on civically active individuals
who were demographically less likely to get involved, Hahrie
Han found that "people's commitment to issues often grew out
of their participation," rather than vice versa.[43] Likewise, a comprehensive survey of research on the long-term effects of participating in extracurricular activities and community organizations
such as 4H and Scouts finds that participation in such experiential civic activities "helps youth incorporate civic involvement
into their identity during an opportune moment in its formative
stages. Participation promotes the inclusion of a civic character
into the construction of identity that, in turn, persists and medi-
ates civic engagement into adulthood."[44]

Just as the experiential component of guided experiential civic
education taps into the strengths of "authentic" educational
practice more generally, action civics programs' approach to
youth as a positive resource—as a source of often untapped
knowledge and strengths rather than a locus of deficits—taps
into the more general strengths of culturally responsive and congruent education. Culturally relevant teaching is "a pedagogy
that empowers students intellectually, socially, emotionally, and
politically by using cultural referents to impart knowledge, skills,
and attitudes. These cultural referents are not merely vehicles for

bridging or explaining the dominant culture; they are aspects of the curriculum in their own right."[45] When youths' own cultural knowledge, habits, and practices are affirmed as having value, they can see themselves as valuable members of the polity more broadly; they also gain confidence in their capacities to navigate obstacles and challenges that arise both inside and outside of school. As Geneva, a student from Atlanta, explained when I interviewed her, "When you know that someone's from the South, or has a similar family background, you know that you can relate cause you're like, you went through what I'm going through, you made an example of what can happen some day. It's kind of like the light at the end of the tunnel, that's what that person means, cause you can relate to them, cause you've been in that tunnel." Geneva shows us how important culturally congruent content and pedagogy are for helping students see themselves in what they're being taught, and hence for seeing themselves as capable of reaching and achieving "the light at the end of the tunnel." Culturally relevant teachers "build intellectually rigorous lessons that are relevant to the real and immediate conditions of their students' lives so that students can think and respond critically for themselves."[46] Action civics directly reflects and applies these practices.

Some may object that these findings, especially those from out-of-school youth community engagement initiatives, are suspect because of self-selection bias. Young people who get involved in community organizing efforts and similar groups are more likely already to be civically motivated and engaged. There's no reason to think that imposing action civics and other forms of guided experiential civic education on other youth, who haven't sought out such experiences on their own, will have the same effect.

There are good reasons, however, to think that they will have some effect—and also that they are among the most promising means of engaging at least some youth who otherwise would remain at the bottom of the civic empowerment gap. Guided experiential civic education in general, and even action civics in particular, will not inspire all young people to become civically engaged and empowered over the long term. No educational intervention works for all students; there's no reason to think that civic engagement would be any different. But the evidence does suggest that these interventions do have significant potential to reduce the civic empowerment gap by setting youth on a path to engagement that they wouldn't have found on their own but will continue down once they're on it.

Consider the twenty-six adult and youth civic leaders I interviewed in de facto segregated, poor and non-White or Arab communities in Boston, Austin, Atlanta, and Dearborn. All of them had grown up (or were growing up) in impoverished circumstances in low-income areas of town and were from historically marginalized ethnoracial groups. Virtually all attributed their initial civic involvement to encouragement from a parent, other relative, or mentor, or a guided civic experience as part of a youth group or similar organization. Only one civic leader attributed his involvement to something else; he attributed his civic interest to having seen a television program on Martin Luther King, Cesar Chavez, and Mahatma Gandhi while he was growing up in the Texas border town of Brownsville. Admittedly, many others may also have been introduced to civic and political activities by a personal contact or youth group experience but failed to pursue additional opportunities on their own. These data do not prove that personal introduction to a civically empowering experience is *sufficient* for engendering civic engagement and empowerment. But they do suggest that such opportunities are *necessary* for doing so, and that a "simple but direct invitation to participate can make a critical difference."[47]

Furthermore, many of the youth and adult civic leaders I interviewed described in detail how unintentional their initial involvement was—even to the point of outright resistance. Gian, for example, explained how he got involved in the Hyde Square Task Force: "Well, I really had nothing to do at my house . . . All

I would do is go to school, go home and then stay home the whole weekend and go out with my parents. I was pretty bored with that. And so like I kind of wanted a job . . . It was the first chance I got, so I took it. My father told me to take it. So I took it." Another organizer at the Hyde Square Task Force, Galicia, explained that she had come in to audition for their dance troupe but filled out a job application that someone handed her and ended up a youth organizer instead. A student leader from Mikva Challenge similarly acknowledged, "I kinda joined because all the other [after school] programs were full, so I thought, 'Hey, why not?'" Lourdes, an adult civic leader with Austin Interfaith, also became involved in reform at her son's school despite herself. "When the organizer came and talked to me I said, you know, whatever. Just someone else coming here to fix things for us. So I was not really interested in it, but I was going to be polite because the principal was getting them to talk to me. I really thought, though, one year and they'll disappear. That will be it. Things will be back to normal. So, for me it was—I had no interest." Although those who stick with youth organizing and other forms of civic engagement are likely different in a variety of ways from those who don't, it seems that initial interest can certainly be made rather than born: in other words, if young people are led or even forced to participate in guided experiential civic activities that are engaging, they may well become more civically engaged in the long run. Self-selection is not a necessary condition for civic experiences to be effective.[48]

MAKING IT REAL

Guided experiential civic education approaches, including action civics, are both possible to enact in public schools and likely to have a significant effect on shrinking the civic empowerment gap. But implementation is challenging. The mock trial I described at the beginning of the chapter, for example, is one of the easiest types of guided experiential civic education in which a teacher can involve her students: it was almost entirely organized by someone else (in this case, the clinical law program at Harvard Law School); it took place mostly after school, on only one day; it required no advance preparation; and student success was virtually guaranteed. Even under these extremely favorable conditions, the endeavor took a fair amount of work to plan and execute. I needed to secure administrative permission for the trip and harangue students to bring in their permission slips, convince parents to let their children stay out until 7 P.M. on a school night and then take the subway home on their own since we didn't have $500 to pay for a school bus, find an additional chaperone, and arrange coverage for my last class period of the day, in addition to teaching, modeling, and monitoring appropriate behavior in public spaces such as the federal courthouse. And despite everything, I was still able to include only about one-quarter of my students. Insofar as most experiential civic education programs are not handed to teachers on a silver platter—the teachers themselves must develop partnerships, fundraise, place students in programs, and possibly run the activity or program themselves—they take even more time, energy, resources, and dedication to be implemented successfully. Furthermore, meaningful experiential education rarely fits into a forty-five-minute or even hour-and-a-half block of time, which tends to be the longest period available in most public middle and high schools. Hence, successful implementation requires not just work and adjustment on the part of the organizing teachers, but also by all of the other teachers who teach those students, and often by administrators and parents as well.

Guided experiential civic education also takes time out of the mandated, standardized curriculum. This is in part because it's time-consuming to have an experience—to travel somewhere, learn one's way around, learn the steps or expectations for a task, talk to people, do collaborative work—especially in comparison simply to reading and completing worksheets about others' experiences. The latter can be accomplished in a fraction of the time required for the former, although I would argue it provides only a fraction of the learning and engagement, too. Curricular trade-offs are also inevitable because although the overall lessons taught through guided experiential civic education can be broadly standards-oriented—teaching about jury duty, for example, or about how a campaign is conducted—often many of the specific lessons are quite local because experiences are grounded in the community: who is running against whom in the city council election, where the federal courthouse in Boston is located, or which interest groups need to be brought on board to turn a vacant lot into a skateboard park. There are nationally organized and sponsored experiential civic education programs, such as Kids Voting USA, Earth Force, and the Center for Civic Education's *We the People: Project Citizen*.[49] But even these appropriately connect students to local candidates and races, as in the case of Kids Voting USA, and to local issues, as in the case of Earth Force and *Project Citizen*. For teachers who are faced with the specter of already-overloaded state standards and potentially high-stakes assessments, this can seem like an untenable trade-off of locally relevant learning, on the one hand, for more general curriculum coverage, on the other.[50] This may explain why less than one-third of all students reported in the 1998 NAEP Civics Assessment that they had participated in mock trials, role playing, or dramas in their social studies class—let alone experienced any such activities beyond the school walls.[51] My firm belief is that this trade-off is more apparent than real, as "coverage" does not equal learning and the richness of authentic student experiences provides a depth and urgency to subsequent in-class learning that is hard to beat. Witness my students' enthusiasm for studying Andrew Jackson in preparation for putting him on trial, for example. I am sure that the spoils system and nullification crisis made a greater impression thanks to "witness" testimony about their effects than they otherwise would have on my crew of fourteen-year-olds. But the sacrifice of some standards-specific instruction is undeniable.

Action civics initiatives take even more time and effort—including time away from the standardized curriculum. They are necessarily longitudinal, taking place over a period of weeks or months. They often require developing partnerships with organizations outside the school. To the extent that they involve youth advocating for change, they run the risk of angering powerful adults both inside and outside the school system. To the extent that they truly follow students' interests, they require teachers to be agile and creative in mastering a wide variety of topics and issues as well as figuring out curricular connections, often on the fly. Students also require a great deal of support and thoughtful facilitation in accomplishing action civics projects. This level of support is difficult if not impossible for one teacher to provide to twenty-five or thirty students in a class, let alone to her entire student load of a hundred or more.

It is hard for me to conceive, for example, of how I could have facilitated my students' citizenship projects successfully had I been the only adult in my classroom, and if my classroom had been the only site where students were supported. At a bare minimum, I had help from my teaching intern each semester, as well as assistance a couple of days a week from two or three City Year corps members. I also recruited my mother to help one semester; another semester I pulled in a former McCormack student, who was by then attending Boston University, to assist for a few weeks. I also depended massively on support from my colleagues. Students drafted their persuasive letters under the guidance of their English teachers, typed them on keyboards borrowed from a special education teacher, edited their presentations with the help of the computer lab teacher, and cajoled teachers all around the building to allow them to use their computers to conduct research and type up their presentations before, during, and after school. Teachers, administrators, custodial staff, cafeteria workers, secretaries, and the school nurse also willingly agreed to be interviewed by students about various topics, allowed students to distribute surveys and pop in and out of their space, and turned a blind eye when they saw my students using cell phones to set up meetings or conduct interviews, although student cell phone use was strictly prohibited by the district. There is no way my students could have accomplished what they did if I had been their sole source of support, or if I had been their only advocate in the school building.[52]

To do guided civic experiential education well, therefore, requires support from within and outside schools. Teachers need assistance with curriculum and program identification and development, as well as coaching to learn how to implement them effectively. Think of how much time I would have saved and how much better my citizenship project curriculum would have been, for example, if I had known what programs were already in existence and had not been inventing so much from scratch! Teachers need time to plan, and time to teach, in longer blocks than forty-three minutes between passing periods. They need supportive colleagues and administrators—including support from principals for trading off curriculum coverage for deeper learning. They need funds to pay for school buses, field trips, and site visits, food for end-of-project exhibitions and celebrations, and other necessary resources. And teachers need assistance in the classroom itself, so thirty students at a time aren't relying on a single adult to guide them through a complex and challenging process.

Teachers also need help from organizations outside schools that develop and support meaningful and high-quality guided civic educational experiences. They need nonprofits as well as political organizations that offer internships, volunteer opportunities, or other experiential placements to young people. They need university partnerships and support. And they need parents and other members of the public who value the work they do, who recognize the importance of guided experiential civic education and action civics rather than viewing it fearfully or suspiciously as "controversial" or partisan work that is inappropriate for public school students to tackle.

How can we ensure that schools get these supports? Frankly,

lists of desired inputs—teacher training, flexible schedules, multiple adults in the classroom—are not popular in the contemporary landscape of education reform. Rather, outputs are what matter: standardized test scores, graduation rates—or in our case, performances on civic empowerment measures, whatever those might be. Furthermore, to the extent that schools are currently being held accountable for outcomes that are not tied at all to addressing the civic empowerment gap, they have little positive incentive—and many negative incentives—to pursue the kinds of resources and practices I have advocated either in this chapter or throughout this book. In the next chapter, I therefore examine if and how standards, assessment, and accountability systems could be used to move schools and educators toward implementing democratically egalitarian and empowering practices.

DEMOCRACY, ACCOUNTABILITY,
AND EDUCATION

7

In the summer of 1999, I'm preparing to teach eighth-grade U.S. history at McCormack Middle School. As I read through Boston Public Schools' Citywide History and Social Science Standards, I become increasingly alarmed. There are thirty separate topics for eighth-grade U.S. history (1815–1890), each broken down into one to five "broad concepts, issues, or ideas," five to eight further "specific objectives," plus additional "key questions" and "performance tasks." With a thirty-six-week school year, I quickly calculate, I have an average of just over one week to spend on each topic. That seems fine for Topic 18: "Scenes of war; battlefield, farm, factory, home, and hospital." We can look at some photographs taken by Mathew Brady during the Civil War and read a couple of letters or diary entries by soldiers or family members. But how am I supposed to cover Topic 11: "Jacksonian Democracy and pre–Civil War reformers: popular politics, abolitionism, women's rights, and schooling" in a week, or even two? Specific objectives for this topic include the spoils system, reformist and abolitionist goals, state's rights theory, and the achievements of William Lloyd Garrison, Harriet Beecher Stowe, Frederick Douglass, Harriet Tubman, Horace Mann, Emma Willard, and Dorothea Dix, among other objectives.

After reading over a few more such topics, equally ambitious in scope—Topic 17 covers "Abraham Lincoln: beliefs, election;

secession and war," while Topic 23 addresses "Reconstruction: aims, obstacles, and phases"—I decide to do some judicious pruning. Mann, Willard, and Dix all disappear from my revised curriculum, as does all of Topic 12: "The emergence of distinctly American religion, art, and literature." I decide further that I'll be happy if we reach 1877, the end of Reconstruction, rather than 1890 by the time the course ends. When I finish mapping out my curriculum, shortly before school begins, I have whittled it down to about twenty-five topics, each taking between three and twelve days to teach. Although I'm sorry to have lost some pieces of the curriculum, I feel good about what I've planned. I'm helped in this regard by my principal's dismissive attitude toward prepping students for the standardized test: the History and Social Science Massachusetts Comprehensive Assessment System, or MCAS. The MCAS is a valuable source of data for understanding our students' strengths and weaknesses, she tells me, but not something we're supposed to jump through hoops to do well on. Just teach students what they should be learning, and the standardized tests will take care of themselves.

My students and I therefore linger on the founding of the American Republic. We have passionate discussions about the proper balance between individual freedom and governmental control in a new country. We compare the Articles of Confederation with the Constitution, as well as examine distributions of power in other countries. For a "report card on the early presidents" project, my students brainstorm categories that presidents should be graded on, such as economic policy or moral leadership, and then work in groups to evaluate their assigned president's failures and accomplishments. All told, we spend about a month exploring the Articles of Confederation through James Monroe.

After this, we start speeding. It turns out that ignoring standardized tests is easier said than done. Over the course of the 1999–2000 school year, my eighth-grade students are subjected to standardized testing on twenty-three separate days of school:

one day each in the fall and spring for the Scholastic Reading Inventory; three days for the Stanford 9 test in reading and math; nine days for the state-wide MCAS in English, math, science, and social studies; four days for district-mandated "benchmark" tests in all four subject areas; two days in January and one day in June for school-developed "writing prompts" in English, science, and social studies; and two days for districtwide math exams. Twenty-three out of 180 days means that students are spending 14 percent of their days in school taking standardized tests—to say nothing of any teacher-developed tests such as quizzes, end-of-unit tests, or even final exams. Hence, a more accurate estimate for the amount of time our eighth-grade students spend taking tests is probably closer to 20 percent. True, I don't spend much time in class focusing on any one standardized test—there are so many, how could I possibly keep track of or focus on one?—but testing takes up so much time, especially during the last six weeks of school, that the lack of mindless test prep feels like small consolation.

Over the next couple of years, the number of standardized tests my students have to take blessedly drops. Because of this, however, my administrators' emphasis on the MCAS increases. Our students need to perform well. By the 2001–2002 school year, therefore, I have eliminated all curricular content that I predict will not be tested, no matter how fascinating and important. I spend only a week total teaching about our nation's first three presidents, because I know from analyzing past tests that questions are never asked about the challenges of governing a new nation, the Half-War, or anything having to do with Thomas Jefferson other than the Louisiana Purchase. I also set aside the three weeks between the end of April vacation and the beginning of the MCAS for review: one week to review American history from prehistory through the Fifteenth Amendment, and two weeks to review the ancient civilizations of Sumer, Mesopotamia, Egypt, India, China, Greece, and Rome, as well as the Neolithic and Paleolithic ages, Judaism, Christianity, Buddhism, and

Taoism. It's true that ancient India is only distantly related to nineteenth-century U.S. history (to say the least!), but it does appear on the MCAS, and students haven't studied it since sixth grade, when they frog-marched through ancient civilizations at a pace of one every three to four weeks.

My husband, a professor at Harvard School of Public Health, is scathing when I mention shifting from the Civil War Amendments to a review of ancient China two weeks before the MCAS. "This is ridiculous!" he bursts out. "We don't test even our graduate students on so much material in their comprehensive exams!" He is right of course, but I still feel that I have a responsibility to my students to prepare them as well as I can for the MCAS, despite the poor effect it has on my teaching.

A few years later, I am simultaneously trying to wrap up my research on the civic empowerment gap and plan my return to teaching eighth grade. I'm really looking forward to teaching again after two years out of the classroom. I become even more enthusiastic about my impending return when I learn from my principal that instead of teaching American History this coming year, I'll get to teach a new course called "Eighth Grade Civics in Action." I'm excited primarily because I now have the opportunity to put my research and ideas about resolving the civic empowerment gap into practice. But I'm also excited because of the newfound freedom it represents from the tyranny of relentless content coverage. I resolve to find out more about Civics in Action and what I can do to help along its development.

Civics in Action turns out to be the brainchild of Sid Smith, Director of Curriculum and Instruction for the Boston Public Schools. Sid tells me he has always been excited about civic education, especially for adolescents who are developmentally primed to discuss, debate, and especially act upon issues of justice, equality, and power. He has managed to introduce this course by exploiting an opening in the newly revised 2004 state history and social studies standards, which fail to specify what eighth graders should learn. His freedom to recommend a new course is also augmented by the state's decision to abandon all MCAS testing in history and social studies. Thanks to No Child Left Behind (NCLB), the federal education law passed in 2001, schools and districts are currently held accountable solely for student achievement in reading and math. They also must test every student in reading and math every year from third to eighth grade. It's therefore just not worth testing history—and frankly, with the redesign of state history standards in 2004, the development of a new set of tests is too contentious.

If teachers and students aren't tied down to the specific content and skills covered in an MCAS exam, then that offers us real freedom for curricular and pedagogical innovation. At the same time, exemption of history and social studies from testing is a mixed blessing. Because reading and math are the two high-stakes domains of knowledge, Boston Public Schools has decided to reduce social studies and science from full-year to half-year courses, with English and math gobbling up the extra instructional time.

Nonetheless, during the course design phase in Spring 2004, I feel quite optimistic about what we can accomplish in civic education across the district, and especially about what I can accomplish as a teacher. Without state standards to guide us, everything seems to be on the table—and anything can be pushed off the table, too. Brimming with ideas from my research leave, I write up a proposal that I present to Sid and his colleagues from the central office. I am wary of overpacking the curriculum, and especially of creating a course that stifles rather than fosters effective civic pedagogies. I hence propose four possible organizing approaches. The first features three essential questions: "What does it mean to make a difference? Why should people (including me) try to make a difference? How can I make a difference?" The next also frames the course around what the district calls "key questions," but with a slightly different tack: "What are the sources of conflict among individuals, groups,

communities, and/or nations? How have conflicts been managed, and how can conflicts be managed, by and among individuals, groups, communities, and nations within a democratic
context?" My third proposal recommends an expanding lens
from *self* (individual rights and responsibilities, character education, conflict resolution), to *community* (service learning, community advocacy, student government), to *polity* (political membership, rights, and responsibilities, voting, serving on a jury,
public service). As a final alternative, I suggest that we could
structure the course around an investigation of democratic civic
values such as justice, equality, liberty, rule of law, opportunity,
democracy, tolerance, stability, and transparency.

To my disappointment but no one's surprise, Civics in Action
does not end up following any of these models. As Sid, another
district administrator, and a team of eighth-grade teachers work
together, we genially but consistently tussle over control. How
much freedom should we have to pilot the course as we see fit,
and how much consistency should there be from class to class
and school to school? How much predetermined content should
we be expected to cover, and how much leeway should we have
to incorporate current events and our students' own interests? If
we pursue a "less is more" philosophy, as I strongly advocate,
how likely is this to turn into "less is less"—or at least, how
fearful is the district administration that merely "less" will result? The final course design we generate at the end of the spring
is driven more by content and less by "big ideas" than I would
like, but it is still much more promising than the overstuffed U.S.
history curriculum I was teaching before. It also features a really
promising partnership with the nonprofit organization Facing
History and Ourselves and includes a requirement that students
take some form of civic action. So I am generally pleased. Sid
seems genuinely excited, too, calling it potentially "the best
course ever."

Interestingly, by the time I return to the classroom in the fall,
the curriculum has grown again, this time thanks to Sid's tinker-

ing. There are more key questions and concepts, more vocabulary words, and overall just more "stuff" to cover. The pilot curriculum now has districtwide objectives, standards, and a recommended curriculum map. I give the map passing attention that fall; it's the 2004 presidential election, which I use as a motivation for structuring much of the content in the course, and I also develop a much more ambitious "citizenship project" (as I described in a previous chapter) than that required by the district. I try to stick to the pacing of the Facing History case study, since we are meeting regularly to talk about its progress, but otherwise I mostly do my own thing.

As I wave goodbye to my first set of students in January 2005 and welcome my next three groups into Civics in Action, I find out that Boston Public Schools has decided to introduce standardized, districtwide midterm and final exams for all eighth-grade civics classes. Suddenly, I become concerned about curriculum coverage. I worry about the fact that I am using a different curriculum map from the draft proffered by Sid. Even though he explicitly encouraged us to try our own thing, I'm feeling concerned that my students won't have learned exactly what they are supposed to have learned by the midterm. If my students do poorly, I fear, then I'll be forced to revert to the curriculum map provided by the district, about which I am less and less enthusiastic.

Over the next two semesters of teaching eighth-grade civics, my anxiety deepens. The materials that I developed to support my students' citizenship projects are adopted for dissemination districtwide and even nationally by City Year, a nonprofit partnering with Boston Public Schools on the civics curriculum. I am also presenting the materials at state and national conferences. But my students' performance on the district midterms and finals is relatively mediocre because I skimp on the mandated curriculum—in Fall 2005, because we spend time on Hurricane Katrina instead, and in Spring 2006 because students want to investigate the increase in youth violence in their neighborhood. I feel I'm doing good work, but I'm constantly worried that given my test results, my principal—or worse, the district—will pull the plug on my "renegade" curriculum.

In this book, I have argued in favor of a particular ideal of civic empowerment and education: one that is egalitarian, collective, engaged, inclusive, eclectic, change-oriented rather than status quo–preserving, responsive to lived experience as opposed to embodying solely theoretical ideals, informed by knowledge, enabled by skills, made consistent by habit, and motivated by efficacious, responsible, and critical attitudes. In the course of this argument, I have told teachers what they should do in their classes, administrators how they should revise school practices, publishers how they should rewrite their textbooks, and parents and students themselves what they should demand from their schools. As the above anecdotes demonstrate, however, telling people what to do is not the same as getting them to do it. I was told very clearly what to do as a teacher: what curriculum to cover, what learning objectives to meet, what order to teach them in. I did not comply. In the case of Civics in Action, in fact, I did my own thing virtually from start to finish even though I had been part of the group that wrote the original curriculum! Given this, what reason do I have to expect that my own ideas will have any greater traction? More specifically, according to what theory of change can I move my recommendations from words on a page to actions on the ground?

In response to this puzzle—"We experts have so many good ideas! Why won't people listen to us and put them into practice?"—many advocates of civic education reform in the United States have seized upon standardized assessment and accountability mechanisms as the way to force change. The practical effects of high-stakes standardized testing on American educational practice are clear. Thanks to such tests, the time allocated to social studies in the Boston Public Schools was cut in half overnight. Thanks to such tests, I cut substantial portions of my American history curriculum in order to focus on those people, events, and ideas that were most frequently assessed. Thanks to such tests, and the significant rewards and punishments that are tied to them, educators and policy makers at all levels have radically reallocated time, money, and training resources to focus on those skills and content for which they will be held accountable: in particular, reading, math, and to some extent science and engineering. If we want to move in from the cold and ensure that all schools focus on providing high-quality civic education to all students, many civic education advocates have argued, then we must push for mandatory standardized civics assessments and high-stakes accountability mechanisms.

I disagree with this approach, because I think it breeds bad teaching. There's little if any evidence that high-stakes testing improves instructional practice in any field. In fact, all the evidence suggests that standardized assessment and high-stakes accountability mechanisms pervert educational practices in unintended but predictable ways. Standardized assessment and accountability systems are especially ill-suited to promoting high-quality civic education practices. High-stakes civics tests would likely expand, not shrink, the civic empowerment gap by working against good civic education everywhere, especially in the poorest schools serving historically marginalized youth. They are thus inappropriate tools for promoting democratic civic education.

Standards, assessments, and accountability measures nonetheless play an essential role in preserving the democratic character of public education. This is because "democratic education" has two intertwined but distinct meanings. The first meaning of democratic education refers to education *for* democracy, *for* empowered citizenship. This is what we have been examining over the course of this book: how schools can help prepare all students to be empowered democratic citizens. Young people are at the center of this conception of democratic education, and their civic empowerment is its primary goal. With respect to this conception of democratic education, I argue, standardized assessment and high-stakes accountability systems have little to offer in practice. Because these latter systems tend to focus on short-term, easily measurable results, they are ill-suited to education for democracy's longer-term goals of transforming the United States into a more equal society in which today's often disempowered youth become tomorrow's critically engaged, efficacious, and empowered adult citizens.

But assessment and accountability mechanisms may play an important legitimating role for education *within* a democracy—in other words, in a democratically justified educational system. This second meaning of democratic education focuses not on youth but on adults, and on the extent to which public schools must be subject to democratic deliberation and citizen control in order to be legitimate.[1] High-quality standards, assessments, and accountability mechanisms in all fields serve the public good. With respect to education *within* democracy in particular, these public goods can be democratically empowering for adults. Assessment and accountability systems potentially both express and foster the nonexpert public's rightful democratic interest in influencing and exercising oversight over public schools by enabling such democratic virtues as equity, transparency, democratic deliberation, and diversity.

Is it possible to create public policies through which expert knowledge about effective civic education for children—education *for* democracy—might be implemented under conditions that still respect adults' democratic control over education—education *within* democracy? What happens when they conflict? To what extent might standards, assessments, and accountabil-

ity measures resolve these challenges, exacerbate them, or neither? Where do teachers fit in? I address these questions in the
rest of this chapter.

STANDARDS, ASSESSMENT, AND ACCOUNTABILITY MECHANISMS AS PUBLIC GOODS

High-quality standards are a public good: in other words, everyone benefits from their existence, and the benefits derived by one
person do not reduce the benefits derived by anyone else.[2] The
existence of strong standards in virtually all domains of life—
from bridge building and telecommunications protocols to food
safety, homebuilding, and automobile design—benefits everyone
equally. It is impossible to imagine living a life, at least in the
early twenty-first century, in which there were no standards governing virtually all fields of endeavor in both the public and private spheres. We all benefit from driving in cars that meet safety
standards on roads and bridges that do the same; this is true
even if we don't ourselves drive, as our safety as pedestrians, for
example, relies in part on others' cars not careening into us due
to careless automobile or road construction. Similarly, we all
benefit equally from eating food that is processed according to
accepted standards and from accessing on-line media that ac-
cord with technical standards for distribution. High-quality
standards for public enterprises in particular—public schools,
the judiciary, the military—are also public goods insofar as they
help ensure the appropriate use and expenditure of scarce public
resources. Governments should not tax people and spend resources on work that is shoddy, massively inefficient, or harmful. Since public resources will always be scarce, it is in the public interest to ensure that they are spent as wisely and effectively
as possible.

Insofar as high-quality standards are necessary for all fields of
endeavor, both public and private, it makes sense to expect that
they would be valuable in education as well. The expenditure of
public resources on education should be made not wantonly but

wisely, not haphazardly but with clear expectations and standards in mind. Furthermore, to the extent that well-developed educational standards establish high-quality educational practice, all citizens benefit. Educational standards, as much as any other standards, are a public good. To say this is not to say anything specific about the kinds, sources, range, or measures that the educational standards should represent. There is appropriately intense disagreement about all of these questions: Who should set standards? What kinds of standards should be set? What should the standards be? Who should assess the achievement of those standards? What should the consequences be for not meeting those standards? But the importance and even necessity of having public educational standards of some form should not itself be questioned.

In this case, we must also accept the necessity of having public educational assessments and accountability measures. This is again for general reasons that don't have to do with education itself, but which do apply to public education as much as to any other public endeavor. Given human fallibility, standards are meaningless if there is no way to determine (via assessment) and ensure (via accountability) that they are being met. "Every meaningful standard offers a realistic prospect of evaluation; if there were no way to know whether anyone was actually meeting the standard, it would have no value or meaning. So, every real standard is subject to observation, evaluation, and measurement."[3] In this respect, standards enable assessment, and assessment enables standards.

A corollary to this is that standards are limited to what can be assessed, and assessments are limited to what can be standardized. As a practical matter, therefore, assessment defines standards in practice. How a standard is assessed ends up guiding the understanding and actions of those attempting to meet the standard far more than any abstract articulation of the standard itself. More constructively, assessment permits the identification of "best practices" to achieve the standards; assessment enables standards to go from being mere expressions of distant dreams to becoming actionable goals. Assessment can also be used for standards-oriented diagnostic purposes—formative assessments, benchmarking, and so forth. All of these relationships between standards and assessments are independent of the role of accountability measures.

Assessments are also crucial, however, in enabling the development and imposition of accountability measures intended to motivate others to meet the standards. Assessments may be used as tools to hold various people or groups accountable for various reasons with respect to standards: in public education, these "accountability holdees" may include students, teachers, administrators, school districts, elected leaders, or citizens as a whole.[4] Teachers may use student assessments to hold themselves or their students accountable; families and even students themselves may use assessments to hold schools accountable; districts may assess to hold teachers or students accountable; citizens may use assessments to hold elected leaders accountable, and so forth. In a celebrated series of state court cases during the 1990s, for example, citizen organizations such as the Campaign for Fiscal Equity used students' wretched test results to hold states responsible for providing an inadequate education to students, particularly in poor and urban districts.[5] In an interesting flip of the accountability stakes, students at The New School in Kennebunk, Maine, use standards to hold teachers accountable. Students and teachers in the school normally decide democratically what courses will be offered each semester, but students may require teachers to offer particular courses on the grounds that students need them to achieve state standards (Maine Learning Results) as demonstrated through their public portfolio presentations.[6] Regardless of who is holding whom accountable for what, the general fact of accountability is necessary to give the standards and assessments "bite"—to make them meaningful guides to educational practice, as opposed to being seen as pesky distractions to the real work of teaching and learning. This dynamic was certainly evident in my own teaching practice.

Standards, assessments, and accountability measures are hence intrinsically interdependent and intertwined. If educational standards are deemed valuable, then educational assessments and accountability within education must be accepted as well. Note that this general statement is "platform independent" with regard to what *kinds* of standards, assessments, and accountability measures should be developed or imposed, by whom, or why. Standards may represent opportunity-to-learn, outcome, or process standards. Assessments might be formative or summative, standardized, portfolio-based, "authentic," norm-referenced or criterion-referenced, quantitative or qualitative. Accountability may be low or high stakes, individual or collective, financial or reputational or professional, negative or positive. These standards, assessments, and accountability (SAA) mechanisms may be developed and applied at various levels: school, district, state, or nation as a whole. All of these distinctions are crucially important in practice, but they come after the prior truth of the necessary relationship among standards, assessment, and accountability.

THE DEMOCRATIC VIRTUES OF SAA MECHANISMS

In addition to serving the public good in general, standards, assessments, and accountability mechanisms can also reflect and promote specifically democratic values and goods. SAAs may enact democratic values in at least six respects. First and probably most important, they reflect democratic principles of equity. By establishing common expectations, whether of goals, opportunities, resources, or outcomes, common standards reflect a commitment to the idea that all young people deserve the same quality education. It is worth noting that this is a fairly radical idea, even within a democracy. Although the United States has been a world leader in asserting the value of universal education and creating "common schools" intended to reflect democratic ideals, what students have learned inside those schools has often intentionally varied wildly. Similarly, schools in different neighborhoods, districts, or states, as well as schools serving different populations of children as determined by race or ethnicity, class, immigration status, first language, and special needs status, for example, also had vastly differing resources and objectives and taught utterly different curricula—appropriately so, many people thought.[7] So the assertion that *all* children should be given equal or at least adequate resources to master a common set of knowledge and skills is a fairly radical embrace of democratic notions of equality. The same can be said of the values underlying contemporary attempts to assess whether each child has in fact mastered the common curriculum and to hold educators, policy makers, or others accountable for children's success in doing so. The democratic significance of these values is important to emphasize even if the empirical outcomes of these policies are less equity-promoting than intended.

Second, SAAs enact the value of efficiency. This is neither solely a democratic value nor by any means the most important democratic value, but it is still important to democracies.[8] It harms the democratic good if scarce resources are used inefficiently, and especially if the public will is only partially realized because of ineffective and inefficient use of resources. Clear standards, assessments that appropriately measure achievement of those standards and enable educators and policy makers to increase achievement, and accountability measures that reward improvement may serve as essential tools for fostering efficiency.

Third, SAAs promote the democratic value of transparency. Instead of obscuring what, why, or how students are learning or confining knowledge of educational expectations to "experts," standards make educational goals and practices transparent to all citizens. Nowadays, it is easy for anyone with internet access to find out exactly what students at every grade level are expected to understand and be able to do in their own state, and to compare these expectations to those set by other U.S. states and by other countries around the world. This is not only because of the power of the internet, but because of the transparency enabled by common standards. As a result, all citizens can get involved in supporting, challenging, or revising the standards that they find. Furthermore, common assessments make transparent to citizens whether their schools and their children are meeting these standards. Instead of being put off with bland reassurances that children are "doing fine," or being bought off with high grades or jazzy bulletin boards that are not true indicators of learning, citizens could use common, objective assessments to determine whether their schools are pursuing equitable goals, providing students equitable opportunities, and achieving equitable outcomes. This level of transparency is powerful, since with these standards and assessments in hand, parents and other citizens in a democracy can hold others accountable—including holding the state accountable in case of failure.

Fourth, the public construction of standards and assessments promotes democratic dialogue and deliberation. When SAA mechanisms are developed via public processes that invite considerable public input and dialogue, democratic relationships are fostered and democratic values are enacted. Such processes may even foster consensus-building about public priorities above and beyond the educational standards and assessments being developed. Individuals may come to the initial debate about what educational standards we should adopt with a diverse and conflicting array of perspectives. But as they discuss what students should learn, and as they relate these discussions to the bigger question of what kind of society we should be creating—to which the question about student learning inevitably connects— then citizens come to engage in a public dialogue and construct at least some common understanding about our public priorities. Under the best circumstances, public dialogue about standards, assessments, and accountability measures may also enable diverse citizens to come together around a common civic vision or democratic culture.

This isn't to say standards adoption always exemplifies the best of deliberative democracy. The Texas State Board of Education's 2010 revisions of Texas's history and social studies standards, which I discussed in Chapter 4, have been rightly reviled as an educational and democratic travesty. Similar outcry both preceded and followed Lynn Cheney and Rush Limbaugh's torching of proposed national history standards in the mid-1990s. In the latter case, Cheney and Limbaugh's wholesale attack on the democratically assembled standards resulted in the unprecedented act of the U.S. Senate voting 99–1 to censure the standards—before they were released and before anyone in the Senate had read them.[9] One reason that both the Texas State Board's and the U.S. Senate's actions are so frustrating, however, is that the standards in both cases were products of an incredibly inclusive and consensus-oriented process that had led to the creation of thoughtful, critical, and balanced curriculum standards. These were eviscerated at the last minute by a group of elected representatives. Given this, it is no accident that both NCLB and the Common Core State Standards in English and math, which have been adopted by almost all states, have been quiet on the subject of history and social studies. Thanks to the Texas State Board of Education's actions, Texas schoolchildren will now be taught that the American Founders believed in a Christian nation and that McCarthyism was justified. But in both cases, the initial state and national history standards developed through inclusive democratic deliberation and debate demonstrated greater breadth of vision than those constructed solely by a narrow slice of experts or by teachers working alone.

Fifth, democratically constructed SAAs can serve as a tool for enabling more robust democratic governance. One important justification of the value of democracy is its capacity to aggregate individuals' vast and diverse array of knowledge and perspectives; because of the range of knowledge and skills brought to bear, better choices are made by the group as a whole than could ever be made by a small cabal of leaders, no matter how intelligent and well-educated they are.[10] Correlatively, they enable (and instruct) teachers to base their practices on collective wisdom or expertise rather than on their individual whims or idiosyncratic knowledge. This was the democratic value that I may have violated in enacting my Civics in Action curriculum as I did. Instead of educating according to the common consensus, I sometimes subjected my students to my individual judgment about what was valuable for them to learn. But if SAA mechanisms work well, they ensure that the democratically expressed will is enacted through public education. The tyranny of the individual teacher exercising her own judgment about what and how to teach is replaced by the authority of the democratic collective.

Sixth and last, by establishing some common goals or characteristics of schools, and common measures of anticipated outcomes, SAAs may foster diversity along other dimensions. This reflects the key liberal democratic values of freedom and diversity. If all schools are held accountable for achieving certain educational outcomes, then they can be left alone to determine their own means of achieving those outcomes. Because their students meet the standards, Big Picture schools can keep class time to a minimum, virtually eliminate specific academic requirements, and place students in compelling internships with photographers, auto mechanics, and biotechnology firms. Because *their* students meet the standards, KIPP schools can lengthen the school day and require Saturday school, mandate schoolwide chants and rules about how to make eye contact, and drill reading and math skills. Montessori schools, expeditionary learning schools, proto-military academies, Deweyan learning communities, Essential Knowledge schools, farm schools, virtual schools that rely entirely on technology-mediated learning: all of these educational enterprises may flourish better in a system that uses common standards, assessments, and accountability mechanisms to ensure that all students are learning than in one that has no SAAs and uses bureaucratic trivialities to control educators' work instead.

THE FAILURES OF SAAS TO SERVE THE DEMOCRATIC PUBLIC GOOD

For every democratic public good that standards, assessment, and accountability systems may promote, however, there is a correlative potential harm. SAAs may be based on collective prejudice and ignorance rather than wisdom; they may elevate public input to such a degree that they inappropriately discount expert knowledge; and they may promote consensus by preserving an exclusionary status quo rather than incorporating diverse voices. They may twist accountability into mistrust and develop standards via political maneuvering rather than public participation. Instead of promoting democratic dialogue, they may dissolve into vitriolic disputes about the "culture wars," promote standards and assessments that stymie youths' development of democratic capacities, and quash learning by overloading standards and expectations with trivia. Assessment and accountability mechanisms may lead even social liberationist schools to adopt "drill and kill" teaching methods, as in the case of Freire Charter School in Philadelphia, which features a photo on its website of individual desks in rows, trumpets its "many, very specific" required classes that leave no room for student input in the first two years, and even requires school uniforms.[11] It's hard to imagine *Pedagogy of the Oppressed* author Paolo Freire embracing his namesake!

Many of these ills characterize SAA mechanisms as they have developed and been applied in the United States over the past few decades. By seeing where SAA mechanisms have diverged from and even undercut their democratic potential, we gain insight into the characteristics and roles that SAA mechanisms need to be democratically justified. Consider, for example, how assessments and accountability measures not only enable the establishment of meaningful standards, but also define and limit such standards. When we conceive of SAAs as the articulation and measurement of discrete bits of knowledge and skills—what we want students to "know and be able to do"—which is the case in the United States today, then we are disabled from setting educational goals about the kinds of people we would like our students to become and the kinds of holistic challenges we would like them to be able to meet. Assessments that are sufficiently objective to enable fair and transparent accountability mechanisms often fail to be sufficiently flexible and context-dependent to measure the kind of standards mastery citizens care about.[12] They also frequently impede high-quality teaching. Accountability measures may promote educators', students', and others' adherence to and achievement of the standards, but pervert incentives and distract educators and students from the real work and value of learning.

These ills arise in large part because SAA mechanisms are necessarily blunt rather than fine-grained. They necessarily cannot specify, assess, or hold students or educators accountable for mastering every piece of knowledge or skill that is considered valuable.[13] When standards are so specific, they quickly overwhelm teachers and students alike. Both of these pathologies were at work during my years teaching American history in the Boston Public Schools. Furthermore, accountability systems that impose consequences for multiple dimensions of student performance may also sink under their own weight. This has been one significant problem with NCLB. It measures schools' "Adequate Yearly Progress" (AYP) with respect to up to twenty-two different subgroups. Failure to make AYP for any one subgroup has resulted in the school's being deemed a failure overall—a result that has afflicted over one-third of all U.S. schools, and nearly half of schools in some states.[14] It is a bit of a Catch-22; the greater the number and rigor of the criteria that students and schools are held accountable for meeting, the greater the chance that students and schools will fail to meet all of the criteria, and the less likely they will be either to build upon their successes or to concentrate on a few high-value domains of improvement. Standards, assessments, and accountability measures are stuck in the Goldilocks dilemma: there can't be so many that they overwhelm students or the system, and there can't be so few that they shrink the curriculum and provide little support for or information about student learning. They need to be "just right." Even then, they still necessarily provide only blunt expectations for and standards of success, which then in turn makes them crude tools for educational evaluation, improvement, or reform. These blunt expectations are further dulled when students and educators are held accountable for their achievement on standardized tests that, because they are comparatively cheap to develop and grade, privilege superficial knowledge and easily measured skills over deep knowledge, complex skills, attitudes, habits, or behaviors.[15] This Goldilocks dilemma accounts in large part for the six-year delay (and counting) in reauthorizing the Elementary and Secondary Education Act, which will replace NCLB. Everyone recognizes what isn't working, but it is much harder to forge a consensus about what could work.

Since standardized assessments end up measuring and accountability systems end up rewarding subsets of what is educationally valued—whether to reduce the cost of developing and scoring the assessments, to reduce the amount of time students spend taking tests, to enable the assessment of the same knowledge and skills over time so as to permit longitudinal comparisons, or other reasons—they risk further perverting educational practice in a variety of ways. Most fundamentally, they skew teachers' instructional efforts toward the narrower content range and even the format and other essentially arbitrary features of the test itself, rather than toward the full range of educational standards or (most importantly) toward student learning.[16] As Robert Behn explains, "'What gets measured gets done' is, perhaps, the most famous aphorism of performance measurement. If you measure it, people will do it. Unfortunately, what people measure often is not precisely what they want done. And people—responding to the explicit or implicit incentives of the measurement—will do what people are measuring, not what these people actually want done."[17]

When I was teaching American history with an eye toward the MCAS, for example, I didn't teach more or better history; I just taught different history—out with the Half War and Emma Willard, in with the Louisiana Purchase and Mesopotamia. My colleagues and I also spent countless hours prepping kids for the exact format of MCAS questions. We used a variation of the MCAS scoring criteria to grade all significant pieces of student writing. We also gave "benchmark" writing prompts in English, math, and social studies three times per year, using questions modeled after MCAS open-response questions and scored using MCAS-based criteria. These tactics often consumed vast amounts of energy to little result. One year, I organized an eighth-grade MCAS quiz bowl in the auditorium using hundreds of questions I had carefully photocopied onto overhead transparencies. The top two teams sat on stage and used buzzers to answer questions about the obstacles facing Lewis and Clark on their westward exploration, Confucius, the Emancipation Proclamation, principles of archaeology, the economic basis for the English colonies, the Rosetta Stone, and so forth. I was really excited about how much the students were learning—until I discovered at the end of the period that our amplifier had cut out about ten minutes into the game. None of the students in the back of the auditorium had been able to hear a thing.

"But they were so attentive," I protested. "They must have been able to follow what was going on!"

"Meira, they were getting to hang out for an hour instead of attending class and doing work," one of my colleagues pointed out. "They weren't going to jeopardize that by cutting up and acting the fool! Anyway," he added consolingly, "it was good for them to see other students being rewarded for their academic knowledge, even if they weren't learning anything themselves."

In all of these ways, SAA mechanisms in the United States typically end up promoting compliance rather than educational improvement. This should not be surprising, Richard Elmore argues, since SAAs are rarely designed with a theory of improvement in mind.

> While state and federal accountability systems may be improvement-oriented in intent, they are often compliance-oriented in practice. In order for an accountability system to be based on improvement, it has to embody an underlying theory of how schools improve their performance. Simply constructing an incentive structure of standards and testing around the expectation of steady improvements in performance is not a theory of improvement. A theory of improvement actually has to account for how people and schools learn what they need to know in order to meet the expectations of the accountability system. By this standard, no existing state or federal accountability system is improvement-oriented.[18]

Evidence from Canada and England reinforces this point. SAAs in and of themselves do not teach educators how to improve their practice; at best, they can motivate educators to seek such improvement and learning through increased professional development, professional learning networks, collaborative observation and analysis of best practices, and other initiatives focused on their own learning.[19] This mismatch between goals and outcomes also partly accounts for the frequent misuse of SAA systems, including making decisions that assessments were not designed to address, drawing conclusions the data cannot support, or imposing high-stakes rewards and punishments on the basis of a single, necessarily imperfect test, all with utter disregard for the measurement limitations inherent in the test.[20]

Furthermore, many of the democratic goods that SAAs have the potential to amplify are equally likely to be diminished thanks to SAAs' power and reach. For example, although SAAs foster some forms of educational diversity, they stymie other equally desirable dimensions of democratic diversity. At the end of the last section, I gave examples of how SAAs enable *pedagogical* and *structural* diversity given common learning goals. But of course, insofar as the learning goals themselves are fixed— insofar as they are codified into standards that all students are expected to achieve—then they necessarily restrict diversity along that very dimension. To the extent that they define a whole rather than just part of schooling, therefore, SAA mechanisms threaten to neglect the authentic range of educational needs and desires among the diverse array of communities and young people within contemporary democratic states. Individual students with a diverse array of passions—for creative writing, chemistry, hip hop, environmental justice, dairy farming, cars, online gaming, mathematics, Navaho history—may be prevented from developing their knowledge and skills because of the lock-step requirements imposed by comprehensive, time-intensive SAA mechanisms. In addition, students and communities that have strengths in domains not recognized or covered by state standards and assessments—strengths such as bilingualism, biculturalism, moral reciprocity, or deep understanding of the natural environment, for example—fail to be "credited" with these capacities or encouraged to build on and develop these strengths further; instead, only their "deficits" in relation to the established standards are noted and "remediated." These failures of SAA systems to foster legitimate and even desirable forms of diversity within a pluralistic democracy harm individuals and the democratic polity alike.

To the extent that standards define and limit what is taught as "common knowledge," the diverse range of knowledge and skills that strengthen democratic deliberation and action may especially be eroded. Christine Sleeter argues, "Allowing for development of diversity and expertise can serve as an intellectual resource for constructive participation in a multicultural democracy and a diverse world. It is to our benefit that we do *not* all learn the same thing, beyond the basic skills. Helping next generations acquire intellectual resources of diverse communities, including those that have been historically silenced, can enable creative dialogue and work, out of which we might better address problems that seem intractable."[21] It is important to recognize here that the critique is not that standards reflect a particular privileged viewpoint (say that of White, Christian males) or that they exclude historically marginalized perspectives. In this case, common standards would be perfectly acceptable so long as they were more inclusive of diverse voices. Rather, the critique is that democracy itself is weakened when all students learn only one set of ideas and skills, no matter how inclusive and worthwhile those ideas and skills are. Also, as standards, assessment, and accountability systems move upstream from individual educators, parents, and communities to higher-level aggregations—whether school districts, states, or even the nation—they run the risk of reducing local democratic control. "Accountable autonomy" measures at the local level can potentially offset this risk by increasing local "empowered participation."[22] But this relationship between local and more distant actors is inherently quite fragile, and it depends on many of the goals (standards), measures (assessments), and accountability outcomes to be set at the local level in a collaborative fashion between public officials and community members.

Furthermore, many people appropriately fear any additional aggregation of power and control by the state, especially over the education of young citizens. As standards, assessments, and accountability measures become ever more tightly linked—a phenomenon that is lauded within education policy circles because such integration represents greater conceptual and organizational coherence—they also inevitably get closer to defining and privileging "official knowledge." Such official knowledge may be partisan and protective of those in power. It may disempower those who hold minority viewpoints or promote otherwise partial and blinkered perspectives. These concerns lead many to argue that the state should not be in the position of defining and hence limiting the scope of knowledge and skills to be acquired by the next generation of citizens. They argue that state control over education reverses the appropriate democratic relationship between the state and citizen, where the citizen exercises voice and power to influence the state and not the other way around. As I have discussed in detail elsewhere, from the child's perspective schooling controlled by a democratic state is probably less limiting than schooling controlled by her parents. I am therefore dubious about this argument on the grounds of individual rights.[23] But I do think this argument has considerable merit from an empirical perspective. Knowledge will inevitably be less limited, less subject to state censorship or control, more representative of the extremes of opinion and not just the inherently conservative "safe middle," and more freely available if there is educational diversity rather than a set of state-imposed hegemonic standards, assessments, and accountability measures.

A final potential threat posed by SAAs to education within a democracy results from their use as both implicit and explicit sorting mechanisms. They sort knowledge and skills, students, teachers, schools, administrators—everything and everyone ends up being assigned a relative value: worthy of inclusion or not, high achieving versus low achieving, effective versus failing, eligible for a specific good like merit pay or grade level promotion or not.[24] Whether or not this sorting can be justified on policy-oriented grounds, it stands in significant tension with democratic values. Democracy entails civic equality among citizens—equality of political voice, and equality before the law. To the extent that standards, assessment, and accountability systems are now sorting young people—young citizens—as early as seven or eight years old and annually after that, we should question the democratic implications of their position in contemporary education.

SAA'S THREAT TO EDUCATING *FOR* DEMOCRACY

SAA mechanisms also pose threats specifically to high-quality civic education: in other words, to education *for* democracy. These threats derive from two contradictions between SAA mechanisms on the one hand and empowering civic pedagogies on the other. First, standardized goals, content, and assessments are uniform and static whereas empowering civic education is context-specific and dynamic. Second, standards, assessments, and accountability mechanisms that are developed by people or groups outside the school—district or state administrators, national expert groups, or even local citizens—and then imposed upon teachers and students in the school inherently undermine good civic education by removing the locus of control from teachers who need to model empowered democratic civic action and students who need to practice it. I address both of these challenges in this section.

Let us begin with a quick review of "best practices" in civic education. I have argued that good civic educational practice in a democracy:

- constitutes an ongoing part of the formal curriculum throughout elementary and secondary school (and beyond) just like math, reading, and other "core" subjects;
- recognizes that students' personal identities interact with their civic and political identities and their civic and political power, both by their own lights and by others';
- enables students to construct historically accurate, personally meaningful, and empowering civic narratives;
- helps students recognize that "ordinary" people can make extraordinary differences by introducing them to local role models, not just to distant and apparently superhuman heroes, and teaching them collective action techniques;
- is responsive to and inclusive of local concerns, contexts, and conditions;
- balances students' development of civic and political knowledge, skills, attitudes, identity, habits, behaviors;
- infuses the life of the school via teachers' use of democratic pedagogies, a procivic school culture, meaningful opportunities for students to exercise their civic and political voice,

and the ready and equal availability of co-curricular and extracurricular activities that promote civic and political engagement and leadership;

- incorporates controversial issues and current events into the curriculum;
- provides students frequent and rich guided civic experiences in which students learn *through* civics and by *doing* civics, not just *about* civics; and
- takes a critical perspective; doesn't merely support or replicate the status quo.

As these qualities remind us, "good civic education" does not mean merely "civics" instruction in the traditional sense: i.e., structures of government; how a bill becomes, or more likely fails to become, a law; individual rights and responsibilities; and a few key court cases. Traditional civics of this sort may be necessary, but it certainly isn't sufficient for achieving the goal of truly moving young people to participate meaningfully and effectively in democratic civic and political life. This latter goal can be met only with a much more ambitious, complex, grounded, and dynamic approach to civic education that contains features such as those I sketch above. The problem with respect to SAAs is that such empowering civic education is contextual and dynamic—two characteristics that are undermined by the standardized and relatively fixed nature of public educational standards and assessments.

If young people are to participate effectively in democratic civic and political life, then they need to master at least some location- and context-specific knowledge and skills. Even within a single state or region, the structures and power dynamics of local civic and political institutions vary widely. Towns may be governed by a strong mayor, a weak mayor in collaboration with the city council, a city manager, or some other structure. The schools, public housing authority, and parks departments may be subject to mayoral control, controlled by the county or state, or function as independent agencies with directly elected governing boards among other possibilities. A city may have a strong and civically involved business community and a thriving civil society, or none at all. Students may live on farms and travel up to twenty-five miles to attend a regional comprehensive high school; alternatively, they may live and be educated in a rural village, a suburban bedroom community, a dying industrial city, or a booming metropolis. These differences matter and need to be taken into account in teaching students how to exercise civic and political power effectively. Whether they want to advocate for more youth summer employment opportunities or get a skateboarding area added to the design for the new park, they need to know whom to work with and how; this will differ from place to place.

It is not only civic and political structures whose particularities matter with respect to civic education. Many of the other good civic education practices listed above also demand significant contextual flexibility and variation. How a school constructs and maintains a "procivic" culture will necessarily vary widely depending on the educational and civic context. A small school with a relatively homogeneous and stable student population will inevitably and appropriately build a different kind of procivic school culture than a large school with a highly transitory and diverse population. Schools in neighborhoods plagued by gang violence and ethnic tensions may work to create a civic school culture that emphasizes safety, mutual respect, and a willingness to identify shared goals across lines of apparent difference. A school located in a highly stable and even insular neighborhood, by contrast, may strive to create a civic culture that provokes (respectful) disagreement and dislodges students from their conformist complacency. Similarly, sensitivity to community context and even individual student variation applies to educators' roles in helping students construct empowering civic narratives that are consistent with their experiences and cultural narratives outside of school.

Finally, the kinds of civic skills and attitudes that young people need in order to become empowered democratic actors vary depending on individual and community context. Minority students and communities may need to be able to codeswitch from Black Vernacular English to Standard American English, from religious to secular language, or from cultural references that are familiar only to the minority group to those that resonate with the majority group as well. The ability to shift like this is key to acquiring and exercising power effectively in a democracy based on majority rule, but it is not an easily standardized goal or practice.[25] On the flip side, members of majority and privileged groups may need to be taught about the existence and persistence of injustice in society; they may also need to learn that these injustices are partly systemic rather than simply examples of individual wrongs done to others. This is an equally crucial component of good democratic education—but is probably as unnecessary in communities with substantial ongoing experiences of injustice as teaching codeswitching is in communities that already speak the "language of power."[26]

High-quality civic education is dynamic as well as contextual. Guided experiential civic education—*doing* civics, not just learning *about* civics—is necessarily an adaptive enterprise. What students experience, how they experience it, what help they will need in making sense of their experiences: all of these are unpredictable and dynamic features of teaching and learning. Good civic education is dynamic also insofar as its content shifts in response to current events and local issues. As I mentioned in my second narrative at the beginning of this chapter, one of the reasons I didn't cover all of the standards that Sid had laid out for Eighth Grade Civics in Action was that important events kept getting in the way. Yes, the structure of the court system is important—but so are the causes and consequences of Hurricane Katrina's devastating attack on the Gulf Coast. As a pedagogical matter, I believe it made sense to take advantage of Katrina as a lengthy "teachable moment." We were able to use something my students actually cared about to explore federalism, the rule of law, separation of powers, individual versus collective responsibility, geography, demographic analysis, media literacy and critical analysis of public rhetoric: "refugees from" versus "survivors of" the hurricane. As a civic matter, too, we were able to orient students' energies and outrage toward constructive and effective action. But we didn't cover the court system, or parliamentary systems, or a number of other items on the school district's curriculum map—and it would be disingenuous to suggest that we likely would have had Hurricane Katrina not occurred. The next year, as I mentioned, we spent time analyzing the horrific rise of violence perpetrated by and against youths in my students' neighborhoods.

The public conversation about crucial civic matters is also continually in flux—not solely because of the unpredictability of current events, but also because democracies promote continued contestation over issues of public import. Diana Hess usefully characterizes one dynamic aspect of this public conversation: namely, the passage of public controversies from being "closed" and settled on one side to being "in the tip" as matters of "open" controversy and then potentially to being "closed" on the opposite side. One potent example of this is the public conversation surrounding the legality and morality of Japanese-Americans' incarceration in internment camps at the hands of the U.S. government during World War II. When Hess started teaching, the matter was mostly closed. Internment camps were seen as a justified response to a wartime necessity. Over the next thirty years, this position slowly came under fire and the internment camps became legitimate matters of controversy. Nowadays there is no controversy again, but only because the camps are fairly universally regarded as a shameful blot on American history. Issues "in the tip" today in the United States include immigrants' civil and social rights, same-sex marriage, and the death penalty. As I discussed in Chapter 5, good civic education in secondary schools will at some point engage with these issues or others like them.[27]

In all of these examples, good civic education is demonstrably contextual, particular, and dynamic—the opposite of the standardized, common, and static nature of standards and assessment systems. To the extent that standards specify exactly what content and skills students will learn, or what issues may be covered, and to the extent that psychometrically valid standardized assessments are then used to assess students' mastery of the standards, these will both in principle and in practice work against the dynamism and contextual grounding of good civic education.

The other way in which standards and assessment systems that apply across schools and districts work against good civic education is by removing the locus of control from those who want and need to model civic action—teachers—and those who want and need to practice civic action—students. When teachers are working in a system that denies them the opportunity to exercise professional judgment or democratic voice or participation, they cannot model the "arts of democratic life."[28] Even more to the point, they can't model *empowerment* if they feel totally disempowered. Similarly, students can't practice democracy, or experience empowerment, if they have no voice and no power in determining what they learn, why, how, or when. In this respect, the imposition of SAA measures upon teachers and students, no matter how carefully considered they are, intrinsically undermines good civic education.

LIMITING SAAS FOR THE SAKE OF DEMOCRACY

When I taught American history in 2002, I attempted to adhere closely to the history standards and assessments that had been developed in a broadly democratic and inclusive process at the state and district level. In doing so, however, I left out anything that I thought wouldn't appear on the test. I dropped social and labor history, as well as the history of women and non-Whites who were not central figures in traditional, moderately triumphalist political narratives. I also neglected an inquiry-based or constructivist approach in favor of curriculum coverage—even going so far as to shift from American history to ancient India and China in the few weeks before the exam. Thus, my efforts to adhere to democratically constructed and implemented SAA mechanisms perversely led me to teach a curriculum that neither lived up to the spirit of the standards, which were much more inclusive than I felt I could be, nor embodied good civic education content or practices.

By contrast, the absence of any state-level democratic consensus about or accountability measures for what I should be teaching in 2004 enabled me to provide quite an effective civic education, but only for half a year with each student since we lost time to high-stakes, heavily tested math and reading instruction. At the same time, this teaching opportunity was made possible only because we happened to have a curriculum director who was personally enthusiastic about civic education, and because I wasn't (yet) getting in trouble for doing poorly on the district exams. Furthermore, even assuming that I was a good civics teacher for those four semesters, it's not clear that my choice to "go rogue" was itself justifiable or democratically legitimate. The 340 or so students I taught over the course of those two years were legally obligated to attend school, and even to pass my specific class in order to move on to high school. I was a public school teacher, a finger of the long arm of the state, unilaterally making decisions about what and how my students should learn in order to become good citizens. My relief at having no state-level oversight and having been spared the potential negative consequences of the district's assessment system—in other words, my relief at not having been disciplined or fired for patently failing to teach many of the items deemed testworthy on the Boston Public Schools' midterm and final exams—may demonstrate the relative democratic illegitimacy of the low-stakes accountability system in place, rather than anything positive about its openness to creativity and innovation.

Alternatively, my pedagogical choices may have represented

the height of democratic legitimacy, insofar as I was partly constructing the civics curriculum with my students rather than merely complying with the demands of elite adults like Sid Smith. My decisions were unilateral from the perspective of school district administrators (or would have been had they been aware of what I was doing), since I did not consult with them at all about my curricular and pedagogical decisions. But they were decidedly collaborative with my students and teaching interns, as well as to a limited extent with local community organizations. My intern Kirsten convinced me that we should devote serious time to Hurricane Katrina in the fall of 2005—a cause that our students enthusiastically embraced. My students' interests and concerns guided our investigation into the history, causes, and consequences of youth violence in their neighborhood. Their "citizenship projects" fostered collaboration between my students and city agencies, local nonprofits, Boston Police, and other organizations. In these respects, by choosing to ignore the districtwide standards and assessments, we were upending the civic empowerment gap both procedurally, insofar as my students exercised greater sway than district administrators, and substantively, as my students gained knowledge and skills that helped them become more empowered citizens.

This is ultimately where the conflict between SAAs' use within schools as expressions of democratic agency among adults and SAAs as tools for promoting young people's development of democratic agency—in other words, between education *within* democracy and education *for* democracy—comes to a head. There are good reasons to have adults democratically involved in setting public educational standards, assessments, and accountability measures. In so doing, adults get to participate in enacting and promoting democratic values through means that also reflect democratic principles. As Terry Moe puts it, rather more contentiously, "The public schools are agencies of democratic government, created and controlled by democratic authorities. They are not free to do what they want. Everything about them, from goals to structure to operations, is a legitimate matter for decision by their democratic superiors and subject to influence by the political processes that determine who those superiors are and how they exercise their public authority."[29] This is a powerful articulation of schools as sites of democratic governance. But at the same time, Moe's assertion reveals how treating the school as a site or tool of democratic governance can subvert students' development of democratic agency. Students' voices are ignored in the formulation above. Neither they nor their teachers are recognized as democratic equals, but instead are treated as subordinates to their "democratic superiors" and to "democratic authorities." Both teachers and students become demoralized and apathetic, waiting for orders from above rather than taking initiative or developing their own sense of self-worth as democratic actors. SAAs' potential to enable collective democratic control over schools thus risks disabling young people's civic development.

These tensions between education *within* and *for* democracy play out in the construction and goals of educational standards, assessments, and accountability mechanisms. Education *within* democracy positions schools as sites and objects of adults' democratic engagement. Educational standards are produced by democratically engaged adults. As such they may

- promote a variety of aims, with civic learning treated merely as one of many goals;
- reflect the status quo, including the interests and perspectives of those currently in power thanks to their position at the top of the civic empowerment gap;
- respond to current civic anxieties rather than representing a vision for a more egalitarian and democratic future;
- express the public will, with expertise derived from the collective wisdom of the engaged democratic populace.

Assessments of these standards are also subject to democratic control by citizens in general. They enable the adult public to exercise ongoing, real-time oversight in order to hold teachers and schools accountable for fulfilling the public will.

By contrast, education *for* democracy positions schools as tools for students' democratic empowerment. Educational standards are created at least in part by experts in civic education because their purpose is to enable high-quality civic education. As such they may

- promote civic learning as one primary aim;
- strive to transform society in order to achieve a revitalized democracy in which citizens are fully engaged and empowered;
- take the long view, with an eye to helping today's students grow into democratically minded and empowered adult citizens in the future;
- derive expertise from elites in the civic education field, including researchers, educators, and policy makers.

Assessments of these standards are treated as tools for determining whether students are mastering the knowledge and skills needed for civic empowerment. In this respect, they are less oversight-oriented and more future-directed. Only time will tell whether schools are effective at empowering their (former) students. Given this, education *for* democracy is ultimately accountable to students themselves, and to the future active citizens they will ideally become.

An ideal system of standards, assessments, and accountability mechanisms would somehow enable and achieve the best of each of these worlds without succumbing to the dangers I've introduced above. They would give us a means of avoiding the kinds of perverse incentives and outcomes that infect education in the United States today. They would also explicitly reflect, enact, and promote the democratic values and principles that lie at the heart of legitimate democratic civic education. Because this utopian ideal is not possible, however, serious reform or implementation of educational standards, assessment, and accountability mechanisms in a democracy must confront these tensions directly.

To start with, we need to reduce educational standards, assessments, and accountability mechanisms' reach over schools. In the United States, they govern virtually every aspect of educational practice. This is not the case in other developed countries. In England, for example, the National Curriculum, along with its associated assessments, is intended to take up approximately two-thirds of students' and teachers' time. This permits (in theory, at least) the collective to exercise some control over schools while also leaving teachers and students free to exercise their own judgment and local control over teaching and learning. If 50–60 percent of students' time was taken up meeting publicly created standards in the United States, that would still leave a lot of time for the kinds of good civic education practices I value. It would also leave room for the kinds of democratic diversity of values, community characteristics, and practices that are threatened by overly comprehensive SAA systems. Furthermore, if some of the SAAs were created distally and some more locally, that might provide the right balance of equity (comparing students in urban and suburban schools along similar dimensions), and community responsiveness (doing what's right by a particular set of students).[30]

When SAAs do force hard choices, we should favor education *for* democracy over education *within* democracy. Schools should serve students' democratic interests in becoming empowered citizens over adults' democratic interests in expressing their values. At the same time, we must recognize that SAAs are neither the sole nor even most effective means of fostering these democratic goods and improving civic education. We cannot standardize and assess ourselves into civic greatness, if for no other reason than that the perverse interactions among standards, assessments, and accountability mechanisms cannot be fully overcome. Rather, SAAs are one small tool among many approaches necessary for fostering good civic education and democratic practice.

These other approaches include: effective teacher recruitment and selection that takes civic propensities and skills into account; extensive professional development at all stages of educators' and administrators' careers; increased resources (time, money, scheduling, instructional minutes/courses); effective and empowering professional networks of educators who are committed to enacting and improving civic education; and public outreach and even "messaging" designed to change the public conversation about the purposes of schooling and the place and models of civic education that we should pursue as a result.

Admittedly, none of these approaches fully addresses the issue that schools are sites of civic engagement, and hence that democratic control is likely to trump these "expert" recommendations. This is essentially a chicken-and-egg problem. Until schools implement high-quality civic education, few adults will likely know or care to advocate for such education. But unless they do, then schools will likely have little motivation or opportunity to improve the civic education that is offered. My hope, nonetheless, is that the recommendations above will help create a virtuous circle in which public schools *within* democracies are enabled and empowered by the citizens who exercise "authority" over them to offer an education *for* democracy.[31]

In a system of education *within* a truly civic democracy, schools would serve as sites of adults' *enlightened* democratic engagement. They would

- serve a variety of aims, but hold civic learning as a central goal;
- reflect a public consensus in favor of robust democratic engagement;
- respond to current aspirations for a robust civic sphere; rely on informed collective wisdom.

Standards would be approached as a means of collaboratively constructing a deliberative public conception of the democratic good. Assessments, likewise, would be conceived of as tools for

Standing Up, Talking Back

Each semester, my eighth-grade students are required to take the Boston Public Schools' End-of-Course Assessment for Civics in Action. One question asks them to select an issue "of importance to your school, your community, the country, the world, and you." They have to present the issue as a question: for example, should United States forces withdraw fully from Iraq this year? Students then have to answer the question from two different perspectives, offering at least three reasons in favor of each perspective. Finally, they have to write an essay that argues in favor of one of the positions they've identified, supporting their thesis with evidence, details, and "a strong conclusion." They are expected to accomplish this, write a second similarly complex essay, and answer twenty-five multiple-choice questions in about an hour.

One spring, my student Jacquari submits the following response, which I have reproduced verbatim.

> Should boston build parks to reduces violence?
> Yes they should build parks to reduces violence
> No they shouldn't build parks to reduces violence
> One reason why they should is to keep the peace the second reason is to have a place for children and the third reason is to have a place were we can run free.

1 reason why they shouldn't is because their will be shoot outs. 2 reason is because people will be smoking and drinking in the park leaving trash behind them 3 reason is because gangs will be hanging out let [late] in the playground and be distroying it with spray paint.

I really think they should be then again they shouldn't because when there are different gangs contacts the fight always be in parks and suppose that there are a hole bunch of little kids in the park and then there are a group of gang members standing or chilling [hanging out] their then they enemies come over and start shouting at the others then some one lose they kid over some one else for nothing. Example when the girl was trying to leave the park in grove hall [a local housing development] because of a gang then as she was walking out the park she got shoot in the back and died.

Jacquari takes this exam June 15, 2005. In the first six months of that year, from January 1 to June 15, there have been twenty-four murders, including six teenagers.

My family and I have lived in Jamaica Plain since 1999. It's part of the city of Boston, about four miles from Jacquari's neighborhood of Dorchester. Although some areas of Jamaica Plain can be dangerous, primary concerns about parks in my corner of the neighborhood include bike path maintenance and the preservation of Boston's Mounted Police unit. Everyone loves the horses and the friendly cops who ride them, and there's ongoing concern about whether the horses will be sold off in the next round of budget cuts. When my daughters and I think about parks, we discuss which ones have good multiage playgrounds, whether the sprinklers will be on yet to combat the summer heat, or why we have to be clandestine about letting our dog swim in Jamaica Pond off-leash. Frankly, by letting our golden retriever cavort leash-free, we constitute the neighborhood ruffians. We frequently run into friends and neighbors at the pond, the Arboretum, and the playground. It would not occur to any of us to view parks as an existential threat—nor even as a potential respite from violence, since violence also does not normally intrude on our day-to-day lives.[1]

Jacquari desperately wants to experience parks in a similarly positive light. "I really think they should be [built]." But to his despair, he concludes that this very civic act endangers kids too much. Not only do parks fail to provide a respite from violence, they provide an excuse for it. He worries about the "bunch of little kids in the park." He doesn't want yet one more kid to be shot in the back. Despite his wish to be optimistic, he is driven to conclude, "Then again they shouldn't."

My family and I live in the same city Jacquari lives in. We are governed by the same mayor and city council. Our neighborhoods even border the same park, the largest in the city. But Jacquari's civic spaces are fraught with fear while ours are not. When Jacquari passes an open space, he sees room for turf wars between rival gangs. When I pass an open space, I see room for a Frisbee game, maybe a picnic. In this respect, Jacquari's city is not the same as my city. I don't see what he sees; I don't live as he lives; and no matter how imaginatively I try to understand the world from others' perspectives, my insights will never match his own.

I have no idea what Jacquari is up to these days. I have not seen him since the Fall 2005 day he came to visit his old middle school teachers to shoot the breeze. He was struggling in high school—no surprise, given his abysmal academic skills. He was sweet and charming as always, but he made it clear he didn't know how long he'd last. He had already been held back in elementary and middle school, so he was an old freshman. Jacquari would turn sixteen in a couple months, and could legally withdraw from school. It is painful to write these words, but I'd be astounded if he made it through high school.

Nonetheless, Boston would be a better place if Jacquari were involved in its governance. Dorchester would be better off if Jacquari had the knowledge, skills, and commitment to work with others to address the problems he identifies in his essay, as well as the many other civic challenges he told me about when he was my student. Jacquari himself would be better off if he could translate his anguish into action—especially into civic action in collaboration with others who also want kids to be able to "run free" in a park rather than watch for a gun at their backs. Furthermore, Jacquari would be better off if he could have translated his knowledge of his own academic weaknesses into empowered engagement, into a declaration that his own education was outrageous and unjust. We owe Jacquari a real education, one in which a fifteen-year-old eighth grader would have had the capacity to write flowing, compelling prose with a mastery of capitalization, spelling, grammar, and mechanics. We owe him an education that would enable him to exercise self-determination: individually, over his own life, and collectively, in collaboration with others, over the life of his community.

It's not that we didn't try. Virtually every teacher at McCormack worked hard to teach every one of our students. But good intentions, and even raw, hard work, are no excuse. It is un-American that Jacquari's childhood experiences led him to flee parks, to fear random shootings, to write a final exam essay with not a single grammatical sentence. And yet, this is the America in which he lives.

Who will right these wrongs? Many adults will try. That is both necessary and appropriate. Many White, middle-class adults will try. That is also necessary and appropriate. But Jacquari, along with Krystal, James, Carmen, Benny, Deyana, Shaniqua, Laquita, Travis, Maria, and their peers—the students whose voices I have tried to amplify within these pages, as a counterpoint to my own—cannot trust solely in adults, let alone well-intentioned White, middle-class adults. They must act themselves—which also, perhaps paradoxically, means that schools must also help enable them to act.

It is fashionable these days to speak of education as the "civil rights issue of our time." President Obama and his secretary of education, Arne Duncan, have both spoken in these terms. So did President George W. Bush and his first secretary of education, Rod Paige. They are joined by university presidents, entertainers, journalists, politicians, business leaders; everyone seems to agree that education is the civil rights issue of our time. As a rhetorical matter I wish we talked about it as the civil rights *struggle* of our time. "Issues" don't scream injustice or demand great sacrifice, which public schools these days require. But rhetoric aside, I am generally pleased by this consensus. Educational injustices are both cause and consequence of broader political, economic, and social injustices in the United States. It is utterly appropriate that we wage a new struggle for civil rights with education at the core.

Oddly, however, we have generally left young people out of the process. Most current and former civil rights movements have been fought by the oppressed themselves—by people fighting for their own rights. They have had allies, but the movements were necessarily and appropriately led by those seeking more rights for themselves. We treat education differently, seeing adults as the appropriate actors on behalf of youth. This shouldn't be the case. Educators should be activists *with* youth. We need to transform schools into places that teach students themselves to take on the civil rights struggle, not just academies that prepare students passively to receive the benefits that the struggle confers. As Charles Cobb, the twenty-year-old designer of the original Freedom Schools curriculum, explained, his goal was to enable students "to stand up in classrooms around the state and ask their teachers a real question" and "make it possible for them to challenge the myths of our society, to perceive more clearly its realities and to find alternatives and ultimately, new directions for action."[2] That is what our schools should be doing today, too. Schools—especially *de facto* segregated schools serving low-income youth of color—should be reconstructed as politically empowering institutions that give young people the tools to fight the civil rights struggles of our and *their* time along-side us.

There is evidence that this is possible. In pockets all around the United States, educators and youth are working together to create a more just nation. In June 2011, for example, members of the United Teen Equality Center testified to the Joint Committee on Education at the Massachusetts State House in favor of a bill they wrote to require high-quality civic education for all public high school students. The civics curriculum would be required to include the "function and composition of the branches of local, state, and federal government, the history of social movements, current events, and community-based action and service-learning projects."[3] Members are primarily low-income youth of color; many are current or former high school dropouts, and many were members or associates of gangs. They have been inspired by their own political empowerment via the United Teen Equality Center to fight for similar opportunities for all Massachusetts teens. As of January 2012, their lobbying and legislative efforts are ongoing.

In Providence, Rhode Island, a group of Generation Citizen students from Hope High School has proposed an amendment that is likely to be passed by the Rhode Island legislature in 2012. "Reciprocity Agreements—Setoff of Personal Income Tax" allows Rhode Island residents to check a box on their tax form that redirects a portion of their state income-tax refund to the Rhode Island Community Food Bank. Ninety-two percent of Hope High School's student body is non-White; over three-quarters qualify for free or reduced-price lunch. Students developed their plan after conducting a survey that demonstrated that many of their peers were affected by hunger. In his description of the students' proposal, one columnist commented admiringly, "It's so simple and it makes so much sense that it's amazing no one came up with it before. A simple check on a tax form could provide substantial help for the Food Bank at a time when its services are more vital than ever."[4] It may be no accident that young people who themselves have experienced hunger generated such a "simple" but "vital" idea. This is what overcoming the civic empowerment gap can accomplish—not only for young people, but for their communities as well.

Young people are also working together to improve their own school communities, often by exercising their voices to transform their school culture. In Chicago, student members of Sullivan High School's Peace and Leadership Council researched and wrote a white paper containing recommendations for improving both student attendance and in-school suspension policies. These are understandable concerns; Sullivan's average daily attendance in 2010 was 81 percent, meaning that a fifth of all kids are absent each day of the year. About 95 percent of the students are low-income and non-White; less than half graduate from high school within five years of entering as freshmen. Sullivan administrators were so excited by the students' insights that they not only requested that the Peace and Leadership Council expand their recommendations specifically with respect to these challenges, but also sought recommendations for increasing student voice across the school. The group, which is sponsored by Mikva Challenge, is understandably thrilled. One of the first initiatives will likely include regular focus groups with students being held in in-school suspension. Students are starting to be seen as collaborative partners for solving problems, not just the sources of trouble themselves.

Back in Boston, the Boston Student Advisory Council worked for three years to secure the Boston School Committee's approval of their student-developed "Student to Teacher Constructive Feedback Policy," also known as the "Friendly Feedback Form." Students can now use this tool in every high school to reflect on their own learning, as well as provide teachers with useful feedback on classroom management and instruction. It will become a formal part of the teacher evaluation and feedback process in 2013. The Boston Student Advisory Council, which is administered by the Boston Public Schools in partnership with Youth on

Board, is now working to get student evaluation of teachers to be part of the formal teacher evaluation process statewide. Their mantra: "We're the ones in the classroom. Ask Us!"

These examples of youth civic action benefit students, their school communities, and their fellow citizens. They demonstrate young people's capacities to make a difference—and remind us that most youth *want* to change the world for the better given the resources and opportunities to do so. They can't do it all on their own. Young people need adult support. They need us to help them master the skills to put their hard-earned knowledge into action. They need us to help them contextualize their historical understanding and their own lived experiences in a way that inspires action rather than disengagement. They need us to help them navigate the arcane and twisting bureaucracies of contemporary public life, and see beyond their personal experiences to a larger, collective whole. But at the same time, young people also need us to understand when we should get out of the way. We need to recognize when it's their turn to make the phone call, speak up at the meeting, or make the video that's destined to go viral. We need to give young people space so that they can start creating their own histories of empowered engagement.

Ultimately, this is for our own benefit as much as theirs. If we want to live in a better world, in a stronger democracy, in a United States that truly stands one day for "justice for all," we need the insights, energy, and knowledge that young people—including low-income youth of color—bring to the struggle. We also need the wisdom they will bring when they are older. Tackling the civic empowerment gap today expands the ranks of active citizens both now and in the future. This long-term, communal, and *equitable* engagement is essential for achieving the "more perfect Union" to which we all aspire. It is time for us to move forward together.

NOTES

PROLOGUE

1. All names of students and teachers in this book have been changed to protect their privacy.

2. Dawson 2006, 248; see also Dawson 1994, 2001.

3. Nielsen Media 2000.

4. Bishop and Cushing 2008; Frankenberg and Lee 2002; Grier and Kunnanyika 2008; Iceland et al. 2002; Irons 2002; Tharp 2001; Anderson and Jones 2002.

5. This isn't quite true, insofar as I was very aware of being one of the very few Jews living in my neighborhood in Austin, Texas. In fact, when I attended Stephen F. Austin High School in the mid-1980s, I was one of four Jewish students out of a student body of 1,600. The other three were my sister, my best friend, and his sister. But that experience felt as if it was due more to sheer numbers—there are a lot more Christians than Jews in Texas—than to outright patterns of segregation.

6. Hilliard et al. 1990; Asante 1998; Hilliard 1998; see also Binder 2002.

7. Levinson 1999.

8. Carter 2005.

9. See Bowles et al. 2009; Kim 2009 for emerging evidence of this from an economic perspective, and Small 2009 for a sociological analysis.

10. Orfield and Lee 2006; see also Orfield et al. 1996; Orfield 2001, tables 14 and 18.

11. Sable et al. 2010, table A8.

12. These findings were calculated using school-level data from district and state websites.

13. Sable et al. 2010, tables A1 and A9.

14. Orfield and Lee 2007, 5–6.

15. Orfield et al. 1996; Orfield 2001; Orfield and Lee 2007.

16. Quotations from Loury 1997 and Ladson-Billings 2004, respectively. See also Shujaa 1996; Walker and Archung 2003; Horsford and McKenzie 2008.

17. KIPP 2011b, 2011a.

18. Grant 2009.

19. Patterson 2001, 192.

20. Bracey 2009, 691. See also Massey and Denton 1993; Hochschild and Scovronick 2003, 48–49.

21. Parents Involved 2007, 15.

22. Ladson-Billings 2009. See also Bell 1980, 2004.

23. U.S. Census Bureau News 2008. See Payne 2008 for a thoughtful discussion of the causes and consequences of this fact.

24. Delpit 1995.

25. There is an increasingly robust debate about the nature and roles of ideal versus nonideal theory in contemporary political philosophy. See, for example, Sher 1997; Murphy 1998; Farrelly 2007; Geuss 2008; Robeyns 2008; Stemplowska 2008; Swift 2008; Simmons 2010. Although I don't explicitly address this literature here, I intend both the form and content of this book to advance the case for nonideal political theory as a valuable and necessary enterprise.

26. Robert Fullinwider draws a very nice distinction between the training of historians and the training of history users. I am definitely in the latter camp. See Fullinwider 1996.

1. THE CIVIC EMPOWERMENT GAP

1. I also discussed my students' response with a few African-American friends and colleagues; they were both less surprised by and less critical of my students than I. They, too, however, were unconvinced by my students' claim that Bush himself had ordered the attack. In retrospect, they tended to agree more with Walter Mosley's comment in the *New York Times Magazine:* "I have never met an African-American who was surprised by the attack on the World Trade Center. Blacks do not see America as the great liberator of the world. Blacks understand how the rest of the world sees us, because we have also been the victims of American imperialism." See Solomon 2004.

2. Wright 2006; Mayer 2009.

3. Shklar 1991; Smith 1997; Foner 1998; Gerstle 2001; Horton 2005.

4. Data about youth come from Lutkus et al. 1999; Baldi et al. 2001b; IES: National Center for Education Statistics 2007; Torney-Purta et al. 2007; U.S. Department of Education et al. 2007; National Center for Education Statistics 2011. For data on adults, see Verba et al. 1995; Delli Carpini and Keeter 1996; The Pew Research Center for the People and the Press 2007.

5. Ayers and Ford 1996; Niemi and Sanders 2004; Students from Bronx Leadership Academy 2 et al. 2008 all provide thoughtful discussions of and evidence of this problem.

6. Hart and Atkins 2002.

7. Galston 2001; Delli Carpini and Keeter 1996.

8. Verba et al. 1995, 305.

9. In 2008, for example, 94 percent of the Black and 98 percent of the White voting-age population were citizens, as compared to only 63 percent of voting-age Hispanics and 68 percent of voting-age Asian Americans. Hence, voting rate disparities combined with citizenship status disparities result in only 32 percent of resident Hispanics and Asian Americans' exercising their voice at the ballot box in the 2008 presidential election, as compared to 65 percent of resident Whites and 61 percent of resident Blacks. U.S. Census Bureau 2010c, table 4b. To the extent that there are group-specific interests or perspectives (a question I take up in Chapter 2), and that voting is one powerful way to express these interests or perspectives, these data suggest that Hispanic and Asian Americans have vastly less national electoral power than Black and White Americans do.

10. Wolfinger and Rosenstone 1980; Verba et al. 1995, chapter 8 and figure 7.2; Nie et al. 1996; Lopez 2003; Lee et al. 2006b; Lopez et al. 2006; Mollenkopf et al. 2006; Pearson and Citrin 2006; Ramakrishnan 2006; National Conference on Citizenship 2008; Corporation for National and Community Service and National Conference on Citizenship 2010a.

11. Corporation for National and Community Service and National Conference on Citizenship 2010a.

12. Specific issues' presence in the political landscape can also shift participatory patterns at least for short periods of time. Immigration reform efforts, including rallies, marches, and protests surrounding support for the DREAM Act and opposition to the 2006 proposed congressional immigration bill and the 2010 Arizona anti-immigrant legislation, mobilized significant numbers of Hispanic and first- and

second-generation immigrant youth and adults. Most likely as a result of these sorts of protests, more youth who were immigrants and children of immigrants reported participating in protests in 2006 than native-born youth. See Lopez et al. 2006; Seif 2010.

13. For more on the civic attitude "chasm," see Smith and Seltzer 2000. Numerous surveys from just the past twenty years have affirmed these findings, including Washington Post et al. 1995; Sigelman and Tuch 1997; Public Agenda 1998; Washington Post et al. 2000, 2001; Baldi et al. 2001a; Dawson 2006. For evidence on race-related civic attitude gaps among young people in particular, see also Dawson 1994; Sidanus et al. 1997; Dawson 2001; Sanchez-Jankowski 2002; Lopez 2003.

14. Putnam 2000, 138.

15. Rosenstone and Hansen 1993; Kinder 1998, 831–832; Uslaner 2002; Chong and Rogers 2005; Mollenkopf et al. 2006.

16. Sharpton 2003.

17. Ladson-Billings 1994.

18. See Rubin 2007 for a powerful description and analysis of this problem. Also, see Chapter 2 for a fuller discussion of these findings about trust.

19. Verba et al. 1995, table 12.14; Lake Snell Perry & Associates and The Tarrance Group 2002; Carnegie Corporation of New York and CIRCLE 2003.

20. Rogowski n.d.

21. Jacobs and Skocpol 2005; Bartels 2008.

22. For evidence of this relationship, see Feinberg 1998, 47; Kinder 1998; Damon 2001, 127, 135. On the other hand, Melissa Williams powerfully challenges this emphasis on identity, arguing instead in favor of replacing "citizenship-as-identity" with a model of "citizenship as membership in a community of shared fate." But even her model of "shared fate" requires that students see themselves and their future as being "enmeshed in relationships" with others. See Williams 2003.

23. Dawson 1994, 2001.

24. Kasinitz et al. 2002; see also Stepick and Stepick 2002.

25. Rubin 2007; Abu El-Haj 2008.

26. Carnegie Corporation of New York and CIRCLE 2003, 4.

27. *Plyler,* (457 U.S. 202).

28. Westheimer and Kahne 2004, 239, 240, table 1.

29. See Bennett 2007; will.i.am 2008; Grossman 2009; Jenkins 2009. By the time this book gets published, I'm sure that even these examples will seem quaint and hopelessly out of date. This is one reason that I have chosen not to devote a whole section or chapter to "digital

citizenship." Although this is an absolutely crucial area of study and action, I am concerned that anything I write would be obsolete within months. Furthermore, I last taught middle school in 2006—ancient history from the perspective of thinking about how to incorporate technology into civic education.

30. See Young 2000 for an especially thoughtful discussion of "expressive action" in politics.

31. Scott 1985, xvi.

32. Powell Jr. 1986; Lijphart 1997, 3; Jaime-Castillo 2009.

33. Feldman 2011.

34. Montgomery 1993; Sachar 1993, 175–176; Skocpol 1999; Skocpol et al. 2000; Montgomery 2001, 1268ff; Freeman 2002.

35. Jeffrey Stout is blistering in this regard: "If our most powerful elites are now essentially beyond the reach of accountability, as they increasingly seem to be, then why suppose that our polity qualifies as a *democratic republic* at all? It appears to function, rather, as a plutocracy, a system in which the fortunate few dominate the rest. And if that is true, then honesty requires that we stop referring to ourselves as *citizens,* and admit that we are really subjects. The question of democratic hope boils down to whether the basic concepts of our political heritage apply to the world in which we now live." See Stout 2010, xv.

36. See Kinder 1998, 831–832, and also Allen 2004. It is possible, of course, to read groups' lack of participation as delivering a judgment about the illegitimacy of contemporary U.S. government. In this case, it is misguided to bemoan unequal levels of participation and representation in conventional political and civic life as creating an illegitimate state, because to do so presumes the underlying legitimacy of the state if people simply participated more equally. Jane Junn argues, for example, that "modes of political participation such as voting or making a campaign contribution are implicitly acts in support of the maintenance of a political system that may not be in the best interests—instrumental or expressive—for people who benefit least from that system . . . Suspending the assumption that groups ought to see participation in the political system as desirable provides the opportunity to train the lens away from the failings of racial mobilizing organizations or inactive citizens, and instead, focus scrutiny on the participatory institutions of democracy that may themselves inhibit the achievement of equality." See Junn 2006, 35.

37. See Ober 2010 for an intriguing discussion of both the value and the challenge of aggregating diverse sources and kinds of knowledge.

38. Bartels 2008, 5.

39. Jacobs and Skocpol 2005, 1.

40. Kahne and Middaugh 2008; Kahne and Sporte 2008; Wilkenfeld 2009 provide powerful evidence about school-level differences. See Cohen and Dawson 1993; Alex-Assensoh 1997; Hart and Atkins 2002; Atkins and Hart 2003; Hart et al. 2004; Wilkenfeld 2009 for research into the geographic influences on civic engagement, identity, and knowledge and skills.

41. See, e.g., Gutmann 1987; Macedo 1990; Gutmann 1995; Callan 1997; Feinberg 1998; Levinson 1999; Brighouse 2000; Blum 2002b; Reich 2002; Levinson and Levinson 2003; American Educational Research Association 2006; Orfield and Lee 2007; *Parents Involved,* 551 U.S. 1 2007 (Stevens, J., dissenting); Ryan 2010; Minow 2010. See Foster 1997 for an important competing view.

42. See Macedo et al. 2005 for a careful examination of the ways in which electoral, municipal, and voluntary sector policies and practices often impede the quantity, quality, and equality of civic engagement in the United States.

43. Numerous books have been written about this travesty, to great rhetorical purpose but little practical avail. Some of the more recent important books include Kozol 2005; Grant 2009; Ryan 2010.

44. Nie et al. 1996; Galston 2003.

45. On civic courses, see Delli Carpini and Keeter 1996; Niemi and Junn 1998; Damon 2001; Galston 2001; Torney-Purta et al. 2001a; Torney-Purta 2002; Carnegie Corporation of New York and CIRCLE 2003, 14; Kahne and Middaugh 2008. On dropout rates, see Chapman et al. 2010.

46. Du Bois 1996 (1903).

47. See Kerr 2002 for a thoughtful discussion of learning about, through, and for citizenship.

48. Rawls 1993.

2. "AT SCHOOL I TALK STRAIGHT"

1. I use the term "ethnoracial" in part because it is simply less cumbersome than "race and ethnicity." More important, however, I use the term to emphasize the indistinction between racial and ethnic group membership. As the opening anecdote reveals, the boundary lines between what we call race and what we call ethnicity are blurry and contested. Some students embrace both ethnic and racial markers, while others assert the racial character of designated ethnic status ("I'm Spanish, not White!"), or alternatively reject any racial designation in favor solely of ethnic group membership ("I'm Cape Verdean, that's it. I'm not White or Black."). Racial and ethnic dividing lines also change over time, with "races" such as Jews or Italians becoming assimilated into

the "White" race and converted into ethnicities instead. This process is but one manifestation of the cultural construction, rather than natural existence, of both race and ethnicity. See Ignatiev 1995.

2. Loury 2008; Alexander 2010.

3. Lee, Ramakrishnan, and Ramírez 2006b.

4. U.S. Census Bureau 2010a.

5. Junn 2006.

6. Chong and Rogers 2005, 65. See also Dawson 1994; Verba et al. 1995; Dawson 2001; Southwell and Pirch 2003; Junn 2006.

7. Young 2000.

8. Smith and Seltzer 2000; Huddy and Feldman 2006.

9. On deliberative democracy's potential to reconfigure political power relationships, see Mansbridge 1980; Gutmann and Thompson 1996; Young 2000. On strategic minority voting, see Guinier 1994.

10. Blum 2002a; Frederickson 2002; Mukhopadhyay et al. 2007.

11. Patterson 1997, 173; see also Zack 1993; Blum 2002a.

12. Appiah and Gutmann 1996; Olsen 1997; Portes and Rumbaut 2006; Chong and Rogers 2005; Jones-Correa 2005; Hochschild 2005; Lee 2005.

13. There is a burgeoning literature—reflecting accelerating facts on the ground—about young people's creative remixing of national, cultural, ethnoracial, religious, and other identities in a display of "flexible citizenship" (Maira 2009). See, for example, Maira 2004; Pollock 2004; Suárez-Orozco 2004; Maira and Soep 2005; Louie 2006; Abu El-Haj 2008; Knight 2011.

14. I also wish to acknowledge, with regret, that I don't even touch on Native Americans in this chapter or the book as a whole. This is in part because the systematic oppression and murder of Native Americans has worked so well that Native Americans now constitute barely 1–2 percent of the U.S. population (U.S. Census Bureau Population Division 2010). It is also because Native Americans are themselves members of sovereign nations toward which they may appropriately direct their civic and political engagement. Native Americans are not the only dual nationals living in the United States, of course. Many immigrants and children of immigrants are dual nationals, with important, apparently positive, consequences for their civic and political involvement in the United States; their political and civic involvement in their home country is positively correlated with their political and civic involvement in the United States (Cain and Doherty 2007). But Native Americans' dual nationality is different insofar as they often live in their sovereign territory; nor, certainly, are they immigrants to the United States. Rather, the United States "immigrated" into their land, with horrific

consequences. Furthermore, U.S. citizenship is itself a contested "good" for many Native Americans. Some scholars and activists, including Porter 2004 and Bruyneel 2004, have argued that awarding of U.S. citizenship to Native Americans in 1924 might plausibly be seen as an act of aggression designed to destroy tribal members' national identity and sovereignty. Given these many complexities of citizenship, history, and identity, and frankly given my lack of expertise in this area, I have chosen not to address issues of Native American political incorporation and empowerment.

15. Levinson 2003b.

16. See Pollock 2004 for a brilliant discussion of many of these challenges.

17. Waters 1999, 26; see also Portes and Zhou 1993; Portes and Rumbaut 2006. See Lee 2005 for a similar description of the "blackening" of Americanized Hmong youth and the "whitening" of "good" Hmong kids who did not adopt hip-hop styles of dress. Dance 2002 illuminates this process among African-American students themselves, while Warikoo 2011 provides a thoughtful comparative analysis of this process among both U.S. and English adolescents.

18. See Hess 2009a, chapter 6 for a thoughtful discussion of the pros and cons of maintaining political neutrality.

19. McIntosh 1990; Harris 1993; Lipsitz 1995; Solomona et al. 2005.

20. See Singleton and Linton 2006; Howard 2006; Pollock 2008 for thoughtful discussions of this problem and suggestions to White educators about how to achieve antiracist pedagogies. In general, however, there's astonishingly little research literature about the effects on students of color of teachers' explicitly acknowledging and encouraging discussion of racism, whether with respect to academic achievement, self-concept, motivation, efficacy, engagement, or any other measure. Two notable exceptions are Ladson-Billings 1994 and Tatum 1992, but both works are now almost twenty years old, and Tatum's addresses college students rather than adolescents. Also with respect to college students, there is some experimental data about the effect of making stereotype threat explicit, which is different from but related to racism. It appears that merely making stereotype threat explicit, without also giving students added coping strategies, tends to worsen its effects. Teaching students positive response strategies may lessen the effect of stereotype threat (Johns et al. 2005). There is also inconclusive research about the effects of parents' preparing their children for ethnoracial bias. See Hughes et al. 2009 for a discussion of and contribution to this literature. Overall, however, the research literature is poor.

21. For evidence of these and many related ills, see Shapiro 2004; Grant 2009; Bonilla-Silva 2010; Jung et al. 2011. For perhaps the most extreme version of the persistence of ethnoracial discrimination in the twentieth century, see Blackmon 2008. This is a devastating account of how local laws and law enforcement were used to enslave Black men through World War II.

22. On voting access, see Friedman 2005; Raskin 2005; Barreto et al. 2009. On fear of arrest or deportation, see Fellner and Compa 2005; Paoletti et al. 2006; Gleeson 2010. For comprehensive coverage, see Jung et al. 2011.

23. Lee 2005, 4.

24. See, for example, Takaki 1993. Johnson et al. 2007 provides a history of anti-Asian discrimination and U.S. citizenship. On implicit attitude tests, see Devos and Banaji 2005. Jost and Banaji 1994 and Jost et al. 2002 address system justification.

25. See Carter 2005 for more on dominant versus nondominant social capital. See also Delpit 1995 and Bourdieu 2006.

26. Sanders 1997; Fung 2004a.

27. Dawson 1994; Smith and Seltzer 2000; Young 2000.

28. Smith and Seltzer 2000, 10; Harris-Lacewell 2007, 41.

29. Dawson 2006; see also Herring 2006; Huddy and Feldman 2006; Harris-Lacewell et al. 2007.

30. See Dyson 2005, 71–72 for an eloquent discussion of this phenomenon.

31. Harris-Lacewell 2007, 34 and 35.

32. Lee 2010.

33. Thomas and Campo-Flores 2005. See Dyson 2005 on beliefs about intentional flooding during Katrina.

34. Thomas and Crouse Quinn 1991; Guinan 1993; CNN.com 1996; Koch 1996; Brandt and Badrich 1997; Siegel et al. 2000; Levinson 2003a. These differences in perception and belief are not confined to the United States. See, for example, the nuanced account in Fassin 2007 of AIDS treatment policies in South Africa.

35. Dyson 2004, 47.

36. In a November 2001 poll, three-quarters of Americans opposed "racial profiling in general," but "fully 66 percent supported such practices for persons of Arab or Middle Eastern descent." See Lee et al. 2006a, 6.

37. Bobo 2001, 281.

38. Haney Lopéz 1996; Delgado and Stefancic 2001; Rothenberg 2002; Bergerson 2003; Lewis 2004.

39. Tatum 2008 provides one of the most comprehensive and

thoughtful research-based discussions of these phenomena. For one account of these dynamics from an antiracist White perspective, see Wise 2008.

40. This ties in with a contrast I have drawn elsewhere (Levinson 2009b) between toleration based on appreciation of commonalities (we all love our children; we both value fidelity) with toleration based on an appreciation of the reasons for one's differences. I suggest that the true basis of mutual respect must be the latter. But I also suggest that toleration—let alone mutual respect—is often most challenged when people are forced to confront reasons that truly do feel different and "other": in other words, beliefs that truly seem opposed to one's own. To paper over these differences on the grounds that the off-putting "other" "must really be trying to say" something consonant with majoritarian perspectives is not what respect means, and it perpetuates majority privilege. This is one of the most powerful critiques of Rawls's original position, that it collapses difference into a solitary person behind the veil who reasons things out from ostensibly objective but in fact culturally and politically situated first principles.

41. Okin et al. 1999; Appiah 2006.

42. Dyson 2004 provides a thoughtful and agonized discussion of this issue; see also Lareau 2003.

43. James Baldwin eloquently rejects this ideal when he laments that "White Americans find it as difficult as white people elsewhere do to divest themselves of the notion that they are in possession of some intrinsic value that black people need, or want. And this assumption—which, for example, makes the solution to the Negro problem depend on the speed with which Negroes accept and adopt white standards—is revealed in . . . the unfortunate tone with which so many liberals address their Negro equals. It is the Negro, of course, who is presumed to have become equal" (Baldwin 1962, 94).

44. Dawson 2001, 288, quoting Glenn Loury.

45. Washington 2004, 129.

46. Dawson 2001, 101, quoting Eugene Rivers.

47. Binder 2002.

48. Du Bois 1996 (1903), 5.

49. See Lee 2005 for an account of the pervasiveness of the equivalence of "White" with "American" among first- and second-generation immigrant Hmong youth.

50. Delpit 1995; Delpit and Dowdy 2002.

51. Carter 2005, 47.

52. Christensen 1994.

53. Baker 2002; Wheeler and Swords 2006; Carter 2005, 30. Such transcription and translation exercises, or "Spoken Language Study," are now a standard part of the English National Curriculum for ninth and tenth graders. Students' capacity to do such work counts for 10 percent of their score on the English Language GCSE—a national, standardized exam that all students take at the end of the tenth grade.

54. Christensen 1994, 145.

55. Lee 2005, 56–57.

56. Fogel and Linnea 2000.

57. Tatum 2007.

58. Levinson 2003a.

59. Junn 2006, 46. See also Chong and Rogers 2005; Mollenkopf et al. 2006; Southwell and Pirch 2003.

60. Chong and Rogers 2005, 45.

61. Zaff et al. 2008.

62. Chong and Rogers 2005; Junn 2006. One form of racial solidarity that has carried particular historical weight among African Americans for more than a century is the philosophy of "racial uplift." Racial uplift invokes a wide and even contradictory range of meanings; it centers, however, on the ideal of racial equality achieved at least in part through African Americans' striving for economic and political equality. Advocates of racial uplift historically disagreed over whether that is best achieved through assimilation, accommodation, or separation. They also disagreed about whether racial uplift was achieved through the elevation of the Black middle class, who could then "reach back" and "pull" lower-achieving Blacks up into the middle class, or whether it was best achieved through collective elevation of all Blacks simultaneously. Finally, some advocates of racial uplift understood it primarily as an individual phenomenon, by which individual Blacks proved to Whites that they—and by extension, other African Americans—were worthy of racial egalitarianism, while others advocated a collective approach to acquiring and using economic and political tools to further the goals of racial equality. Contemporary scholars have also attacked philosophies of racial uplift for being proto-colonialist, classist, and sexist, among other sins. See Moore 2003. For all of these reasons, I do not address racial uplift in the main text, nor do I advocate it as a philosophy that schools should teach in service of closing the civic empowerment gap. But it is nonetheless a powerful current in African-American solidaristic thought and political education. See Gaines 1996 for a thoughtful and searching analysis of racial uplift in Black twentieth-century thought.

63. Ginwright and James 2002 discuss this phenomenon with respect to youth organizing.

64. DeSipio 2001; Jones-Correa 2005; Wong 2006; Bloemraad 2006.

65. Miller 2000, 41.

66. This claim obviously raises a huge range of normative considerations, from affirmative action to group rights to equality of opportunities versus outcomes. Because I can say nothing satisfactory about these issues in an endnote, and to address them in the main text would take us too far off course, I will simply let them dangle—tantalizing but unresolved.

67. McAdam 1988.

68. Southwell and Pirch 2003.

69. Seider 2008a, 2008b.

3. "YOU HAVE THE RIGHT TO STRUGGLE"

1. This same school reform model has now been embraced by U.S. Secretary of Education Arne Duncan under his "Race to the Top" initiative.

2. I address codeswitching in detail in Chapter 2.

3. Tamara Beauboeuf-Lafontant frames this succinctly when she explains that "consciously focusing our attention on the political rather than cultural experiences of students provides us with the way of productively engaging with the reality of a majority white female teaching force educating and increasingly nonwhite public-school population. If we consider that the successful education of poor students and students of color, hinges on *political* congruence between teachers and students, rather than on cultural similarity, we become interested in helping teachers identify and reflect on their political convictions and their pedagogy as manifestations of their stance toward the positive struggle for democracy. The history of good black segregated schools and the teachers fondly recalled in the schools is important to the concept of political relevance because it evidences this positive struggle, and demonstrates that politically relevant teaching has a long and proud past" (Beauboeuf-Lafontant 1999, 719).

4. See Barton 1995; Epstein 1997, 1998, 2000; Wineburg 2001; Epstein 2001; VanSledright 2002; Barton and Levstik 2004 for further evidence of this attitude and approach.

5. Torney-Purta 2002; Haste 2004; Torney-Purta et al. 2007. Adults, too, ignore or reject depersonalized authorities—books, television programs, in-school curricula, teachers who seem to be mere transmission

agents for received wisdom—in favor of direct experiences such as personal experience, stories told by family members, or direct interaction with historical artifacts in museums or historical sites. See Rosenzweig and Thelen 1998.

6. Albert Shanker Institute 2003, 14.

7. Craig 2003.

8. Quoted in Albert Shanker Institute 2003, 13. See also Ravitch 1994; Cheney 1994; Cheney et al. 1995; Damon 1995.

9. Stotsky 2004, 12.

10. Tyack 2003, 53.

11. Gibbon 2002a; see also Avery and Simmons 2000; Damon 2001.

12. Ravitch 2003, 151; see also Schlesinger Jr. 1998.

13. Albert Shanker Institute 2003, 18.

14. To her credit, Diane Ravitch is absolutely clear about the importance of influences outside of school. "[T]he schools are not a total institution. They do not control every aspect of children's lives. Children are influenced not just by what they read in their textbooks and what they encounter on tests, but by their families, their friends, their communities, their religious institutions, and—perhaps more than anything else—the popular culture" (Ravitch 2003, 159).

15. Torney-Purta et al. 2007, 113; see also Torney-Purta 2002, 206.

16. Rosenzweig and Thelen 1998. Even media are often de facto segregated, tailored to and consumed by a narrow demographic audience. A comparison of Nielsen ratings for the top ten broadcast television shows among African Americans, Hispanics, and the general population, for example, demonstrates the division of media attention. Less than half appear simultaneously on the overall list and the African American list on the day I am writing this (October 8, 2010: data are for the week of September 27, 2010), and there is no overlap at all with the top shows among Hispanic viewers (Nielsen Media Research 2010).

17. Epstein 1998, 408, 419; see also Seixas 1993; Barton 1995; Epstein 2000, 2001, 2009.

18. Wright 2003.

19. On African-American churches, see Alex-Assensoh and Assensoh 2001. On African-American fraternal organizations, see Skocpol et al. 2006.

20. Hughes 1994.

21. Obama 2008a. For for powerful evidence of slavery's ongoing support by the federal government, its persistent national rather than

sectional character, and even its effective perpetuation until the early years of World War II, see Fehrenbacher 2001; Blackmon 2008; Hahn 2009.

22. Obama 2008a.

23. Fullinwider 1996, 206.

24. Baldwin 1962, 81. See also Rosenzweig and Thelen 1998, 159.

25. Mosley-Braun 2003.

26. Perry 2003.

27. Morehouse College 2007; Black Excel 2007.

28. Ironically, because many historically Black colleges and universities were founded, led, and especially funded by Whites until relatively recently, these institutions in general may have been less consistent at promoting a distinctive African-American civic narrative than were de jure and even some de facto segregated K–12 schools. See Gasman 2007; Watson and Gergory 2005. For example, John Hope, the first African-American president of what became Morehouse College, "imbued Morehouse College with a spirit of race leadership—of commitment, obligation, and personal responsibility." This was new to Morehouse: "No previous president . . . had ever been as socially active; of course, all the previous presidents had been white" (Davis 1998, 199). See also Manley 1995, 15–90 and Watson and Gergory 2005, 32 for a similar description of Spelman students' shifts in "political awareness, solidarity, and activism" once Spelman appointed its first African-American president.

29. Foster 1997, 34, 35. See also hooks 1994; Perry 2003.

30. Foster 1997, 38.

31. Johnson 2000.

32. Payne 2003, 25.

33. Payne 1995, chapter 10; see also Chilcoat and Ligon 1999.

34. Payne 2003.

35. Watson's comment echoes Rosenzweig and Thelen's findings: "When we asked what common history they [African Americans] shared with other Americans, they generally avoided the conventional sentiments about freedom and democracy. Instead, they found common ground in the history of migration or struggle against oppression— identifying with other immigrants and poor Americans rather than with the dominant social groups or mainstream political ideals" (Rosenzweig and Thelen 1998, 157).

36. Steele 2009.

37. This appropriation can potentially go both ways. Rosenzweig and Thelen found in their interviews with African-American adults that African Americans "generally avoided the conventional sentiments

about freedom and democracy. Instead, they found common ground in the history of migration or struggle against oppression—identifying with other immigrants and poor Americans rather than with the dominant social groups or mainstream political ideals" (Rosenzweig and Thelen 1998, 157).

38. Verba et al. 1995.

39. See Payne 2003 for arguments in this vein.

40. Johnson 2000.

41. It also depends on *collective* struggle, not just individual heroism, as I discuss more in the next chapter.

42. This seems to be what the historian Gary Nash and his colleagues have in mind when they suggest the following: "Can a plurality of stories and jarring perspectives fit into a coherent understanding of the American past? Quite simply, the particularities of social history *can* be mainstreamed readily enough by changing the governing narrative from the rise of democracy, defined in terms of electoral politics, to the struggle to fulfill the American ideals of liberty, equal justice, and equality. This new narrative, arising out of a democratized historical practice, would speak to contests and conflicts over power and how such contests reflect the long struggles among various groups to elbow their way under the canopy of the nation's founding promises. This narrative is as simple as the opening words of the Constitution: "to create a more perfect union" (Nash et al. 2000, 101).

43. Payne 2003, 27.

44. Baldwin 1962, 101.

45. Cheney 1987, 7.

46. 107th Congress 2002.

47. Albert Shanker Institute 2003, 3–4, 14.

48. Zimmerman 2002.

49. Haste 2004, 420.

50. See Allen 2004 for an argument in this regard, pointing out that we want to create a "whole" polity, but not "one" people.

51. Staff and Partners of the Center for Democracy and Citizenship 2011 (1995). See also Boyte and Kari 1996; Boyte 2005. In Chapter 6, I discuss some experiential civic education programs that are built around this narrative of "public work." These include Public Achievement, Earth Force, and Youth Build.

52. See, for example, Boix-Mansilla and Jackson 2011.

53. Moreau 2003, chapter 7; see also Zimmerman 2002.

54. Ravitch 2003, 156.

55. Stout 2010, xviii. Marshall Ganz has similarly put telling one's own story, listening to others' stories, and co-constructing stories that

motivate action at the center of his political organizing work. See Ganz 2007. Under Ganz's and others' tutelage, thousands of Obama for America volunteers were trained during the 2008 presidential campaign to tell their "story of self," a "story of us," and a "story of now," and to elicit such stories from others.

4. RETHINKING HEROES AND ROLE MODELS

1. The professors are Jesus Francisco de la Teja, Professor and Chair, Department of History, Texas State University; Daniel L. Dreisbach, Professor, American University; Lybeth Hodges, Professor, History, Texas Woman's University; and Jim Kracht, Associate Dean and Professor, College of Education and Human Development, Texas A&M University (Texas Education Agency 2009). David Barton is founder and president of WallBuilders, an organization dedicated to "Presenting America's forgotten history and heroes with an emphasis on our moral, religious, and constitutional heritage," and whose goals are "(1) educating the nation concerning the Godly foundation of our country; (2) providing information to federal, state, and local officials as they develop public policies which reflect Biblical values; and (3) encouraging Christians to be involved in the civic arena" (WallBuilders 2009). Finally, Peter Marshall is founder and president of Peter Marshall Ministries, which is "dedicated to helping to restore America to its Bible-based foundations through preaching, teaching, and writing on America's Christian heritage and on Christian discipleship and revival" (Peter Marshall Ministries 2009a). He is concerned about "a loss of our collective memory," and argues "that in order to restore America we have to recover the truth about America's Christian heritage, and God's hand in our history" (Peter Marshall Ministries 2009b).

2. Marshall 2009, 8–9.

3. WallBuilders 2009.

4. Barton 2009, 19.

5. See Alinsky 1945, 1971.

6. Cargill 2009.

7. Shorto 2010.

8. Newport 2006; see also Wineburg and Monte-Sano 2008.

9. Bond 1993.

10. Bernsen 2009.

11. Peter Marshall Ministries 2009a.

12. See Levinson 2009a for a much more comprehensive account.

13. Wecter 1941, 99.

14. Ibid., viii.

15. "Heroification" is the term used by Loewen 1995, 19. As Sam

Wineburg and Chauncey Monte-Sano put it, "We doubt that many high school students in an all-white classroom in Montana (or anywhere else) would recognize the King who told David Halberstam in 1967 'that the vast majority of white Americans are racists, either consciously or unconsciously'; the King who linked American racism to American militarism, calling both, along with economic exploitation, the 'triple evils' of American society; the King who characterized the bloodbath in Vietnam as a 'bitter, colossal contest for supremacy' with America as the 'supreme culprit'; or the King who in a speech two months before his assassination accused America of committing 'more war crimes almost than any nation in the world'" (Wineburg and Monte-Sano 2008, 1201). Also see Dyson 2004, 287–305, for a provocative analysis of King's "ambiguous heroism," and Kammen 1991 for a comprehensive account of heroification and the reconstruction of historical memory.

16. Dimond and Pflieger 1974, 7.

17. McClenaghan 1953, 23.

18. To test this impression, I analyzed the sidebars and images in five contemporary civics textbooks. All five exemplify this careful patterning. Davis et al. 2005; Hartley and Vincent 2005; McClenaghan 2003; Wolfson 2005; Glencoe/McGraw-Hill 2005.

19. Webster 1790, 23.

20. Tyack 2001, 337.

21. Ibid.

22. Wecter 1941, 111, see also chapter 6 passim.

23. Ibid., 139.

24. Tyack 2001, 356.

25. Schwartz 1990, 98.

26. Wecter 1941, viii; see also Kammen 1991.

27. Zimmerman 2002.

28. Davis et al. 2005.

29. James 1880; Schlesinger Jr. 1968 (1958); Gibbon 2002b.

30. Schlesinger Jr. 1968 (1958), 350.

31. Gibbon 2002b, xxi.

32. Giraffe Heroes Project 2008a, 2008b.

33. Gibbon 2002b, 13.

34. Gallup and Lyons 2002. Unfortunately, there's little way to get a longitudinal view of young people's attitudes toward heroes—at least with regard to their selection of a family member or other person known to themselves—since prior to 2000, the poll question specifically excluded family and friends from the list of possible answers: "What one man (woman) that you have heard or read about, alive today in any part of the world, do you admire the most, not including any of your

relatives or personal friends?" Data are also unavailable on the percentage of youth who declined to name any person they admired prior to 2000.

35. Lyons 2008.

36. Axthelm 1979; Hanson 1996; Marr 1998; Silverman 2003; Truchard 2005; McDorman et al. 2006; Browne and Fishwick 1983; Edelstein 1996; Fishwick 1969; Wecter 1941; Klapp 1949.

37. Wecter 1941, 489.

38. Churchill 1925.

39. Ibid.

40. Cowen 2000.

41. Gibbon 2002b, 11.

42. CNN 2008.

43. Addis 1996, 1381; see also Gibbon 2002b, 12.

44. Addis 1996; see also Kemper 1968; Speizer 1981; Lockwood and Kunda 1997, 2000.

45. In 1949, when the question was first asked and coded for this kind of response, only 1 percent of survey respondents named a family member or friend as the man that they "have heard or read about, living today, in any part of the world" whom they admired the most. Three percent of survey respondents similarly named a family member or friend when asked about their most admired woman. These numbers stayed steady in 1955, the next year that results were broken down in this way. By 1966, however, the numbers started creeping up—3 percent for men and 5.6 percent for women—and they more than doubled again for men by 2006, when a full 9 percent of those identified were family or friends. Women have held steady at around 6 percent since the 1970s; I conjecture this is because of a shrinking gender gap with respect to recognition and publicity of public figures. Findings calculated by author using Gallup Organization 1949, 1955, 1966, 1977, 2006.

46. Averett 1985; Porpora 1996, 222; Bucher 1997; Anderson and Cavallaro 2002; Yancy et al. 2002; Robison 2003; Pomper 2004, 22; Bricheno and Thornton 2007.

47. I found identical results in a survey I conducted with approximately 100 young people in four communities. One of the survey questions asked them to complete the sentence, "My role model(s) is (are) . . ." *Ninety-three* percent of those who answered included at least one family member or friend and/or a religious figure such as God, Muhammed, or Jesus—someone with whom the students also seemed to feel a direct, personal relationship. Again, this is not because students were unaware of the more famous or extraordinary exemplars. They

uniformly mentioned leaders such as Martin Luther King and others in listing four people "everybody from the United States has heard of." Rather, these data strongly reinforce the notion that personal relationships totally trump as a practical matter abstract knowledge of distant heroes with respect to role model identification.

48. Marr 1998; Kelly 2003.

49. Pomper 2004; see also Kelly 1997. By contrast, Thomas Carlyle would be appalled, albeit unsurprised, by this utter rejection of heroes' desirability in a democratic society. He famously castigated "Democracy, which means despair of ever finding any Heroes to govern you, and contented putting up with the want of them" (Carlyle 1918 [1843], 249).

50. Pomper 2004, 4–5; see also Hook 1943, 229.

51. Loewen 1995, 216.

52. Marr 1998.

53. Obama for America 2008; Obama 2008b.

54. Schlesinger Jr. 1968 (1958).

55. Kahne and Westheimer 2003 offer good empirical evidence of the promise of this approach.

56. Wolfson 2005; McClenaghan 2003; Glencoe/McGraw-Hill 2005; Hartley and Vincent 2005; Davis et al. 2005.

57. I discuss the effects of standardized curricula and assessments on civic education in Chapter 7.

58. Bond 1993.

59. Wineburg and Monte-Sano 2008, 1201–1202.

60. Zinn 1980; Kohl 1995; West and Glaude 2006.

61. Obama 2009.

62. Kerr 2002.

5. HOW TO SOAR IN A WORLD YOU'VE NEVER SEEN

1. Flanagan et al. 2007, 428.

2. See Dewey 1990 (1900), 18 for a compelling account of the school as "a miniature community, an embryonic society." Flanagan et al. 2007 provides a comprehensive summary of the empirical research literature supporting this claim.

3. Gibson 1988; Sizer and Sizer 1999; Torney-Purta et al. 2001b; Flanagan et al. 2007.

4. Sue et al. 2007, 271.

5. Yosso et al. 2009, 661. See also Pierce 1995; Solorzano et al. 2000; Sue et al. 2007a, 2009.

6. According to the Bureau of Justice's National Center for Education Statistics 2009 report on Indicators of School Crime and Safety,

schools whose student body is majority non-White and/or over 75 percent poor (eligible for free or reduced price lunch) are four to ten times more likely to subject their students to random and/or daily metal detector checks than schools with a majority-White and/or nonpoor student body. Urban schools are likewise far more likely to conduct such checks than suburban or rural schools (Dinkes et al. 2009, table 20.22, p. 136).

7. Dreeben 1968; Jackson 1968; Spring 1971; Bowles and Gintis 1976; Carnoy and Levin 1985.

8. Flanagan et al. 2007, 422, 428–429.

9. Webster 1790; Macedo 1990.

10. Verba et al. 1995, 425.

11. Dinkes et al. 2009, 136, table 20.22.

12. Cramer and Samuels 2005. Similarly, a teacher in the Chicago Public Schools reported to me that in response to a 2011 schoolwide survey, students in her high school reported they wanted *more* security guards rather than fewer; they also favored higher rates of suspension, because they felt they learned more when certain students were suspended from school. These responses speak to a complex civic reality. While students may well be right that they learn more and are safer when punitive discipline and police surveillance are increased, this is arguably because the school community is already in tatters. If students' social, emotional, and academic needs were uniformly met, it is likely that many of the "bad kids" would turn out to be quite "good" kids. They wouldn't "need" to be suspended. If the school community felt more like a family than like a factionalized zone in which everybody has to be on guard, then security patrols might not be required for peace to prevail.

13. See Foote 2008 for an account of similar dilemmas faced by students in Los Angeles.

14. Dillon 2010. This problem is not limited to Los Angeles. In Chicago, for example, thirty-two children were killed and another 226 shot, specifically while they were going to or coming from school during the 2009–10 school year alone (Saulny 2010). Since Chicago Public Schools were open only 172 days that year, this means that the act of traveling to or from school claimed the life of a child every five days, and subjected one or more children to injury by gunfire every single school day. Chicago Public School students have been better protected in 2010–11, thanks to an emergency federal infusion of money into the "Safe Passage" program in response to a virally spread cell phone video of the brutal 2009 beating death of Derrion Albert. Thanks to Safe Passage, "yellow jackets"—community members, often parents, wearing

yellow safety vests—are paid $10 per hour to stand at designated street corners before and after school and keep watch as students walk to or from school. Safe Passage also pays for a massive police presence around various high schools. "A police helicopter often flies over potential hot spots for after-school violence around the city, and tactical police units can be moved to certain schools or neighborhoods in anticipation of possible fights or shootings based on tips from gang- and school-based intelligence." Understandably, some community members—and even the former police commissioner herself—are worried about the establishment of a "police state" surrounding low-income students of color (Schaper 2011). At the same time, many educators and students are wondering whether such an expensive program has any hope of being retained.

15. Again, see Foote 2008, chapter 4 for a compelling description of Los Angeles students' fears in this regard.

16. Dinkes et al. 2009, 136, table 20.22.

17. Meier 1995, 122.

18. This vision admittedly exhibits a somewhat "deficit-oriented" approach to the students' communities and even families. Although it could be more proactively engaged with students' families and communities rather than merely plotting their flight, it nonetheless reflects a real recognition of the risks and impediments that young people growing up in the Fourth Ward faced, and that they and their families alike were eager for them to escape.

19. On the importance of "everyday" experiences and challenges in schools, see Pollock 2004; Abu El-Haj 2006; Pollock 2008.

20. Perkins 1998; Bransford et al. 1999.

21. I discuss these in detail in Chapter 2.

22. Admittedly, students in schools driven by standardized tests often don't get to observe or emulate true readers, writers, or mathematicians, either. They instead engage in a simulacrum of such activities, corresponding to the shadows of these disciplines that are reflected on the test. But these students arguably also do not actually master the complex knowledge, skills, efficacious attitudes, or habits of being good writers, mathematicians, and readers.

23. Meier 2003, 16–17; see also Kahne and Westheimer 2003.

24. See Chapter 6 for a discussion of the empirical evidence in favor of this cycle.

25. Rowe 1986 shows how such techniques help "previously 'invisible' people become visible" (Rowe 1986, 45). Homana et al. 2006 and Torney-Purta et al. 2006 provide useful analysis of the interplay among pedagogies for students' civic empowerment.

26. Torney-Purta et al. 2001b, 137. See also Hess 2009b.

27. On overall civic and political knowledge, see Blankenship 1990; Hahn 1999; Torney-Purta et al. 2001b; Campbell 2008. Torney-Purta et al. 2001b, figure 8.1 and table 8.2 reveal intent to vote. On likelihood of being an informed voter, see Campbell 2005, while Kahne and Sporte 2008 address expectation of engaging in other political and civic actions. Blankenship 1990; Hahn 1999; Baldi et al. 2001b; Gimpel et al. 2003; Perliger et al. 2006 all address expression of political efficacy and civic duty. See Hibbing and Theiss-Morse 2002; Hess 2009a on comfort with civic and political conflict, Blankenship 1990; Hahn 1999 on interest in politics and attentiveness to current events, and Carnegie Corporation of New York and CIRCLE 2003 on critical thinking and communications skills. For international data, see Hahn 1998; Torney-Purta et al. 2001b.

28. Verba et al. 1995; Andolina et al. 2003; Campbell 2008; Wilkenfeld 2009; Kahne and Sporte 2008.

29. See Torney-Purta et al. 2001c, 9–10 for compelling data from around the world. Almost 90 percent of U.S. students reported on one nationally representative survey that "the most frequent instructional methods when studying civic-related topics were reading textbooks and studying worksheets, the more rote types of learning activities," while less than half of the students reported such active pedagogies as debates, discussions, or role-playing exercises (Torney-Purta 2002, 209). NAEP data are consistent with this portrait: 83 percent of fourth-grade students reported using the social studies textbook at least weekly, and over two-thirds of fourth graders completed worksheets on a weekly or daily basis. The only other instructional methods to come close to this frequent level of use were using quantitative data, charts, or graphs (81 percent) and hearing a teacher's lecture (66 percent). These same four relatively passive, teacher-focused pedagogies were also the only methods reported used on a weekly or daily basis by at least three-quarters of eighth graders; the only significant difference is that 95 percent of eighth graders reported daily or weekly use of the social studies textbook (Lutkus et al. 1999, 91).

30. Cazden 2001; see also Mehan 1979.

31. Hess 2009a, 36.

32. Kahne et al. 2000; Baldi et al. 2001a; Campbell 2008; Wilkenfeld 2009; Kahne and Sporte 2008, 755. See also Kahne and Middaugh 2008 for corroborative data from a large-scale study of young people's civic learning opportunities in California.

33. This discussion about an open classroom climate strongly echoes portions of the vast literature in political philosophy and social science

on deliberative democracy. For reasons of space and focus, I do not think, however, that this would be a productive direction for future work by those interested in deliberative democracy. As a starting place, Rosenberg 2007 brings together excellent examples of both theoretical and empirical work on the topic.

34. Parker and Hess 2001, 273; see also Hess 2009a, chapter 4.

35. See Wiggins and McTighe 2005 for more about essential questions.

36. Hess 2009a, 67–68.

37. Egelko 2007.

38. Mayer v. Monroe County Municipal School Corp. 2007. See also Moran 2009 for a discussion of the political and pedagogical "minefield" associated with discussing politics, especially during an election season, and suggestions for how to navigate the minefield.

39. See Hess 2009b for an interesting discussion of this very question.

40. See Stout 2010.

41. Rawls 1993, 9.

42. Ibid., Lecture VI.

43. On restorative justice, see Elliott and Gordon 2005; Wadhwa 2010. On youth councils and youth court, see Owadokun and Avilés 2005; Fraser 2005. On the design, implementation, and effect of zero tolerance policies, see Martin II 2001; Skiba 2000; Skiba et al. 2000, June; Advancement Project and The Civil Rights Project at Harvard University 2000; Advancement Project 2010.

44. McFarland and Thomas 2006; Kahne and Sporte 2008; Zaff et al. 2008; Thomas and McFarland 2010.

45. Torney-Purta and Wilkenfeld 2009.

46. John 2000; Owadokun and Avilés 2005; Governor's Statewide Youth Council 2009; Mutseyekwa 2009.

6. THE CASE FOR ACTION CIVICS

1. For these reasons, guided experiential civic education seems very likely to increase students' overall mastery of "twenty-first-century skills" sought by civic and business leaders alike. See Torney-Purta and Wilkenfeld 2009.

2. Numerous examples, analyses, and evaluations of such approaches are available from practitioners and civic education organizations as well as the research literature. See Weis and Fine 2000; Darling-Hammond et al. 2002; Westheimer and Kahne 2002; Kahne and Westheimer 2003; Lay and Smarick 2006; Noguera et al. 2006; Apple and Beane 2007; Schultz 2008; Cammarota and Fine 2008; Delgado and

Staples 2008; Hess 2009a. The Campaign for the Civic Mission of Schools 2010 provides information about and links to over 100 well-vetted curricula, programs, and organizations.

3. Learn and Serve America's National Service-Learning Clearinghouse 2010.

4. Learn and Serve America's National Service-Learning Clearinghouse 2008; Corporation for National and Community Service 2009. Service learning ended up on the chopping block, however, in federal budget negotiations in summer 2011.

5. Chicago Public Schools 2007; Learn and Serve America's National Service-Learning Clearinghouse 2008; Corporation for National and Community Service 2008.

6. Walker 2000; Bass 2004.

7. Hepburn et al. 2000; Walker 2002; Lopez et al. 2006. This is not to suggest that *no* service-learning programs attempt to encourage activism or long-term change. Earth Force, for example, characterizes itself as a service-learning program but takes an explicitly policy-oriented approach.

8. Stoneman 2002; Kahne and Westheimer 2003, 2006; Winerip 2006.

9. Westheimer and Kahne 2004a.

10. Hibbing and Theiss-Morse 2002, 134–137; Carnegie Corporation of New York and CIRCLE 2003.

11. Walker 2002, 186; Zaff and Michelsen 2002. Hart et al. 2007 found a significant positive correlation between twelfth graders' participation in voluntary or required school-based community service and their voting participation as adults eight years later, but in failing to control for multiple factors that have apparent significance (such as gender, since girls tend to volunteer more than boys), the results are at best merely suggestive.

12. It is worth noting that avoidance of controversy is not confined to American civic education. An international study of fourteen-year-olds' civic attitudes in twenty-eight countries found that "activities that imply conflict of opinions (political party membership and political discussion) are not highly rated on average," a result which presumably is linked to many schools' avoidance of "discussing partisan conflict" (Torney-Purta et al. 2001b, 79, 89).

13. Galston 2001, 220; see also Andolina et al. 2002; Galston 2003.

14. Walker 2000, 2002; Keeter et al. 2002; Kahne and Westheimer 2003; Zukin et al. 2006; Lopez et al. 2006.

15. Boyle-Baise et al. 2006; Stoecker and Tryon 2009.

16. National Action Civics Collaborative 2010.

17. For evidence of Public Achievement's and Earth Force's effectiveness in promoting empowering civic outcomes, see RMC Research Corporation 2007; Melchior 2010. Research on the other organizations is underway.

18. Mikva Challenge 2010; see also Earth Force 2010; Public Achievement 2010.

19. Miller 2010.

20. Fine and Weis 2000; Ginwright and James 2002; Noguera et al. 2006; Cammarota and Fine 2008; Kirshner 2008.

21. Kirshner 2006.

22. Cammarota and Fine 2008, 2.

23. YPAR Think Tank 2010.

24. Duncan-Andrade 2006, 167.

25. Kirshner et al. 2003; Fine 2009.

26. Stoneman 2002, 223; see also Kirshner 2006; O'Donoghue and Kirshner 2008.

27. Philadelphia Student Union 2010.

28. On Cabrini Green, see Schultz 2008. See Gordon 2011 for a description and analysis of Cesar Chavez Public Charter Schools. Other initiatives are described in Noguera et al. 2006; Bixby and Pace 2008; and of course schools' and programs' own websites.

29. Mikva Challenge 2011. See McIntosh et al. 2010 for example of others districts' work.

30. Rothman 2010.

31. YPAR Think Tank 2010 shows the prevalence of the topic among urban youth in the United States. In reading about and working with civic educators around the world, I have also encountered youth striving to improve school bathrooms in Mexico, Columbia, India, England, Australia, and elsewhere.

32. Rubin 2007.

33. It's intriguing to think about how I might do this now, with the availability of YouTube, wikis, Ning sites, Facebook groups, and other technologies that facilitate making one's work public. Given the paucity of computers and ubiquity of annoying internet filters in my school, as in others around the nation, however, my guess is that I would have stuck with the in-person presentations. See Reich 2009 on computer restrictions in schools.

34. Strobel et al. 2008.

35. Duncan-Andrade 2005, 2006; Tatum 2008; Certo et al. 2008; Murphy 2009; Powers 2009.

36. O'Donoghue and Kirshner 2008, 238.

37. Yates and Youniss 1999; Westheimer and Kahne 2004b; Ives and Obenchain 2006; Feldman et al. 2007; O'Donoghue and Kirshner 2008; Syvertsen et al. 2009.

38. Delli Carpini and Keeter 1996 offer the first term in each set of two. Verba et al. 1995 propose the second term in each set as part of their Civic Voluntarism Model. Although there are some subtle differences between them, I will treat them as interchangeable for my purposes. See also Niemi and Junn 1998.

39. Snow et al. 1980; McAdam 1988; Hart et al. 2007; Bishop and Cushing 2008; McAdam and Paulsen 2010.

40. Hart et al. 2007.

41. O'Donoghue and Kirshner 2008, 244. See also Yates and Youniss 2002.

42. See Allen 2004 for an argument that sacrifice is at the heart of democracy.

43. Han 2009, 102.

44. Youniss et al. 1997, 624; see also Yates and Youniss 1999, 2002.

45. Ladson-Billings 1994, 18. See also Perry et al. 2003; Banks 2004; Banks et al. 2005; Nieto 2005; Sleeter 2005; Duncan-Andrade and Morrell 2008; Hall et al. 2009.

46. Duncan-Andrade 2007, 627.

47. Keeter et al. 2002, 35.

48. See Flanagan et al. 2007 for corroborating evidence.

49. Center for Civic Education and National Conference of State Legislatures 1996.

50. Gagnon 2003.

51. Lutkus et al. 1999, 91.

52. See Kanner 2005 for confirmation of the importance of a supportive school environment for civic educators to be effective.

7. DEMOCRACY, ACCOUNTABILITY, AND EDUCATION

1. In her seminal book *Democratic Education,* Amy Gutmann sets goals based on both conceptions of democratic education without necessarily recognizing their potential contradiction. She articulates the goal of what I call education *for* democracy as follows: "all citizens must be educated so as to have a chance to share in self-consciously shaping the structure of their society" (Gutmann 1987, 46). In this formulation of democratic education, she is arguing that young people should learn the knowledge and skills necessary to be civically empowered. Earlier, however, she claims, "A democratic theory of education focuses on what might be called 'conscious social reproduction'—the

ways in which citizens are or should be empowered to influence the education that in turn shapes the political values, attitudes, and modes of behavior of future citizens" (Gutmann 1987, 14). In this formulation of democratic education, she is arguing that adults should be able to exercise democratic power over education. This is education *within* a democracy, not education *for* a democracy.

2. I should note that I am packing a lot into the adjective "high-quality." It's clear that the standards themselves need to surpass a certain level: meat-packing standards, for example, shouldn't be so low that contaminated meat could get through despite full compliance with the standards. But they also should be themselves designed to serve a public good. Hiring standards that are designed to reward nepotism over competence, or house lot size standards that intentionally price middle-class and poor homeowners out of the neighborhood are both examples of standards that are designed to serve private rather than public goods. So not all standards are a public good; but high-quality ones—i.e., those that set an appropriately high bar for the activity or output and that are themselves oriented toward a worthwhile aim—are public goods. I am grateful to Randall Curren for pressing this point with me.

3. Ravitch 1996, 9.

4. Behn 2003 introduces the term "accountability holdees." Gloria Ladson-Billings provides an especially interesting example of holding citizens as a whole accountable in her redescription of the individual "achievement gap" as a collective "education debt." See Ladson-Billings 2006 for more details.

5. See Rebell 2009.

6. Students and Faculty of The New School 2010; see also The New School 2010.

7. Reuben 2005; see, e.g., Powell et al. 1985; Tyack and Cuban 1995; Tyack 2001; Oakes 2005.

8. Stein 2001.

9. Nash et al. 2000.

10. Surowiecki 2005; Ober 2010.

11. Freire Charter School 2010.

12. Darling-Hammond 2004.

13. Archbald and Newmann 1988; Wasserman 2001; Koretz 2008.

14. Darling-Hammond 2004; Wiley et al. 2005, ii; Dillon 2009, 2.

15. Sacks 2000; Herman 2003; Darling-Hammond 2004; Toch 2006; Winerip 2006; Koretz 2008; Ulluci and Spencer 2009.

16. Koretz 2008.

17. Behn 2003, 569.

18. Elmore 2005, 294.

19. O'Day 2002; Fullan 2007; Levin 2008.

20. Linn 2000; Curren 2004; Fuhrman and Elmore 2004; Koretz 2008.

21. Sleeter 2005, 7.

22. Fung 2004b.

23. Levinson 1999.

24. Sacks 2000.

25. Chapter 2 develops these ideas in more detail.

26. Delpit 1995; Cross Jr. et al. 1999; Delpit and Dowdy 2002; Carter 2005.

27. Hess 2009a, chapter 7.

28. Meier 2003, 16. I detail these concerns in Chapter 5.

29. Moe 2000, 127.

30. The new Common Core Standards in English and math may end up supporting these goals. They are very promising on paper; the question now is how they will translate both to educational practice and to assessment and accountability design.

31. Moe 2000, 127.

EPILOGUE

1. This isn't to say that we are totally shielded. Three young men were murdered in 2010 at our favorite pizza place in an apparent gang-related conflict. There have also been a few shootings near my daughters' school. But these are shocking outliers in an otherwise peaceful and safe existence.

2. Payne 2003, 25–26.

3. Massachusetts Senate 2011.

4. Kerr 2011.

REFERENCES

Abu El-Haj, Thea Renda (2006). *Elusive Justice: Wrestling with Difference and Educational Equity in Everyday Practice.* New York: Routledge.

——— (2008). "'I Was Born Here, but My Home, It's Not Here': Educating for Democratic Citizenship in an Era of Transnational Migration and Global Conflict." *Harvard Educational Review* 77(3): 285–316.

Addis, Adeno (1996). "Role Models and the Politics of Recognition." *University of Pennsylvania Law Review* 144(4): 1377–1468.

Advancement Project (2010). *Test, Punish, and Push Out: How 'Zero Tolerance' and High-Stakes Tests Funnel Youth into the School-to-Prison Pipeline.* Washington, D.C. and Los Angeles: Advancement Project.

Advancement Project and The Civil Rights Project at Harvard University (2000). "Opportunities Suspended: The Devastating Consequences of Zero Tolerance and School Discipline Policies." Civil Rights Project, Washington, D.C., and Harvard University. Retrieved June 13, 2011, from www.eric.ed.gov/PDFS/ED454314.pdf.

Albert Shanker Institute (2003). "Education for Democracy." Washington, D.C.: Albert Shanker Institute.

Alex-Assensoh, Yvette (1997). "Race, Concentrated Poverty, Social Isolation, and Political Behavior." *Urban Affairs Review* 33(2): 209–227.

Alex-Assensoh, Yvette, and A. B. Assensoh (2001). "Inner-City Contexts, Church Attendance, and African-American Political Participation." *Journal of Politics* 63(3): 886–901.

Alexander, Michelle (2010). *The New Jim Crow.* New York: New Press.

Alinsky, Saul David (1945). *Reveille for Radicals.* Chicago: University of Chicago Press.

———— (1971). *Rules for Radicals: A Practical Primer for Realistic Radicals.* New York: Vintage Books.

Allen, Danielle S. (2004). *Talking to Strangers: Anxieties of Citizenship since* Brown v. Board of Education. Princeton: Princeton University Press.

American Educational Research Association (2006). "Amicus Curiae 10." Retrieved July 11, 2007, from www.aera.net/uploadedFiles/News_Media/AERA_Amicus_Brief.pdf.

Anderson, Elizabeth, and Jeffrey Jones (2002, September). "The Geography of Race in the United States." Retrieved June 24, 2009, from www.umich.edu/~lawrace/.

Anderson, Kristin J., and Donna Cavallaro (2002). "Parents of Pop Culture? Children's Heroes and Role Models." *Childhood Education* 78: 161–168.

Anderson, Noel S., and Haroon Kharem, eds. (2009). *Education as Freedom: African American Educational Thought and Activism.* Lanham, MD: Lexington Books.

Andolina, Molly W., et al. (2002). "Searching for the Meaning of Youth Civic Engagement: Notes from the Field." *Applied Developmental Science* 6(4): 189–195.

Andolina, Molly W., et al. (2003). "Habits from Home, Lessons from School: Influences on Youth Civic Engagement." *PS: Political Science and Politics* 36(2): 275–280.

Appiah, Kwame Anthony (2006). *Cosmopolitanism: Ethics in a World of Strangers.* New York: W. W. Norton.

Appiah, K. Anthony, and Amy Gutmann (1996). *Color Conscious: The Political Morality of Race.* Princeton: Princeton University Press.

Apple, Michael W., and James A. Beane, eds. (2007). *Democratic Schools: Lessons in Powerful Education.* Portsmouth, NH: Heinemann.

Archbald, Doug, and Fred Newmann (1988). *Beyond Standardized Testing: Assessing Authentic Achievement in the Secondary School.* Reston, VA: National Association of Secondary School Principals.

Asante, Molefi Kete (1998). *The Afrocentric Idea,* rev. and exp. ed. Philadelphia: Temple University Press.

Atkins, Robert, and Daniel Hart (2003). "Neighborhoods, Adults, and the Development of Civic Identity in Urban Youth." *Applied Developmental Science* 7(3): 156–164.

Averett, Joy (1985). "Facets: Today's Kids and Hero Worship, Who Can They Look Up To?" *English Journal* 74(5): 23.

Avery, Patricia G., and Annette M. Simmons (2000). "Civic Life as Conveyed in United States Civics and History Textbooks." *International Journal of Social Education* 15(2): 105–130.

Axthelm, Pete (1979, August 6). "Where Have All the Heroes Gone?" *Newsweek*, 44.

Ayers, William, and Patricia Ford (1996). *City Kids, City Teachers.* New York: New Press.

Baker, Judith (2002). "Trilingualism." In *The Skin That We Speak: Thoughts on Language and Culture in the Classroom,* ed. Lisa Delpit and Joanne Kilgour Dowdy, 49–61. New York: New Press.

Baldi, Stephane, et al. (2001a). "What Democracy Means to Ninth-Graders: U.S. Results From the International IEA Civic Education Study." Washington, D.C.: U.S. Department of Education and National Center for Education Statistics.

Baldi, Stephane, et al. (2001b). "What Democracy Means to Ninth-Graders: U.S. Results from the International IEA Civic Education Study." *Education Statistics Quarterly* 3(2): 89–96.

Baldwin, James (1962). *The Fire Next Time.* New York: Vintage International.

Banks, James A. (2004). "Teaching for Social Justice, Diversity, and Citizenship in a Global World." *Educational Forum* 68(4): 296.

Banks, James A., et al. (2005). "Education and Diversity." *Social Education* 69(1): 36–40.

Barreto, Matt A., Mara Cohen-Marks, and Nathan D. Woods (2009). "Are All Precincts Created Equal? The Prevalence of Low-Quality Precincts in Low-Income and Minority Communities." *Political Research Quarterly* 62(3): 445–458.

Bartels, Larry M. (2008). *Unequal Democracy: The Political Economy of the New Gilded Age.* New York: Russell Sage Foundation.

Barton, David (2009). "2009 TEKS Review." Memo sent to Miriam Martinez, Director of Curriculum Texas Education Agency. Retrieved July 24, 2009, from ritter.tea.state.tx.us/teks/social/Barton current.pdf.

Barton, Keith C. (1995). "'My Mom Taught Me': The Situated Nature of Historical Understanding." Paper presented at Annual Meeting of the American Educational Research Association, Chicago.

Barton, Keith C., and Linda S. Levstik (2004). *Teaching History for the Common Good.* Mahwah, NJ: Lawrence Erlbaum Associates.

Bass, Melissa (2004). "Civic Education through National Service: Lessons from American History." CIRCLE Working Paper 12. College Park, MD: Center for Information and Research on Civic Learning and Engagement. Retrieved September 25, 2010, from www.civic youth.org/PopUps/WorkingPapers/WP12Bass.pdf.

Beauboeuf-Lafontant, Tamara (1999). "A Movement Against and Beyond Boundaries: 'Politically Relevant Teaching' among African American Teachers." *Teachers College Record* 100(4): 702–723.

Behn, Robert D. (2003). "Why Measure Performance? Different Purposes Require Different Measures." *Public Administration Review* 63(5): 556–576.

Bell, Derrick A., ed. (1980). *Shades of Brown: New Perspectives on School Desegregation.* New York: Teachers College Press.

——— (2004). *Silent Covenants:* Brown v. Board of Education *and the Unfulfilled Hopes for Racial Reform.* Oxford: Oxford University Press.

Bennett, W. Lance, ed. (2007). *Civic Life Online: Learning How Digital Media Can Engage Youth.* Cambridge, MA: MIT Press.

Bergerson, Amy Aldous (2003). "Critical Race Theory and White Racism: Is There Room for White Scholars in Fighting Racism in Education?" *International Journal of Qualitative Studies in Education* 16(1): 51–63.

Bernsen, James (2009, April 28). "State Board of Education Pulls Reins on 'Radical' Curriculum Group." *Texas Republic News.* Retrieved July 20, 2009, from www.texasinsider.org/?p=8341.

Big Picture Learning (2010). "Big Picture Learning Cycle Reference Guide." Retrieved June 13, 2011, from www.bigpicture.org/products-page/publications/big-picture-learning-cycle-reference-guide/.

Binder, Amy J. (2002). *Contentious Curricula: Afrocentrism and Creationism in American Public Schools.* Princeton: Princeton University Press.

Bishop, Bill, and Robert G. Cushing (2008). *The Big Sort: Why the Clustering of Like-Minded America Is Tearing Us Apart.* New York: Houghton Mifflin Harcourt.

Bixby, Janet S., and Judith L. Pace, eds. (2008). *Educating Democratic Citizens in Troubled Times: Qualitative Studies of Current Efforts.* Albany: State University of New York Press.

Black Excel (2007). "Morehouse College Profile." Retrieved August 6, 2007, from www.blackexcel.org/morehous.htm.

Blackmon, Douglas A. (2008). *Slavery by Another Name: The Re-Enslavement of Black People in America from the Civil War to World War II.* New York: Doubleday.

Blankenship, Glen (1990). "Classroom Climate, Global Knowledge, Global Attitudes, Political Attitudes." *Theory and Research in Social Education* 43(4): 363–386.

Bloemraad, Irene (2006). *Becoming a Citizen: Incorporating Immigrants and Refugees in the United States and Canada.* Berkeley: University of California Press.

Blum, Lawrence (2002a). *"I'm Not a Racist, But . . .:" The Moral Quandary of Race.* Ithaca, NY: Cornell University Press.

——— (2002b). "The Promise of Racial Integration in a Multicultural Age." In *Moral and Political Education,* ed. Stephen Macedo and Yael Tamir. New York: New York University Press.

Bobo, Lawrence D. (2001). "Racial Attitudes and Relations at the Close of the Twentieth Century." In *America Becoming: Racial Trends and Their Consequences,* vol. 1, ed. Neil J. Smelser et al., 264–301. Washington, D.C.: National Academy Press.

Boix-Mansilla, Veronica, and Anthony Jackson (2011). *Educating for Global Competence: Preparing Our Youth to Engage the World.* Washington, D.C.: Council of Chief State School Officers and the Asia Society.

Bond, Julian (1993, April 4). "Remember the Man and the Hero, Not Just Half the Dream." *Seattle Times.* Retrieved August 21, 2008, from seattletimes.nwsource.com/special/mlk/perspectives/reflections/bond.html.

Bonilla-Silva, Eduardo (2010). *Racism without Racists: Color-Blind Racism and the Persistence of Racial Inequality in the United States,* 3rd ed. Lanham, MD: Rowman and Littlefield.

Bourdieu, Pierre (2006). "Cultural Reproduction and Social Reproduction." In *Inequality: Classic Readings in Race, Class, and Gender,* ed. David B. Grusky and Szonja Szelenyi, 257–272. Cambridge, MA: Westview Press.

Bowles, Samuel, and Herbert Gintis (1976). *Schooling in Capitalist America.* London: Routledge and Kegan Paul.

Bowles, Samuel, Glenn C. Loury, and Rajiv Sethi (2009). "Group Inequality." Economics Working Papers, Institute for Advanced Study, School of Social Science, Princeton. Retrieved May 24, 2011, from econpapers.repec.org/RePEc:ads:wpaper:0088.

Boyle-Baise, Marilynne, et al. (2006). "Learning Service or Service Learning: Enabling the Civic." *International Journal of Teaching and Learning in Higher Education* 18(1): 17–26.

Boyte, Harry Chatten (2005). *Everyday Politics: Reconnecting Citizens and Public Life.* Philadelphia: University of Pennsylvania Press.

Boyte, Harry Chatten, and Nancy N. Kari (1996). *Building America: The Democratic Promise of Public Work*. Philadelphia: Temple University Press.

Bracey, Gerald W. (2009). "Our Resegregated Schools." *Phi Delta Kappan* 90(9): 691–692.

Brandt, Daniel, and Steve Badrich. (1997, January–March). "Pipe Dreams: The CIA, Drugs, and the Media." NameBase NewsLine. Retrieved October 18, 2010, from www.namebase.org/news16 .html.

Bransford, John D., Ann L. Brown, and Rodney R. Cocking, eds. (1999). *How People Learn: Brain, Mind, Experience, and School*. Washington, D.C.: National Academies Press.

Bricheno, Patricia, and Mary Thornton (2007). "Role Model, Hero, or Champion? Children's Views Concerning Role Models." *Educational Research* 49(4): 383–396.

Brighouse, Harry (2000). *School Choice and Social Justice*. Oxford: Oxford University Press.

Browne, Ray B., and Marshall W. Fishwick (1983). *The Hero in Transition*. Bowling Green, OH: Bowling Green University Press.

Bruyneel, Kevin (2004). "Challenging American Boundaries: Indigenous People and the 'Gift' of U.S. Citizenship." *Studies in American Political Development* 18(1): 30–43.

Bucher, Anton A. (1997). "The Influence of Models in Forming Moral Identity." *International Journal of Educational Research* 27(7): 619–627.

Cain, Bruce, and Brendan Doherty (2007). "The Impact of Dual Nationality on Political Participation." In *Transforming Politics, Transforming America: The Political and Civic Incorporation of Immigrants in the United States*, ed. Taeku Lee et al., 89–105. Charlottesville: University of Virginia Press.

Callan, Eamonn (1997). *Creating Citizens*. Oxford: Oxford University Press.

Cammarota, Julio, and Michelle Fine (2008). *Revolutionizing Education: Youth Participatory Action Research in Motion*. New York: Routledge.

Campaign for the Civic Mission of Schools (2010). "Educational Resources—Civic Mission of Schools." Retrieved April 14, 2010, from civicmissionofschools.org/cmos/site/resources/edresources.

Campbell, David (2008). "Voice in the Classroom: How an Open Classroom Climate Fosters Political Engagement among Adolescents." *Political Behavior* 30(4): 437–454.

Campbell, David E. (2005). "Voice in the Classroom: How an Open Classroom Environment Facilitates Adolescents' Civic Development." CIRCLE Working Paper 28. College Park, MD: Center for Information and Research on Civic Learning and Engagement. Retrieved January 17, 2012, from www.civicyouth.org/popups/workingpapers/WP28campbell.pdf.

Cargill, Barbara (2009, April). "The Cargill Connection." Retrieved July 20, 2009, from www.thsc.org/thscpac/BarbaraCargill4-25-09.htm.

Carlyle, Thomas (1918 [1843]). *Past and Present.* New York: Charles Scribner's Sons.

Carnegie Corporation of New York and CIRCLE (2003). "The Civic Mission of Schools." New York: Carnegie Corporation of New York and Center for Information and Research on Civic Learning and Engagement. Retrieved November 12, 2011, from www.civicmissionofschools.org/site/campaign/documents/CivicMissionofSchools.pdf.

Carnoy, Martin, and Henry M. Levin (1985). *Schooling and Work in the Democratic State.* Stanford: Stanford University Press.

Carter, Prudence (2005). *Keepin' It Real: School Success Beyond Black and White.* New York: Oxford University Press.

Cazden, Courtney (2001). *Classroom Discourse: The Language of Teaching and Learning,* 2nd ed. New York: Heinemann.

Center for Civic Education and National Conference of State Legislatures (1996). *We the People . . . Project Citizen.* Calabasas, CA: Center for Civic Education.

Certo, Janine L., et al. (2008). "An Argument for Authenticity: Adolescents' Perspectives on Standards-Based Reform." *High School Journal* 91(4): 26–39.

Chapman, Chris, Jennifer Laird, and Angelina KewalRamani (2010). "Trends in High School Dropout and Completion Rates in the United States: 1972–2008." IES, National Center for Education Statistics, U.S. Department of Education. Retrieved June 14, 2011, from nces.ed.gov/pubs2011/2011012.pdf.

Cheney, Lynne V. (1987). "American Memory: A Report on the Humanities in the Nation's Public Schools." Washington, D.C.: National Endowment for the Humanities.

——— (1994, October 20). "The End of History." *Wall Street Journal,* 224: A22.

Cheney, Lynne, et al. (1995, February 6). "Correspondence." *New Republic* 212(6): 4–5.

Chiaravalloti, Laura A. (2009). "Making the Switch: Lightbulbs, Literacy, and Service-Learning." *Voices from the Middle* 17(1): 24–33.

Chicago Public Schools (2007). "Service Learning: Strategy Description." Retrieved May 22, 2010, from www.cpstoolkit.com/StrategyPage.aspx?id=58#FAQ1.

Chilcoat, G. W., and J. A. Ligon (1999). "'Helping to Make Democracy a Living Reality': The Curriculum Conference of the Mississippi Freedom Schools." *Journal of Curriculum and Supervision* 15(1): 43–68.

Chong, Dennis, and Reuel Rogers (2005). "Reviving Group Consciousness." In *The Politics of Democratic Inclusion*, ed. Christina Wolbrecht and Rodney E. Hero, 45–74. Philadelphia: Temple University Press.

Christensen, Linda (1994). "Whose Standard? Teaching Standard English." *Rethinking Our Classrooms: Teaching for Equity and Justice*, vol. 1, ed. Bill Bigelow, 142–145. Milwaukee, WI: Rethinking Schools.

Churchill, Winston (1925). "Mass Effects in Modern Life." Retrieved August 16, 2008, 2008, from www.teachingamericanhistory.org/library/index.asp?documentprint=1032.

CNN.com (1996, October 13). "Nation of Islam Investigates Possible CIA Crack Connection." Retrieved October 18, 2010, from www.cnn.com/US/9610/13/farrakhan/.

——— (2008, February 21). "CNN Heroes: A Note to Educators." Retrieved August 16, 2008, from www.cnn.com/2008/LIVING/studentnews/02/08/heroes.educator.note/index.html.

Cohen, Cathy J., and Michael C. Dawson (1993). "Neighborhood Poverty and African American Politics." *American Political Science Review* 87(2): 286–302.

Corporation for National and Community Service (2008). "Community Service and Service-Learning in America's Schools." Retrieved May 22, 2010, from nationalservice.gov/pdf/08_1112_lsa_prevalence_factsheet.pdf.

——— (2009). "President Obama Signs Landmark National Service Legislation." Retrieved May 22, 2010, from www.nationalservice.gov/about/newsroom/releases_detail.asp?tbl_pr_id=1301.

Corporation for National and Community Service and National Conference on Citizenship (2010a). "Civic Life in America: Data on the Civic Health of the Nation." Civic Life in America. Retrieved June 1, 2011, from civic.serve.gov/national.

——— (2010b). "Civic Life in America: Key Findings on the Civic

Health of the Nation." Civic Life in America. Retrieved June 2, 2011, from www.ncoc.net/index.php?download=103kcfl378.

Cowen, Tyler (2000, May) "The New Heroes and Role Models." *Reason*. Retrieved August 15, 2008, from findarticles.com/p/articles/mi_m1568/is_1_32/ai_62162015/pg_1?tag=artBody;col1.

Craig, Bruce (2003, May 2). "SEDIT-L archives—May 2003 (no. 1)." *NCH Washington Update* 9(19). Retrieved May 18, 2007, from https://listserv.umd.edu/cgi-bin/wa?A2=ind0305&L=sedit-l&O=A&P=52.

Cramer, Maria, and Adrienne P. Samuels (2005, December 30). "Boston's Homicides 2005: A Boston Globe Special Report." *Boston Globe*. Retrieved June 28, 2010, from www.boston.com/news/specials/homicide2.

Cross, William E., Jr., Linda Strauss, and Peony Fhagen-Smith (1999). "African-American Identity Development across the Life Span: Educational Implications." In *Racial and Ethnic Identity in School Practices: Aspects of Human Development,* ed. Rosa Hernández Sheets and Etta R. Hollins, 29–47. Mahwah, NJ: Lawrence Erlbaum Associates.

Curren, Randall R. (2004). "Educational Measurement and Knowledge of Other Minds." *Theory and Research in Education* 2(3): 235–253.

Damon, William (1995). *Greater Expectations: Overcoming the Culture of Indulgence in America's Homes and Schools.* New York: Free Press.

——— (2001). "To Not Fade Away: Restoring Civil Identity among the Young." In *Making Good Citizens,* ed. Diane Ravitch and Joseph P. Viteritti, 123–141. New Haven: Yale University Press.

Dance, Lory Janelle (2002). *Tough Fronts: The Impact of Street Culture on Schooling.* New York: Routledge.

Darling-Hammond, Linda (2004). "From 'Separate But Equal' to 'No Child Left Behind': The Collision of New Standards and Old Inequalities." In *Many Children Left Behind: How the No Child Left Behind Act Is Damaging Our Children and Our Schools,* ed. Deborah Meier and George Wood, 3–32. Boston: Beacon Press.

Darling-Hammond, Linda, Jennifer French, and Silvia Paloma Garcia-Lopez, eds. (2002). *Learning to Teach for Social Justice.* Multicultural Education Series. New York: Teachers College Press.

Davis, James E., Phyllis Fernlund, and Peter Woll (2005). *Civics: Government and Economics in Action.* Upper Saddle River, NJ: Prentice Hall.

Davis, Leroy (1998). *A Clashing of the Soul: John Hope and the Dilemma of African American Leadership and Black Higher Education in the Early Twentieth Century.* Athens: University of Georgia Press.

Dawson, Michael C. (1994). *Behind the Mule: Race and Class in African-American Politics.* Princeton: Princeton University Press.

—— (2001). *Black Visions: The Roots of Contemporary African-American Political Ideologies.* Chicago: University of Chicago Press.

—— (2006). "After the Deluge: Publics and Publicity in Katrina's Wake." *Du Bois Review* 3(1): 239–249.

Delgado, Melvin, and Lee Staples (2008). *Youth-Led Community Organizing: Theory and Action.* Oxford: Oxford University Press.

Delgado, Richard D., and Jean Stefancic (2001). *Critical Race Theory: An Introduction.* New York: New York University Press.

Delli Carpini, Michael, and Scott Keeter (1996). *What Americans Know about Politics and Why It Matters.* New Haven: Yale University Press.

Delpit, Lisa (1995). *Other People's Children.* New York: New Press.

Delpit, Lisa, and Joanne Kilgour Dowdy, eds. (2002). *The Skin That We Speak: Thoughts on Language and Culture in the Classroom.* New York: New Press.

DeSipio, Louis (2001). "Building America, One Person at a Time: Naturalization and Political Behavior of the Naturalized in Contemporary American Politics." In *E Pluribus Unum? Contemporary and Historical Perspectives on Immigrant Political Incorporation,* ed. Gary Gerstle and John Mollenkopf, 67–106. New York: Russell Sage Foundation.

Devos, Thierry, and Mahzarin R. Banaji (2005). "American = White?" *Journal of Personality and Social Psychology* 88(3): 447–466.

Dewey, John (1990 [1900]). *The School and Society and The Child and the Curriculum.* Chicago: University of Chicago Press.

Dillon, Erin (2009, September) "Moving Targets: What It Now Means to Make 'Adequate Yearly Progress' under NCLB." *Explainer.* Retrieved February 10, 2010, from www.educationsector.org/usr_doc/EXP_AYP_UPDATE.pdf.

Dillon, Sam (2010, June 25). "School Is Turned Around, but Cost Gives Pause." *New York Times,* A1, A3.

Dimond, Stanley E., and Elmer F. Pflieger (1974). *Civics for Citizens: Annotated Edition.* Philadelphia: J. B. Lippincott.

Dinkes, Rachel, et al. (2009). "Indicators of School Crime and Safety: 2009." National Center for Education Statistics and Bureau of Justice Statistics, U.S. Department of Justice. Retrieved June 28, 2010, from bjs.ojp.usdoj.gov/index.cfm?ty=pbdetail&iid=1762.

Dreeben, Robert (1968). *On What Is Learned in School*. Reading, MA: Addison-Wesley.

Du Bois, W. E. B. (1996 [1903]). *The Souls of Black Folk*. New York: Penguin.

Duncan-Andrade, Jeffrey (2005). "An Examination of the Sociopolitical History of Chicanos and Its Relationship to School Performance." *Urban Education* 40(6): 576–605.

——— (2006). "Urban Youth, Media Literacy, and Increased Critical Civic Participation." In *Beyond Resistance! Youth Activism and Community Change,* ed. Shawn Ginwright et al., 149–169. New York: Routledge.

——— (2007). "Gangstas, Wankstas, and Ridas: Defining, Developing, and Supporting Effective Teachers in Urban Schools." *International Journal of Qualitative Studies in Education* 20(6): 617–638.

Duncan-Andrade, Jeffrey, and Ernest Morrell (2008). *The Art of Critical Pedagogy: Possibilities for Moving from Theory to Practice in Urban Schools*. New York: Peter Lang.

Dyson, Michael Eric (2004). *The Michael Eric Dyson Reader*. New York: Basic Civitas.

——— (2005). *Come Hell or High Water: Hurricane Katrina and the Color of Disaster*. New York: Basic Civitas.

Earth Force (2010). "Earth Force: Programs: The Earth Force Framework." Retrieved March 30, 2010, from www.earthforce.org/section/programs/caps.

Eaton, Susan (2006). *The Children in Room E4: American Education on Trial*. Chapel Hill, NC: Algonquin Books.

Edelstein, Alan (1996). *Everybody Is Sitting on the Curb: How and Why America's Heroes Disappeared*. New York: Praeger.

Egelko, Bob (2007, October 2). "Supreme Court Denies Hearing for Fired 'Honk for Peace' Teacher." *San Francisco Chronicle,* A7.

Elliott, Elizabeth, and Robert M. Gordon, eds. (2005). *New Directions in Restorative Justice: Issues, Practice, Evaluation*. Portland, OR: Willan.

Elmore, Richard F. (2005). "Agency, Reciprocity, and Accountability in Democratic Education." In *The Public Schools,* ed. Susan Fuhrman and Marvin Lazerson, 277–301. New York: Oxford University Press.

Epstein, Terrie (1997). "Sociocultural Approaches to Young People's Historical Understanding." *Social Education* 61: 28–31.

——— (1998). "Deconstructing Differences in American-American and European-American Adolescents' Perspectives on U.S. History." *Curriculum Inquiry* 28(4): 397–423.

——— (2000). "Adolescents' Perspectives on Racial Diversity in U.S. History: Case Studies from an Urban Classroom." *American Educational Research Journal* 37(1): 185–214.

——— (2001). "Racial Identity and Young People's Perspectives on Social Education." *Theory into Practice* 40(1): 42–47.

——— (2009). *Interpreting National History: Race, Identity, and Pedagogy in Classrooms and Communities.* New York: Routledge.

Farrelly, Colin (2007). "Justice in Ideal Theory: A Refutation." *Political Studies* 55(4): 844–864.

Fassin, Didier (2007). *When Bodies Remember: Experiences and Politics of AIDS in South Africa.* Berkeley: University of California Press.

Fehrenbacher, Don E. (2001). *The Slaveholding Republic: An Account of the United States Government's Relations to Slavery.* New York: Oxford University Press.

Feinberg, Walter (1998). *Common Schools/Uncommon Identities.* New Haven: Yale University Press.

Feldman, Lauren, et al. (2007). "Identifying Best Practices in Civic Education: Lessons from the Student Voices Program." *American Journal of Education* 114(1): 75–100.

Feldman, Noah (2011, June 13) "Praise the Arab Spring, Prepare for the Arab Fall." *Bloomberg.* Retrieved June 17, 2011, from www.bloomberg.com/news/2011-06-13/praise-the-arab-spring-prepare-for-the-arab-fall-noah-feldman.html.

Fellner, Jamie, and Lance Compa (2005). "Immigrant Workers in the United States Meat and Poultry Industry." Submission by Human Rights Watch to the Office of the United Nations High Commissioner for Human Rights Committee on Migrant Workers. Human Rights Watch, Geneva. Retrieved October 11, 2010, from www2.ohchr.org/english/bodies/cmw/docs/hrw.doc.

Fine, Michelle (2009). "Postcards from Metro America: Reflections on Youth Participatory Action Research for Urban Justice." *Urban Review* 41: 1–6.

Fine, Michelle, and Lois Weis, eds. (2000). *Construction Sites: Excavating Race, Class, and Gender among Urban Youth.* New York: Teachers College Press.

Fishwick, Marshall William (1969). *The Hero, American Style.* New York: D. McKay.

Flanagan, Constance A., et al. (2007). "School and Community Climates and Civic Commitments: Patterns for Ethnic Minority and

Majority Students." *Journal of Educational Psychology* 99(2): 421–431.

Fogel, Howard, and Ehri Linnea (2000). "Teaching Elementary Students Who Speak Black English Vernacular to Write in Standard English: Effects of Dialect Transformation Practice." *Contemporary Educational Psychology* 25(2): 212–235.

Foner, Eric (1998). *The Story of American Freedom.* New York: W. W. Norton.

Foote, Donna (2008). *Relentless Pursuit: A Year in the Trenches with Teach for America.* New York: Alfred A. Knopf.

Foster, Michele (1997). *Black Teachers on Teaching.* New York: New Press.

Frankenberg, Erica, and Chungmei Lee (2002). *Race in American Public Schools: Rapidly Resegregating School Districts.* Cambridge, MA: Civil Rights Project of Harvard University.

Fraser, Katie (2005). "Youth Courts." *Insights on Law and Society* 5(2): 20–21.

Frederickson, George M. (2002). *Racism: A Short History.* Princeton: Princeton University Press.

Freeman, Joshua B. (2002). "Red New York." *Monthly Review* 54(3): 36–42.

Freire Charter School (2010). "Freire Charter School Home." Retrieved March 3, 2010, from www.freirecharterschool.org/index.htm.

Friedman, Anne Kiehl (2005). "Voter Disenfranchisement and Policy toward Election Reforms." *Review of Policy Research* 22(6): 787–810.

Fuhrman, Susan, and Richard Elmore, eds. (2004). *Redesigning Accountability Systems for Education.* New York: Teachers College Press.

Fullan, Michael (2007). *The New Meaning of Educational Change,* 4th ed. New York: Teachers College Press.

Fullinwider, Robert K. (1996). "Patriotic History." In *Public Education in a Multicultural Society,* ed. Robert K. Fullinwider, 203–227. Cambridge: Cambridge University Press.

Fung, Archon (2004a). "Deliberation's Darker Side: Six Questions for Iris Marion Young and Jane Mansbridge." *National Civic Review* (Winter): 47–54.

——— (2004b). *Empowered Participation: Reinventing Urban Democracy.* Princeton: Princeton University Press.

Gagnon, Paul (2003). *Educating Democracy: State Standards To Ensure a Civic Core.* Washington, D.C.: Albert Shanker Institute.

Gaines, Kevin Kelly (1996). *Uplifting the Race: Black Leadership, Politics, and Culture in the Twentieth Century.* Chapel Hill: University of North Carolina Press.

Gallup Organization (1949). "Survey by Gallup Organization, December 2–December 7, 1949." Lincoln, NE: Gallup Organization; Storrs, CT: The Roper Center for Public Opinion Research.

——— (1955). "Survey by Gallup Organization, December 8–December 13, 1955." Gallup Poll # 557. Lincoln, NE: Gallup Organization; Storrs, CT: The Roper Center for Public Opinion Research.

——— (1966). "Survey by Gallup Organization, December 8–December 13, 1966." Gallup Poll # 738. Lincoln, NE: Gallup Organization; Storrs, CT: The Roper Center for Public Opinion Research.

——— (1977). "Survey by Gallup Organization, December 9–December 12, 1977." Gallup Poll # 990. Lincoln, NE: Gallup Organization; Storrs, CT: The Roper Center for Public Opinion Research.

——— (2006). "Survey by Gallup Organization, December 11–December 14, 2006." Lincoln, NE: Gallup Organization; Storrs, CT: The Roper Center for Public Opinion Research.

Gallup Organization and Linda Lyons (2002). "No Heroes in the Beltway." Retrieved August 18, 2008, from www.gallup.com/poll/6487/Heroes-Beltway.aspx.

Galston, William A. (2001). "Political Knowledge, Political Engagement, and Civic Education." *Annual Reviews Political Science* 4: 217–234.

——— (2003). "Civic Education and Political Participation." *Phi Delta Kappan* 85(1): 29–33.

Ganz, Marshall (2007). "What Is Public Narrative?" Harvard Kennedy School of Government. Retrieved June 8, 2011, from www.hks.harvard.edu/organizing/tools/Files/What%20Is%20Public%20Narrative.3.8.07.doc.

Gasman, Marybeth (2007). *Envisioning Black Colleges: A History of the United Negro College Fund.* Baltimore: Johns Hopkins University Press.

Gecan, Michael (2002). *Going Public: An Organizer's Guide to Citizen Action.* New York: Anchor Books.

Gerstle, Gary (2001). *American Crucible: Race and Nation in the Twentieth Century.* Princeton: Princeton University Press.

Geuss, Raymond (2008). *Philosophy and Real Politics.* Princeton: Princeton University Press.

Gibbon, Peter (2002a, October 1). "Panel Discussion: Why Is U.S. History Still a Mystery to Our Children?" Retrieved May 18, 2007, from www.aei.org/events/filter.,eventID.131/transcript.asp.

———— (2002b). *A Call to Heroism: Renewing America's Vision of Greatness*. New York: Atlantic Monthly Press.

Gibson, Margaret A. (1988). *Accommodation without Assimilation: Sikh Immigrants in an American High School*. Ithaca, NY: Cornell University Press.

Gimpel, James G., J. Celeste Lay, and Jason E. Schuknecht (2003). *Cultivating Democracy: Civic Environments and Political Socialization in America*. Washington, D.C.: Brookings Institution Press.

Ginwright, Shawn A., Pedro Noguera, and Julio Cammarota, eds. (2006). *Beyond Resistance! Youth Activism and Community Change: New Democratic Possibliities for Practice and Policy for America's Youth*. New York: Routledge.

Ginwright, Shawn A., and Taj James (2002). "From Assets to Agents of Change: Social Justice, Organizing, and Youth Development." *New Directions for Youth Development* 96: 27–46.

Giraffe Heroes Project (2008a). "Kids Page—Guided Tour Stop 1." Retrieved December 5, 2008, from www.giraffe.org/guidedtour1_text.html.

———— (2008b). "Kids Page—Guided Tour Stop 2." Retrieved December 5, 2008, from www.giraffe.org/guidedtour2_text.html.

Gleeson, Shannon (2010). "Labor Rights for All? The Role of Undocumented Immigrant Status for Worker Claims Making." *Law and Social Inquiry* 35(3): 561–602.

Glencoe/McGraw-Hill (2005). *Civics Today: Citizenship, Economics, and You*. New York: Glencoe.

Gordon, Pamela Jane (2011). *Developing Citizenship: Examining the Experiences of Youth from a Civic Focused School*. Ed.D. diss., Graduate School of Education, Harvard University.

Governor's Statewide Youth Council (2009). "The Governor's Statewide Youth Council Midterm Report." Boston, MA: Governor's Office, State of Massachusetts.

Grant, Gerald (2009). *Hope and Despair in the American City: Why There Are No Bad Schools in Raleigh*. Cambridge, MA: Harvard University Press.

Grier, Sonya A., and Shiriki K. Kunnanyika (2008). "The Context for Choice: Health Implications of Targeted Food and Beverage Marketing to African Americans." *American Journal of Public Health* 98(9): 1619–1629.

Grossman, Lev (2009, June 17) "Iran Protests: Twitter, the Medium of the Movement." *Time Magazine*. Retrieved July 30, 2009, from www.time.com/time/world/article/0,8599,1905125,00.html.

Guinan, M. E. (1993). "Black Communities' Belief in 'AIDS as Genocide': A Barrier to Overcome for HIV Prevention." *Annals of Epidemiology* 3(2): 193–195.

Guinier, Lani (1994). *The Tyranny of the Majority: Fundamental Fairness in Representative Democracy.* New York: Free Press.

Gutmann, Amy (1987). *Democratic Education.* Princeton: Princeton University Press.

——— (1995). "Civic Education and Social Diversity." *Ethics* 105(3): 557–579.

Gutmann, Amy, and Dennis F. Thompson (1996). *Democracy and Disagreement.* Cambridge, MA: Belknap Press of Harvard University Press.

Hahn, Carole L. (1998). *Becoming Political.* Albany: State University of New York Press.

——— (1999). "Citizenship Education: An Empirical Study of Policy, Practices and Outcomes." *Oxford Review of Education* 25(1–2): 231–250.

Hahn, Steven (2009). *The Political Worlds of Slavery and Freedom.* Cambridge, MA: Harvard University Press.

Hall, Lani, et al. (2009). "Essential Elements of the 4-H Experience: Generosity." *Arizona Cooperative Extension:* 1–3. Retrieved May 23, 2010, from cals.arizona.edu/pubs/family/az1495d.pdf.

Han, Hahrie (2009). *Moved to Action: Motivation, Participation, and Inequality in American Politics.* Stanford, CA: Stanford University Press.

Haney Lopéz, Ian (1996). *White by Law: The Legal Construction of Race.* New York: New York University Press.

Hanson, Christopher (1996). "Where Have All the Heroes Gone?" *Columbia Journalism Review* 34(6): 45–48.

Harris, Cheryl I. (1993). "Whiteness as Property." *Harvard Law Review* 106(8): 1707–1791.

Harris-Lacewell, Melissa (2007). "Do You Know What It Means . . . : Mapping Emotion in the Aftermath of Katrina." *Souls* 9(1): 28–44.

Harris-Lacewell, Melissa, Kosuke Imai, and Teppei Yamamoto (2007). "Racial Gaps in the Responses to Hurricane Katrina: An Experimental Study." Princeton University. Retrieved October 20, 2010, from imai.princeton.edu/research/files/katrina.pdf.

Hart, Daniel, and Robert Atkins (2002). "Civic Competence in Urban Youth." *Applied Developmental Science* 6(4): 227–236.

Hart, Daniel, et al. (2004). "Youth Bulges in Communities: The Effects of Age Structure on Adolescent Civic Knowledge and Civic Participation." *Psychological Science* 15(9): 591–597.

Hart, Daniel, et al. (2007). "High School Community Service as a Predictor of Adult Voting and Volunteering." *American Educational Research Journal* 44(1): 197–219.

Hartley, William H., and William S. Vincent (2005). *Holt American Civics*. New York: Holt, Rinehart and Winston.

Haste, Helen (2004). "Constructing the Citizen." *Political Psychology* 25(3): 413–439.

Hepburn, Mary A., Richard G. Niemi, and Chris Chapman (2000). "Service Learning in College Political Science: Queries and Commentary." *PS: Political Science and Politics* 33(3).

Herman, Joan (2003). "The Effects of Testing on Instruction." In *Redesigning Accountability Systems for Education*, ed. Susan Furhman and Richard Elmore, 141–166. New York: Teachers College Press.

Herring, Cedric (2006). "Hurricane Katrina and the Racial Gulf: A Du Boisian Analysis of Victims' Experience." *Du Bois Review* 3(1): 129–144.

Hess, Diana E. (2009a). *Controversy in the Classroom : The Democratic Power of Discussion*. New York: Routledge.

——— (2009b). "Teaching about Same-Sex Marriage as a Policy and Constitutional Issue." *Social Education* 73(7): 344–349.

Hibbing, John R., and Elizabeth Theiss-Morse (2002). *Stealth Democracy: Americans' Beliefs about How Government Should Work*. New York: Cambridge University Press.

Hilliard, Asa G. (1998). *SBA: The Reawakening of the African Mind*, rev. ed. Gainesville, FL: Makare.

Hilliard, Asa G., et al. (1990). *Infusion of African and African American Content in the School Curriculum: Proceedings of the First National Conference, October 1989*. Morristown, N.J.: Aaron Press.

Hochschild, Jennifer (2005). "From Nominal to Ordinal: Reconceiving Racial and Ethnic Hierarchy in the United States." In *The Politics of Democratic Inclusion*, ed. Christina Wolbrecht and Rodney E. Hero, 19–44. Philadelphia: Temple University Press.

Hochschild, Jennifer, and Nathan Scovronick (2003). *The American Dream and the Public Schools*. Oxford: Oxford University Press.

Homana, Gary, Carolyn Barber, and Judith Torney-Purta (2006). "Assessing School Citizenship Education Climate: Implications for the Social Studies." CIRCLE Working Paper 48. College Park, MD: Center for Information and Research on Civic Learning and Engagement. Retrieved January 17, 2012, from www.civicyouth.org/popups/workingpapers/WP48homana.pdf.

Hook, Sidney (1943). *The Hero in History: A Study in Limitation and Possibility*. New York: John Day.

hooks, bell (1994). *Teaching to Transgress: Education as the Practice of Freedom.* New York: Routledge.

Horne, Tom (2007, June 11). "An Open Letter to the Citizens of Tucson." Department of Education, Office of the Superintendent of Public Instruction, State of Arizona. Retrieved July 5, 2010, from www.ade.state.az.us/; www.ade.state.az.us/administration/superintendent/AnOpenLettertoCitizensofTucson.pdf.

Horsford, Sonya Douglass, and Kathryn Bell McKenzie (2008). "'Sometimes I Feel Like the Problems Started with Desegregation': Exploring Black Superintendent Perspectives on Desegregation Policy." *International Journal of Qualitative Studies in Education* 21(5): 443–455.

Horton, Carol A. (2005). *Race and the Making of American Liberalism.* New York: Oxford University Press.

Howard, Gary R. (2006). *We Can't Teach What We Don't Know: White Teachers, Multiracial Schools.* New York: Teachers College Press.

Huddy, Leonie, and Stanley Feldman (2006). "Worlds Apart: Blacks and Whites React to Hurricane Katrina." *Du Bois Review* 3(1): 1–17.

Hughes, Diane, et al. (2009). "Received Ethnic-Racial Socialization Message and Youths' Academic and Behavioral Outcomes: Examining the Mediating Role of Ethnic Identity and Self-Esteem." *Cultural Diversity and Ethnic Minority Psychology* 15(2): 112–124.

Hughes, Langston (1994[1925]). "I, Too, Sing America." In *The Collected Poems of Langston Hughes.* New York: Knopf.

Iceland, John, Daniel H. Weinberg, and Erika Steinmetz (2002). "Racial and Ethnic Residential Segregation in the United States: 1980–2000." Series CENSR-3, U.S. Census Bureau.

IES: National Center for Education Statistics (2007). "NAEP Data Explorer." Retrieved July 9, 2007, from nces.ed.gov/nationsreport card/nde/.

Ignatiev, Noel (1995). *How the Irish Became White.* New York: Routledge.

Irons, Peter (2002). *Jim Crow's Children: The Broken Promise of the Brown Decision.* New York: Viking Penguin.

Ives, Bob, and Kathryn Obenchain (2006). "Experiential Education in the Classroom and Academic Outcomes: For Those Who Want It All." *Journal of Experiential Education* 29(1): 61–77.

Jackson, Philip W. (1968). *Life in Classrooms.* New York: Holt, Rinehart, and Winston.

Jacobs, Lawrence R., and Theda Skocpol, eds. (2005). *Inequality and*

American Democracy: What We Know and What We Need to Learn. New York: Russell Sage Foundation.

Jaime-Castillo, Antonio M. (2009). "Economic Inequality and Electoral Participation: A Cross-Country Evaluation." Paper presented at Comparative Study of the Electoral Systems (CSES) Conference, Toronto. Retrieved November 11, 2010, from www.cses.org/plancom/2009Toronto/CSES_2009Toronto_JaimeCastillo.pdf.

James, William (1880). "Great Men, Great Thoughts, and the Environment." *Atlantic Monthly* 46(276): 441–459.

Jenkins, Henry (2009). *Confronting the Challenges of Participatory Culture: Media Education for the 21st Century.* Cambridge, MA: MIT Press.

John, Mary (2000). "The Children's Parliament in Rajasthan: A Model for Learning About Democracy." In *Citizenship and Democracy in Schools: Diversity, Identity, Equality,* ed. Audry Osler, 169–175. Stoke-on-Trent, UK: Trentham.

Johns, Michael, Toni Schmader, and Andy Martens (2005). "Knowing Is Half the Battle: Teaching Stereotype Threat as a Means of Improving Women's Math Performance." *Psychological Science* 16: 175–179.

Johnson, James Weldon (2000). *Lift Every Voice and Sing.* New York: Penguin.

Johnson, Kevin R., et al. (2007, August 4). "ImmigrationProfBlog: Asian Exclusion Laws." ImmigrationProf Blog. Retrieved October 20, 2010, from lawprofessors.typepad.com/immigration/2007/08/asian-exclusion.html.

Jones-Correa, Michael (2005). "Bringing Outsiders In: Questions of Immigrant Incorporation." In *The Politics of Democratic Inclusion,* ed. Christina Wolbrecht and Rodney E. Hero, 75–102. Philadelphia: Temple University Press.

Jost, John T., and Mahzarin R. Banaji (1994). "The Role of Stereotyping in System-Justification and the Production of False Consciousness." *British Journal of Social Psychology* 33: 1–27.

Jost, John T., Brett W. Pelham, and Mauricio R. Carvallo (2002). "Non-Conscious Forms of System Justification: Implicit and Behavioral Preferences for Higher Status Groups." *Journal of Experimental Social Psychology* 38: 586–602.

Jung, Moon-Kie, João H. Costa Vargas, and Eduardo Bonilla-Silva (2011). *State of White Supremacy: Racism, Governance, and the United States.* Stanford: Stanford University Press.

Junn, Jane (2006). "Mobilizing Group Consciousness: When Does Ethnicity Have Political Consequences?" In *Transforming Politics,*

Transforming America: The Political and Civic Incorporation of Immigrants in the United States, ed. Taeku Lee et al., 32–47. Charlottesville: University of Virginia Press.

Kahne, Joseph, et al. (2000). "Developing Citizens for Democracy? Assessing Opportunities to Learn in Chicago's Social Studies Classrooms." *Theory and Research in Social Education* 28(3): 331–338.

Kahne, Joseph, and Ellen Middaugh (2008). "Democracy for Some: The Civic Opportunity Gap in High School." CIRCLE Working Paper 59. College Park, MD: Center for Information and Research on Civic Learning and Engagement. Retrieved November 12, 2011, from www.civicyouth.org/PopUps/WorkingPapers/WP59Kahne.pdf

Kahne, Joseph E., and Susan E. Sporte (2008). "Developing Citizens: The Impact of Civic Learning Opportunities on Students' Commitment to Civic Participation." *American Educational Research Journal* 45(3): 738–766.

Kahne, Joseph, and Joel Westheimer (2003). "Teaching Democracy: What Schools Need to Do." *Phi Delta Kappan* 85(1): 34–40, 57–66.

——— (2006). "The Limits of Efficacy: Educating Citizens for a Democratic Society." *PS: Political Science and Politics* 39(2): 289–296.

Kammen, Michael G. (1991). *Mystic Chords of Memory: The Transformation of Tradition in American Culture.* New York: Knopf.

Kanner, Elisabeth (2005). *Doing Democracy: A Study of Nine Effective Civic Educators.* Ed.D. diss., Graduate School of Education, Harvard University.

Kasinitz, Philip, John Mollenkopf, and Mary C. Waters (2002). "Becoming Americans/Becoming New Yorkers: The Experience of Assimilation in a Majority Minority City." *International Migration Review* 36(4): 1020–1036.

Keeter, Scott, et al. (2002). "The Civic and Political Health of the Nation: A Generational Portrait." College Park, MD: Center for Information and Research on Civic Learning and Engagement. Retrieved November 12, 2011, from www.civicyouth.org/research/products/Civic_Political_Health.pdf.

Kelly, Christopher (1997). "Rousseau's Case For and Against Heroes." *Polity* 30(2): 347–366.

——— (2003). *Rousseau as Author: Consecrating One's Life to the Truth.* Chicago: University of Chicago Press.

Kemper, Theodore D. (1968). "Reference Groups, Socialization, and Achievement." *American Sociological Review* 33: 31–45.

Kerber, Linda K. (1998). *No Constitutional Right to Be Ladies:*

Women and the Obligations of Citizenship. New York: Hill and Wang.

Kerr, Bob (2011, May 11) "These Students Found a Way to Make a Difference." *Providence Journal*. Retrieved June 17, 2011, from www.projo.com/news/bobkerr/kerr_column_11_05-11-11_LFO 0K3P_v12.311df66.html.

Kerr, David (2002). "Citizenship Education: An International Comparison across Sixteen Countries." *International Journal of Social Education* 17(1): 1–15.

Kim, Young Chul (2009). "Lifetime Network Externality and the Dynamics of Group Inequality." Munich Personal RePEc Archive (MPRA) Paper. University Library of Munich. Retrieved May 24, 2011, from mpra.ub.uni-muenchen.de/18767/1/MPRA_pa per_18767.pdf.

Kinder, Donald R. (1998). "Opinion and Action in the Realm of Politics." *Handbook of Social Psychology*, 4th ed., ed. Daniel T. Gilbert et al., 778–867. Boston: McGraw-Hill.

KIPP (2011a). "KIPP about KIPP." Retrieved June 13, 2011, from www.kipp.org/about-kipp.

——— (2011b). "KIPP Five Pillars." Retrieved June 13, 2011, from www.kipp.org/about-kipp/five-pillars.

Kirshner, Ben (2006). "Apprenticeship Learning in Youth Activism." In *Beyond Resistance! Youth Activism and Community Change*, ed. Shawn A. Ginwright et al., 37–57. New York: Routledge.

——— (2008). "Guided Participation in Three Youth Activism Organizations: Facilitation, Apprenticeship, and Joint Work." *Journal of the Learning Sciences* 17(1): 60–101.

Kirshner, Ben, Karen Strobel, and Maria Fernández (2003). "Critical Civic Engagement among Urban Youth." *Penn GSE Perspectives on Urban Education* 2(1): 1–20.

Klapp, Orrin E. (1949). "Hero Worship in America." *American Sociological Review* 14(1): 53–62.

Knight, Michelle (2011). "It's Already Happening: Learning from Civically Engaged Transnational Immigrant Youth." *Teachers College Record* 113(6): 1275–1292.

Koch, Kathleen (1996, Oct. 23). "CIA Disavows Crack Connection; Many Skeptical." CNN. Retrieved October 18, 2010, from www .cnn.com/US/9610/23/cia.crack/.

Kohl, Herbert (1995). *Should We Burn Babar? Essays on Children's Literature and the Power of Stories*. New York: New Press.

Kohn, Alfie (2002). "Education's Rotten Apples." *Education Week* 22(3): 48.

Koretz, Daniel (2008). *Measuring Up: What Educational Testing Really Tells Us.* Cambridge, MA: Harvard University Press.

Kozol, Jonathan (2005). *The Shame of the Nation: The Restoration of Apartheid Schooling in America.* New York: Crown.

Ladson-Billings, Gloria (1994). *The Dreamkeepers: Successful Teachers of African American Children.* San Francisco: Jossey-Bass.

—— (2004). "Landing on the Wrong Note: The Price We Paid for *Brown.*" *Educational Researcher* 33(7): 3–13.

—— (2006). "From the Achievement Gap to the Education Debt: Understanding Achievement in U.S. Schools." *Educational Researcher* 35(3): 3–12.

—— (2009, June 9) "Inching toward Equity." *Forum for Education and Democracy.* Retrieved August 3, 2009, from www.forumfor education.org/node/477.

Lake Snell Perry and Associates, and the Tarrance Group (2002). "Short-Term Impacts, Long-Term Opportunities: The Political and Civic Engagement of Young People in America." College Park, MD: Center for Information and Research on Civic Learning and Engagement and The Center for Democracy and Citizenship and the Partnership for Trust in Government at the Council of Excellence in Government.

Lareau, Annette (2003). *Unequal Childhoods: Class, Race, and Family Life.* Berkeley: University of California Press.

Lay, J. Celeste, and Kathleen J. Smarick (2006). "Simulating a Senate Office: The Impact on Student Knowledge and Attitudes." *Journal of Political Science Education* 2(2): 131–146.

Learn and Serve America's National Service-Learning Clearinghouse (2008). "Policy: K–12 Service Learning." Retrieved May 22, 2010, from www.servicelearning.org/instant_info/fact_sheets/k-12_facts/policy/.

—— (2010). "What is Service-Learning?" Retrieved May 22, 2010, from www.servicelearning.org/what_is_service-learning/service-learning_is.

Lee, Stacey J. (2005). *Up against Whiteness: Race, School, and Immigrant Youth.* New York: Teachers College Press.

Lee, Taeku, S. Karthick Ramakrishnan, and Ricardo Ramírez (2006a). "Introduction." In *Transforming Politics, Transforming America: The Political and Civic Incorporation of Immigrants in the United States,* ed. Taeku Lee et al., 1–16. Charlottesville: University of Virginia Press.

——, eds. (2006b). *Transforming Politics, Transforming America:*

The Political and Civic Incorporation of Immigrants in the United States. Charlottesville: University of Virginia Press.

Lee, Trymaine (2010, August 27). "Rumor to Fact in Tales of Post-Katrina Violence." *New York Times.* Retrieved October 5, 2010, from www.nytimes.com/2010/08/27/us/27racial.html?ref=hurricane_katrina.

Levin, Ben (2008). *How to Change 5000 Schools: A Practical and Positive Approach for Leading Change at Every Level.* Cambridge, MA: Harvard Education Press.

Levinson, Meira (1999). *The Demands of Liberal Education.* Oxford: Oxford University Press.

——— (2003a). "Challenging Deliberation." *Theory and Research in Education* 1(1): 23–49.

——— (2003b). "The Language of Race." *Theory and Research in Education* 1(3): 267–281.

——— (2009a). "'Let Us Now Praise. . . ?' Rethinking Heroes and Role Models in an Egalitarian Age." In *Philosophy of Education in the Era of Globalization,* ed. Yvonne Raley and Gerhard Preyer, 129–161. New York: Routledge.

——— (2009b). "Mapping Multicultural Education." In *Oxford Handbook of Philosophy of Education,* ed. Harvey Siegel, 420–442. New York: Oxford University Press.

Levinson, Meira, and Sanford Levinson (2003). "'Getting Religion': Religion, Diversity, and Community in Public and Private Schools." In *School Choice: The Moral Debate,* ed. Alan Wolfe, 104–125. Princeton: Princeton University Press.

Lewis, Amanda E. (2004). "'What Group?' Studying Whites and Whiteness in the Era of 'Color-Blindness.'" *Sociological Theory* 22(4): 623–646.

Lijphart, Arend (1997). "Unequal Participation: Democracy's Unresolved Dilemma." *American Political Science Review* 91(1): 1–14.

Linn, Robert R. (2000). "Assessments and Accountability." *Educational Researcher* 29(2): 4–16.

Lipsitz, George (1995). "The Possessive Investment in Whiteness: Racialized Social Democracy and the 'White' Problem in American Studies." *American Quarterly* 47(3): 369–387.

Lockwood, Penelope, and Ziva Kunda (1997). "Superstars and Me: Predicting the Impact of Role Models on the Self." *Journal of Personality and Social Psychology* 73(1): 91–103.

——— (2000). "Outstanding Role Models: Do They Inspire or Demoralize Us?" In *Psychological Perspectives on Self and Identity,* ed. Abraham Tesser et al., 147–171. Washington, D.C.: American Psychological Association.

Loewen, James W. (1995). *Lies My Teacher Told Me: Everything Your American History Textbook Got Wrong.* New York: New Press.

Lopez, Mark Hugo (2003). "Electoral Engagement among Latino Youth." CIRCLE Fact Sheet. College Park, MD: Center for Information and Research on Civic Learning and Engagement. Retrieved November 12, 2003, from www.civicyouth.org/PopUps/Electoral %20%20Engagement%20Among%20Latino%20Youth.pdf.

Lopez, Mark Hugo, et al. (2006). *The 2006 Civic and Political Health of the Nation: A Detailed Look at How Youth Participate in Politics and Communities.* College Park, MD: Center for Information and Research on Civic Learning and Engagement. Retrieved January 17, 2012, from www.civicyouth.org/popups/2006_CPHS_Report_update.pdf.

Louie, Vivian Shuh Ming (2006). "Growing Up Ethnic in Transnational Worlds: Identities among Second-Generation Chinese and Dominicans." *Identities* 13(3): 363–394.

Loury, Glenn C. (1997, April 23). "Integration Has Had Its Day." *New York Times,* A23. Retrieved August 3, 2009, from www.nytimes.com/1997/04/23/opinion/integration-has-had-its-day.html?scp=1&sq=&st=nyt.

——— (2008). *Race, Incarceration, and American Values.* Cambridge, MA: MIT Press.

Lutkus, Anthony D., et al. (1999). "NAEP 1998 Civics Report Card for the Nation." Washington, D.C.: U.S. Department of Education, Office of Educational Research and Improvement, and National Center for Education Statistics.

Lyons, Linda (2008). "Results for Teens, Ages 13–17, Most Admired Men + Women," fax to author.

Macedo, Stephen (1990). *Liberal Virtues.* Oxford: Oxford University Press.

Macedo, Stephen, et al. (2005). *Democracy at Risk : How Political Choices Undermine Citizen Participation and What We Can Do about It.* Washington, D.C.: Brookings Institution Press.

Maira, Sunaina (2004). "Imperial Feelings: Youth Culture, Citizenship, and Globalization." In *Globalization: Culture and Education in the New Millenium,* ed. Marcelo M. Suárez-Orozco and Desirée Baolian Qin-Hilliard, 203–234. Berkeley: University of California Press.

——— (2009). *Missing: Youth, Citizenship, and Empire after 9/11.* Durham, NC: Duke University Press.

Maira, Sunaina, and Elisabeth Soep (2005). *Youthscapes: The Popular, the National, the Global.* Philadelphia: University of Pennsylvania Press.

Manley, Albert E. (1995). *A Legacy Continues: The Manley Years at Spelman College, 1953–1976.* Lanham, MD: University Press of America.

Mansbridge, Jane J. (1980). *Beyond Adversary Democracy.* New York: Basic Books.

Marr, Andrew (1998, October 2). "Where Have All of the Heroes Gone?" *New Statesman,* 25–26.

Marshall, Peter (2009) "Feedback on the Current K–12 Social Studies TEKS." Memo to Miriam Martinez, Curriculum Director, Texas Education Agency. Retrieved July 9, 2009, from ritter.tea.state.tx.us/teks/social/Marshallcurrent.pdf.

Martin, Ralph C., II (2001). "ABA Juvenile Justice Policies: Zero Tolerance Policy Report." American Bar Association. Retrieved October 29, 2011, from www.abanet.org/crimjust/juvjus/zerotolreport.html.

Massachusetts Senate (2011). "An Act to Design, Pilot, and Implement Civics as a High School Graduation Requirement." Massachusetts Senate Bill 00183.

Massey, Douglas S., and Nancy A. Denton (1993). *American Apartheid: Segregation and the Making of the Underclass.* Cambridge, MA: Harvard University Press.

Mayer, Jane (2009). *The Dark Side: The Inside Story of How the War on Terror Turned into a War on American Ideals.* New York: Anchor.

Mayer v. Monroe County Municipal School Corp., 474 F.3d 477 (7th Cir.), *cert. denied,* 552 U.S. 823 (2007).

McAdam, Doug (1988). *Freedom Summer.* New York: Oxford University Press.

McAdam, Doug, and Ronnelle Paulsen (2010). "Specifying the Relationship between Social Ties and Activism." In *Readings on Social Movements: Origins, Dynamics, and Outcomes, Second Edition,* ed. Doug McAdam and David A. Snow, 277–293. New York: Oxford University Press.

McClenaghan, William A. (1953). *Magruder's American Government.* Boston: Allyn and Bacon.

——— (2003). *Magruder's American Government,* rev. ed. Needham, MA: Prentice Hall.

McDorman, Todd F., et al. (2006). "Where Have All the Heroes Gone?" *Journal of Sport and Social Issues* 30(2): 197–218.

McFarland, Daniel A., and Reuben J. Thomas (2006). "Bowling Young: How Youth Voluntary Associations Influence Adult Political Participation." *American Sociological Review* 71 (June): 401–425.

McIntosh, Hugh, Sheldon Berman, and James Youniss (2010). "A Five Year Evaluation of a Comprehensive High School Civic Engagement Initiative." CIRCLE Working Paper No. 70. Medford, MA: Center for Information and Research on Civic Learning and Engagement. Retrieved September 20, 2011, from www.civicyouth. org/PopUps/WorkingPapers/WP_70_McIntosh_Berman_Youniss. pdf.

McIntosh, Peggy (1990). "White Privilege: Unpacking the Invisible Knapsack." *Independent School* 49(2): 31.

Mehan, Hugh (1979). *Learning Lessons.* Cambridge, MA: Harvard University Press.

Meier, Deborah (1995). *The Power of Their Ideas: Lessons for America from a Small School in Harlem.* Boston: Beacon Press.

——— (2003). "So What Does It Take to Build a School for Democracy?" *Phi Delta Kappan* 85(1): 15–21.

Melchior, Alan (2010). "Earth Force Evaluation Data Tables: CAPS Data 2008–2009." Center for Youth and Communities, Heller School for Social Policy and Management, Brandeis University. Retrieved May 27, 2010, from www.earthforce.org/files/2447_file _2008_2009_CAPS_Results.v1.pdf.

Mikva Challenge (2010). "Issues to Action: The Six Steps." Retrieved November 13, 2011, from www.mikvachallenge.org/site/files/719/ 58688/237214/328068/SixSteps_IssuesToAction_%282%29.pdf.

——— (2011). "Classroom Activism." Retrieved November 13, 2011, from www.mikvachallenge.org/activism.

Miller, David (2000). *Citizenship and National Identity.* Oxford: Oxford University Press.

Miller, Yawu (2010, May 13). "Hyde Square Task Force Study: "No Mutual Respect" between MBTA Police and Youths; Vow to Offer Solution." *Bay State Banner* 45, 40. Retrieved May 25, 2010, from www.baystatebanner.com/local11-2010-05-13.

Minow, Martha (2010). *In Brown's Wake: Legacies of America's Educational Landmark.* New York: Oxford University Press.

Moe, Terry M. (2000). "The Two Democratic Purposes of Public Education." In *Rediscovering the Democratic Purposes of Education,* ed. Lorraine M. McDonnell et al., 127–147. Lawrence: University Press of Kansas.

Mollenkopf, John, et al. (2006). "Politics among Young Adults in New

York: The Immigrant Second Generation." In *Transforming Politics, Transforming America: The Political and Civic Incorporation of Immigrants in the United States,* ed. Taeku Lee et al., 175–193. Charlottesville: University of Virginia Press.

Montgomery, David (1993). *Citizen Worker: The Experience of Workers in the United States with Democracy and the Free Market during the Nineteenth Century.* Cambridge: Cambridge University Press.

———— (2001). "Presidential Address: Racism, Immigrants, and Political Reform." *Journal of American History* 87(4): 1253–1274.

Moore, Jacqueline M. (2003). *Booker T. Washington, W. E. B. Du Bois, and the Struggle for Racial Uplift.* Wilmington, DE: Scholarly Resources.

Moran, Martin (2009). "The Politics of Politics in the Classroom." *Schools: Studies in Education* 6(1): 57–71.

Moreau, Joseph (2003). *Schoolbook Nation: Conflicts over American History Textbooks from the Civil War to the Present.* Ann Arbor: University of Michigan Press.

Morehouse College (2007). "Freshman Orientation/Morehouse College." Retrieved August 7, 2007, from www.morehouse.edu/academics/degree_requirements/freshman_orientation.html.

Mosley-Braun, Carol (2003). "Democratic Presidential Debate: Closing Debate." Fox News Transcript.

Mukhopadhyay, Carol C., Rosemary Henze, and Yolanda T. Moses (2007). *How Real Is Race? A Sourcebook on Race, Culture, and Biology.* Lanham, MD: Rowman and Littlefield.

Murphy, Liam B. (1998). "Institutions and the Demands of Justice." *Philosophy and Public Affairs* 27(4): 251–291.

Murphy, Stephen H. (2009). "Real Authentic Learning." *Principal Leadership (High School Ed.)* 9(6): 6–8.

Mutseyekwa, Tapuwa (2009, November 6). "Zimbabwe Children's Parliament Speaks Out on Rights Issues." UNICEF. Retrieved June 30, 2010, from www.unicef.org/infobycountry/zimbabwe_51659.html.

Nash, Gary B., Charlotte Crabtree, and Ross E. Dunn (2000). *History on Trial: Culture Wars and the Teaching of the Past.* New York: Vintage.

National Action Civics Collaborative (2010). "Action Civics: A Declaration for Rejuvenating Our Democratic Traditions." National Action Civics Collaborative. Retrieved June 10, 2011, from www.centerforactioncivics.org.

National Center for Education Statistics (2011). "The Nation's Report

Card: Civics 2010." Institute of Education Sciences, U.S. Department of Education. Retrieved June 1, 2011, from nces.ed.gov/na tionsreportcard/pdf/main2010/2011466.pdf.

National Conference on Citizenship (2008). "2008 Civic Health Index: Beyond the Vote." National Conference on Citizenship and CIR-CLE. Retrieved May 1, 2009, from www.ncoc.net/download.php ?file=2kccfl36&ext=pdf&name=2008%20Civic%20Health%20 Index.

Newport, Frank (2006, July 16). "Martin Luther King Jr.: Revered More After Death Than Before." Gallup News Service. Retrieved August 18, 2008, from www.gallup.com/poll/20920/Martin-Luther-King-Jr-Revered-More-After-Death-Than-Before.aspx.

New School, The (2010). "The New School—Curriculum." Retrieved July 22, 2010, from www.tnsk.org/TNS/curriculum.htm.

Nie, Norman H., Jane Junn, and Kenneth Stehlik-Barry (1996). *Education and Democratic Citizenship in America*. Chicago: University of Chicago Press.

Nielsen Media (2000). "Top Prime-Time Programs: African-American Homes." Retrieved February 17, 2003, from www.nielsenmedia .com/ethnicmeasure/african-american/programsAA.html.

Nielsen Media Research (2010, September 27). "Top TV Ratings." Retrieved October 8, 2010, from en-us.nielsen.com/content/nielsen/ en_us/insights/rankings/television.html.

Niemi, Richard G., and Jane Junn (1998). *Civic Education: What Makes Students Learn*. New Haven: Yale University Press.

Niemi, Richard G., and Mitchell S. Sanders (2004). "Assessing Student Performance in Civics: The NAEP 1998 Civics Assessment." *Theory and Research in Social Education* 32(3): 326–348.

Nieto, Sonia (2005). "Public Education in the Twentieth Century and Beyond: High Hopes, Broken Promises, and an Uncertain Future." *Harvard Educational Review* 75(1): 43–64.

Oakes, Jeannie (2005). *Keeping Track: How Schools Structure Inequality*, 2nd ed. New Haven: Yale University Press.

Obama, Barack (2008a, March 18). "A More Perfect Union." Speech delivered in Philadelphia. Retrieved April 10, 2009, from www.npr .org/templates/story/story.php?storyId=88478467.

——— (2008b, February 5). "Remarks of Senator Barack Obama: Super Tuesday." Chicago. Retrieved December 8, 2008, from www .barackobama.com/2008/02/05/remarks_of_senator_barack_ obam_46.php.

——— (2009). "Inaugural Address." Washington, D.C.: The White

House. Retrieved May 23, 2011, from www.whitehouse.gov/blog/
inaugural-address/.

Obama for America (2008). "Barack Obama and Joe Biden: The
Change We Need" (Obama's campaign home page). Retrieved December 7, 2008, from www.barackobama.com.

Ober, Josiah (2010). *Democracy and Knowledge: Innovation and
Learning in Classical Athens*. Princeton: Princeton University Press.

O'Day, Jennifer (2002). "Complexity, Accountability, and School Improvement." In *Redesigning Accountability Systems for Education*,
ed. Susan Fuhrman and Richard Elmore, 15–46. New York: Teachers College Press.

O'Donoghue, Jennifer L., and Ben Kirshner (2008). "Engaging Urban
Youth in Civic Practice: Community-Based Youth Organizations as
Alternative Sites for Democratic Education." In *Educating Demo-
cratic Citizens in Troubled Times: Qualitative Studies of Current
Efforts*, ed. Janet S. Bixby and Judith L. Pace, 227–251. Albany:
State University of New York Press.

Okin, Susan Moller, et al. (1999). *Is Multiculturalism Bad for Women?*
Princeton: Princeton University Press.

Olsen, Laurie (1997). *Made in America: Immigrant Students in Our
Public Schools*. New York: New Press.

107th Congress (2002). "Recognizing the Importance of Teaching
United States History and Civics in Elementary and Secondary
Schools, and for Other Purposes." *H. Con. Res. 451.* October 1,
2002. Retrieved April 10, 2009, from bulk.resource.org/gpo.gov/
bills/107/hc451eh.txt.pdf.

Orfield, Gary (2001). "Schools More Separate: Consequences of a Decade of Resegregation." Cambridge, MA: Civil Rights Project at
Harvard University.

Orfield, Gary, Susan Eaton, and The Harvard Project on Desegregation
(1996). *Dismantling Desegregation: The Quiet Reversal of* Brown
v. Board of Education. New York: New Press.

Orfield, Gary, and Chungmei Lee (2006). "Racial Transformation and
the Changing Nature of Segregation." Cambridge, MA: Civil
Rights Project at Harvard University.

———— (2007). "Historic Reversals, Accelerating Resegregation, and
the Need for New Integration Strategies." Civil Rights Project/
Proyecto Derechos Civiles, UCLA. Retrieved May 1, 2009, from
www.civilrightsproject.ucla.edu/research/deseg/reversals_reseg
_need.pdf.

Owadokun, Remi Manoela, and Pearlie Avilés (2005). "Somerville

Youth Council." *New Directions for Youth Development* 106 (Summer): 85–90.

Paoletti, Sarah, et al. (2006, November 1). "Petition Alleging Violations of the Human Rights of Undocumented Workers by the United States of America." Report to the Inter-American Commission on Human Rights, Organization of American States. Retrieved October 11, 2010, from www.aclu.org/images/asset_upload_file 946_27232.pdf.

Parents Involved in Community Schools v. Seattle School District No. 1, 551 U.S. 1 (2007).

Parker, Walter C., and Diana E. Hess (2001). "Teaching With and For Discussion." *Teaching and Teacher Education* 17(3): 273–289.

Pateman, Carole (1970). *Participation and Democratic Theory.* Cambridge: Cambridge University Press.

Patterson, James T. (2001). Brown v. Board of Education: *A Civil Rights Milestone and Its Troubled Legacy.* Oxford: Oxford University Press.

Patterson, Orlando (1997). *The Ordeal of Integration: Progress and Resentment in America's "Racial" Crisis.* New York: Civitas/Counterpoint.

Payne, Charles M. (1995). *I've Got the Light of Freedom: The Organizing Tradition and the Mississippi Freedom Struggle.* Berkeley: University of California Press.

——— (2003). "More Than a Symbol of Freedom: Education for Liberation and Democracy." *Phi Delta Kappan* 85(1): 22–28.

——— (2008). *So Much Reform, So Little Change: The Persistence of Failure in Urban Schools.* Cambridge, MA: Harvard Education Press.

Pearson, Kathryn, and Jack Citrin (2006). "The Political Assimilation of the Fourth Wave." In *Transforming Politics, Transforming America: The Political and Civic Incorporation of Immigrants in the United States,* ed. Taeku Lee et al., 217–242. Charlottesville: University of Virginia Press.

Perkins, David (1998). "What Is Understanding?" In *Teaching for Understanding: Linking Theory with Practice,* ed. Martha Stone Wiske, 39–44, 51–57. San Francisco: Jossey-Bass.

Perliger, Arie, Daphna Canetti-Nisim, and Ami Pedahzur (2006). "Democratic Attitudes among High-School Pupils: The Role Played by Perceptions of Class Climate." *School Effectiveness and School Improvement* 17(1): 119–140.

Perlstein, Linda (2007). *Tested: One American School Struggles to Make the Grade.* New York: Henry Holt.

Perry, Theresa (2003). "Up from the Parched Earth: Toward a Theory of African-American Achievement." In *Young, Gifted, and Black: Promoting High Achievement among African-American Students,* ed. Theresa Perry et al., 1–108. Boston: Beacon Press.

Perry, Theresa, Claude Steele, and Asa Hilliard III (2003). *Young, Gifted, and Black: Promoting High Achievement among African-American Students.* Boston: Beacon Press.

Peter Marshall Ministries (2009a). "Peter Marshall Ministries, America's Christian Heritage, Restoring America, Christian Homeschool Material and Curriculum." Retrieved July 20, 2009, from peter marshallministries.com.

——— (2009b). "Peter Marshall Ministries, America's Christian Heritage, Restoring America, Christian Homeschool Material and Curriculum Index." Retrieved July 20, 2009, from petermarshallminis tries.com/about/index.cfm.

Pew Research Center for the People and the Press (2007). "What Americans Know: 1989–2007. Public Knowledge of Current Affairs Little Changed by News and Information Revolutions." Retrieved August 4, 2009, from people-press.org/reports/pdf/319.pdf.

Philadelphia Student Union (2010). "Vision Statement (Draft)." Retrieved April 16, 2010, from home.phillystudentunion.org/About-Us/Vision-Statement-Draft.html.

Pierce, Chester (1995). "Stress Analogs of Racism and Sexism: Terrorism, Torture, and Disaster." In *Mental Health, Racism, and Sexism,* ed. C. Willie et al., 277–293. Pittsburgh: University of Pittsburgh Press.

Plyler v. Doe, 457 U.S. 202 (1982).

Pollock, Mica (2004). *Colormute: Race Talk Dilemmas in an American School.* Princeton: Princeton University Press.

———, ed. (2008). *Everyday Antiracism: Getting Real about Race in School.* New York: New Press.

Pomper, Gerald M. (2004). *Ordinary Heroes and American Democracy.* New Haven: Yale University Press.

Porpora, Douglas V. (1996). "Personal Heroes, Religion, and Transcendental Metanarratives." *Sociological Forum* 11(2): 209–229.

Porter, Robert Odawi (2004). *Sovereignty, Colonialism, and the Future of the Indigenous Nations.* Durham, NC: Carolina Academic Press.

Portes, Alejandro, and Rubén G. Rumbaut (2006). *Immigrant America: A Portrait,* 3rd ed., rev., expanded, and updated. Berkeley: University of California Press.

Portes, Alejandro, and Min Zhou (1993). "The New Second Generation: Segmented Assimilation and Its Variants among Post-1965

Immigrant Youth." *American Academy of Political and Social Sciences* 530: 74–96.

Powell, Arthur G., Eleanor Farrar, and David K. Cohen (1985). *The Shopping Mall High School: Winners and Losers in the Educational Marketplace.* New York: Houghton Mifflin.

Powell, G. Bingham, Jr. (1986). "American Voter Turnout in Comparative Perspective." *American Political Science Review* 80(1): 17–43.

Powers, Beth Haverkamp (2009). "From National History Day to Peacejam: Research Leads to Authentic Learning." *English Journal* 98(5): 48–53.

Public Achievement (2010). "Public Achievement—Practice—Teacher Guide." Retrieved March 30, 2010, from www.augsburg.edu/cdc/publicachievement/TeacherGuide/SixStagesIntro.html.

Public Agenda (1998). *A Lot to Be Thankful For: What Parents Want Children to Learn about America.* New York: Public Agenda.

Putnam, Robert D. (2000). *Bowling Alone: The Collapse and Revival of American Community.* New York: Simon and Schuster.

Ramakrishnan, S. Karthick (2006). "But Do They Bowl? Race, Immigrant Incorporation, and Civic Voluntarism in the United States." In *Transforming Politics, Transforming America: The Political and Civic Incorporation of Immigrants in the United States,* ed. Taeku Lee et al., 243–259. Charlottesville: University of Virginia Press.

Raskin, Jamin (2005). "Lawful Disenfranchisement." *Human Rights: Journal of the Section of Individual Rights and Responsibilities* 32(2): 12–16.

Ravitch, Diane (1994). "Standards in U.S. History: An Assessment." *Education Week* 14: 48.

——— (1996). "50 States, 50 Standards." *Brookings Review* 14(3): 6–9.

——— (2003). *The Language Police: How Pressure Groups Restrict What Students Learn.* New York: Alfred A. Knopf.

Rawls, John (1993). *Political Liberalism.* New York: Columbia University Press.

Rebell, Michael A. (2009). *Courts and Kids: Pursuing Educational Equity through the State Courts.* Chicago: University of Chicago Press.

Reich, Justin (2009, July 10). "In Schools, a Firewall That Works Too Well." *Washington Post.* Retrieved April 27, 2010, from www.washingtonpost.com/wp-dyn/content/article/2009/07/10/AR2009071003459.html.

Reich, Rob (2002). *Bridging Liberalism and Multiculturalism in American Education.* Chicago: University of Chicago Press.

Reuben, Julie (2005). "Patriotic Purposes: Public Schools and the Education of Citizens." In *The Public Schools,* ed. Susan Fuhr man and Marvin Lazerson, 1–24. Oxford: Oxford University Press.

RMC Research Corporation (2007). "Public Achievement 2005–2006 Evaluation Brief." Retrieved May 27, 2010, from www.augsburg .edu/democracy/documents/2005-06EvaluationBri.pdf.

Robeyns, Ingrid (2008). "Ideal Theory in Theory and Practice." *Social Theory and Practice* 34(3): 341–362.

Robison, Jennifer (2003, June 10). "Teens Search for Role Models Close to Home." Gallup. Retrieved August 17, 2008, from www .gallup.com/poll/8584/Teens-Search-Role-Models-Close-Home .aspx.

Rogowski, Jon C. (n.d.). *Political Alienation and Government Trust in the Age of Obama.* Memo. Mobilization Change and Political and Civic Engagement, and Black Youth Project. Retrieved November 11, 2011, from www.2008andbeyond.com/wp-content/uploads/ E08B_Memo_Alienation_Trust.pdf.

Rosenberg, Shawn W., ed. (2007). *Deliberation, Participaton and Democracy: Can the People Govern?* Basingstoke, England: Palgrave Macmillan.

Rosenstone, Steven J., and John Mark Hansen (1993). *Mobilization, Participation, and Democracy in America.* New York: Macmillan.

Rosenzweig, Roy, and David Thelen (1998). *The Presence of the Past: Popular Uses of History in American Life.* New York: Columbia University Press.

Rothenberg, Paula S., ed. (2002). *White Privilege: Essential Readings on the Other Side of Racism.* New York: Worth.

Rothman, Andrew (2010). "Schools and Justice in Boston: A Historical Case Study." Cambridge, MA: Harvard Graduate School of Education and Boston: Another Course to College.

Rowe, Mary Budd (1986). "Wait Time: Slowing Down May Be a Way of Speeding Up!" *Journal of Teacher Education* 37(1): 43–50.

Rubin, Beth C. (2007). "'There's Still Not Justice': Youth Civic Identity Development amid Distinct School and Community Contexts." *Teachers College Record* 109(2): 449–481.

Ryan, James E. (2010). *Five Miles Away, a World Apart: One City, Two Schools, and the Story of Educational Opportunity in Modern America.* New York: Oxford University Press.

Sable, Jennifer, Chris Plotts, and Lindsey Mitchell (2010). "Characteristics of the 100 Largest Public Elementary and Secondary School Districts in the United States: 2008–09." Statistical analysis report.

Institute of Educational Sciences, National Center for Education Statistics. Retrieved November 7, 2011, from nces.ed.gov/pubs 2011/2011301.pdf.

Sachar, Howard (1993). *A History of the Jews in America*. New York: Vintage.

Sacks, Peter (2000). *Standardized Minds: The High Price of America's Testing Culture and What We Can Do to Change It*. Cambridge: Da Capo.

Sanchez-Jankowski, Martin (2002). "Minority Youth and Civic Engagement: The Impact of Group Relations." *Applied Developmental Science* 6(4): 237–245.

Sanders, Lynn M. (1997). "Against Deliberation." *Political Theory* 25(3): 347–376.

Saulny, Susan (2010, July 2). "Graduation Is the Goal, Staying Alive the Prize." *New York Times*, 159: A1, 15. Retrieved June 14, 2011, from www.nytimes.com/2010/07/02/us/02chicago.html.

Schaper, David (2011, March 24). "Chicago's Silent Watchmen Guard School Route." Morning Edition, National Public Radio. Retrieved June 12, 2011, from www.npr.org/2011/03/24/134798564/chicagos-silent-watchmen-guard-school-route.

Schlesinger, Arthur, Jr. (1998). *The Disuniting of America: Reflections on a Multicultural Society,* rev. and enlarged ed. New York: W. W. Norton.

Schlesinger, Arthur M., Jr. (1968 [1958]). "The Decline of Heroes." In *Heroes and Anti-Heroes: A Reader in Depth,* ed. Harold Lubin. San Francisco: Chandler.

Schultz, Brian D. (2008). *Spectacular Things Happen along the Way: Lessons from an Urban Classroom*. New York: Teachers College Press.

Schwartz, Barry (1990). "The Reconstruction of Abraham Lincoln." In *Collective Remembering,* ed. David Middleton and Derek Edwards, 81–107. London: Sage.

Scott, James C. (1985). *Weapons of the Weak: Everyday Forms of Peasant Resistance*. New Haven: Yale University Press.

Seider, Scott (2008a). "'Bad Things Could Happen': How Fear Impedes the Development of Social Responsibility in Privileged Adolescents." *Journal of Adolescent Research* 23(6): 647–666.

——— (2008b). "Resisting Obligation: How Privileged Adolescents Conceive of Their Responsibilities to Others." *Journal of Research in Character Education* 6(1): 3–19.

Seif, Hinda (2010). "The Civic Life of Latina/o Immigrant Youth: Challenging Boundaries and Creating Safe Spaces." In *Handbook* of *Research on Civic Engagement in Youth,* ed. Lonnie R. Sherrod et al., 445–470. Hoboken, NJ: John Wiley and Sons.

Seixas, Peter (1993). "Historical Understanding among Adolescents in a Multicultural Setting." *Curriculum Inquiry* 23: 301–327.

Shapiro, Thomas (2004). *The Hidden Cost of Being African American.* Oxford: Oxford University Press.

Sharpton, Al (2003, October 26). "Democratic Presidential Debate: Closing Debate." Fox News Transcript. Retrieved November 12, 2011, from www.foxnews.com/story/0,2933,101269,00.htm.

Sher, George (1997). *Approximate Justice: Studies in Non-Ideal Theory.* Lanham, MD: Rowman and Littlefield.

Shklar, Judith (1991). *American Citizenship: The Quest for Inclusion.* Cambridge, MA: Harvard University Press.

Shorto, Russell (2010, February 14). "How Christian Were the Founders?" *New York Times Magazine,* 32ff. Retrieved June 8, 2011, from www.nytimes.com/2010/02/14/magazine/14texbooks-t.html.

Shujaa, Mwalimu J. (1996). *Beyond Desegregation: The Politics of Quality in African Americsn Schooling.* Thousand Oaks, CA: Corwin.

Sidanius, Jim, et al. (1997). "The Interface between Ethnic and National Attachment." *Public Opinion Quarterly* 61: 102–133.

Siegel, K., D. Karus, and E. W. Schrimshaw (2000). "Racial Differences in Attitudes toward Protease Inhibitors among Older HIV-Infected Men." *AIDS Care* 12(4): 423–434.

Sigelman, Lee, and Steven A. Tuch (1997). "Metastereotypes: Blacks' Perceptions of Whites' Perceptions of Blacks." *Public Opinion Quarterly* 61: 87–101.

Silverman, William M. (2003). "Where Have All the Heroes Gone?" *Journal of the American Osteopathic Association* 103(1): 27–28.

Simmons, A. John (2010). "Ideal and Nonideal Theory." *Philosophy and Public Affairs* 38(1): 5–36.

Singleton, Glenn E., and Curtis Linton (2006). *Courageous Conversations about Race: A Field Guide for Achieving Equity in Schools.* Thousand Oaks, CA: Corwin.

Sizer, Theodore R., and Nancy Faust Sizer (1999). *The Students Are Watching: Schools and the Moral Contract.* Boston: Beacon Press.

Skiba, Russell J. (2000). "Zero Tolerance, Zero Evidence: An Analysis of School Disciplinary Practice." Indiana Education Policy Center Publications, Safe and Responsive Schools Project. Retrieved October 20, 2010, from www.indiana.edu/~safeschl/publication.html.

Skiba, Russell J., Robert S. Michael, and Abra Carroll Nardo (2000, June). "The Color of Discipline: Sources of Racial and Gender Disproportionality in School Punishment." Indiana Education Policy Center Publications, Safe and Responsive Schools Project. Retrieved October 20, 2010, from www.indiana.edu/~safeschl/publication .html.

Skocpol, Theda (1999). "How Americans Became Civic." In *Civic Engagement in American Democracy,* ed. Theda Skocpol and Morris P. Fiorina, 27–80. Washington, D.C.: Brookings.

Skocpol, Theda, Marshall Ganz, and Ziad Munson (2000). "A Nation of Organizers: The Institutional Origins of Civic Voluntarism in lthe United States." *American Political Science Review* 94(3): 527–546.

Skocpol, Theda, Ariane Liazos, and Marshall Ganz (2006). *What a Mighty Power We Can Be: African American Fraternal Groups and the Struggle for Racial Equality.* Princeton: Princeton University Press.

Skrla, Linda, and James Joseph Scheurich, eds. (2003). *Educational Equity and Accountability: Paradigms, Policies, and Politics.* Studies in Education/Politics. New York: RoutledgeFalmer.

Sleeter, Christine E. (2005). *Un-Standardizing Curriculum: Multicultural Teaching in the Standards-Based Classroom.* New York: Teachers College Press.

Small, Mario Luis (2009). *Unanticipated Gains: Origins of Network Inequality in Everyday Life.* New York: Oxford University Press.

Smith, Robert C., and Richard Seltzer (2000). *Contemporary Controversies and the American Racial Divide.* Lanham, MD: Rowman and Littlefield.

Smith, Rogers (1997). *Civic Ideals: Conflicting Visions of Citizenship in U.S. History.* New Haven: Yale University Press.

Snow, David A., Lewis A. Zurcher, and Sheldon Eckland-Olson (1980). "Social Networks and Social Movements: A Microstructural Approach to Differential Recruitment." *American Sociological Review* 45 (October): 787–801.

Solomon, Deborah (2004, February 8). "Questions for Walter Mosley: It's the Money, Stupid." *New York Times Magazine,* 17.

Solomona, R. Patrick, et al. (2005). "The Discourse of Denial: How White Teacher Candidates Construct Race, Racism and 'White Privilege.'" *Race, Ethnicity and Education* 8(2): 147–169.

Solorzano, Daniel, Miguel Ceja, and Tara Yosso (2000). "Critical Race Theory, Racial Microaggressions, and Campus Racial Climate: The Experiences of African American College Students." *Journal of Negro Education* 69(1/2): 60–73.

Southwell, Priscilla L., and Kevin D. Pirch (2003). "Political Cynicism and the Mobilization of Black Voters." *Social Science Quarterly* 84(4): 906–917.

Speizer, Jeanne J. (1981). "Role Models, Mentors, and Sponsors: The Elusive Concepts." *Signs* 6(4): 692–712.

Spring, Joel (1971). *Education and the Rise of the Corporate State.* Boston: Beacon Press.

Staff and Partners of the Center for Democracy and Citizenship, University of Minnesota Extension (2011 [1995]). "Reinventing Citizenship: The Practice of Public Work." Retrieved June 7, 2011, from www.extension.umn.edu/distribution/citizenship/dh6586.html.

Steele, Michael (2009, March 4). "State of the Black Union Roundtable." CSPAN. Retrieved March 9, 2009, from www.youtube.com/watch?v=ojO-4zvULaM.

Stein, Janice Gross (2001). *The Cult of Efficiency.* Toronto: House of Anansi Press.

Stemplowska, Zofia (2008). "What's Ideal about Ideal Theory?" *Social Theory and Practice* 34(3): 319–340.

Stepick, Alex, and Carol Dutton Stepick (2002). "Becoming American, Constructing Ethnicity: Immigrant Youth and Civic Engagement." *Applied Developmental Science* 6(4): 246–257.

Stoecker, Randy, and Elizabeth A. Tryon (2009). "The Unheard Voices: Community Organizations and Service Learning." In *The Unheard Voices: Community Organizations and Service Learning,* ed. Randy Stoecker and Elizabeth A. Tryon, 1–18. Philadelphia: Temple University Press. Stoneman, Dorothy (2002). "The Role of Youth Programming in the Development of Civic Engagement." *Applied Developmental Science* 6(4): 221–226.

Stotsky, Sandra (2004). "The Stealth Curriculum: Manipulating America's History Teachers." Thomas B. Fordham Foundation, Washington, D.C. Retrieved June 28, 2007, from www.edexcellence.net/doc/StealthCurriculum%5BFINAL%5D04-01-04.pdf.

Stout, Jeffrey (2010). *Blessed Are the Organized: Grassroots Democracy in America.* Princeton: Princeton University Press.

Strobel, Karen, et al. (2008). "Qualities That Attract Urban Youth to After-School Settings and Promote Continued Participation." *Teachers College Record* 110(8): 1677–1705.

Students and Faculty of the New School, Kennebunk, ME (2010, April 28). "Panel Discussion: Alternatives in Schooling." Seminar Presentation, Harvard Graduate School of Education.

Students from Bronx Leadership Academy 2, et al. (2008). *SAT Bronx: Do You Know What Bronx Kids Know?* New York: Next Generation Press.

Suárez-Orozco, Carola (2004). "Formulating Identity in a Globalized World." In *Globalization: Culture and Education in the New Millenium*, ed. Marcelo M. Suárez-Orozco and Desirée Baolian Qin-Hilliard, 173–202. Berkeley: University of California Press.

Sue, Derald Wing, et al. (2007a). "Racial Microaggressions and the Asian American Experience." *Cultural Diversity and Ethnic Minority Psychology* 13(1): 72–81.

Sue, Derald Wing, et al. (2007b). "Racial Microaggressions in Everyday Life: Implications for Clinical Practice." *American Psychologist* 62(4): 271–286.

Sue, Derald Wing, et al. (2009). "Racial Microaggressions and Difficult Dialogues on Race in the Classroom." *Cultural Diversity and Ethnic Minority Psychology* 15(2): 183–190.

Surowiecki, James (2005). *The Wisdom of Crowds*. New York: Random House.

Swift, Adam (2008). "The Value of Philosophy in Nonideal Circumstances." *Social Theory and Practice* 34(3): 363–387.

Syvertsen, Amy, et al. (2009). "Using Elections as Teachable Moments: A Randomized Evaluation of the Student Voices Civic Education Program." *American Journal of Education* 116(1): 33–67.

Takaki, Ronald T. (1993). *A Different Mirror: A History of Multicultural America*. Boston: Little, Brown.

Tatum, Alfred W. (2008). "Adolescents and Texts: Overserved or Underserved? A Focus on Adolescents and Texts." *English Journal* 98(2): 82–85.

Tatum, Beverly Daniel (1992). "Talking about Race, Learning about Racism: The Application of Racial Identity Development Theory in the Classroom." *Harvard Educational Review* 62(1): 1–24.

———— (1997). *"Why Are All the Black Kids Sitting Together in the Cafeteria?" and Other Conversations about Race*. New York: Basic Books.

Texas Education Agency (2009, July 2). "TEA—Curriculum—Social Studies Expert Reviewers." Retrieved July 24, 2009, from ritter.tea .state.tx.us/teks/social/experts.html.

Tharp, Marye (2001). *Marketing and Consumer Identity in Multicultural America*. Thousand Oaks, CA: Sage.

Thomas, Evan, and Arian Campo-Flores (2005, October 3). "The Battle to Rebuild: In a Fierce Cultural Storm, the Future of the Lower Ninth Is Buffeted by Race and Politics." *Newsweek*.

Thomas, Reuben J., and Daniel A. McFarland (2010). "Joining Young, Voting Young: The Effects of Youth Voluntary Associations on Early Adult Voting." CIRCLE Working Paper no. 73. Medford MA:

Center for Information and Research on Civic Learning and Engagement. Retrieved June 13, 2011, from www.civicyouth.org/featured-extracurricular-activities-may-increase-likelihood-of-voting/.

Thomas, Stephen B., and Sandra Crouse Quinn (1991). "The Tuskegee Syphilis Study, 1932 to 1972: Implications for HIV Education and AIDS Risk Education Programs in the Black Community." *American Journal of Public Health* 81(11): 1498–1505.

Toch, Thomas (2006). "Margins of Error: The Education Testing Industry in the No Child Left Behind Era." Education Sector, Washington D.C. Retrieved July 20, 2008, from www.educationsector.org/usr_doc/Margins_of_Error.pdf.

Torney-Purta, Judith (2002). "The School's Role in Developing Civic Engagement: A Study of Adolescents in Twenty-eight Countries." *Applied Developmental Science* 6(4): 202–211.

Torney-Purta, Judith, Carolyn H. Barber, and Britt Wilkenfeld (2007). "Latino Adolescents' Civic Development in the United States: Research Results from the IEA Civic Education Study." *Journal of Youth and Adolescence* 36: 111–125.

Torney-Purta, Judith, Carole L. Hahn, and Jo-Ann M. Amadeo (2001a). "Principles of Subject-Specific Instruction in Education for Citizenship." In *Subject-Specific Instructional Methods and Activities*, ed. Jere Brophy, 373–410. New York: JAI Press.

Torney-Purta, Judith, et al. (2001b). *Citizenship and Education in 28 Countries: Civic Knowledge and Engagement at Age Fourteen.* Amsterdam: International Association for the Evaluation of Educational Achievement.

Torney-Purta, Judith, et al. (2001c). *Citizenship and Education in 28 Countries: Civic Knowledge and Engagement at Age Fourteen, Executive Summary.* Amsterdam: International Association for the Evaluation of Educational Achievement.

Torney-Purta, Judith, and Britt S. Wilkenfeld (2009). "Paths to 21st Century Competencies through Civic Education Classrooms: An Analysis of Survey Results from Ninth-Graders." Campaign for the Civic Mission of Schools and American Bar Association Division for Public Education, Washington D.C. Retrieved June 14, 2011, from www.civicyouth.org/?p=360.

Torney-Purta, Judith, Susan Vermeer Lopez, and Education Commission of the States (2006). "Developing Citizenship Competencies from Kindergarten through Grade 12: A Background Paper for Policymakers and Educators." Education Commission of the States. Retrieved August 2, 2011, from www.ecs.org/html/IssueSection.asp?issueid=19&s=Selected+Research+%26+Readings.

Truchard, James (2005) "Where Have All the Heroes Gone?" *Control Engineering* 3 (March 1). Retrieved December 4, 2008, from www .controleng.com/article/CA509812.html.

Tumulty, Karen, and Ed O'Keefe (2010, July 21). "Fired USDA Official Receives Apologies from White House, Vilsack." *Washington Post.* Retrieved October 11, 2010, from www.washingtonpost.com/wp-dyn/content/article/2010/07/21/AR2010072103871.html.

Tyack, David (2001). "School for Citizens: The Politics of Civic Education from 1790 to 1990." In *E Pluribus Unum? Contemporary and Historical Perspectives on Immigrant Political Incorporation,* ed. Gary Gerstle and John Mollenkopf, 331–370. New York: Russell Sage Foundation.

———— (2003). *Seeking Common Ground: Public Schools in a Diverse Society.* Cambridge, MA: Harvard University Press.

Tyack, David, and Larry Cuban (1995). *Tinkering Toward Utopia: A Century of Public School Reform.* Cambridge, MA: Harvard University Press.

U.S. Census Bureau (2008). "An Older and More Diverse Nation by Midcentury." U.S. Census Bureau. Retrieved August 3, 2009, from www.census.gov/Press-Release/www/releases/archives/population/ 012496.html.

———— (2010a). "Table 7: Nativity and Citizenship Status by Sex, Hispanic Origin, and Race: 2010." Retrieved June 14, 2011, from www.census.gov/population/socdemo/hispanic/cps2010/CPS-2010-table07.xls.

———— (2010b, Nov. 9). "Voting and Registration in the Election of November 2004—Detailed Tables." Voting and Registration Population Characteristics (P20) Reports. Retrieved May 27, 2011, from www.census.gov/hhes/www/socdemo/voting/publications/p20/ 2004/tables.html.

———— (2010c, Nov. 9). "Voting and Registration in the Election of November 2008—Detailed Tables." Retrieved May 27, 2011, from www.census.gov/hhes/www/socdemo/voting/publications/ p20/2008/tables.html.

U.S. Census Bureau Population Division (2010). "Annual Estimates of the Resident Population by Sex, Race, and Hispanic Origin for the United States: April 1, 2000 to July 1, 2009 (NC-EST2009-03)." U.S. Census Bureau. Retrieved Sep. 29, 2010, from www.census .gov/popest/national/asrh/NC-EST2009-srh.html.

U.S. Department of Education, et al. (2007). "Average scale scores with percentages for civics, grade 8, Race/ethnicity used in NAEP reports after 2001 [SDRACE] × Natl School Lunch Prog eligibility

(3 categories) [SLUNCH3]: By jurisdiction, 2006 (NAEP Data Explorer)." NAEP 2006 Civics Assessment. Retrieved July 9, 2007, from nces.ed.gov/nationsreportcard/nde/viewresults.asp?pid=4-2-8-CIV-National-10-SDRACE,SLUNCH3-20063-CR-MN,RP-2-1-1-1-0-2-3-0-1.

Ulluci, Kerri, and Joi Spencer (2009). "Unraveling the Myths of Accountability: A Case Study of the California High School Exit Exam." *Urban Review* 41: 161–173.

Uslaner, Eric M. (2002). *The Moral Foundations of Trust.* Cambridge: Cambridge University Press.

VanSledright, Bruce (2002). "Confronting History's Interpretive Paradox while Teaching Fifth Graders to Investigate the Past." *American Educational Research Journal* 39(4): 1089–1115.

Vaznis, James (2010, October 1). "Boston Agrees to Help Non-English-Speakers in Classroom." *Boston Globe.* Retrieved October 11, 2010, from www.boston.com/news/local/breaking_news/2010/10/boston_agrees_t.html?comments=all#readerComm.

Verba, Sidney, Kay Lehman Schlozman, and Henry E. Brady (1995). *Voice and Equality: Civic Voluntarism in American Politics.* Cambridge, MA: Harvard University Press.

Wadhwa, Anita (2010). "'There Has Never Been a Glory Day in Education for Non-Whites': Critical Race Theory and Discipline Reform in Denver." Cambridge, MA: Harvard Graduate School of Education.

Walker, Tobi (2000). "The Service/Politics Split: Rethinking Service to Teach Political Engagement." *PS: Political Science and Politics* 33(3).

——— (2002). "Service as a Pathway to Political Participation: What Research Tells Us." *Applied Developmental Science* 6(4): 183–188.

Walker, Vanessa Siddle, and Kim Nesta Archung (2003). "The Segregated Schooling of Blacks in the Southern United States and South Africa." *Comparative Education Review* 47: 21–40.

WallBuilders (2009). "Wallbuilders Overview." Retrieved July 24, 2009, from www.wallbuilders.com/ABTOverview.asp.

Warikoo, Natasha Kumar (2011). *Balancing Acts: Youth Culture in the Global City.* Berkeley: University of California Press.

Washington, Booker T. (2004[1895]). "The Atlanta Compromise." In *Ripples of Hope: Great American Civil Rights Speeches,* ed. Josh Gottheimer, 128–131. New York: Basic Civitas.

Washington Post, Kaiser Family Foundation, and Harvard University (1995). *The Four Americas: Government and Social Policy Through the Eyes of America's Multi-racial and Multi-ethnic Society.* Washington, D.C.: *The Washington Post.*

———— (2000). *Washington Post/Kaiser Family Foundation/Harvard University National Survey on Latinos in America.* Washington, D.C.: *The Washington Post.*

———— (2001). *Race and Ethnicity in 2001: Attitudes, Perceptions, and Experiences.* Washington, D.C.: *The Washington Post.*

Wasserman, Selma (2001). "Quantum Theory, the Uncertainty Principle, and the Alchemy of Standardized Testing." *Phi Delta Kappan* 83(1): 28–40.

Waters, Mary (1999). *Black Identities: West Indian Immigrant Dreams and American Realities.* New York: Russell Sage Foundation and Cambridge, MA: Harvard University Press.

Watson, Yolanda L., and Sheila T. Gergory (2005). *Daring to Educate: The Legacy of the Early Spelman College Presidents.* Sterling, VA: Stylus.

Webster, Noah (1790). "On the Education of Youth in America." In Webster, *A Collection of Essays and Fugitiv Writings on Moral, Historical, Political, and Literary Subjects.* Boston: I. Thomas and E. T. Andrews.

Wecter, Dixon (1941). *The Hero in America: A Chronicle of Hero-Worship.* New York: Charles Scribner's Sons.

Weis, Lois, and Michelle Fine (2000). *Construction Sites: Excavating Race, Class, and Gender among Urban Youth.* New York: Teachers College Press.

West, Cornel, and Eddie S. Glaude, Jr. (2006). "Standard Covenant Curriculum: A Study of Black Democratic Action." Covenant with Black America. Retrieved December 10, 2008, from www.covenant withblackamerica.com/resources/covenant_StandardCovenantCur riculum.doc.

Westheimer, Joel, and Joseph Kahne (2002). "Educating for Democracy." In *Democracy's Moment: Reforming the American Political System for the 21st Century,* ed. Ronald Hayduck and Kevin Mattson, 91–107. Boulder: Rowman and Littlefield.

———— (2004a). "Educating the 'Good' Citizen: Political Choices and Pedagogical Goals." *PSOnline: Political Science and Politics* 37(2).

———— (2004b). "What Kind of Citizen? The Politics of Educating for Democracy." *American Educational Research Journal* 41(2): 237–269.

Wheeler, Rebecca, and Rachel Swords (2006). *Code-Switching: Teaching Standard English in Urban Classrooms.* Urbana, IL: National Council of Teachers of English.

Wiggins, Grant, and Jay McTighe (2005). *Understanding by Design,* exp. 2nd ed. Alexandria, VA: Association for Supervision and Curriculum Development.

Wiley, Edward W., William J. Mathis, and David R. Garcia (2005, September) "The Impact of the Adequate Yearly Progress Requirement of the Federal 'No Child Left Behind' Act on Schools in the Great Lakes Region." Great Lakes Center. Retrieved February 7, 2010, from greatlakescenter.org/docs/early_research/g_l_new_doc/EPSL-0505-109-EPRU.Great_lakes.pdf.

Wilkenfeld, Britt (2009). "Does Context Matter? How the Family, Peer, School and Neighborhood Contexts Relate to Adolescents' Civic Engagement." CIRCLE Working Paper 64. Medford, MA: Center for Information and Research on Civic Learning and Engagement. Retrieved May 6, 2010, from www.civicyouth.org/PopUps/WorkingPapers/WP64Wilkenfeld.pdf.

will.i.am (2008). "Yes We Can." Adobe Flash video. Retrieved August 25, 2010, from www.youtube.com/watch?v=jjXyqcx-mYYDOI: July 30, 2009.

Williams, Melissa (2003). "Citizenship as Identity, Citizenship as Shared Fate, and the Functions of Multicultural Education." In *Citizenship and Education in Liberal-Democratic Societies: Teaching for Cosmopolitan Values and Collective Identities*, ed. Kevin McDonough and Walter Feinberg, 208–247. Oxford: Oxford University Press.

Wineburg, Sam, and Chauncey Monte-Sano (2008). "'Famous Americans': The Changing Pantheon of American Heroes." *Journal of American History* 94(4): 1186–1202.

Wineburg, Samuel S. (2001). *Historical Thinking and Other Unnatural Acts: Charting the Future of Teaching the Past*. Philadelphia: Temple University Press.

Winerip, Michael (2006, March 22) "Standardized Tests Face a Crisis Over Standards." *New York Times*. Retrieved February 9, 2010, from www.nytimes.com/2006/03/22/education/22education.html?_r=3&pagewanted=1.

Wise, Tim (2008). *White Like Me: Reflections on Race from a Privileged Son*, rev. and updated. Brooklyn: Soft Skull Press.

Wolfinger, Raymond E., and Steven J. Rosenstone (1980). *Who Votes?* New Haven: Yale University Press.

Wolfson, Steven C. (2005). *Civics for Today: Participation and Citizenship*, rev. ed. New York: Amsco School Publications.

Wong, Janelle (2006). *Democracy's Promise: Immigrants and American Civic Institutions*. Ann Arbor: University of Michigan Press.

Wright, Jeremiah (2003, April 13). "Confusing God and Government." Sermon delivered at Trinity United Church of Christ, Chicago. Retrieved April 10, 2009, from www.sluggy.net/forum/view
topic.php?p=315691&sid=4b3e97ace4ee8cee02bd6850e52f50b7.

Wright, Lawrence (2006). *The Looming Tower: Al-Qaeda and the
Road to 9/11*. New York: Knopf.

Yancy, Antronette, Judith M. Siegel, and Kimberly L. McDaniel
(2002). "Role Models, Ethnic Identity, and Health-Risk Behaviors
in Urban Adolescents." *Archives of Pediatrics and Adolescent Med-
icine* 156(1): 55–61.

Yates, Miranda, and James Youniss (1999). *Roots of Civic Identity: International Perspectives on Community Service and Activism in
Youth*. New York: Cambridge University Press.

——— (2002). "Community Service and Political Identity Development in Adolescence." *Journal of Social Issues* 54(3): 495–512.

Yosso, Tara, et al. (2009). "Critical Race Theory, Racial Microaggressions, and Campus Racial Climate for Latina/o Undergraduates."
Harvard Educational Review 79(4): 659–690.

Young, Iris Marion (2000). *Inclusion and Democracy*. New York: Oxford University Press.

YPAR Think Tank. (2010, March 20). "YPAR in the Classroom: Rut-
gers Urban Teaching Fellows Followed by Michelle Fine." Adobe
Flash video. Retrieved April 2, 2010, from www.ustream.tv/
recorded/5585858.

Zack, Naomi (1993). *Race and Mixed Race*. Philadelphia: Temple University Press.

Zaff, Jonathan F., and Erik Michelsen (2002, October). "Encouraging
Civic Engagement: How Teens Are (or Are Not) Becoming Responsible Citizens." *Child Trends Research Brief*. Retrieved November
3, 2003, from www.childtrends.com.

Zaff, Jonathan F., Oksana Malanchuk, and Jacquelynne S. Eccles
(2008). "Predicting Positive Citizenship from Adolescence to Young
Adulthood: The Effects of a Civic Context." *Applied Developmental Science* 12(1): 38–53.

Zimmerman, Jonathan (2002). *Whose America? Culture Wars in the
Public Schools*. Cambridge, MA: Harvard University Press.

Zinn, Howard (1980). *A People's History of the United States*. New
York: Harper and Row.

Zukin, Cliff, et al. (2006). *A New Engagement? Political Participation,
Civic Life, and the Changing American Citizen*. Oxford: Oxford
University Press.

ACKNOWLEDGMENTS

I started pondering the issues I discuss in this book in 1999. Unsurprisingly, I've garnered a lot of debts in the intervening twelve years. I am grateful to the following friends, students, and colleagues who provided comments on specific chapters, help with particular problems, or the pointed question at just the right time: Richard Alba, Michelle Bellino, Celina Benavides, Sigal Ben-Porath, Shelley Billig, Alexandra Binnenkade, Janie Bradley, Chris Buttimer, Gregory Bynum, Eamonn Callan, Liz Canner, Mario Carretero, Prudence Carter, Jean Comaroff, John Comaroff, Andrew Scott Conning, Eileen Coppola, Ernesto Cortes, Nancy Crowe, Randall Curren, Jeff Dolven, Jack Dougherty, Leslie Duhaylongsod, Aaliyah El-Amin, Drew Faust, Walter Feinberg, Heidi Fessenden, Constance Flanagan, James Forman, Luis Fraga, Julie Friedberg, Marybeth Gasman, Hunter Gelbach, Carl Glickman, Roger Goddard, Pamela Gordon, Susan Griffin, Jacquelyn Dowd Hall, Hahrie Han, David Hansen, Kate Harrigan, Dan Hart, Helen Haste, Thomas Healy, Diana Hess, Lindy Hess, Frederick Hess, Chris Higgins, Monica Higgins, Darlene Clark Hine, Jennifer Hochschild, Kenneth Holdsman, Mala Htun, John Jost, Joseph Kahne, Elisabeth Kanner, Roi Kawai, Judith Keneman, Jimmy Kim, Jane King, Heather Kirkpatrick, Lauren Kleutsch, Daniel Koretz, Muriel Leonard, Richard Light, David Lublin, Linda Lyons, Michael Marder, Susan McClendon, Michael Merry, Meredith Mira, Michele Moody-Adams, Thomas Nikundiwe, James Noonan, Tiffany Nova, Kelly Nuxoll, Patricia Ouellet, Alexander Packard, Alison Packard, Diane Palmer, Denis Phillips, Mica Pollock, Richard Primus, Richard Rabinowitz, Brendan Randall, Justin Reich, Rob Reich, Susan Reverby, Reuel Rogers, Lisa Rosen, Beth Rubin, Anna Rosefsky Saavedra, Donna San Antonio, Gino Segre, Carla Shalaby, Amy Shine, Julie Sloan, Rogers Smith, Lester Kenyatta Spence, Marc Stears,

Laurel Stolte, Adam Strom, Lorella Terzi, lê thi diem thúy, Judith Torney-Purta, Julia Van Alst, Judith Vichniac, Anita Wadhwa, Richard Weissbourd, Melissa Williams, Ajume Hassan Wingo, Kendall Wood, Jennifer Worden, Rebecca Yacono, James Youniss, Jon Zaff, and Karen Zawisza. Merely listing names is a poor proxy for a proper acknowledgment. It fails to convey the pages filled with commentary and suggestions, the hours spent at a favorite café hashing out ideas, or the phone conversations about draft chapters squeezed in between children's and adults' bedtimes. Many on this list shaped my research, thinking, writing, and teaching in profound ways. To do justice to each person's contribution, however, would require more pages than the book itself, so I regretfully leave the particulars unspecified.

Natalie Addison, Celina Benavides, Chris Buttimer, Melissa Chabran, Alexandra Rose Clifton, Shari Dickstein, Aaliyah El-Amin, Pamela Gordon, Saundra Murphy Hamilton, Laura Hsu, Phil Jones, Katondra Verese Lee, Jasmine Mahmoud, Meredith Mira, James Noonan, Vanessa Rodriguez, Sarah Tsang, Julia Van Alst, and Caihong Wei provided expert research assistance. They were frequently assisted by the incredible staff of the Harvard Graduate School of Education (HGSE) Gutman Library, especially Carla Lillvik and Edward Copenhagen. My faculty assistants, Lisa Betty, Korrey Lacey-Buggs, and in particular Leslee Friedman, also provided top-notch support. To think what I could have accomplished as an eighth-grade teacher with the same level of assistance!

I am an extroverted thinker: I think best (and tend to write only) when I can engage others in conversation. I thus benefited from giving talks at numerous academic institutions and conferences. Participants in the Stanford-Illinois Philosophy of Education Summer Institutes and the Young Faculty Leadership Forum, in particular, provided essential insights in the early years of the project. William Galson, Stephen Macedo, Robert Putnam, and Ted McConnell also pulled me into and guided me through the newly resurgent field of civic education. Cornell's Young Scholar Symposium in the Program in Ethics and Public Life provided me the impetus to write the first two chapters of this book. The constructive comments I received there from Lawrence Blum, Robert Fullinwider, Michele Moody-Adams, and the symposium participants were essential. Furthermore, those two chapters represented only the first of many to which Larry graciously responded. In the end, he critiqued every chapter at least once, and in some cases, two or three times. His patience, generosity, and gentle insights are boundless.

Thea Abu El-Haj also read the complete manuscript, providing an empathetic and useful critique of each chapter. Sara Bershtel's influence is similarly deeply felt. After reading a sprawling version of the manuscript a year ago, she helped me figure out what the manuscript could do well, what aims I should postpone for the next book I write, and how to tell the difference. Belying his protestations, Michael Aronson offered invaluable editorial advice through two rounds of manuscript revision. I also benefited from the comments of two anonymous reviewers for Harvard University Press, as well as Katherine Brick's expert copyediting and Brendan Randall's peerless proofreading and indexing skills.

Having already provided crucial feedback on nascent ideas and chapters, Peter Levine generously read the entire manuscript this spring. His comments were typically incisive, cutting to the heart of my claims about theory, empirical research, and educational practice. Although in his modest fashion he "asked" only seven questions, I found myself stymied by three of them. They will keep me busy well into my next book. Peter has also influenced this book through his leadership of CIRCLE, which nourishes an indispensible nationwide community of scholars, policy makers, and activists in the field. An early grant from CIRCLE funded all of my primary data collection in four de facto segregated communities in Boston, Atlanta, Austin, and Dearborn.

I wish I could thank by name each of the 125 individuals I interviewed in these four cities. They were incredibly generous with their time, wisdom, and especially their trust. Although I include fewer direct quotations from the interviews and focus groups than I had anticipated, the insights that I gained were crucial in shaping every aspect of this book. They reinforce my conviction that political and educational philosophy are made better by direct engagement with the world, especially in conversation with people outside one's normal circles. I am particularly grateful to Todd McDowell for enabling my entry into Zavala Elementary, and to Tahsine Bazzi for organizing incredible meetings with Fordson High students and parents, imams, and other community leaders in Dearborn. I also want to thank Austin Independent School District and Dearborn Public Schools.

I of course owe immense gratitude to my former students and colleagues in Boston and Atlanta Public Schools. They were unfailingly supportive of my oscillation between the roles of teacher and researcher, and generously agreed to interviews in some cases years after I had last been in touch. More important, they helped me grow as an educator and a person, offering hearty doses as needed of humor, teaching techniques, materials, empathy, respect, and realism. My students and colleagues alike tolerated my mistakes, put up with my crazy schemes, cheered our joint successes, and continually renewed my faith in the value of teaching and learning together. I realize that my depictions of Walden and McCormack show hardship and failure as well as triumph. I hope that these are understood in a context of deep respect and love.

Four colleagues at Harvard also read the entire book manuscript and provided endless intellectual, professional, and personal guidance. Howard Gardner supported this project from its inception, providing at various times advocacy for my cause, office space, publishing advice, career counseling, and inimitable honesty. Robert Selman read the manuscript last summer, tactfully emphasizing its strengths while prodding me (mostly unsuccessfully) to take a more developmentally nuanced approach. Appropriately, given his own research, Bob's most valuable contribution has been perspective: on HGSE, the career path at Harvard, civic and moral development, work-family balance, and life in general. I cherish his mentorship.

As chair of my hiring and promotion committees, Julie Reuben is most directly responsible for my transition from Boston Public Schools to Harvard—and for my not (yet) transitioning back again. She is also a valued writing group colleague, mentor, and friend. I shudder to think how many times she's read versions of this book. Throughout it all, she has offered unstinting support, incisive and substantive commentary, and essential recommendations about structure and organization. Jal Mehta, the other member of our writing group, is a treasured friend and thought partner. He has read almost every word I've written over the past three years and prodded me to make each one better: more exact, livelier, more daring. Although he remains dubious about some arguments in the book, Jal's influence can be felt on every page. I look forward to our continued intellectual exchange and collaboration.

I am lucky beyond belief to have been part of three intensely generative intellectual communities during the decade or so I've been working on this book. The first is my Spencer/National Academy of Education Postdoctoral Fellowship cohort. Many of the names sprinkled throughout this book are those of close friends and colleagues whom I first met through the Spencer/NAE meetings. These gatherings provided welcome intellectual stimulation that enriched the book both directly and by example. Radcliffe Institute for Advanced Study facilitated another of the most intellectually stimulating periods of my life, thanks to the miraculous group of scholars, composers, artists, writers, and activists brought together under Drew Faust's leadership. I was introduced to a whirlwind of ideas, methodologies, questions, and ways of engaging with the world that influence me still. Financial support from Spencer/ NAE and from Radcliffe also enabled me to take two years off from teaching middle school to read and write. This book would not exist without that time and funding.

Most recently, I have felt immensely privileged to be part of the Harvard Graduate School of Education community. Dean Kathleen McCartney has fostered an atmosphere of generous collaboration, as well as consistent support for junior faculty, that stimulates intense intellectual and professional growth. I am particularly indebted to her and many others for their support of the Civic and Moral Education Initiative. HGSE's masters and doctoral students have also taught me a great deal, including specifics about how to improve this manuscript. I am especially indebted to LevLab members, who waded through very rough material to help me write a better book.

This network of professional relationships would be neither possible nor fulfilling without the support of my family. I have now spent more than half of my life in partnership with my husband, Marc Lipsitch. I would not be the teacher, scholar, friend, colleague, daughter, or mother that I am without his encouragement and influence. He keeps me challenged, engaged, and grounded. Although Marc has not read *No Citizen Left Behind,* he has lived it alongside me. Most crucially, Marc has made sure the book has kept its rightful place as a secondary rather than primary aspect of our lives together as a family.

Our two daughters, Rebecca and Gabriella, will be nine and almost six when *No Citizen Left Behind* is published. I started working on it before they were born. The fact that they feel beloved rather than neglected is thanks in no small measure to their grandparents, Susan and Ian Lipsitch and Cynthia and Sanford Levinson. There is no way that I could have pursued my teaching, research, and writing without their unwavering support. Neither could I have gone to work each day had it not been for Christine Murphy, nanny and early childhood educator extraordinaire. She has made our professional lives possible, and our personal lives more colorful. I am also grateful to Jussara Cabral for providing exemplary childcare during the final year of writing and editing.

In addition to shoring up the domestic front, my parents provided intellectual guidance at every stage of this book's development. I long ago lost track of the number of proposals, chapter outlines and drafts, articles, and fellowship and job applications they have read and responded to—often turning them around in less than a day. We have talked about the ideas and dilemmas contained in these pages for hundreds of hours: over meals, over the phone, overnight . . . Their feedback tended to be complementary, with my father getting excited about the big picture and my mother methodically tackling structure, tone, clarity, and evidence. But they have always been united in their faith in the book: both in its value and in my capacity to write it. I am grateful to them beyond compare. I also want to thank my sister and brother-in-law, Rachel and Ariel Levinson Waldman, for their probing conversations and enthusiasm. Although their daughter Sarah is too young to have contributed anything to the book, she deserves mention, along with Rebecca, Ella, and their other cousins Sara and Leah, as altogether splendid human beings.

Finally, I wish to acknowledge the use of the following previously published material I have written: parts of the Prologue and Chapters 1, 3, 4, and 6 have appeared in "The Civic Empowerment Gap: Defining the Problem and Locating Solutions," in *Handbook of Research on Civic Engagement in Youth*, edited by Lonnie R. Sherrod, Judith Torney-Purta, and Constance A. Flanagan (John Wiley and Sons, 2010, reprinted with permission); parts of Chapter 2 have appeared in "Challenging Deliberation," *Theory and Research in Education* 1(1): 23–49; parts of Chapter 4 have appeared in "Let Us Now Praise . . . ? Rethinking Role Models and Heroes in an Egalitarian Age," in *Philosophy of Education in the Era of Globalization,* edited by Yvonne Raley and Gerhard Preyer (Routledge, 2009, reprinted with permission); and parts of Chapter 7 have appeared in "Democracy, Accountability, and Education," *Theory and Research in Education* 9(2): 125–144.

Given all of this assistance, I need to take sole personal responsibility for two important errors: first, those people I have forgotten to acknowledge, and second, all remaining mistakes of fact and interpretation. I hope the former will accept my apology in deference to my lousy memory. I hope those who find the latter will offer sympathetic correction and invite me into conversation. The book is complete, but the intellectual journey continues.

INDEX

Abu El-Haj, Thea, 41
Academic achievement gap, 31–32, 48, 292
Action civics, 224–230, 235–236, 241–242, 246–248
Action research. *See* Youth participatory action research
Afghanistan War, 196
African Americans, 9, 40, 60–62, 67, 68, 69, 77–79; and multicultural curriculum, 6, 7, 114, 123; civic engagement, 35, 36, 38, 39, 65, 93, 127; counternarratives, 117–118–119, 124; teachers, 120–121
Afrocentric curriculum. *See* Curriculum, Afrocentric
Agha-Soltan, Neda, 45
Albright, Madeleine, 148
Alinsky, Saul, 139
Al Jazeera, 47
American Dream, 146, 185
American Political Science Association, 49
American Textbook Council, 111
Anderson, Marian, 6, 8, 12

Angelou, Maya, 6
Arab American Political Action Committee, 125
Arab Spring, 45, 47
Asian Americans. *See* Ethnoracial categories; Ethnoracial identity
Assessments. *See* High-stakes assessments; Standardized assessments; Standards, assessments, and accountability mechanisms
Assimilation, 82, 84, 91, 175
Atlanta Public Schools, 1, 5, 7, 8, 12, 14, 101, 121
Austin, Texas, 22, 195, 243, 299n5
Austin Interfaith, 244

Bacharach, Burt, 2, 3
Baker, James, 141
Baldwin, James, 118, 129, 308n43
Bambara, Toni Cade, 6
Bartels, Larry, 49
Barton, David, 139, 140, 141, 142, 143
Behn, Robert, 270

82, 96; dominant/non-dominant, 90, 206; civic, 160, 175, 183, 186, 187, 190, 191. *See also* Cultural capital

Obama, Barack, 33, 40, 45, 73, 74, 117, 165; as hero, 158–159; and education, 292–293
Old Fourth Ward. *See* Fourth Ward
Open classroom, 192–198, 200, 202

Paige, Rod, 293
Parents Involved v. Seattle, 15, 19
Parks, Rosa, 6, 165
Payne, Charles, 129
Payzant, Thomas, 63
Penn, William, 138
Persian Gulf War, 32
Peter Marshall Ministries, 138
Plessy v. Ferguson, 16
Political participation. *See* Civic action
Political theory, 18–22, 95, 96, 206
Politics of race, 63–64. *See also* Ethnoracial politics
Postraciality, 69, 73. *See also* Colorblindness
Power, 12, 21, 28, 31, 33, 37, 86, 108, 122; and ethnoracial identity, 73, 75, 82; culture of, 87; language of, 87, 90, 91, 92, 279; collective, 92–93, 117, 164, 219, 220, 232
Power analysis, 86–87, 225, 226–227
Prejudice, 218–219. *See also* Discrimination; Racism

Presidential elections, 33–34, 40
Public Achievement, 224
Public good, 30, 259, 263, 268
Public goods, 259, 260–261
Public reason, 205–206
Public servants, 30–33, 49–50, 77, 185, 226, 234, 274
Putnam, Robert, 37

Race, 64–82, 97–98. *See also* Ethnoracial categories
Racial identity. *See* Ethnoracial identity
Racial isolation. *See* De facto segregation
Racial uplift, 309n62
Racism, 31, 70, 72, 73–74, 77, 111, 123, 131, 136, 144, 147. *See also* Discrimination; Prejudice
Ravitch, Diane, 112, 133
Rawls, John, 205–206, 308n40
Religion, 51, 67, 160, 203–204. *See also* Civil religion
Ringgold, Faith, 6
Rivers, Eugene, 83
Rivlin, Alice, 148
Role models, 138–166, 174–175, 188, 191, 209, 218, 276
Roosevelt, Theodore, 143, 146, 152
Rubin, Beth, 41
Rush, Benjamin, 145

Sadiq (student), 61, 89
Same-sex marriage, 201–205, 280
Schlafly, Phyllis, 141
Scholastic Reading Inventory, 252
School reform, 52, 257, 270, 285–286